JOURNEY INTO THE HEART OF REALITY

Journey into the Heart of Reality

Spiritual Guide to Divine Ecstasy of Self-Realization

Shiva Somadev

Journey into the Heart of Reality 1st edition 2020
Published by Prana Rider

Layout and cover design by Shiva Somadev
www.shivasomadev.com

ISBN-13: 978-1-5272-5839-6

To those who longs to know Her Majesty Divine Truth.

'The Self is not known through study of the scriptures, nor through subtlety of the intellect, nor through much learning. But by him who longs for Him is He known. Verily unto him does the Self reveal His True Being.'

~ *Katha Upanishad* ~

Table of contents

Foreword... 1

Introduction 4

Invocation 11

Sat-Chit-Ananda (Being-Consciousness-Bliss)...................... 13

Death.. 18

The Truth 24

Beyond the Limitations of Logic... 25

The Fourth Way.. 29

Man-Machine.. 35

Three and Seven – The Fundamental Laws.............................. 41

The Ray of Creation 44

Quantum Mechanics 47

Do – Ti – La – Sol – Fa – Mi – Re – Do 57

The Human Chemical Factory 63

The Birth of Imperfection.. 72

From Shiva Down to Earth 74

Working With the 'Fourth Way' Ideas 78

All Haqq (I am the Truth)... 85

Meeting Teacher 89

Inner Jesus Prayer, Zikr and Mantra-Japa 94

Growing Intimacy with The Beloved 96

Confusing Sexual Games with Teacher................................... 99

False Prophesy and Cancellation of the 'Sex Exercise' 103

New Adventures 106

Russian Mafia in a French Prison...................................... 116

The Magic Mushroom Portal... 128

Three Weeks in Oakland Jail 130

Farewell Wife, Friends, School, and Welcome the Unknown 133

The First Lesson of Magic Mushrooms - Pranayama 138

The Second Lesson of the Magic Mushrooms - Hell 146

The Flood of Happiness 150

The Headless Way 156

The Hell of Oneness 158

Maya 161

Arunachala – Shiva. The Heart of The Universe 166

Meeting Tarananda 168

Negative Shock on My Return from India 172

The Power of Mantra 174

Victor 182

Liberty Caps, a Black Hole and Singularity 188

Back to Beloved Mother India 197

Margarita 211

Satsang 215

1.21 Gigawatts into a Flux Capacitor 218

The Mysterious Language of Chemistry 223

Astonishing DMT World 228

New Darshan of Mother India 238

A Brief Visit to Nepal 244

A Growing Desire to Become a Sadhu 246

The Rewards of the Fasting Tapas 250

A Magical Journey into the Land of Shiva 254

Shiva's Messenger 257

The Life and Sadhana of Sadhus in a Himalayan Cave 259

Fairies of Renuka – Rivendell 270

The Conquest of Mind or Twenty-one Days to Nirvana 274

Solar Eclipse and a Brief Visit to Hell 280

Epiphany and Marriage 284

Forty Days of Fasting 290

Holotropic Breathing 293

I Do Believe in Fairies 299

Man = Tension 304

Fright and Temptations 305

Dream-reality 308

Healthy Diet and Breatharianism 314

Satsangs and Prana Yoga 319

Ayahuasca, Magic Mushrooms and a Vision of Ganesha 326

Labour of Love 331

Kumbhaka Prana Yoga 336

Shabda Brahman 370

Lessons from the Dying Process 374

Samavesha (Divine Possession) 376

Virtual Reality and Simulation Theories 394

Light on Common Misconceptions 404

Parting Words of Advice 412

Appendix 1 417

Appendix 2 419

Appendix 3 424

Glossary of Sanskrit Terms 428

Foreword

The book you about to read contains an exquisitely raw and searingly honest account of Shiva Somadev's voyage to the heart of reality. Expounding upon philosophical gems he's garnered through the course of his life; he shares his findings beginning with a breakdown of the philosophical systems which has shaped his understanding of the path from its rocky beginnings.

Hungry for truth in the spiritually deprived wasteland of communist Russia before the age of internet, Shiva is driven by a spiritual starvation and finds his way under the tutelage of a "teacher" who opens the doors to self-discovery while providing him with a foundation and a community with whom to practice. With an innate ability to discover truth, Shiva sifts the gold from the slag, revealing kernels of wisdom which prove invaluable as the course upon his maiden voyage is set. Taking things lightly and focusing intently on what's beneficial he dives headfirst, immersing himself in the Gurdjieff's teachings.

Having tasted the fruits of a spiritual opening within the context of a school that has arisen like a mirage in the spiritual desert, Somadev gives himself completely to this path and the school, embracing the light, while remaining blissfully ignorant to the hidden dangers lurking in its midst. What ensues is a story of innocence lost at the hands of megalomaniac teacher who takes advantage of young Somadev's naivety and hunger for truth.

In spite of the events that transpire, and the teachers abuse of power which he uses to satiate a monstrous ego and appetite, Shiva's rebellious soul refuses to let go of the torch. Blazing his path and following the light of his soul, he turns the poison churned up in the wake of his teacher's ravenous greed into the fuel to carry on, a sacrifice by which light is shed upon a path to freedom. As Shiva begins to renounce the life he's been conditioned to in the wake of a sobering captivity and sentence within a French prison, he takes the time to stare into the abyss and to deeply reflect upon all that has brought him to this point in life.

Shiva is a man of extremes and from the spell of hedonism he begins to awaken to the strength of his truest self and to shed the outworn skins which bind his soul and trap his light. While the events that unfold keep the reader completely engrossed, they also remind us the importance of pulling over and taking our own life's inventory, looking into the darker corridors before the next disaster looms large enough to claim its next victim. This bare bone telling provides seekers with a cautionary tale of dangers lurking within the spiritual landscapes.

As Shiva begins to awaken and take the steps needed to extradite himself from the web in which he's become bound, deeply enmeshed in the threads of community, the next phase of the journey begins.

Shiva discovers the resilience to continue his journey by any means, even if it means passing through hells depth and turning his back on his community in order to stay true to himself and to experience the wisdom of the newfound teachings unfolding within his highest levels of awareness.

The practice that begins to reveal itself is one of very ancient origins known as Kumbhaka. In the utilization of these methods developed over thousands of years, sages and visionaries have recorded volumes of experiences, bringing back stories of their quests throughout the infinite layers of reality.

Kumbhaka Prana Yoga is a unique system developed by the author throughout his lifetimes journeys in consciousness and dedication to spiritual growth. Brought about through personal revelations, spontaneously revealed through psychedelic and meditative practices, the path revealed is one of pure prana or life-force, wherein Shiva passes through the gates of "death", retaining his breath in order to find the spiritual treasures hidden within the depths of the sea of consciousness. Taking from this ancient practice and the revelations he's had in the wake of shamanic states, Shiva makes use of the ever-increasing prana, riding wave upon wave of this universal energy in order to discover and utilize the alchemical gold of spirit he seeks.

Differentiated from other yogic practices, *Kumbhaka Prana Yoga* makes full use of the life-force in order to go beyond the physical asanas most commonly associated with yogic practice.

In Shiva's utilization of the techniques of prolonged dynamic, intuitive breathing he is brought into sublime moments, where the doors of perception are opened to the infinite. He knows this gift which has been imparted will become his life's work and thus brings it back to craft his practice and initiate others.

As the name Kumbhaka implies, taking us on a breath-taking journey of incredible beauty and richness, he plunges again and again to the depths, to unveil the deepest layers of his soul, offering the fruits of his journeys to the benefit of all seekers.

Shiva's personal approach narrates a path to the core, which both amuses and amazes as he shares his personal discoveries, and deep insights which come in the wake of a passionate and uncompromising dedication to the spirit guiding him. Shiva shares the distillation of his wisdom as his soul passes through its dark night and awakens to the brilliance of the undying light.

This courageous and personal telling of his own life story is bound to captivate and cause readers to take closer looks into their own life narratives, discovering universal threads of truth which remind us of our own deeper truths and fuel our hunger to push the boundaries of exploration.

Shiva's groundbreaking discoveries, integrating his psychedelic revelations within his expansive system of *Kumbhaka Prana Yoga* are bound to act as a lighthouse for those who've set sail upon their own uncharted waters, giving us glimpses of a tapestry both ancient and modern. This book is a must read for all truth seekers.

~ Kailasam Berke ~

Introduction

What is the greatest treasure of all, which once discovered, forever fulfils all desires?
What is that which grants absolute satisfaction and unalloyed happiness?

One doesn't have to be a genius, to notice that everything external to oneself is bound to pass, even life itself. Those who seek happiness and fulfilment in external objects will inescapably end up in disappointment and pain when the objects of their love, desire and affection will disappear or are taken away from them.

Is there anything everlasting in this flux of appearances?

What about you, my dear reader? Do you really believe that after this fascinating flash in eternity called life, you will forever cease to exist?

What is more enduring: the world which appears in your consciousness, or you, the conscious agent (or maybe consciousness itself) who perceives this world? Would this world exist at all if you were not conscious of it? And even if it existed somewhere, somehow, but you weren't aware of it, even in your memory, would such a non-existent world matter to you at all? Let me put it boldly: if you were not, nothing would be!

Our greatest problem, that which gives us sense of incompletion, unfulfillment and unsatisfaction lies in our ignorance about our true nature. Therefore, the greatest spiritual teachings call us to 'know thyself'!

Most people are wrongly convinced, deluded by the most powerful 'Maya' (illusion), that they are either their bodies, or the individuals within their bodies, and with the death of that body they shall cease to exist.

Not inquiring into the true nature of reality and their own selves, taking their mortal bodies living their temporary lives to be the only reality, they are searching for happiness, peace and satisfaction in transitory things.

We all, by nature, seek more and more happiness. We aspire for more intense, more durable, more intoxicating, more satisfying joy. In our ordinary lives, however, happiness is always preceded or followed by pain and sorrow.

Most of us think that money, power, or fame can provide us with happiness and satisfaction. Certainly, money, power and fame can enrich the quality of our lives, make it more interesting, give us greater freedom to explore the world, give us temporary security and pleasures, but can they fulfil all our desires and give us total satisfaction and ultimate happiness?

No mortal is lucky enough to have unwavering satisfaction and happiness. Our happiness is always challenged by the highs and lows of our circumstances and it is often the case that we work very hard towards the happiness and satisfaction, only to find it to be temporary and not worth the struggle.

On this imperfect plane of existence, which most of us take to be the only reality, it is simply impossible to obtain an all-satisfying perfection. The idea of the possibility of such perfection, however, is ingrained in the essential nature of our consciousness.

'This isn't it!' said the then-rich and famous George Harrison. 'Fame is not the goal. ... To be able to know how to get peace of mind, how to be happy, is something you don't just stumble across. You've got to search for it.'

And where is it that absolute satisfaction and unalloyed happiness can be found? How can we tap into that perennial flood of purest joy? How do we rid ourselves of disappointment, misery, boredom, suffering, pain, unfulfilled desires and unsatisfaction and be established in the flooding nectar of unconditional love and the radiance of utmost joy?

The highest bliss, the incomparable ecstasy, the never-ending amazement, the aliveness, the tears of gratitude, the heavenly euphoria, the rapture of joy, the childlike wonder, the divine knowledge, the greatest wisdom, the sweetest honey of purest love, the boundless freedom, the magnificence of supreme intelligence, the astonishment, the perfection, the eternity, the infinity... What is their source?

If our happiness depends on anything outside of us, it's not a real happiness, my friend, but rather dependency and slavery. The treasure and joy which can be taken away or disappear, leaving you with nothing but frustration and misery is not a real treasure or joy, but merely a teaser, a borrowed thing.

True happiness belongs to the self-sufficient!

Real and great treasure, true unalloyed happiness, everlasting joy and absolute satisfaction can only be found within your true immortal Self, my dear reader, that which is identical to God – the Absolute – the Highest Reality.

Ironically, instead of searching for the eternal, we strive to fulfil ourselves with the temporary.

For most people, the possibility of freeing themselves from all limiting conditions and finding the absolute satisfaction will never even arise in all their lifetimes. Only a handful of fortunate ones (this includes you, my dear reader) will come across the clues and become interested in discovering the Ultimate Truth. And only eternal Truth can grant eternal bliss.

Can the Ultimate Truth be found somewhere outside of yourself?

Of course not, my dear friend, for you must be there to experience it.

Now you know where to find the greatest treasure of all. It is the open secret almost everyone overlooks.

The greatest treasure can only be found within your True Self.

One day, my dear reader, after looking very attentively with great love and growing clarity at your own Self, the realisation will dawn on you: 'it is only You at all times!'

You are the dearest friend, lover, love and beloved to your Self.

All else crumbles away, losing its importance. Only the eternal essence of all – your True Self is forever your true beloved.

Upon realising this, you will be falling ever more deeply in love with your Self, until all imaginary veils of separation are ablaze with the ecstasy of realisation and union.

The True Self is the reality. To know the Self is to know God. By knowing the Self, everything else is known. By attaining the

Introduction

Self, nothing else could be desired, for the Self is the most desirable of all. Even those who are not aware of it desire the Self.

I was extremely fortunate to receive the gift of curiosity and inquiry into the true nature of reality. I was blessed with the unquenchable longing for the Ultimate Truth.

Even as a young lad, I was always attracted to eternal questions, philosophy, the esoteric and magic. Many late evenings with my philosophy-inclined friends were dedicated to pondering over the true nature of reality and solving the great mysteries of existence. Having no gurus or spiritual teachers on the horizon, I consumed knowledge from the pages of philosophical and esoteric books, which I was lucky to find.

Unfortunately, growing up in Soviet Russia, in an era before the internet, we were greatly deprived of esoteric knowledge. On the other hand, this 'spiritual starvation' involuntarily stirred a great hunger in the hearts and minds of many Russian people – a holy hunger for spiritual knowledge and the Ultimate Truth.

After digesting many books on psychology, philosophy, mysticism, tarot, Kabbala, Gnosticism, etc…, the book *In Search of the Miraculous* by P.D. Ouspensky illuminated my mind with its radical ideas and led me to join the 'Fourth Way' esoteric school, which was formed on and was working with the ideas of great mystic – G.I.Gurdjieff.

I was very lucky to have as my first spiritual teacher the enigmatic and humorous English actor Robert Taylor. After being in school less than three months, I experienced, with his guidance, what could be described as 'Cosmic Consciousness'.

Triggered by the intense 'Self-remembering' (a spiritual technique which I describe later), utilising and transforming the release of the tremendous energy of my fear, my consciousness was catapulted out of a tiny cocoon of four dimensions into the ecstatic freedom and clarity of higher dimensions.

This Divine experience – a verification of higher levels of consciousness – became my vantage point from which I could see the secrets of reality with far greater clarity. However, this experience was just the first shy kiss of enlightenment and the very beginning of a love affair with the Beloved Truth, which led me through a series of Divine revelations to the absolute ecstasy of Self-realisation!

Introduction

Love, sex, drugs, relationships, betrayal of trust, being in a cult, serving sentences and learning great lessons in French and American prisons, discovering the great spiritual teachings (Christian mysticism, Fourth way, Sufism, Zen, Advaita Vedanta, Kashmir Shaivism etc.), living as a sadhu (holy man) in Himalayan caves and on the tops of the holy hills, many days of fasting and isolation, countless experiments with the consciousness-expanding substances, shamanic journeys under heroic doses of my major teachers - magic mushrooms revealing their unique astonishing knowledge, excursions into the alien worlds, hells and heavens... all this and much, much more you will find in this captivating and highly adventurous book, my dear reader.

Most importantly of all, however, is that this amazing story is not only entertaining, but a guidance towards the Divine ecstasy of Self-realisation!

Kumbhaka Prana Yoga, which came to me as a series of Divine revelations and which I will describe fully towards the end of this book is probably the most powerful spiritual vehicle towards the ecstasy of Truth, known to man!

With the power and grace of *Kumbhaka Prana Yoga*, I have been divinely blessed to break through all the coverings and illusions to the highest of heights. I have been allowed to enter the Sanctum Sanctorum.

I have lost my imaginary shackles and boundaries. I have lost my dream world, my dream body and my ego in the supreme ecstasy of the Eternal Truth!

Self-realisation is perfect bliss. It is the greatest gain of all games. It is the abode of the most beautiful and the most desirable Universal love. It is the flood of excessive joy. It is the kingdom of unalloyed happiness. It is the radiance of Self-knowledge.

No amount of earthly or heavenly pleasures can ever come close to the Divine ecstasy of Self-realisation.

For those lucky souls who have had even a glimpse of such Divine revelations, the search for Truth is over, for experiencing it first-hand, all other knowledge found in books or from the lips of gurus, however wise, is only secondary.

Although there is no end to the depth of God's intelligence, the blessed ones who experience revelations of Divine Truth discover the direct path to God and become initiated into her Divine

Introduction

Mysteries at their deepest levels! The practical knowledge of the direct path to the heart of the ultimate reality is far more important than all conclusive logic and descriptive knowledge rooted in words. It is even more important than the deepest understanding.

My dearest reader... If you allow me, I would like to take you with me on a most fascinating journey through the incredible events of my adventurous life. This is the story of searching for her Majesty Truth, which shall take you to the summit of spiritual mountain, the majestic view from which shall fill your heart with unalloyed happiness and absolute satisfaction. This is a journey into the very heart of infinite reality, a journey of the discovery of the greatest treasure of all – Self-knowledge. Upon obtaining this, you will be filled with unending, unsurpassable bliss, supreme joy and unbelievable ecstasy.

Only the arrival at the Absolute Truth can set all our doubts at rest and give us total satisfaction. The half-truth, or a quarter of truth cannot do it... In fact, partial truths can be far dangerous than outrageous lies.

Leaving the scaffolding of theoretical knowledge behind in the first part of this book, we will move to the main structure – a practical application: the means and methods for regaining True Knowledge and the establishment in the Absolute Truth – otherwise known as Self-realisation, Self-recognition, God-realisation, Awakening, Buddha Nature, Enlightenment, Liberation, Emancipation, Repose, Moksha, Nirvana, Kaivalya etc....

Although the intellectual knowledge and understanding of reality is a very important step towards the realisation of the Absolute Truth, it is not enough just to understand the truth, for the truth is beyond words, understanding, beliefs, or even wildest imagination. No amount of intellectual knowledge, regardless how high, deep and sophisticated, can give you direct knowledge and experience of reality. Words, at best, can only point in the direction of the Truth.

Intellectual knowledge must be applied and put into intelligent efforts, spiritual practice (Sadhana), and self-sacrifice (Tapas). One must develop unshakable courage and willpower for gaining true wisdom, and then go beyond even that...

The collection of thoughts and spiritual experiments on which this book is based is my adventure, my life story. It could be

9

described as my ultimate search for Truth. I hope you can join me on this quest, and in it, find your own story, your own truth and ultimately, happiness.

> *'Camerado, I give you my hand! I give you my love more precious than money, I give you myself before preaching or law; Will you give me yourself? Will you come travel with me? Shall we stick by each other as long as we live?'*

~ Walt Whitman ~

Invocation

Om Gum Ganapataye Namaha.

O! The fountainhead of supreme knowledge, radiating Divine wisdom through the mysterious sacred geometry, numbers, vibrations, sounds and letters.

O! The revealer of the magnificent Universe!

O! Lord of gunas (ever-changeful qualities of prakriti – nature)!

Enlighten my intellect with thy splendorous light of Divine wisdom, remove distracting activities of rajas (agitation) and darkness of tamas (dullness), but allow me to be established in pure sattva (clarity), for the accomplishment of the task of writing a book, that can elevate individual soul to the recognition of the absolute truth, shatter the imaginary walls of separation and limitations, wipe away debilitating objective knowledge (knowledge of limitations) and help one to be established in the infinite ecstasy of pure reality....

O! Almighty Shakti – the Divine mother of all that is! The infinite bliss that is thy true nature cannot have any limitations, radiating as purest love willing myriads of universes into existence. Everything is done by thy unimpeded will with the aid of thy supreme knowledge.

O! Omniscient One, who presides over each letter of the Divine alphabet, open wide my heart and let thy unconditional love flow through it, as refreshing and cleansing as streams of divine poetry, washing off feelings of apathy, boredom and sadness. Guide my thoughts and lead my fingers to type sequences of letters, words and sentences, arranging them in such a way that they draw away the shadows of uncertainty, fear and doubt, and illuminate one's spiritual heart with thy magnificent light. Make my writing eloquent and clear...

O! Absolute Shiva! May all the rays of thy magnificent consciousness return to their radiant source and experience thy wonderful glory! May all beings be able to know thee – the substratum of all, as their very own Self...

Sat-Chit-Ananda (Being-Consciousness-Bliss)

'Do I contradict myself? Very well, I contradict myself, I am large, I contain multitudes.'

~ Walt Whitman ~

My dear reader, the book you are holding is just one of the numerous clues that your own intelligence-energy has created for you. It is a reminder of your real nature, about which you've forgotten, when you drunk the magic waters from the lake of forgetfulness while you were wandering in the Bardo (intermediate between death and rebirth) state. This book is one of the countless clues serving as your 'wake up to Reality' call.

Reality itself is beyond words, imagination, descriptions, or any comparisons, because there nothing exists apart from It, and so It can never be compared. Nevertheless, It is the substratum of all existence – the unborn, undying, ever-existing Absolute Being - your True Nature.

This Absolute Reality, without shadow of a doubt, can, and when the time is ripe, will be known and experienced by you, for your True Self is not different from It. You are identical with It. Atman (Soul) is Brahman (Absolute)...

Of course, this vast world with its multiplicity of various forms, sounds, objects, living beings, stars, galaxies, history and countless activities, appears to be very real and separate from you, existing

13

Sat-Chit-Ananda (Being-Consciousness-Bliss) independently of your perceptions of it. It seems to be an objective reality, governed by the laws of nature, or by the laws of a supreme being with an infinitely superior intelligence and power than yours. Your senses and mind, which themselves are the instruments of Maya (illusion), constantly confirm the status of the world as objective reality. Moreover, it seems to be filled with meaning, purpose, love, beauty and happiness, inevitably paired with its opposites: the meaninglessness, purposelessness, hatred, ugliness and sadness. Your human intelligence seems to be very limited in comparison with the intelligence of the One who creates the cosmos and life.

However, it is your True Self, which is the same as Divine Consciousness, Supreme Intelligence-Energy, the grand unified field of all possibilities, or God, that creates this apparent manifestation, this dream in which you appear as a limited individual confined within your body-cage.

That reality, which exists eternally, without beginning or end, is incomprehensible by the mind or senses. It is unbroken, undivided, indestructible, formless, prior to any appearances, the nameless One... But for the convenience of somehow giving it a definition, we can call it 'Existence' or 'Being'.

This 'Being' cannot not be! It always is. Such is its nature.

'Non-being' by its very definition, does not exist.

This Being – God – stands above of all the recognisable world. To understand God, to know God, one must become God, or realise one's total identity within God, not through the intellect only, but through the totality of one's being. This infinite Being cannot be comprehended by the finite mind or senses, but because it is reality itself, it can be experienced and realised directly by the entirety of your whole being, as your own True Identity!

The nature of this 'Being' is the Supreme Intelligence – Absolute Consciousness!

This fundamental Being-Consciousness does not require space or time for its existence, rather, non-fundamental space and time themselves derive their existence from this unfathomable Absolute Being.

This Being-Consciousness did not suddenly spring into existence from the 'non-being'. Self-existent, beginning-less, origin-less, eternal, it is the origin of everything.

Sat-Chit-Ananda (Being-Consciousness-Bliss)

This Being-Consciousness has never ever been absent. It never began, and it will never end.

In its highest, or primal state, the nature of this Being-Consciousness is bliss beyond belief. The ancient Hindu scriptures describe this reality as Sat Chit Ananda (Being-Consciousness-Bliss). This Supreme Reality, in Hindu tradition, is also known by the name Brahman or Shiva.

Shiva is the infinite ocean of all possibilities. In his highest, or primal state, he is omnipresent, omniscient and omnipotent. There is nothing impossible for Shiva – the Absolute.

The Divine intelligence of Absolute Shiva is far beyond the limitations of the human mind and logic.

What seems to be impossible for the mind and logic is possible for this Absolute being.

The Absolute is a storehouse of contradictions and paradoxes. This infinite being is not only Supreme Intelligence (Consciousness), but also the Infinite Energy. This Supreme Intelligence-Energy is the very essence of Shiva – his manifesting abilities, his creative nature, his wish-fulfiller, who in the scriptures is called Shakti.

Just as an artist, musician, poet, or lover cannot contain creative energy within themselves, and burst to express it in the form of a beautiful painting, music or poetry, so does the extreme joy, the unrestrained ecstasy, the insane euphoria of the Shiva-Shakti union pour out into the creation process…

The Universe is created from the ripples and waves of pure excessive joy!

In the very core of your radiant heart, in the source of all manifestations, in the mysterious sunya (great void) that is pregnant with infinite possibilities and energy, Shiva-Shakti, the supreme energy-intelligence, the very Self of all, is timelessly immersed in an ecstatic, orgasmic, blissful dance of union, totally free, amazed at its own might, soaked in Soma-Amrit (ambrosial nectar), and filled with Sugandhim (sweet smell, fragrance of fragrances). This supreme energy-intelligence splits itself into particles and anti-particles, into the 'observer' and the 'observed', in the paradoxical, ungraspable by the senses and mind, the infinite 'singularity.' From this tireless, effortless, ecstatic dance, Divine knowledge cascades as a flood of love, transforming itself into Para and Pashyanti Vak

Sat-Chit-Ananda (Being-Consciousness-Bliss) (Divine Language), sequences of mantras and Matrikas (misunderstood divine mothers – deities presiding over the letters of divine alphabet), and into the sequences of numbers intertwined with sacred geometry. Thus the 'laws of nature' – Prakriti – are effortlessly created.

Trapped in the cobwebs of his own granddaughter – Maya (illusion) – through the identification with a character of his and his Shakti's own illusory creation, rotating on a wheels of Samsara (repetitive existence), the shrunken into an individual, consciousness of Shiva, gradually learns the truth from the clues; such as the scriptures, words of the enlightened sages, shamans, rishis, gurus, and the revelations of sacred plants and substances, which were deliberately left in the 'story' in order to find the way back home.

Then he overcome fear and self-imposed limitations, rises above Maya with the help of sacred Sadhana (spiritual effort), shakes off illusory conditionings and limitations, purifying his intelligence from the dust of doubts and thoughts, and learns from his own life-force (Prana Sakti) the greatest secrets of reality. He purges himself of the 'unreal', spits out all objective limiting knowledge of differences, frees himself from the 'matrix' of illusion, and returns home to a true eternal kingdom of bliss-love-joy. He regains the astonishing clarity of supreme consciousness – intelligence, laughs at his own unbelievable divine jokes, wonders at his own infinite might and the absolute freedom to be, to know, to do, to manifest anything and everything effortlessly. Seemingly wandering here and there, Shakti unites with her Beloved Shiva in never-ending, delightful, ecstatic dance of pure love....

Shiva (the Absolute transcendence, peace that passes understanding) and Shakti (infinite energy/creativity) are one inseparable being. Like heat is the nature of fire and wetness is the nature of water, so the Supreme Intelligence and the Infinite Energy is the nature of Reality. Shiva is beyond the 'laws' of nature. He is the greatest outlaw. He is also the very Self of all and is described as vaster than the cosmos yet smaller than an atom, immovable, yet moving with infinite speed, one without second, yet full of diversity and differentiations, far away and yet closer than the heartbeat, in a state of total repose and relaxation, yet filled with the infinite density of energy.

Sat-Chit-Ananda (Being-Consciousness-Bliss)

This supremely intelligent and infinitely energetic (powerful) being is both; non-manifest, formless, spaceless, timeless, attributeless reality, and the creator of all forms, activities, lives, all manifestations and the most minute particles of everything as well.

To describe somehow in a human language this indescribable being, we can try to imagine some of the essential qualities of its primal state.

First and the foremost is the Absolute freedom!

The Absolute has no boundaries, no impediments, no objections, no restrictions of body, no time, no space, no gravity, no directions, no restrictions of thought, nor doubt, nor fear, nor taboos, nor any laws..., nothing exists to oppose the Absolute. Nothing is impossible for the Absolute. Everything is possible...

The next quality of the Absolute is perfect contentment. Because the Absolute is one without a second, nothing exists which is not the Absolute. No desire can arise in the Absolute, because the nature of the Absolute is such that if there was the possibility for a desire, it would be immediately fulfilled without any passage of time.

Because it is supreme intelligence and infinite energy in a state of the absolute freedom and contentment, the Absolute is filled with unimaginable bliss. It is the source of all joy and ultimate bliss itself. As though surprised by its own infinite power, the Absolute is in a state of perpetual wonder, ever fresh, ever new. It contains within itself all possibilities. Shakti - the infinite energy of Shiva, known at this point as Ananda Sakti (bliss-energy); shining, throbbing, radiating, emanating this bliss, this unconditional love.

Because reality is infinite, everything is possible. It is even possible to create a substance (matter) out of energy, or pure intelligence. The Absolute is self-sufficient, independent (not depending on anything at all), the sovereign ruler of his Eternal Kingdom of Highest Bliss.

Death

*'The Hereafter never rises before the
thoughtless child (the ignorant), deluded by the
glamour of wealth. 'This world alone is, there
is none other': thinking thus, he falls under my
sway again and again.'*

*~ Lord Yama (Lord of Death) 'Katha
Upanishad' ~*

A mong the many uncertainties and unpredictability of life,
one thing is definite: life inevitably leads to death.
Our body, regardless of how well and how long it was
functioning, will eventually break down and will be left
behind as a lifeless corpse.

Our life energy (Prana-Shakti), which has been animating the
body, will eventually snap the link between the body and
consciousness and, upon leaving the body and familiar world
behind, will return to its disembodied state.

Obviously, it is impossible to say, my dear reader, what exactly
is going to happen to you at that moment and after death, for there
are not many people with the claim that they have been reborn and
can remember what was happening to them in the intermediate
state between death and rebirth.

Do not be deceived, however, by the popular clichés of new-
age gurus who simply repeat like parrots that 'death is not real'.
When the time comes to leave your body and the familiar world
behind, you will see how real death truly is.

Death

In facing death, which inescapably is going to occur, no friends or relatives can save or protect us. It will be only you and death! Such is the law. I am sorry, but no-one will help you if you haven't already helped yourself by making an early acquaintance with death by means of spiritual sadhana, tapas and meditation, or at least followed the way of Dharma (righteous living). All the tricks, tactics, pretences and lies, which helped us avoid punishment in our life won't work with death, for she can see through us. It will be too late for begging and crying. Justice will triumph despite our protests, and we'll get exactly what we deserve. To be more precise, it is not that some external entity will penalize us, but due to our own ignorance and non-inquiry into the Truth, our own mind will punish us. Our own mirrors will judge us.

It is not God who punishes man, but it is man who punishes himself. His poisonous pride and vanity lead him to think that he knows that there is no God, and therefore he separates himself from God, thus abandoning God. By abandoning God, he abandons his very Self – the real source of joy, love and compassion. Atheists and materialists who do not believe in God are crucifying themselves and inflicting great suffering on their own heads. Is it any wonder then, that these deeply rooted delusions, vanity and pride, can only be purified by the heat of intense suffering in Purgatory?

Death is the greatest guru, unveiler and revealer. Nothing and no one can hide from her incessant gaze. Death is not a bearer of darkness but the bearer of light. Its mighty scythe cuts down even the tallest and the thickest of thickets, leaving no underbrush for us to slink and slither away into. No, death exposes us in the fullness of the light, and any time we face death is a tremendous opportunity to truly see ourselves, for all manner of hidden and insidious demons will be brought to the surface. Just as pure white light reveals the true colours of reality, so too does the light of death bring out our true colours.

Death mercilessly destroys the false conviction that earthly life is the only reality.

In the *Bardo Thodol (Liberation Through Hearing During the Intermediate State),* known in the West as *The Tibetan Book of Death,* which I regard as one of the most important books ever written, with the profound knowledge of 'bardo' (the intermediate state between death and rebirth), it is said that after one's losing senses, intrinsically connected to the five great elements (Mahabhutas), one by one, and therefore losing connection with the familiar world, after the intense inner battle for safety and sanity, the moment arises when one simply cannot struggle any longer. Having no choice, one surrenders to whatever is going to happen.

At this moment, a sense of carelessness arises, and in that carelessness 'luminosity' (the undeferential radiance of an empty mind) presents itself.

The *Bardo Thodol* describes the dissolution of the self and the falling away of external reality. The consciousness that remains experiences the true nature of mind as the dazzling light of luminosity. This is Bardo of Dharmakaya, all phenomena unmanifested are free of characteristics and distinctions here.

Some, who deeply long for union with Truth can recognise luminosity as their very Self and be absorbed into it. For others, luminosity might last only for the duration of finger snap, for its light, due to non-recognition would appear as a most terrifying thing.

Falling out of luminosity, one experiences 'second light' – suddenly seeing a room with a body lying on a bed and relatives weeping. One will now understand that it is his body on the bed and that he is dead. But no number of attempts to enter the body will succeed and upon hearing the roaring thunder and obliteration of the 'second light' vision, one will enter the next stage of the after-death scenario.

The first bardo after the moment of death and Luminosity, called Sambhogakaya, can bestow rewards on those souls who were engaged in spiritual practices. Within the dazzling array of lights of many colours and visions of peaceful and wrathful deities, those in the bardo are challenged to be not afraid of these visions and recognize that in reality they are projections of one's own mind. But the recognition of this truth is not an easy one. It is mainly determined by the previous spiritual practice of Self-recognition (Pratyabhijna Hrdaya). If the second bardo is experienced with fear, confusion, and nonrealisation, the bardo of becoming begins. Projections of karma appear that will cause rebirth in one of the Six Realms: gods, demi-gods, humans,

animals, hungry ghosts, and hells. This is the bardo of
Nirmanakaya.[1]

I am not intending to frighten, you my dear reader, but rather to
simply state the truth, without trying to dress it in pretty clothes.
This is a truth that can warn you of the consequences of ignorance
and help you make the right choices in life.

A true friend is not one who feeds your ego with sweet lies to
keep you temporary asleep, but one who exposes lies, calling upon
and leading you towards the liberating Truth.

Isn't it bizarre that we regularly make strenuous efforts to
achieve some fleeting reward in life and yet make no investigation
or preparation for meeting the greatest examiner and bestower of
greatest rewards or punishments – death?

Knowing well that life is short, and death is inevitable, the
majority of human beings, nevertheless, are like ostriches, burying
their heads in the sand, naively pretending that death won't find
them. They completely ignore the fact of death. Why?

For some, even talk, or reminder of death is taboo – a forbidden
subject. It is an unpleasant and frightening thought, safer to keep at
bay.

It seems that a large number of people have a very well-
established materialistic view on reality, that is: 'I am the body, the
world is objective reality, I perceive it due to consciousness
produced by the neurons firing in my brain and when my body and
brain dies, I will cease to exist and perceive anything.'

Many people, however, feel instinctively that existence does
not end with the end of life, and there is something bigger and far
more intelligent than them governing the events in the cosmos and
beyond and that their souls will be the subject of God's judgment
and will be sent either to Heaven or Hell. Not knowing how to
directly approach the Truth and even rejecting such possibility,
they settle into their 'beliefs systems' as best as they can, following
moral codes and commandments. At least, due to fear of being
punished for sins and being rewarded for good actions they try as
best as they can to be and to do good.

The majority of people have a blind faith, believing in what the
scriptures, founders or elders say, without major investigations,

---

[1] "Bardo Thodol" (The Tibetan Book of the Dead) Padmasambhava.

casting off all other opinions and religious views and discouraging investigation into the Truth.

Faith is a very powerful force, and without it even the attempts of the realisation of truth are not possible. To undertake the proper investigation of truth by the means of meditation, sadhana, tapas, or other spiritual experiments, one, first of all, must have faith in the possibility of the direct realisation of Truth.

In eastern religious and philosophical traditions such as Hinduism and Buddhism, people believe in reincarnation driven by the karmic forces: 'what you sow you shall reap.' Such a view of reality invites individuals to follow the ways of Dharma – righteous conduct. It also encourages people to engage in various yogas: Karma Yoga – selfless service to God and humankind, Bhakti Yoga – devotion to the Beloved, surrender and self-sacrifice, and Jnana Yoga – inquiry into the true nature of reality – inquiry into the Self.

Those who have had a near-death experience, even though it may have only lasted five or ten minutes, usually return to life completely transformed and dedicate the rest of their lives to service, sharing love and kindness.

For those rare beautiful souls who in their deep longing for the Beloved Truth sacrifice their ego and their very sanity, and dive into the utmost depths of inner reality with the help of spiritual sadhana, death is a long-awaited opportunity to drop self-imposed limitations of the body and the world illusion and awake into the Divine rapture and ecstasy of the Highest Truth!

They receive Diksha (Direct Sight) and Upadesha (Teaching) from the best teacher of all – Lord Yama (Lord of Death).

The Truth, however, is above and beyond of even death. Death is only a humble servant of Her Majesty Truth, separating countless realms of infinite reality.

Truth simply cannot be known through the investigation of only one tiny fraction of infinite reality – called 'Earthly life.'

Not knowing what is beyond death, one simply cannot know the Truth.

To know the Truth and to be established in the Truth, one must embrace death, learn from death and, with the grace of her precious teachings, go beyond the rotating wheel of Samsara (cyclic repetitive existence), into the timeless reality – the Divine Ecstasy of Immortal Truth.

Nothing in infinite existence is more valuable, precious and beautiful than Her Majesty Supreme Truth!

The Truth

'All things perish, Truth alone remains'

~ Nachiketa ~ Katha Upanishad ~

As the moon and the stars fade away with the rising of the sun, so does the mind with its display of the Universe fade away, evaporating in the proximity of the brilliant light of Purest Love and melting in the Divine Ecstasy of naked Truth.

When beloved Shakti strips herself of her beautiful clothes to reveal her nakedness to a chosen one, one realises that the naked Truth is the most beautiful thing in all the worlds. Beloved Shakti begins her love dance within every atom of one's body-cosmos.

This utmost intimacy with the naked Truth is Divine Ecstasy!

Is there anything in the whole Universe and beyond that is higher, longer lasting, more important, more satisfying, more desirable than Absolute Truth?

Truth is the highest, the greatest, the everlasting, the only satisfying, the most important, the imperishable, the most desirable! Truth is God! Truth is Reality! Truth is Love!

Stick to the Truth and the Truth shall set you free.

There is a deep wisdom behind this famous saying. For in knowing, or rather abiding in Truth and as Truth, one is free from falsities, lies, deception, pretences, and doubt. However, the truth that we are seeking, the truth that grants ultimate liberation, must be the highest, the Absolute Truth. Half-truths, or the relative truths cannot give us total satisfaction, neither liberation, moreover, they will be found as non-truths on higher levels of infinite reality.

24

The Truth

If you have this unquenchable longing for the Absolute Truth, my dear reader, if you feel that nothing but the Absolute Truth can satisfy you, you are the lucky one, you are the chosen one, for this noble desire is the most important force in this most beautiful quest. As is said in Katha Upanishad: 'The Self is not known through the study of scriptures, nor through the subtlety of the intellect, nor through much learning. But by him who longs for Him is He known. Verily unto him does the Self reveals His true being....'

But is it at all possible to know the Absolute Truth? And if so, how? What are the ways, the means and methods to realise this sublime Truth?

There are two major methods of investigation into reality.

The first method known as a 'scientific method of investigation'.

Most of us love science and rely on science and scientists for explanations of how the universe works. The problem with science, however, is that it still has no idea of what consciousness is. It is based on the study of objective phenomena. When scientists try to understand what is happening within individualised consciousness, conducting experiments, which they think can bring the light of understanding to the workings of the human brain and other body systems and their connections, they are still studying the objective phenomenon – an appearance. The scientific method of investigation, therefore, is an indirect method of studying reality.

The only direct method of studying reality is the investigation of the subject – the Self!

And this can be achieved only by the intelligent efforts of self-investigation, self-introspection and self-inquiry. This is known as the 'Yogic method'.

I will be extensively elaborating on the 'Yogic method' later in this book.

But first, let's amuse ourselves with the eternal philosophical questions.

Beyond the Limitations of Logic

I remember somewhere around the age of thirteen, my rebellious cousin Victor and I were in a highly philosophical mood. We had a burning question about the nature of space. I am sure that at a certain point in your youth you had these questions too. The question troubling our young minds was the question: 'is the universe infinite, or finite?' Of course, we've heard several times that the universe as space is limitless, infinite, but despite of all our efforts to wrap our minds around it, it was frankly not possible to grasp, to comprehend the actual image of this statement. It is simply not possible 'not to have an end of space', but it is equally impossible to have an end also, for then, the question still remains; 'what is beyond that ending?'

Having learned some mathematics and geometry in school, we decided to try to solve the hard 'problem' by the method usually used in geometry, called 'proof by contradiction'. Hanging on a wall above the bed in Victor's room was a rug with various patterns on it, limited by a circle close to the edge of this rug. We used this rug as a representation – a map of the universe.

Suppose, we said, the universe has an end, and we pointed at the circle. The question then arises: what is beyond this limit? Suppose, we said, it is a sort of a 'kingdom of spirit'. And what are the means to experience that, which is beyond the limits of space? How can we experience that kingdom of spirit? And we came to what seemed at that time a revelational conclusion: to experience that which is beyond the limits of space, or beyond the limitations

26

of mind's abilities to comprehend, we need to lose our limited minds, to go beyond mind's logic...

A few years later, when I was searching for truth in the texts of Kabbala and tarot cards, my attention was drawn to the fifteenth major arcana' of the Tarot cards, known as The Devil.

The Devil – 'Baphomet' – has harpy feet, ram horns, bat wings, a reverse pentagram on the forehead, a raised right hand, and a lowered left hand holding a torch. He sits on a square pedestal with two naked human demons – one male, one female, with tails – chained to it...[2]

The words 'Fate' and 'Logic' also refer to this arcana. The Hebrew hieroglyph of this arcana is 'Samech', that is 'an arrow flying perpetually in a circle'. I thought of its significance as it is logic that keeps one within this circle, within the limited perception of the mind. It is logic that is the arrow, aiming at one, if one tries to escape the circle of limitations...

In fact, as we will see further, our perceptions of the world and the events developing in time is largely due to our special type of cognitive process, based on the projection of restrictions upon unrestricted reality by our logic and our thought processes that are rooted in language.

Even now, after much learning, inquiries and direct insights into the true nature of reality, this is still true: the finite mind cannot comprehend neither the idea of infinity, nor the idea of finality. This applies not only to space, but also to time. In fact, if we look more closely, we will see that space cannot exist without time. Space, for its existence needs the duration of time. If we proceed questioning then: what is time? obviously, we will discover, that our perception of time is that of a past, present and future. If we consider our usual perceptions – beliefs that the past is already gone, and exists only in our memories, and the future has not arrived yet and does not exist yet as an actual experience, but only as a potentiality, which may, but most probably won't actualise itself as we expect it to, then, the question is: what is this 'present', which we call reality?

How long is the duration of this 'present now'?

---

[2] "The Pictorial Key to the Tarot" Arthur Edward Waite.

Beyond the Limitations of Logic

Relying on 'logic', which we are going to apply for now, before we can go altogether 'beyond logic', there are few possibilities of the mystery of time-space, or space-time continuum. One of these possibilities is that the future already exists, but we cannot perceive it due to our limited abilities of perception. Also, there is the possibility that many branches of future exist already, and which one will actualise as the 'present' will be determined by the choices one makes in the 'present'. Almost the same thing applies to the 'past'. It is possible, that the 'past' did not disappear into nothing, but still exists in the vaster 'now' and if we could speed up our abilities to perceive reality, we might break through the limitations of our perceptions of the space-time continuum, separate ourselves from our bodies, our life stories and our four-dimensional reality, and perceive the past, the present and the future simultaneously, as a time-body stretching from birth to death of a physical body, and beyond...

In fact, the experience of being outside our usual perception of the space-time continuum happened to me for the first time some years ago, when I was an active member of the so-called 'Fourth Way' school...

The Fourth Way

After many years of active search for the Ultimate Truth through the study of the ideas of great philosophers, psychologists, Gnostics, and other sources of esoteric and exoteric knowledge, I came across the book of P.D. Ouspensky, *In Search of the Miraculous*. It captured my attention and at the time seemed to me a great revelation. Within the pages of this book I found a bookmark displaying photographs of Gurdjieff and Ouspensky, the logo of the Fourth Way – the Enneagram – the name of the school – Fellowship of Friends – and a phone number. I gave them a call and was invited to attend three prospective meetings, to see if I would like to join the school.

I must admit I was impressed with the content, the presentation and above all the energy of these meetings and the people involved.

Mind you, these events took place in Moscow, just a few years after *perestroika* and *glasnost* (rebuilding and free speech), at a time when many Russian people were so hungry for spiritual knowledge after seventy years of starving for it during the Soviet regime. In those times, together with the authentic schools and groups, many pseudo schools, cults and sects began to flourish in Russia and had a very good 'harvest' of young people searching for truth…

After paying ten percent of my earnings (monthly payment to teacher), I joined the school and became a very active member. The school, its ideas and the practical work I did on myself became more important to me than any other life events, pre-school friends and even family. Almost from the very beginning, I plunged myself into the inner circle of the school. I wasn't just a passive observer attending occasional meetings, but voluntary and absolutely naturally took the responsibility for sharing the knowledge that I was rapidly assimilating into my very being, and sincerely helping other members to clear their doubts and climb the ladder of spiritual clarity.

I was very fortunate to have as my first spiritual teacher, for a period of about a year and a half, the very charismatic and humorous English actor Robert Taylor. The meetings with Robert were always filled with the electrifying energy of a real presence. Arranging very wisely and meticulously the positions of students (for the benefit of greater explosion of spiritual energy), he would have us sit in a perfect circle and face each other. He then invited us to look into each other's eyes, to look through the eyes of the person on the opposite end as the observer, into the 'one who sees'. He invited us to feel the sensations of our feet touching the floor, the sensations of the palms of our hands resting on our knees, to hear all sounds simultaneously, to see everything at once with panoramic vision, to expand our awareness to the extreme so that one may be able to perceive all at once. He encouraged us then to stop our thoughts and just be pure awareness. After some ten to fifteen minutes of total silence, within the increasingly sparkling, crackling energy, he would ask: 'when you are in love, where would you like to be?'

Someone would answer from the high state they were in: 'With my Beloved!' Robert would then say: 'Your Beloved is Here! Feel it. Where else He could be?'

I had been in the school for about three months when an extraordinary revelation happened. It was the second part of a meeting. After the break, we were divided into three small groups. The clarity and the energy were already heightened after the first part of the meeting. Around fourteen people were in our small group. The meeting started and I was trying to comprehend, without a thought construct, all impressions at once. I was looking into and through the eyes of my friends who were sharing with me these magical moments. Exactly opposite me sat a new student. I'd seen him only once before, very briefly, and hadn't had a chance to talk to him. He had this very masculine body type and energy that I found difficult to immediately open to.

I noticed that when my eyes met his eyes, they involuntarily moved their focus, trying to escape this challenging connection.

Noticing that, I asked myself: what am I afraid of? And so I decided to overcome this instinctive fear by keeping my gaze on his eyes. Truly, the eyes are the windows to our souls. Our eyes met, and we continued gazing into each other. We didn't just coldly stare with closed shutters behind our eyes.

No, our shutters – our lenses – our already dilated pupils were opening wider and wider, allowing our souls to meet! I shifted the sense of my identity onto him. Becoming him, I was looking through his eyes back into the space where my own head was located, the space behind my eyes from where I was looking. I felt simultaneously that I was he, gazing at 'me', gazing at him. I allowed him to penetrate my very heart with his gaze, into my very vulnerable essence. I also, was silently, by the power of intention, speaking to him: 'Do not just see only me, but expand your consciousness, see, hear, and feel all at once. Without moving your gaze, include in the field of your cognition, the people sitting on the left and on the right of you.'

It was fear! Fear which I somehow was able to accept, endure and transform, that suddenly released its tremendous energy. It was the condensed energy of fear, courage, and love, as also sexual energy that suddenly exploded from some hidden place.

The room and all objects in it began to metamorphose. The light and colours flashed in synchronicity with the pulsations of my rapidly beating heart. As in psychedelic works of art, I began to see everything in inverse colours; blacks swapped their positions with whites, reds were flashing as green, blue as orange, and so on... The forms and objects, including people, started to float in the air, losing their solidity, transforming into the abstract waves of radiant energy. It brought me to a critical point – the precipice of the great and scary Unknown. I was about to lose all understanding of everything. My mind, with all its objective knowledge and familiar perceptions, was about to detonate in one Big Bang!

At this terrific moment, an inner voice appeared, a voice which belongs to that part of intelligence that protects the body and mind from death.

This voice said: 'Stop here! If you go any further, you may never come back. You have no knowledge of what lies ahead. You've never been there before. Without 'knowledge', you cannot know what is going to happen. It could be far more terrifying than Death itself, it could be total and irreversible insanity!!!'

But the other, stronger (at this moment) part of me – a different type of intelligence – said: 'Go! Plunge deeper into the Unknown, it is the only way back home. This is your chance! Don't miss it. Be brave! I have seen all that is based on knowledge, and I am ready to go beyond knowledge. I am ready to die!!!'

And so, I seized this tremendous energy of fear and directed it into the ever-expanding consciousness of the Self. In the next instant, I was catapulted out of the space-time continuum, or maybe it's better to say: my consciousness broke through the illusion of four dimensions into the higher dimension beyond space and time.

Suddenly, I could comprehend simultaneously my whole life story: my body just being born, my body dying, and all moments in between. I could move freely into the past and the future. Of course, it is impossible to adequately describe the experience of that which is beyond human language. Words are too pale to transmit the energy of the miracle, but here are a few notes of this brief enlightenment:

True Knowledge presents itself not because we think hard and are trying to expand our knowledge, but, on the contrary, through movement in the opposite direction – stopping our thought process and plunging deeper into the great unknown.

Beyond the space-time continuum, there is a sun of Absolute knowledge that is shining, radiating True knowledge. This knowledge is received by touch, or by being, not by thinking.

If the real 'I' (that which emerged from the dream of the space-time continuum) is present, it is totally satisfied. No desire can arise for the real 'I', for if the real 'I' had a desire, then this desire would be immediately fulfilled without any passage of time, and so, the real 'I' is perpetually in a state of repose and absolute contentment.

Only when the real 'I' is present, is there the realisation of true doership. Before that, the perceptions, that I (the body-mind) was doing something, making an effort, etc, were simply imagination. When the real 'I' is present it rules over the unfolding of a 'play'. Just as how the organic life on Earth flourishes without the Sun's visible hand in it, so when the real 'I' is present, it does all spontaneously, without desire, without thought and without hands...

After a while, my expanded consciousness shrunk back to the perception of the continuation of a life story.

This experience of a higher realm of reality became my true teacher from then on. It was the summit of the spiritual mountain, from where I could see the landscapes of objective knowledge and the valleys of life stories with greatest clarity. As Leonardo da Vinci said, 'Wisdom is the daughter of Experience' and 'Experience is the teacher of teachers.'

Despite my present opinion that the teachings of Mr. G. I. Gurdjieff, known as the 'Fourth Way' are incomplete, sometimes contradictory, and at certain times even ridiculous, I feel it would be a shame not to include some of its most valuable points in this book, for there are many good ideas which cannot be found in any other teachings, and which are in harmony with my direct experiences and understanding.

Moreover, I feel that without these ideas, which filtered through my efforts and assimilated into my very being during of eight and a half years of life in the Fourth Way school, this book would be incomplete. Gurdjieff's ideas are very practical, and so you, my dear reader, can extract wisdom and a spiritual gain from them. In fact, for many seekers of Truth who are filled with the theoretical knowledge of highest advaita (nonduality), it could be very useful to step into the practicality of the Fourth Way. I have had encounters with many people who can talk the talk of highest wisdom but lack elementary self-observation skills and cannot walk the walk.

Finally, the beginning of my story of the search for Truth has so much to do with the Fourth Way's ideas, practice and its specific language, that I don't see how I can adequately express my ideas and experiences without tying them to the essence of Gurdjeff's teaching. Although it is not easy to be very brief, due to a special Fourth Way terminology, I promise to be very concise, separate wheat from chaff, and present here only those ideas which help me give you a better picture of the true nature of reality, along with some practical methods to help with Self -knowledge.

I must, however, warn you my dear reader, that the next twenty pages or so, could be described as 'technical', requiring special attention, due to their specific language. Obviously, my dear reader, less than anything I wish to bore you with my writings. Nevertheless, I have left these pages here, and if you get lost in them, you can skip them altogether, returning to the more interesting parts of my story. These pages can serve you as references, if you find unfamiliar words in further reading.

Man–Machine

'Man, such as we know him, the 'man-machine' the man who cannot 'do', and with whom and through whom everything 'happens', cannot have a permanent and single I. His I changes as quickly as his thoughts, feelings and moods, and he makes a profound mistake in considering himself always one and the same person; in reality he is always a different person, not the one he was a moment ago.'

~ G. I. Gurdjieff ~

A human being is a machine. A machine working on a principle of stimulus and response, taught Gurdjieff. Though he considers himself to be always the same, a human being does not have a permanent 'I'. Triggered by different external and internal stimuli, many different 'I's come to the surface of his awareness. And although they all differ, man identifies himself with each 'I' that he feels himself to be at any given moment. This explains many inner contradictions, love/hate attitudes at different times, 'I's that make decisions, and 'I's that experience the consequences of every action and decision.

To soften these inner contradictions, man unknowingly builds up 'buffers' that prevent these contradictory groups of 'I's from seeing each other.

When baby is born, it represents pure 'essence'. Although this essence already has certain tendencies for future developments, the mind is as pure as a blank sheet of paper. There are, of course, exceptions to these rules, and some individuals are born with the memories of past lives. With the growing process of learning, imitation, education and other influences of their surrounding environment, a baby accumulates and gradually builds around its vulnerable essence a sort of defence mechanism, shielding it from the dangers of the outside world: that which is known in Gurdjeff's system as 'personality'. With the further development of personality, the sense of 'identity' of a young human being begins to shift its gravity from the pure essence towards a 'borrowed from the surrounding influences' personality.

When child feels that he has done something wrong, and is going to be punished for it, to avoid the pain of punishment, he could create a momentary lie, which might save him for the time being. Feeling saved once, he can then use another lie to escape, or at least postpone punishment. These lies, and also the ideas and behavioural patterns, borrowed from the people surrounding this child, build up to create a form of protection for the vulnerable essence, which gradually turns into a prison.

The personality, which is supposed to safeguard and protect the essence from the harmful intrusions of the external world, grows into a mighty prison guard who stops allowing access to the essence, not only to 'enemies' with the weapons, but also to friends with nourishing food. The sense of identity of the individual shifts further and further from the essence into personality, which in the Fourth Way is called 'false personality'. The essence, that needs nourishment, is blocked by the false personality, stops getting enough attention, and in some cases, even dies. Gurdjieff said that there are many people walking this earth, who are internally dead...

Without the permanent single 'I', the man-machine does not have a true single will, and although man imagines that he is in control of his destiny, everything just 'happens' to him, in the same way that the weather just happens. And so, the man-machine is only under the illusion of free will.

The other very important statement of this system is that the man-machine does not remember himself. In other words, most of the time he is not conscious of himself. His awareness of himself is lost, so to speak, in the perceptions of the external world...

Man-Machine

The many 'I's that man-machine takes to be his real 'I', come to the surface of his awareness from different places of his 'apparatus'.

We have seen already the division of essence and false personality. The next very important point to grasp in this system is that man does not have just one 'brain' – one centre of intelligence. He has several centres, which are responsible for different types of intelligence, work at different speeds, and consume different types of fuel for their performance. Gurdjieff gives us the definitions of five so-called 'lower centres' associated with the functions of the 'machine' and of two higher centres, associated with higher intelligence, or consciousness, which is fully developed and constantly 'at work', but with which the man-machine has no conscious connection.

The five lower centres are as follows: 1) the intellectual centre, 2) the emotional centre, 3) the moving centre, 4) the instinctive centre, and 5) the sexual centre. Each centre is further divided into three parts: 1) intellectual, 2) emotional, and 3) mechanical. The division of these centres into the three parts represent a different level of attention with which they are working. The mechanical parts of these centres work with the minimum level of attention, where the attention is almost automatic or mechanical.

To give you a very brief example, let's look at the mechanical part of a moving centre. Moving centres are responsible for the body's movements. This does not include respiration, yawning, sneezing and other involuntary body movements; these are governed by the instinctive centre. When learning of a certain movement, for example, learning to walk, or to tie shoes laces, or ride a bicycle, or drive a car, etc., one must bring into the learning process the maximum attention, and in the beginning the desired movements are very difficult and slow. This is an example of the workings of the intellectual part of the moving centre.

With practice and repetition, one begins to master these movements and in succeeding in them, feels joy. This indicates the working of the emotional part of the moving centre.

When the desired movements become very natural, habitual patterns, one is no longer required to paying much attention to the movements, they just happen automatically. This indicates the working of the mechanical part of the moving centre – the part requiring the minimum level of attention.

Similar examples apply to all the lower centres. The mechanical part of the instinctive centre, which does not require any attention is responsible for all those invisible mechanical processes within the body such as the growing of bones, nails, hairs etc., the circulation of blood, the secretion of hormones, digestion, etc....

Within the emotional part of the instinctive centre there is joy and appreciation of the sensual instinctive pleasures, and also repulsion from unpleasant sensations and pain.

The intellectual part of the instinctive centre requires special attention, for this part is said to have a special type of intelligence responsible for the protection of the human machine from harm, danger and death. This intelligence is said to be very ancient (reptilian) and highly developed. Certain types of intuition and some psychic powers are said to be a part of this intelligence. One thing that Gurdjieff points out is that this part of human beings is not interested in 'awakening'. Awakening is something that the intellectual part of the instinctive centre is frightened of.

It is this intelligence of the intellectual part of the instinctive centre, which in Fourth Way jargon is called the King of Clubs that was speaking to me in the above story: 'Stop! Don't go there! You may never come back, for you don't know what lies ahead!' The only part of human intelligence, which can be stronger than King of Clubs is the King of Hearts – the intellectual part of the emotional centre.

The King of Hearts is that part of a human being that can, firstly, control the lower parts of the emotional centre, preventing the wastage of energy through the identification with and expression of negative emotions; and secondly, gather the energy and direct it towards something higher than itself, namely the higher centres, which it even can sacrifice itself for. As an example, in the story above, the King of Hearts was that part of me which said: 'Go! Plunge yourself deeply into the unknown! It is the only way Home!' The King of Hearts is the part that can 'feel' God!

It is also the part which can work with the highest speed and on the most refined fuel. It can utilise and transform the energy of instinctive fear, or extreme beauty into ever-expanding consciousness...

The slowest part of the human machine is the intellectual centre, responsible for thought processes. The mechanical part of the intellectual centre was called by Gurdjieff a 'formatory apparatus'. This part – the Jack of Diamonds is a sort of a library in which the information is stored. The Jack of Diamonds collects, without great deal of a selectivity, all sorts of useful and useless information. Very often the false personality is based around this formatory apparatus.

The work of the Jack of Diamonds is not a real thinking process, but a sort of operation of the memory bank. It is a search and matching of already accumulated information and clichés, borrowed from external sources. A good example of the working of the mechanical part of the intellectual centre is a quiz show, in which one must find an answer to a certain question within a short period of time. Very often, those people who can answer quickly are considered by many to be very intelligent beings.

But all their knowledge in fact is borrowed knowledge; not the result of their thinking, but rather their ability to quickly pick up certain information stored in their memory.

The other type of intelligence which belongs to the function of the intellectual part of the intellectual centre is a different type of thinking. It is the ability to look at a question from many different perspectives, giving extensive thought to a chosen subject. But most importantly, this King of Diamonds, like the King of Hearts can also sacrifice himself, cut off the chain of associative, or opposite thinking, and experience a state free of thought...

It is worth mentioning that each part of each centre is further divided into positive and negative parts. The best example of these divisions is in the emotional parts of centres. The Queen of Hearts (the emotional part of the emotional centre) very often flips between love and hate. She is a drama queen. This part of the human machine works very fast and with lots of energy, which can be easily spilled out as an expression of negativity. Only the King of Hearts can catch this extremely fast throwing of energy, seize this energy and transform it into love, gratitude and ever-expanding consciousness.

Man-Machine

All centres work with different speeds and consume different types of fuel. The slowest centre, as I have already mentioned, is an intellectual centre, followed by the moving and instinctive centres. However, the King of Clubs can work at very high speeds and, in the moments of real danger and life-threatening situations, can even snatch all the energy from all other centres, in order to save a body. There are many stories of people performing extraordinary actions, without remembering them, in situations of great danger.

One part of the human machine that works with a big amount of refined energy is the emotional part of the emotional centre. Unfortunately, this refined energy is very often lost through expressions of negativity. The Queen of Hearts loves the drama of love/hate relationships. Expressing negative emotions is one of the major ways for the machine to lose or get rid of excessive energy, which could otherwise be used for a higher purpose – namely, the connection with the higher centres.

One lower centre which I haven't mentioned yet, is the sexual centre. According to Gurdjieff, the sexual centre produces and works with a very high energy which can be used for the reconnection with the higher centres, but this energy is constantly getting used by the activities of all the other lower centres. The energy is lost through the unnecessary excitements and activities of the different parts of the human machine, such as physical exertion, mental rehearsing and replaying of certain scenarios, unnecessary talking, imagination, expressions of negative emotions etc....

In the next step in this brief look at the Fourth Way ideas, I want to display the way the 'human chemical factory' refines and transmutes food substances into higher substances and energies. To understand these processes however, I must introduce a few other Fourth Way ideas.

Three and Seven – The Fundamental Laws

To understand Gurdjieff's teaching, we must understand the two fundamental laws that govern processes in the universe. The combination and interconnectedness of these laws are very beautifully presented graphically in the Enneagram – the main symbol of the Fourth Way system of knowledge. These laws are *the law of three* and *the law of seven*...

The law of three postulates that Newton's law of motion – for every action, there is an equal and opposite reaction – is incorrect, for there are not two forces that produce action, but three: active, passive and neutralising. The system says that if there were only two forces in nature, they simply would cancel each other out, and so the action would stop. The system says that the active and the passive (or reactive) forces are usually obvious, but the third force (the neutralising force) is often invisible. And yet it is the third force that helps active or passive forces proceed in one or another direction.

We can find the principle of 'trinity' in practically every religion, as well as in sacred geometry and in theories of the creation of the universe. We will come back to further exploration of the law of three and the Holy Trinity later in this book...

The second fundamental law, about which I would like to talk extensively is the law of seven. To understand the meaning of this law, we should look upon the universe as consisting of vibrations of different density, proceeding from different sources in various directions and interacting with each other; colliding, strengthening,

41

weakening, arresting one another and so on. This law states that a view that vibrations are continuous (meaning that they proceed, ascend, or descend uniformly and gradually if they do not interact with another force) is incorrect.

The law of seven introduces the discontinuity of vibrations. It postulates that the vibrations develop not uniformly, but with periodical accelerations and retardations. The examples of workings of this law we can find in different sorts of vibrations, such as light, heat, chemistry, or magnetism, but the easiest way to see it is in the vibrations of sound.

A study of the seven-tone musical scale gives us a very good foundation for understanding this cosmic law – the law of octaves. It has been found through the observations of sound vibrations, that between the lower note 'do' and the higher 'do' (in which there is twice the amount of vibrations of the lower 'do') there are two places where a retardation in the increase of vibrations takes place. These retardations take place in the intervals between 'mi' and 'fa' and between 'ti' and the higher 'do' notes.

We can find the applications of the law of octaves in our everyday life. For example, when we are inspired to start a certain project, we feel so much energy and a great potential at the very beginning. This new beginning is the 'do' of a new ascending octave. We start working on a project and are still filled with the energy of original inspiration – the original 'do' of an octave. And so we proceed through 're' and 'mi', but at this point we begin to feel tired and bored with the project. Here we have reached the interval in this ascending octave where the progression slows down and started to deviate from the original direction. We can get stuck there until better times come, or we can find a third force (the law of three) in the form of new knowledge, new insight, new inspiration etc. If we can find a third force, we can 'bridge the interval' between 'mi' and 'fa'. We can give an additional power to our ascending octave in such a way, that it will continue to ascend all the way through 'fa' 'sol' 'la' 'ti', almost to the very end, where the second retardation, or deviation of the octave takes place. It is often the case that when we are almost at the end of the project, a new interval between 'ti' and the higher 'do' takes place, which can be 'bridged' by the additional vibrations of extra effort, a strong motivation etc....

Three and Seven – The Fundamental Laws

All this knowledge of bridging intervals and finding a third force can be quite helpful for success in life, but the true reason, I am including this system of knowledge in this book lies in further elaboration of 'vibrations'...

I am using these brief examples from Gurdjieff's teachings to lay down the foundation for our beautiful building of knowledge, which we are going to dismantle in the end, like Buddhist monks destroying a stunning mandala after its completion. For despite the beauty of objective knowledge, this knowledge rooted in words and logic is itself only a prison. In fact, as we will see further, the letters, the vibrations of the sounds of letters, the words and sentences they create, themselves are the building blocks of the illusion of the appearance. True knowledge, as well as real beauty is prior, or beyond words, and the only aim of these writings is to show you how to break through the walls of this seemingly beautiful illusion and prepare you for the miraculous transition from the unreal to the real.

The Ray of Creation

The next of Gurdjieff's ideas, the Ray of Creation may seem very naïve, if taken literally. Gurdjieff paints a rather primitive picture with the Ray of Creation. If the Absolute is like a radiant sun, then our Milky Way galaxy, our sun, our planets, our Earth and moon are all only one ray of creation, one ray of this sun – the Absolute.

The next manifestation, emanating from the Absolute is 'all worlds', the next 'all suns', the next 'our sun', the next 'planets', the next 'Earth' and lastly 'the moon'. According to Gurdjieff, the moon is an unborn planet, which is getting ready to be born. It is gradually getting warmer and in some short astrological time will become a planet itself. I am not going to comment on this limited view, but rather will go into the different aspect of this theory of creation. According to Gurdjieff, and as we will see further, many other sources of knowledge, the three forces (the active, the passive and the neutralising), although they appear to have different functions, constitute one whole Absolute...

"In forming one independent whole, the three forces possess a full and independent will, full consciousness, full understanding of themselves and of everything they do. The idea of the unity of the three forces in the Absolute forms the basis of many ancient teachings – consubstantial and indivisible Trinity, Trimurti – Brahma, Vishnu, and Shiva, and so on.

The three forces of the Absolute, constituting one whole, separate and unite at their own will and by their own decision, and at these junctions they create phenomena, or 'worlds'. These worlds, created by the will of the Absolute, depend entirely upon this will for everything that concerns their own existence. In each of these worlds the three forces again act. However, since each of these worlds is now not a whole, but only a part, then the three forces in them do not form a single whole. It is now a case of three wills, three consciousnesses, three unities. Each of the three forces contains within it the possibility of all three forces, but at the meeting point of the three forces each of them manifests only one principle – the active, the passive, or the neutralising. The three forces together form a trinity which produces new phenomena. But this trinity is different, it is not that which was in the Absolute, where the three forces formed an indivisible whole and possessed one single will and one single consciousness. In the worlds of a second order, the three forces are now divided, and their meeting points are now of a different nature. In the Absolute, the moment and point of their meeting is determined by their single will. In the words of the second order, where there is no longer a single will but three wills, the points of issue are each determined by a separate will, independent of the others, and therefore the meeting point becomes accidental or mechanical. The will of the Absolute creates the worlds of the second order and governs them, but it does not govern their creative work, in which a mechanical element makes its appearance."[3]

At the source of all creation there is a single independent will of the Absolute in which the three forces are not separate from the Absolute and they create the 'worlds' fashioned by the will of the Absolute. Gurdjieff calls these highest orders of creation 'world one' and 'world three'. But as creation progresses, new secondary orders of creation take place, in which three forces appear, in addition to the three forces acting as an expression of the single will of the Absolute. This second order of creation called 'world six'. In the third order of creation, where in addition to the three forces of the Absolute and the three forces of a secondary order, another six more mechanical forces appear. This is called 'world twelve'.

To summarise, the Ray of Creation according to Gurdjieff appears as follows: 1) Absolute – world one, 2) all worlds – world three, 3) all suns – world six, 4) our sun – world twelve, 5) planets

---

[3] "In Search of the Miraculous: Fragments of an Unknown Teaching" P.D.Ouspensky.

– world twenty-four, 6) Earth – world forty-eight, 7) moon – world ninety-six.

Although this elementary scheme undoubtedly appears very primitive, if looked at it from a different angle, it gives us a better understanding...

Quantum Mechanics

*'If quantum mechanics hasn't profoundly
shocked you, you haven't understood it yet'*

~ Neils Bohr ~

A t this point, I would like to introduce into this book just a very few concise ideas of the branch of science called quantum mechanics. I am not a mathematician or a scientist myself, so I am not going to claim a faultless precision and absolute accuracy on this subject but will nevertheless give you the essence of it in an easy-to-digest language. I am not going to analyse every little detail of it, use scientific terminology, or mathematical equations, but outline the key points of quantum mechanics in a language that can be easily understood.

It must be clear that the science at best can provide us only with the models of reality, not the reality itself. All these models of reality lie within the domain of language and symbols – interpretations of reality. Infinite reality can never be understood by a finite mind but can only be realised by total identity with it through direct experience.

Scientists, at least at present, do not know how reality works. They only hypothesise and build theories about reality, based on the rational thinking and logic that results from the experiments they perform and mathematical equations they solve. Science and mathematics break down when approaching Infinity.

Supreme intelligence – God Absolute – the source of all laws and all appearances, the source from which space-time and all things emerged, itself has never been born or created, it didn't have a beginning and it is never going to end. The finite mind can never comprehend this truth.

The main reason I am going to write about the scientific theories is that, being part of your own creation, scientific discoveries can also serve as a helpful clue, pointing you in right direction if you dig deep into their true meaning. Pioneering science, specifically quantum mechanics, point to ideas similar to what ancient scriptures and maharishis were saying a long time ago; that what we perceive as reality is an illusion, it only appears to be that way to our senses and mind, but the appearance itself covers the truth. At the deepest levels, reality has its own rules, which do not obey the physical laws of so-called 'local realism.'

If we look at the Ray of Creation as an emergence of creation from what is known in quantum mechanics as a 'quantum field', 'zero-point energy field', 'vacuum', or 'grand unified field of infinite possibilities', then the Ray of Creation starts to make more sense.

Creation did not begin in some far removed place in time 'past'; some thirteen point eight billion years ago with the explosion of a singularity, triggered by a quantum fluctuation known as the 'Big Bang', but is continuously emerging – emitting from the 'Eternal Presence', the grand unified field of infinite possibilities. If we believe those scientists who are holding on to the Big Bang, the question still remains: wasn't there time before the Big Bang?

To go into the beginning of time, we do not need to go into the far removed past, but to zoom into the very 'Presence' – before the perceptions of the space-time continuum formed. We must zoom inwards towards the source of perceptions, as we would follow fractals stretching into ever-narrowing units of time, which, with the process of penetration into it, paradoxically will widen, expand and explode with a new heightened clarity of intelligence and the increasing energy of inner dimensions of infinite reality.

A good illustration here would be the movie *Inception*, in which certain individuals induce and penetrate the hierarchical depths of dream states. With each deeper level within the dream realities, the time gap widens exponentially. We can say that the whole length of this movie, with all its extraordinary stories happens within the narrow time gap of a car falling from a bridge into the river.

Scientists (quantum mechanics) penetrate the narrow units of time with the help of hadron colliders. They are able to accelerate the speed of particles to near the speed of light, then let them to collide. They are able to take pictures of the moment of collision. Studying the trajectories of the smaller particles after they have smashed in the special photo chamber, they then have some insights into the nature of behaviour of the 'very small' – the building blocks of reality, and also the origin of time.

As I mentioned earlier however, the scientific method of investigation of reality is an indirect method, for what it studies falls into the category of phenomena, or appearance. To investigate reality directly, one must study oneself – the very source of awareness-consciousness and all appearances within it.

Are there any scientists out there who are not the product of your creative consciousness, my dear reader? Isn't it you who allows them to appear within your consciousness? Would they be there if you weren't aware of them? And if they were there but you were completely oblivious of them, would they matter to you at all?

Even when scientists are trying to study consciousness itself by studying of workings of a body-cosmos, such as studying brain functions, neuron activities, DNA structures, hormone secretions, etc., they are still studying only appearances. Even when they are studying in their experiments the neuron and microtubules activities of a person under the influence of consciousness-expanding substances, such as psilocybin mushrooms or DMT, they are still studying the phenomena and not the source.

There is simply no other way to study consciousness than to study oneself – the source of consciousness!

However, we should not completely ignore all scientific research, for they appear within your consciousness for a certain purpose; they are the clues that Creator left in this dream-appearance – to trace your way back home to your true nature, to wake up from the limitations of the illusory dream-reality into the unlimited freedom of Highest Reality.

If you are willing to question and to learn from appearances, if you are willing to look at and accept every event of your life as a teacher, who, if you allow it to, can teach you something every time that you haven't realised before, or simply forgot, something more insightful and profound about your true nature, you are on the right track for Self-discovery.

And so, quantum mechanics gives us a clue about our real nature, pointing out that; 'It is conscious observation, that is causing a wave function to collapse into a particle' in other words: it is you who creates the appearance of the material world by observing it. It is you who is causing the infinite potentialities – the quantum ocean of infinite possibilities – to collapse into only one of all possible patterns. The conscious observer creates the world as he/she goes along by the very act of conscious observation.

So, here we come to the very interesting point on the nature of that which is known as the 'present', or 'reality'. We see that in comparisons with the highest speeds of subatomic particles, our perception or cognition of our created reality is very slow. If things begin to move very fast, they leave only traces, like the circular movement of a firebrand. We do not perceive the actual movement of firebrand, just the ring of fire-glow. If the speed increases, moving objects disappear completely from our view. We cannot perceive jumps from one photo frame to the next while we are watching a movie in a cinema, but instead we perceive a smoothly unfolding story. We cannot perceive the changing colours of every pixel on a TV screen, but instead perceive a whole picture. The human ear cannot perceive frequencies of sound lower than twenty hertz, or higher than twenty thousand hertz. The analogies could go on and on... Our ordinary perceptions of 'waking reality', our perceptions of what we call a 'present moment' are within the boundaries of the speed of our cognition. Or to put it in other words: it is our special type of a cognitive process that projects restrictions called 'the world' upon unrestricted reality...

From the moment of the eternal 'NOW' to the moment of human cognition of what we consider as 'now' is an astronomically long time. What we consider as the 'present moment' – 'now' – is in fact a 'past'.

Everything has a different lifespan, a universe, a galaxy, a star, a planet, organic life, a human being, a living cell, a molecule, an atom, an electron, a subatomic particle, a virtual photon etc. When we are talking about the quantum field and the lifespan of virtual particles and antiparticles, we are talking about infinitesimally small scales. These scales appear infinitesimally small to our human perception, but for subatomic particles themselves it is a lifetime.

When we are approaching a 'quantum world', all our usual physical laws start to break down.

Quantum mechanics undoubtedly points to the idea that at the very foundation, at the very core of reality, at this 'eternal moment', before the void begins to split itself into asymmetrical particles and antiparticles, there is oneness and nonlocality. The principle of superposition, for example, claims that while we do not know what the state of any object is, it is in all possible states simultaneously, as long as we don't look to check.

It is the process of observation, or a measurement itself, that causes the object to be limited to a single possibility.

The famous 'double-slit' experiment gives us very interesting insights into the nature of light. The first part of this experiment shows us that light behaves like a wave. This experiment was performed by Thomas Yung a century before quantum mechanics were born. The simple presentation of this experiment is as follows; if the light passes through one slit, then on a screen behind this slit we find, as expected, one band of light. But if the light passes through the double slit (two slits close to each other), then surprisingly on the screen behind the slits we observe instead of two bands of light a different pattern – pattern that is known as the 'interference pattern', which we usually find in situations where the waves are passing through two gaps near each other. But the most surprising results were found in the second part of the double-slit experiment, which was performed much later with the development of quantum mechanics and technology.

When scientists decided to look and measure what was happening when the light passed through the double slit, instead of the 'interference pattern', which indicates a wave function of light, they found two streaks of light, which indicates that light now behaved as particles. This experiment has been performed countless times since then, with additional modifications such as firing electrons or photons through the slits one at the time etc. The results are always the same; i.e. if the light passes through the double slit without being measured, it behaves as a wave, if measuring devices are trying to 'see' which slit the photon or electron is passing through, it behaves as a particle.

These experiments gave a foundation for the famous 'Copenhagen interpretation of quantum mechanics', devised by Neils Bohr and Werner Heisenberg. The essence of this is: the act of measurement affects the system, causing the set of probabilities to reduce to only one of the possible values immediately after the measurement, or in other words; conscious observation causes the wave function to collapse into a particle.

Of course, the Copenhagen interpretation is debatable and not the only quantum theory. Albert Einstein, for example could not accept the idea that 'if I don't look at the moon, there is no moon, or the moon is everywhere in a quantum superposition state, and only if I look at the moon, the moon is materialised.' Neither he could accept the idea of quantum entanglement, calling it a 'spooky action at distance'.

In quantum entanglement, it appears that one particle of an entangled pair 'knows' what measurement has been performed on the other, and to what outcome, even though there is no known means for such information to be communicated between particles, which at the time of measurement may be separated by arbitrarily great distances.

In the EPR (Einstein, Podolsky, Rosen) thought experiment, which came to be known as the 'EPR paradox', Einstein and others considered such behaviour to be impossible, as it violates the 'local realist' view of causality and argued that the accepted formulation of quantum mechanics must therefore be incomplete. Later however, the counterintuitive predictions of quantum mechanics were verified experimentally. Experiments have been performed involving measuring the polarisation or spin of entangled particles in different directions, which – by producing violations of Bell's inequality – demonstrate statistically that the local realist view cannot be correct. This has been shown to occur even when the measurements are performed more quickly than light could travel between the sites of measurement: there is no light speed or slower influence that can pass between the entangled particles. Recent experiments have measured entangled particles within less than one-hundredth of a percent of the travel time of light between them.

According to the formalism of quantum theory, the effect of measurement happens instantly.

Quantum entanglement proposes – and it has been experientially proven – that if on one of the two 'tween particles', or entangled particles, that were sent in different directions, even as far as the different ends of the universe, changed polarity or spin, the other entangled particle would change polarity or spin instantaneously. This means that at the quantum level, information does not require time to propagate, it travels faster than the speed of light, it travels instantaneously.

"In 1964, J.S. Bell published a mathematical proof which came to be known as Bell's theorem. Bell's theorem is a mathematical construct which, as such, is indecipherable to the non-mathematician. Its implications, however, could affect profoundly our basic world view. Some physicists are convinced that it is the most important single work, in the history of physics. One of the implications of Bell's theorem is that at a deep and fundamental level, the 'separate parts' of the universe are connected in an intimate and immediate way. In short, Bell's theorem and the enlightened experience of unity are very compatible. In 1972, John Clauser and Stuart Freedman at the Lawrence Berkeley laboratory performed an experiment to confirm or disprove the predictions of the theorem. They found that the statistical predictions upon which Bell based his theorem are correct.

Bell's theorem not only suggests that the world is quite different than it seems, it demands it!

There is no question about it. Physicists have proven that our rational ideas about the world in which we live are profoundly deficient. In short, Bell's theorem shows that the principle of local causes, however reasonable it sounds, is an illusion!"[4]

Of course, the Copenhagen interpretation is not the only interpretation, or theory of quantum mechanics. There are many other theories speculating on the mechanism of how reality works. Among them is Hugh Everett's many-worlds interpretation. The many-worlds interpretation asserts the objective reality of the universal wavefunction and denies the actuality of wavefunction

---

[4] "The Dancing Wu Li Masters: An Overview of the New Physics" Gary Zukav.

collapse. Many-worlds implies that all possible alternate histories and futures are real, each representing an actual 'world' (or 'universe'). The hypothesis states there is very large – perhaps infinite – number of universes, and everything that could possibly have happened in our past, but did not, has occurred in the past of some other universe or universes. Before many-worlds, reality had always been viewed as a single unfolding history. Many-worlds, however, views reality as a many-branched tree, wherein every possible quantum outcome is realised.

In many-worlds, the subjective appearance of wavefunction collapse is explained by the mechanism of 'quantum decoherence' – a sort of leaking of the universal wavefunction into the environment, and this is supposed to resolve all the paradoxes of quantum theory, since every possible outcome of every event defines or exists in its own 'history' or 'world'. The many-worlds interpretation treats the other histories or worlds as real since it regards the universal wavefunction as the basic physical entity or 'the fundamental entity'.

The idea of many worlds is very attractive and reminds me a famous treatise attributed to sage Valmiki – Yoga Vasishta, in which there are worlds within worlds, stories within stories, parallel realities, stretching or shrinking of time and the infinite possibilities of infinite consciousness, which would seem to be impossible for the rational mind, taking place.

There are many other interpretations and theories speculating on how reality works. Among them the ideas of holographic reality, multiple big bangs, organic universes, virtual reality, or digital reality, etc…

One of the very popular theories is superstring theory. Some physicists believe that, at the 'beginning of the universe' (up to 0.000000000000000000000000000000000000000001 of a second after the Big Bang), the four fundamental forces were once a single fundamental force. According to string theory, every particle in the universe, at its most microscopic level (Planck length), consists of varying combinations of vibrating strings (or strands) with preferred patterns of vibration. String theory claims that it is through these specific oscillatory patterns of strings that a particle of unique mass and force charge is created (that is to say, the electron is a type of string that vibrates one way, while the up-quark is a type of string vibrating another way, and so forth).

Superstring theory proposes that the fundamental fabric of reality consists of one-dimensional strings vibrating in an 11-dimensional space. The superstring theory, with its further development, gave rise to what is known as the second superstring revolution, leading to the birth of M-theory. 'M' stands for the open interpretation of 'magic', 'mystery', or 'membrane'. M-Theory, like the many-worlds theory, proposes the existence of parallel realities. In this sense, the reality can be considered not as the only universe, but rather as part of a 'multiverse'. String theory and M-theory require the presence of 10 or 11 space-time dimensions respectively. The extra 6 or 7 dimensions may either be compactified on a very small scale, or our universe may simply be localised on a dynamic (3+1)-dimensional object, a 'D3-brane'. This opens up the possibility that there are other 'branes' which could support other universes. This is unlike the universes in the quantum multiverse, but both concepts can operate at the same time. Some scenarios postulate that our 'Big Bang' was created, along with our universe, by the collision of two branes.

There exist countless other theories concerning the nature of reality and the processes of creation. As Ramana Maharshi once said: 'There may be any number of theories of creation. All of them extend outwardly. There will be no limit to them, because time and space are unlimited. They are however only in the mind. If you see the mind, time and space are transcended and the Self is realised.'[5]

After this brief excursion into the weird worlds of quantum mechanics, which to the ordinary folks appear more like science-fiction, but nevertheless it is science at its best, let us return for a while to Gurdjeff's idea of the Ray of Creation.

But before we do, I would like to point out certain similarities between Gurdjeff's teaching and superstring theory, as well as M-theory.

All these theories also harmoniously correspond with the principle of 'Spanda' of the Kashmir Shaivism tradition and Tantric philosophy. 'Spanda' according to an ancient texts of

---

[5] "Be As You Are: The Teachings of Sri Ramana Maharshi" David Godman

Kashmir Shaivism tradition is the creative vibration, the heartbeat of Shiva. It is the radiance, the thrill, the throb, the pulsation of consciousness, the vibration of Shiva and Shakti's ecstatic union, the sacred tremor of our spiritual heart from which countless creations are rippling, bubbling, sparkling, cascading into existence.

Let us look now again at the Ray of Creation that is throbbing, vibrating, shining countless worlds into existence, not from the viewpoint of a primordial past on a macro-scale, not from an ancient Big Bang, but from the Big Bangs of the 'Eternal Present' – from this awesome, pregnant with energy and intelligence timeless void, which splits itself into particles and antiparticles, from this grand unified field of infinite possibilities, prior to human cognition of 'world appearance'.

Note that from the moment of the real timeless 'now', prior even to the 'planck scale' (0.0000000000000000000000000000000000000000001 of a second) to the moment of cognition of the so called 'present moment' by a human being (0.04 of a second according to some scientists), is 'light years'.

Do – Ti – La – Sol – Fa – Mi – Re – Do

As stated by Gurdjieff, from the point of view of law of three – (Holy Trinity/active-passive-neutralising forces) combined with the law of seven (law of discontinuity and asymmetry of vibrations), creation begins with the first note 'Do', which is conductor of the active force. The active force which creates the note 'Do' in the Absolute represents the maximum frequency of vibrations or the greatest density of vibrations.

This first note 'Do' could be compared with the Pranava – the mystical sound AUM or OM from which creation originates according to Vedas and the Visionaries of Reality – the maharishis (great seers). AUM or OM is said to be the primordial sound, which is also called Shabda-Brahman – the essence and the source of ultimate reality.

The expression 'density of vibrations' corresponds to the frequency of vibrations and is used as the opposite to 'density of matter'. In other words, the higher the density of matter, the lower the density of vibrations, and, vice versa; the higher the density of vibrations the lower the density of matter. The greatest density of vibrations is found in the finest, most rarefied matter. The active force in the Absolute represents the maximum density of vibrations, while the matter in which these vibrations proceed represents the minimum density of matter.

In his presentation of the Ray of Creation, Gurdjieff says that three forces of the Absolute, following the law of octaves, act within the three types of matter of different density. Gurdjieff

Do – Ti – La – Sol – Fa – Mi – Re – Do

names these as Carbon (C), Nitrogen (N) and Oxygen (O), also creating a new form of substance, phenomena or world which Gurdjieff calls Hydrogen (H). Beginning with 'Hydrogen 6'-'World 6', the descending order of creation gradually becomes more mechanical, producing worlds of lower order (H – 12), (H – 24), (H – 48), (H – 96) …

Again, according to Gurdjieff: the terms 'carbon', 'nitrogen', 'oxygen' and 'hydrogen' used here have a very broad meaning. It is not the same 'hydrogen' that is known in chemistry. 'Hydrogen', as a child of 'carbon', 'nitrogen' and 'oxygen', forms and completes the family, so to speak. Any simple element is a 'hydrogen', but any combination of elements which possesses a definite function, either in the world or in the human organism is also a 'hydrogen'. This definition of matters enables us to classify them in the order of their relationship to life and to the functions of a human organism. Each 'hydrogen' includes an enormous number of different substances connected together and representing a definite 'cosmic group'. Gurdjieff suggests that all 'hydrogens', beginning with the highest density of vibrations (H6) and ending with the lowest density of vibrations (H3072) can be found and play a part in human organisms and in the world, we are living in.

In a way, these interactions of elements through the notes of the octave remind me very much of the ideas of Hindu philosophy regarding the play of gunas. Rajas can be compared to an active force, Tamas to the resisting force and Sattva to a neutralising force. And although gunas begin their ever-changing dance only at the level of Prakriti (Nature), in the pure order of creation, preceding the play of gunas, we also find play of trinity (three forces); Brahma – Vishnu – Shiva, Shiva – Shakti – Nara (individual), Para (highest) – Parapara (medium) – Apara (lower), Father – Son – Holy Ghost etc…

Each level of world-order is saturated or impregnated with energies and influences of all levels above. The universe is brought into being by the will of a Supreme Creator of inconceivable and ineffable intelligence through a series of world-orders of increasingly detailed manifestation. Because of this sequence, each world-order is directed not only by its own intelligence, but is also subject to the laws of all higher orders, so that the whole creation is

Do – Ti – La – Sol – Fa – Mi – Re – Do

a living structure continuously vivified by the influence of the Absolute which permeates all the inferior levels.

Just like a computer programmer sets the rules, instructions and algorithm (code) for the computer program to run and if those set of instructions are efficient enough, they (the instructions) can proceed on their own, creating and propagating fractal patterns, virtual games or virtual realities, so does the Absolute create a general plan for the rest of the universe, which then further develops, mechanically driven by the set of rules. The will of the Absolute cannot directly manifest itself in subsequent worlds apart from this plan, and, in manifesting itself in accordance with this plan, it takes the form of mechanical laws. Should the Absolute decide to manifest its true essence upon a subsequent order of creation, it would destroy the 'game'.

Gurdjieff then proceeds to say that the density of vibration corresponds to the level of intelligence. The highest frequency of vibration indicates greater intelligence. I will elaborate further on this point, for this will bring us to the idea of a 'hierarchical structure of reality', or hierarchy of the levels of intelligence, and also hierarchy of the levels of lucidity and the hierarchy of the perceivers, references to which we can find in ancient yogic and tantric scriptures.

When scientists equipped with the latest technology focus their attention on the world of infinitesimally small spaces and infinitesimally small measures of time, they do not see the astral, mental, archetypal, metaphysical worlds, but instead they perceive the worlds of living cells, molecules, atoms, electrons, quarks, virtual photons and other subatomic particles.

Through zooming within themselves with introverted attention and awareness, yogis, rishis, sages, visionaries, or people who have broken through the threshold of ordinary perception with the help of the wisdom of sacred plants, on the other hand, instead of perceiving cells, molecules, atoms or subatomic particles are amazed to perceive countless 'more real, than real' inner worlds of a shockingly magnificent nature. They see and experience worlds of aliens, archetypes, parallel realities, worlds of sacred geometry and dancing sequences of numbers, terrifying hells, delightful paradises, angels, gods, goddesses, divine beings, dances of the letters of the Divine alphabet etc....

Do – Ti – La – Sol – Fa – Mi – Re – Do

And so, the studying of a fundamental reality by scientists and studying of fundamental reality by yogis follows a different route and leads to different discoveries.

Although the great minds of the scientific world are gradually coming to the same conclusions concerning the fundamental nature of reality, that is that reality is different to what it appears to be, and that the foundation of reality – the very source of it – is consciousness, they are still missing the most important point, that consciousness – the foundation of reality – is the subject; the Self. It cannot be found in external objects, be these objects sentient or insentient. Infinite consciousness cannot be understood by finite minds and the source of all appearances – the Greatest Mystery – reality, cannot be rationalised but can only be directly realised within oneself by the subject him/herself, who is none other than God Absolute.

Returning to the Ray of creation: 'Hydrogen', for easier understanding, is the substance (the energy-intelligence of a certain density of vibration) permeating and operating within the corresponding 'worlds'. These orders of 'worlds' with the corresponding 'hydrogens' are not only found outside of the body world, but also within the human organism, and also within the psychic, or psychological body, so to speak.

Gurdjieff for example says, that the Sun is 'world 12', planets are 'world 24', the Earth is 'world 48' and the moon is 'world 96'. The numbers corresponding to these worlds show the numbers of laws operating within these worlds. But these worlds and the number of laws operating within these worlds, also can be found within the human.

The pure 'essence', uncontaminated by the process of education, imitations and thought formation, is said to be 'world 24', which also corresponds to and is in harmony and mutual connection with 'nature'. The essence is in harmonious resonance and a simple joyful relationship with nature, as also it feeds on nature, so to speak, for a beautiful nature is filled with 'hydrogen 24' and the 'essence' resonates with the same vibrations and is wide open to receive its food (the impressions), before it begins to be covered by the false personality.

The 'false personality' on the other hand is said to be 'world 96', the world under the influence of additional mechanical laws.

Do – Ti – La – Sol – Fa – Mi – Re – Do

The quality of the energy of this world of the 'false personality' is much heavier, so to speak, than that of the 'pure essence'. The essence surely has more freedom than the false personality, which buries itself under the weight of additional restrictions. The 'essence' gravity, so to speak, lies in the emotional centre. The gravity of the 'false personality' on the other hand centres around the intellectual centre.

Nevertheless, the simple and beautiful 'essence' is not the highest part in a human being. Our real 'I', is said to be the 'world 12 and 6'.

To reconnect with the real 'I', and to establish one's identity with this 'I', one must do the intelligent work on oneself.

The work on oneself often begins with the creating of the so-called 'true personality', which said to be 'world 48'. 'True personality' is a 'group of 'I's', that is interested in the inner evolution of man, and is centred on 'work on oneself'. The work on oneself usually begins with the processes of self-observation. The man-machine does not know itself but assumes that it knows itself very well. In the beginning of the work, a man should create an 'observer'. He has to separate a part of himself from the machine and personality without judgment, and, without going into the analyses, simply observe and make mental pictures of the behaviour of the machine, registering not only the movements of the machine, but the work of all lower centres (emotions, thoughts, sensations, etc.).

The 'observer' (witness) gradually grows into a 'steward' and a preparing machine for the arrival of a 'Master'- the Real 'I'. Together with the process of self-observation, which allows one to study oneself and to know the mechanics of one's machine better, one begins to work on cleaning of its parts (lower centres) from improper workings and contamination by the wrong knowledge. One should notice and prevent the leakages of energy in order to bring the work of the lower centres into a more efficient order, to educate the uneducated 'essence', to work on creating willpower, and so on...

An ordinary man, who mistakenly takes himself to be free, is in reality a prisoner. He is a prisoner of his thoughts, emotions, swinging moods, desires, habits, opinions of others, planetary influences, karmic forces and all mechanical laws governing life on

Do – Ti – La – Sol – Fa – Mi – Re – Do

Earth etc… Although, he thinks that he knows himself, has choices and the willpower to do things, to move in a chosen direction and achieve his goals etc., he is just a toy of higher forces.

When a man begins to observe himself, as though for a first time, he starts to see, recognise and understand that he is a prisoner. With this revelatory knowledge, he has a chance now to ask himself: 'how can I escape from this mechanical prison?' and begin to work towards his liberation. He has a chance to free himself!

To be able, however, to free himself from all the mechanical laws he is under now, he should study and understand the main principles of work of his apparatus, he should get all the necessary tools for escape, and he must find someone (a teacher, or guru), who is already became free and who knows how to escape.

Together with the self-observation and self-remembering, man must learn not to identify himself with his body and his problems, not to express negative emotions, and in latter stages, transform the energy of negative emotions into love, light, gratitude and higher states of consciousness.

As my first spiritual teacher Robert Taylor used to say: if your heart is filled with negativity, but you want to invite God in your life, it is just like saying 'dear God, please come to me, we will drink cold tea from dirty cups…'

God loves clean things, so one must clean and polish first one's heart to rid it of negativity.

The Human Chemical Factory

Each centre (brain) of the machine, and each part of the centres work at different speeds and consume different types of fuel (energy). These types of fuel are different types of 'hydrogens'.

We can look now at the human organism as a chemical factory, receiving different types of food from the surrounding environment, assimilating this food, and transforming this food into higher substances and energies (hydrogens). It is possible with certain knowledge and work on oneself to make one's 'chemical factory' work more efficiently, so that it will begin to produce additional amounts of higher substances, which according to Gurdjieff, will settle in the body and bring the whole organism to a higher level, onto a higher plane of being. These additional higher hydrogens then will allow a special type of 'crystallisation' into the higher subtle bodies. Higher hydrogens, which have greater density of vibrations and higher speeds are also necessary for reconnection with the higher centres, to shift one's identity onto higher levels of consciousness. Higher centres (consciousness), although connected to the 'functions' of the machine (lower centres), are at the same time independent of them.

In ordinary circumstances, however, all higher 'hydrogens' that the human 'chemical factory' produces are consumed by the needs of this factory itself, or else this higher energy leaks out of the 'factory' via negative emotions, wastage of precious attention, identifying with problems, objects or thoughts, imagination, unnecessary talk and other activities.

63

The Human Chemical Factory

Gurdgieff then proceeds to say that there are three types of food that the human chemical factory consumes: 1) the ordinary food we eat, 2) the air we breathe, 3) the impressions we receive. He then invites us to look at the human organism as a three-storey building. The upper floor of this factory consists of a man's head; the middle floor, the chest; and the lower, the stomach, back, and the lower part of the body.

According to Gurdjieff, physical food (all substances which can serve as food for man) is 'hydrogen 768' (H768). This 'hydrogen' enters the lower storey of the human chemical factory as 'oxygen' with the vibrations of note 'do 768'. Remember that 'hydrogen' is not only a substance, but also a certain density of vibrations, and that all ascending or descending octaves begin with the note 'do' and proceed to develop as per the law of seven, or law of octaves, having intervals between the notes 'mi' and 'fa', and further between notes 'ti' and the note 'do' of the next octave.

'Oxygen' – 'do 768' meets with 'carbon 192' which is present in the organism. From the union of O768 and C192 nitrogen 384 (N384) is obtained. N384 is the next note 're'. 'Re'384 which becomes 'oxygen' in the next triad meets with 'carbon' 96 in the organism and together with it produces a new 'nitrogen 192', which is the note 'mi' 192.

The transmutation or alchemical refinement of 'do 768' into 'mi 192' is the process of breaking food down into its simplest form by the digestive system, the absorption by the wall of small intestines of valuable nutrients, the entering of nutrients into the bloodstream and delivering them to each cell of the body. But poorly oxygenated blood needs to return to the lungs for a boost of oxygen, for without oxygen our brain, liver, and other organs can be easily damaged.

As is known from the law of octaves 'mi' cannot pass independently to 'fa' in an ascending octave; an 'additional shock' is necessary. If an 'additional shock' is not received, the substance 'mi 192' cannot by itself pass to the full note 'fa'.

At the given place in the organism where 'mi 192' ought to appear, there enters the 'second food'- air, in the form of 'do 192'. The note 'do' possesses all the necessary semitones, that is, all the energy necessary for the transition to the next note, and it gives a part of its energy to the note 'mi' which has the same density as

64

itself. The energy of 'do' gives 'mi' 192 force enough, while uniting with 'carbon 48' already in the organism, to pass into 'nitrogen 96'. 'Nitrogen 96' will be the note 'fa'.

To give a more vivid picture of this process and the place in the organism where the 'second food' - air enters the body as 'do 192' and gives the necessary additional energy and additional vibrations (bridging the interval) to the place of the interval of the 'first food' octave, between 'mi 192' and 'fa 96', you can visualise the venous blood pumped to the lungs to receive the necessary 'oxygen'. And so, the venous blood gets oxygenated and changes its quality into arterial blood. Oxygen burns the fuel (sugar and fatty acids) in our cells to produce energy!

Then the 'first food' octave proceeds its refinement process through 'fa 96', 'sol 48', 'la 24' up to the 'ti 12'. And so, the 'ti 12' is the highest substance produced in the organism from physical food with the help of the 'additional shock' obtained from the air.

'Ti 12' is known as sexual or seminal energy!

As it is said in the Shree Vidya tradition, describing the highest Goddess Tripura Sundari or Lalita to whom we will be returning as the book progresses: 'Each chakra is presided over by a Yogini whose function relates to the transmutation of food, which is alchemy of the food factory. The chakra of the Absolute or semen/ova itself has 1000 letters or petals. Semen is conceived of as residing here because of its alchemical nature as an elixir produced by the synthesis of the forms of food'.[6]

As the great exponent of Trika philosophy of the Kashmir Shaivism tradition, sage Abhinavagupta also says in his Para-trisika-Vivarana (the secret of tantric mysticism): '"Whatever enters the inner psychic apparatus or the outer senses of all beings, that abides as sentient Life-energy in the middle channel i.e., sushumna whose main characteristic is to enliven all the parts of the body.'

That Life-energy is said to be 'ojas' (vital lustre), that is then diffused as an enlivening factor in the form of common seminal energy to all parts of the body. Then, when an exciting visual or auditory perception enters the percipient, on account of its existing power, it fans the flame of passion in the form of agitation of

---

[6] "Shri Yantra Lalita Tripurasundari"

seminal energy. Sense organs by themselves, without this union with the seminal energy cannot acquire full expansion. Beautiful objects entering sense organs agitate seminal energy which creates a sense of delight. If there is an absence of delight, it only spells insentience. Excessive delight is possible only to those whose heart is expanded by seminal energy, which has the boundless capacity to strengthen sensibility. When there is the dissolution of Prana (air of exhalation) and Apana (air of inhalation) in susumna, which as the central channel is full of the energy of all the senses, then one's consciousness enters the stage of the great central sushumna channel where it unites with the pulsation of one's Shakti. Then all sense of duality dissolves and there is the perfect I-consciousness, generated by the abundance of the perfection of one's own inherent Shakti."[7]

'Do 192' (air) entering the middle storey of the factory in the character of 'oxygen' and giving part of its energy to 'mi 192' unites at a certain place with 'carbon 48' which is present in the organism and passes into 're 96'. 'Re 96' passes into 'mi 48' with the help of 'carbon 24' and with this, the development of the second octave (air octave) comes to a stop. For the transition of 'mi' into 'fa', an 'additional shock' is necessary, but at this point nature has not prepared any 'additional shock' and the second octave cannot develop further. In the ordinary conditions of life, it does not develop further.

The third octave (the octave of impressions), begins with 'do 48'. Impressions enter the organism in the form of 'oxygen 48'. 'Do 48' has sufficient energy to pass into the following note, but at that place in the organism where 'do 48' enters, the 'carbon 12' necessary for this is not present. At the same time, 'do 48' does not come into contact with 'mi 48' so it can neither pass into the next note nor give part of its energy to 'mi 48'.

Under the conditions of normal existence, the production of the fine 'matters' by the factory come to a stop at this point and the third octave sounds as 'do' only. The highest substance produced by the factory is 'ti 12' (sexual or seminal energy) and for all its higher functions the factory is able to use only this higher 'matter'.

---

[7] "Para-trisika-Vivarana" (The secret of Tantric Mysticism) Abhinavagupta translated by Jaideva Singh

The Human Chemical Factory

For the 'air octave', which stopped its development on the note 'mi 48', and the 'impressions octave', which stopped at the note 'do 48' to proceed further, we need to create an 'artificial shock' at the point where the beginning of the third octave is arrested. The note 'do 48' designates the moment when an impression enters our consciousness. An 'artificial shock' at this point means a certain kind of effort made at the moment of receiving the impression!

Although from the first glance, the first conscious shock of Self-remembering and 'divided attention' doesn't seem like a big deal, I assure you that in favourable situations this conscious effort can trigger the expansion of energy and consciousness to a truly miraculous degree of the comprehension of reality.

In ordinary circumstances, the power of our attention-awareness is mechanically glued to objects of perceptions. Our attention jumps from one impression to the next, from one object to another object. Moreover, it is frequently broken by a stream of thought.

If now, receiving impressions we divide our attention (we perceive the objects and simultaneously we perceive the subject 'self', perceiving the objects), we are doubling the quantity of impressions, and also agitating seminal energy, bringing necessary carbon 'ti 12' to the place of entry of impressions, and by this act, are forcing the 'impressions octave' to proceed from the note 'do 48', through 're 24', to 'mi 12'. At the same time, the additional energy of this, so-called 'first conscious shock' gives enough power to the 'air octave', which stopped at 'mi 48', to proceed further through 'fa 24', 'sol 12', to 'la 6'. And so, with one additional 'first conscious shock', which in this system is known as 'Self-remembering', our human factory begins to produce the additional amount of refined substances, energies. Although 'ti 12' and 'mi 12' have the same numbers, the quality of their energy is different. The 'ti 12' is the finest substance produced from the 'physical food octave' with the additional shock from the 'air octave' representing the sexual energy. The 'mi 12' is the finest substance produced from the 'octave of impressions' and with the help of an additional 'conscious shock' is the 'emotional energy' (love, gratitude, feeling of connectedness with the higher reality and God).

The Human Chemical Factory

Although all these plays of numbers or substances and the energies they represent seems very academic and dry, with enough practice one can easily discern between different levels of hydrogens or energies, for each field of hydrogens or energies has a very definite taste or a quality attached to it. Also, the food of impressions is not always hydrogen 48, but it varies from the lower quality of impressions of hydrogen 96 to higher ones such as hydrogen 24 or even hydrogen 12 in the case of refined conscious art, music or architecture.

For the octaves to proceed with their development any further, we need to introduce a 'second conscious shock'. Understanding the nature of this 'shock' is not as simple as the nature of a 'first conscious shock'. P.D. Ouspensky tell us in his book on Gurdjeff's teaching *In Search of the Miraculous* that the nature of this 'second conscious shock' relates to the emotional life. It has to do with the transformations or transmutations of negative emotions into the positive ones!

Before one becomes capable of transforming negative emotions and suffering into love and light, however, one must learn how to catch them and not to express them, which requires a certain amount of alertness, for the movements of the emotions are very fast. When, however, one wakes up to a certain degree and begins to see things with a greater degree of clarity, one begins to recognise that every event and every moment of one's life, regardless if this moment appears blissful or painful, is a Divine gift. And so, one becomes grateful for everything. This constant gratitude helps one catch one's energy that is about to be spilled through the expression of negativity, and turn it into love, light, gratitude and higher states of consciousness.

For the one who has become a master of the transformation of negativity and suffering into love and light, everything, regardless of its nature, appears as a gift! Moreover, what appears as suffering becomes food for the awakening soul!

In fact, one of the practices of the Fourth Way is called a 'voluntary suffering', sometimes called 'intentional suffering'. Robert Taylor often encouraged us to practice a little 'voluntary suffering', such as holding one foot in about an inch above the floor while sitting on a train, or bus, or in other conditions. This little 'intentional suffering' serves a few purposes. Firstly, it gives you a better chance to remember yourself, and secondly, it is a sort of advanced payment, an expression of gratitude towards the Creator, and so it is the beginning of a connection with God!

Robert Taylor often used to say that any effort made in any 'centre' (moving, instinctive, intellectual) affects the emotional centre. And it is through the development of the emotional centre, specifically the intellectual part of it, that one begins to regain connections with the higher centres and God.

As I mentioned earlier, every centre, and each part of it work with the different energy (hydrogens) and at different speeds. The slowest of all is said to be the intellectual centre, which works on 'hydrogen 48'. The moving and the instinctive centres are much faster and working with 'hydrogen 24'. The emotional centre can work at very high speeds, using 'hydrogen 12' as its fuel, but very rarely does so, and in ordinary conditions works with 'hydrogen 24'.

One line of work on oneself is the development, or the awakening of the King of Hearts (the intellectual part of the emotional centre), for this is the highest part in man, full of true love, understanding, wisdom and compassion. The King of Hearts is that part which can feel the presence of something higher than itself, can feel the great plan of the cosmic architect. It is also this part that stands above and can see the uselessness of flat (two dimensional) relationships (a human drama), in which the Queen of Hearts (the emotional part of the emotional centre) finds pleasure. The King of Hearts intuitively knows (feels) a new vertical dimension – a dimension towards God!

But with all its beauty, intuition and understanding, the King of Hearts must sacrifice himself for the higher centres to be born. And although it is not easy to do so, for the great dragons of fear are guarding the portals between the two worlds, a strong King of Hearts is able to release tremendous energy, allowing for greater expansion, and sacrifice himself to the unknown.

The higher emotional centre is said to be working with 'hydrogen 12' at far greater speeds than the lower centres. To make a temporary, or even permanent connection with this type of higher intelligence, one must work on the refinement and balance of the lower centres and especially on the development of the intellectual parts (kings) of the centres. As we have seen above, one of the highest substances produced in the human organism is 'hydrogen ti 12'.

The other lower centres, due to improper functioning, steal, so to speak, and use this precious energy for their own needs. A big amount of this precious energy is used in such functions, as imagination (not useful creative imagination, but uncontrolled fantasies), and identification with certain problems or objects of desire, in which the power of attention is wasted. This valuable energy can be thrown out with the explosion of anger, or slowly leak out with feelings of dissatisfaction, judgement, apathy or boredom.

Scenery of outstanding beauty is said to be filled with the high hydrogens, and if one, at the moments of witnessing of such majestic beauty, creates a 'first conscious shock', by remembering oneself (the simultaneous perception of the objects and the subject – seer – Self, observing objects), one's King of Hearts emerges and utilises the energy of this sublime beauty into the ever-expanding consciousness!

It feels love and gratitude towards the whole creation and specifically towards the Creator of such awe-inspiring beauty. The 'hydrogen mi 12' is in operation now, which in itself is the higher order of creation. The speed of perceptions accelerates at these pregnant with higher possibilities moments, which allows one a temporary connection with the higher emotional centre. To jump onto the fast-moving train of the higher emotional centre, one should accelerate the speed of one's own vehicle that is moving in the same direction equal to the speed of the train.

On the other hand, moments of sudden explosion of the energy of immense fear, can either knock one out of consciousness (fainting) or send one into an 'out of body experience' in the realm of the higher intellectual centre – 'world six'. 'World six' is removed from our ordinary perceptions even further than the 'world twelve' of the higher emotional centre. In such cases of what can be called a 'mystical experience', the revelations that one perceives in these higher realms of reality are so intense and incomparable with anything else known to our ordinary level of perceptions, that no words exist to describe these experiences, as the shrunken-back-to-ordinary-perceptions intelligence usually cannot recreate, or even remember the vastness and significance of such an experience.

The other very important point I would like to draw your attention to, and which truly was the main reason of my bothering with the introduction into this book of the idea of the Ray of Creation, is that reality is hierarchical.

I have noticed in recent years a tendency, greatly induced by self-proclaimed 'neo-advaita' gurus and spiritual teachers, to oversimplify our understanding of the principles on which reality works. Many of these oversimplified notions seem to be based on the interpretations, taken out of context, of such iconic and popular sages, such as Ramana Maharshi and Nisargadatta Maharaj. The basic notion of these teachings suggests that reality can be reduced to two basic things, namely consciousness and its content. The universe is the content, the object of consciousness, or a superimposition upon consciousness, and consciousness stands as the subject and the silent witness of the universal display. Consciousness is then compared to a screen on which the phenomena is displayed, or a blank sheet of paper on which life stories are written.

Those who have crossed over the 'world appearance frequency field' into the higher frequencies of inner dimensions know without a shadow of a doubt, that 'our universe' is just one of the many realities of infinite intelligence, and that the inner dimensions are far more real than our familiar 'world appearance'. Moreover, those yogis, and those courageous souls, who plunge ever deeper into the bottomless ocean of inner realities, have discovered for themselves that reality is hierarchical, i.e., there are layers and layers of the levels of intelligence, levels of lucidity and levels of perceivers.

The ideas of hierarchical reality or the hierarchy of intelligence we can find not only in Gurdjieff's teaching, but in many other mystical esoteric traditions and ancient scriptures. To give you a few examples of the descending order of creation in which the birth of imperfection takes place I would like to cite couple of passages from the Gnostic gospel *The Apocryphon of John (The Secret Book of John/ The Secret Revelation of John)*, which impressed me profoundly when I was in my twenties.

The Birth of Imperfection

After the initial words about the ineffable infinite all-giving nature of Absolute Reality, (see appendix 1), follows the passage which describes the birth of imperfection.

'And the Sophia of the Epinoia, being an aeon, conceived a thought from herself and the conception of the invisible Spirit and foreknowledge. She wanted to bring forth a likeness out of herself without the consent of the Spirit – he had not approved – and without her consort, and without his consideration. And though the person of her maleness had not approved, and she had not found her agreement, and she had thought without the consent of the Spirit and the knowledge of her agreement, [yet] she brought forth. And because of the invincible power, which is in her, her thought did not remain idle, and something came out of her which was imperfect and different from her appearance, because she had created it without her consort. And it was dissimilar to the likeness of its mother, for it has another form.

'And when she saw [the consequences of] her desire, it changed into a form of a lion-faced serpent. And its eyes were like lightning fires which flash. She cast it away from her, outside that place, that no one of the immortal ones might see it, for she had created in ignorance. And she surrounded it with a luminous cloud, and she placed a throne in the middle of the cloud that no one might see it except the Holy Spirit, who is called the mother of the living. And she called his name Yaltabaoth. And when the light had mixed with the darkness, it caused the darkness to shine. And when the darkness had mixed with the light, it darkened the light and it became neither light nor dark, but it became dim'[8]

Similar stories of the loss of perfection are also found in the bible. One of these stories is the story of the expulsion of Lucifer from heaven due to his pride (anava mala), another is the story of the expulsion of Adam and Eve from Eden due to the breaking of God's law, (do not eat fruit from the tree of knowledge), which resulted in the birth of the knowledge of good and evil, otherwise known as the knowledge of duality. It is said in certain scriptures that the root 'ma' of the word 'Maya', (that which is not, yet appears), can be translated as 'to measure'. When the measurement (comparison) begins, the infinity (immeasurable reality) gets broken, or veiled.

---

[8] "Apocryphon of John: Secret Book of John"

From Shiva Down to Earth

In the Shaiva system of philosophy and yoga known as Agama Shastra, which is considered to be of Divine origin (i.e. a revelation by Shiva, or Shakti), the descending of the levels of reality from the Absolute down to Earth takes place through the 36 Tattvas. Tattva can be translated as 'thatness', or 'suchness'. It is a certain quality of a certain level or plane of reality. The Kashmir Shaivism tradition, especially at its very heart, known as the 'Trika' system, indicates a triad consisting of:

1) Para – the highest (supreme energy existing in transcendence),

2) Parapara – identity in difference (supreme/un-supreme Sakti, existing both in transcendence and immanence)

3) Apara – difference (un-supreme energy, existing in immanence),

or

1) The Supreme Transcendent – Siva

2) The Supreme Creative Energy – Sakti

3) nara (man) – the bound soul, or anu, shrunken into an infinitesimally small point of consciousness (microcosmic spiritual atom)

This tradition also speaks of the trinity of energies:

1) Iccha Sakti – the energy of will

2) Jnana Sakti – the energy of knowledge

3) Kriya Sakti – the energy of action.

"The Ultimate reality is said to be non-relational consciousness (Cit or Parasamvit). In it, there is no distinction between subject and object, or of 'I' and 'This'. The other Sanskrit word the Trika system of the Kashmir Shaivism tradition uses to describe Reality

is 'Prakasa-Vimarsa'. Prakasa is the Eternal Light, without which
nothing can appear. It is luminous, undifferentiated consciousness.
It is Siva. Vimarsa is Sakti, the Svabhava, which literally means
'own being', or 'own becoming' – the intrinsic essential nature of
Siva. Vimarsa is, so to speak, the mirror in which Siva realises His
own grandeur, power and beauty. Vimarsa is the power of doership
of Siva. Vimarsa is that aspect of Prakasa by which it knows itself.
Vimarsa is an immediate awareness of 'I', it is this I-consciousness
of Ultimate Reality that is responsible for the manifestation,
maintenance, and re-absorption of the universe. Vimarsa has been
named variously as ParaSakti, Kartrtva, Sphuratta, Sara, Hrdaya,
Spanda and Svatantrya. Each of these names describes a specific
attribute of the Ultimate Reality. For example, Svatantrya (Sva =
self, tantram = dependency) points out self-dependency, complete
self-sufficiency, divine unimpeded sovereignty and the perfect
limitless freedom of the Absolute. Svatantrya Sakti is the free will
of Siva, of which nothing can oppose or limit it, and there is no sort
of deficiency in its potency. Svatantrya is described as an energy
that emanates from the Supreme ParamaSiva, a wave of motion
inside consciousness (Spanda – creative pulsation, vibration,
throbbing, thrilling, vibration of ecstasy of the Siva-Sakti union, the
heartbeat of Siva). Svatantrya, which is nothing other than perfect
freedom of Siva expresses itself into Iccha Sakti (will), which
immediately translates into Jnana Sakti (knowledge) and Kriya
Sakti (action). The Ultimate Reality is not only pure consciousness,
but also the supreme spiritual energy or power. This all-inclusive
universal consciousness is also called Anuttara, the Highest
Reality, the Absolute. It is both transcendental and immanent.

Creativity is the very essence of divinity. It is in the very nature
of ultimate reality: to manifest. If the Highest Reality did not
manifest, it would not be the Highest Power, Self or
Consciousness. Ultimate Reality is 'prakasavimrsamaya'. In this
primal state of being there is no differentiation between 'I' and
'This'. The 'I' is Prakasa and the 'This' is Vimarsa, but there are
no distinctions between the two, they exist in a state of unity. This
Vimarsa is Svatantrya, or the unimpeded sovereign power or Sakti.
This Sakti is not contentless. It contains all that is to be. Parama
Siva has infinite powers, but the following may be considered to be
the main ones:

From Shiva Down to Earth

1) Cit – the power of Self-revelation, the changeless principle of all changes. In this aspect, the Supreme is known as Siva.

2) Ananda – Absolute Bliss. This is also called Svatantrya. In this aspect, the Supreme is known as Sakti.

Cit (Consciousness) and Ananda (Bliss) are the very 'Svarupa', or nature of Parama Siva. Highest Reality is often described as Sat-Cit-Ananda – Being-Consciousness-Bliss. The rest can be considered as His Sakties.

3) Iccha or Will. In this aspect, He is known as Sadasiva.

4) Jnana or Knowledge. In this aspect, He is known as Isvara.

5) Kriya – Action, the power of assuming any and every form. In this aspect, He is known as Sadvidya or Suddha Vidya."[9]

For a detailed description of tattvas, see Appendix 2).

The descending from the Highest Siva down to Earth orders of Tattvas, which we may also call the Ray of Creation, allows us to look at the process of yoga as the reverse process of ascendance through the hierarchical ladder of Reality towards the higher principle (tattva). This process sees the simultaneous dissolution of the lower tattvas sequentially through the levels of 'perceivers' up to Parama Siva or the True Self.

For those who maintain that the world appearance is governed directly by the will of the Absolute and therefore is perfection itself, and for those who think that enlightenment is a shift of consciousness into a 'witnessing' mode, I and many scriptures which I regard as the highest knowledge, say that there are many layers of Reality with qualitatively different levels of 'perceivers', and that the world-appearance is an impure order of creation.

The will of the Absolute does not manifest directly on the Earth plane, but manifests here through the 48 mechanical laws', and freedom therefore is freedom from these mechanical laws, according to Gurdjieff.

As Rainer Maria Rilke expressed it so well in his 'First Duino Elegy':

> *'Who, if I cried out, would hear me among*
> *the angels' hierarchies?*

---

[9] "Siva Sutras" Vasugupta translated by Jaideva Singh

From Shiva Down to Earth

And even if one of them pressed me suddenly
against his heart:

I would be consumed in that overwhelming
existence.

For beauty is nothing but the beginning of
terror, which we are still just able to endure,

and we are so awed because it serenely
disdains to annihilate us.

Every angel is terrifying. [10]

We must understand that if God-Absolute decides to reveal His/Her true being to us, then not only us, but all steps in the hierarchy of creation would be annihilated by His/Her terrific beauty.

When Krishna began to show His true Majestic and terrifying form to Arjuna: 'If the splendour of thousands of suns were to blaze forth all at once in the sky, even that would not resemble the splendour of that exalted being'. (11.12). 'Arjuna saw the entire universe, divided in many ways, but standing as (all in) One (and One in all) in the body of Krishna, the God of Gods.' (11.13). Arjuna with his hair standing on their ends and trembling with fear, began to beg Krishna for mercy to return to his human form.'[11]

Leaving for a while quantum mechanics, the Ray of Creation and Siva Sutras, let's return to my life story.

---

[10] "Duino Elegies" (First Duino Elegy) Rainer Maria Rilke
[11] "Bhagavad Gita" 11:12

77

Working With the 'Fourth Way' Ideas

Most of my life now was centred around Gurdjeff's ideas from the Fourth Way school. I began to see the triviality and uselessness of ordinary existence. I lost interest in spending my precious time with my pre-Fourth Way friends.

I entered the inner circle of the school. This was not a matter of a special initiation, but rather the result of gratitude for the received knowledge and guidance I had received, which had led me to experience higher states of consciousness. One who enters the inner circle is not one who passively attends meetings, not one who is concerned any longer with the receiving of help and knowledge, but one who had become filled with a deeper understanding through the verification of the higher states of consciousness. It is one who starts to feel responsible for the school at large, one who, filled with love and gratitude, desires to share the knowledge and understanding, and help friends take next step on the evolutionary ladder.

When one is given the tools for awakening and begins to use these tools, when one begins to make sincere zealous efforts for the betterment and purifying of oneself, making oneself more conscious, one is repaying, so to speak, both to the school and to God. When these efforts bring one closer and closer to a state of unity with God and the whole creation, one begins to feel flooded with the Divine love and gratitude that seeks its expression in new sacrifices, efforts and repayments.

There is an idea of 'three lines of work' in the Fourth Way:

Working With the 'Fourth Way' Ideas

1) work on oneself for oneself
2) work for others
3) work for a school at large or work for a higher force or God.

This idea is rooted in the principle of bridging intervals in one's work. Working on the 'three lines' I finally came to realisation that the three lines are truly only one, for if one begins to work on oneself, one inevitably works also for others and for God, and when working for others, one is truly working for oneself and for God, and when working for God or higher forces, one truly works for oneself and for others. An understanding of the unity and oneness of all manifestation began to blossom in my heart.

Experiences of higher states of consciousness started to appear more frequently. One of the most powerful practices for the penetration of the expanded states of consciousness was 'Self-remembering', which Gurdjieff sometimes called 'Self-recollection' and P.D. Ouspensky sometimes called 'divided attention'. 'Divided attention' is the effort towards comprehension of a maximum quantity of impressions including the 'perceiver' and the 'I' simultaneously.

In our ordinary condition, we do not perceive all impressions at once, but only a small fraction of the total field of impressions at any one time. We can hear a particular sound and see the object in front of us but are not aware at the same time of the sensations of our feet touching the floor, or our breathing process. The next moment we are aware of a sudden thought, but have lost the impression of sound etc. Attention in our ordinary condition jumps from one impression to the next. With the practice of divided attention, one begins to activate all 'four kings' – the intellectual parts of the 'centres' simultaneously.

As described above, the different parts of the centres work with the different levels of attention; jacks work with the minimum level of attention (mechanical attention), queens work with attracted attention (all attention goes to the object of attention, which can be also called identification), and kings can work with divided attention (one is aware not only of objects, but also of the subject – the perceiver). The working intellectual part of a moving centre (the King of Spades), for example, can visualise a separate-from-the-body 'I' – an observer simultaneously perceiving the totality of visual impressions with expanded panoramic vision. The King of

Diamonds (the intellectual part of the intellectual centre) can arrest the thought process. The King of Hearts (the intellectual part of emotional centre) activates the emotion of gratitude and love, for it begins to see real beauty and feel God's presence. The King of Clubs (the intellectual part of the instinctive centre) can become aware of the totality of sensations within the body, and also of the surrounding energy. Working the four kings simultaneously opens the 'doors of perception', as William Blake said in his 'The Marriage of Heaven and Hell'; 'If the doors of perception were cleansed everything would appear to man as it is, Infinite. For man, has closed himself up, till he sees all things thro' narrow chinks of his cavern.'[12]

What I began to observe and experience with these efforts of 'being aware of maximum impressions and sensations simultaneously', is that at the beginning it was not so easy, or even possible to comprehend and hold the totality of awareness on all impressions at once. The focus of my attention jumped from one sensation to the next. But with perseverance, there was suddenly a miraculous entrance into a state of a total comprehension. The most surprising thing in this process was that when this breakthrough happened, the necessity of effort was completely gone. And there you are fully present, effortless, comprehending the totality of external and internal impressions (object and subject) at once, and not only comprehending, but fully embodying the experience as 'I am This'. In this state of expanded consciousness, no doubts, or wrongdoing is possible, for everything that appears is governed by the Higher Self. The efforts of the four kings to divide attention, to perceive the maximum number of impressions at once accelerates the speed of cognition and allows the higher emotional centre to emerge.

I remember very well one of the meetings led by Robert Taylor. As we progressed with the usual 'stopping thoughts and dividing attention techniques', Robert asked everyone to say one, two, or three words directly describing the nature of the experience, such as: 'bird singing', or 'hands touching knees', or 'breathing' etc. All the others should include or add this experience to what they already aware of. The energy in the room was rising and glowing.

---

[12] "The Marriage of Heaven and Hell" William Blake.

Everything was the expression of this shimmering radiant energy. When it seemed that this pulsating energy had reached its crescendo, Robert said: 'now, let it go, let go of all efforts, let go of this energy'. I sincerely tried to let go of this energy, let go of this all-embracing state, but I simply couldn't. There was no effort, just pure relaxation and yet this glowing presence just stayed there, invincible. This was a pure miracle.

Establishment in this state of 'witnessing consciousness', this ability to be always present is pronounced by many gurus as enlightenment. It seems that there is nothing deeper, or higher than this pure witnessing, for it seems to be so complete and does not allow any doubts about its completeness. Many are deluded here. The majority of world gurus and their disciples are stuck here. Of course, it is not a bad state to be established in, but it is not true 'awakening', for this 'presence' is still within the illusion of appearance.

In his book *Tertium Organum*, P. D. Ouspensky proposes that the sense of time is the imperfect perception of higher-dimensional space. In other words, if the speed of perceptions increases dramatically, one can 'freeze time', so to speak, or break through the illusion of time into the perception of the fourth, fifth and sixth higher dimensions of space-time.

I began to hypothesise that the structure of what we know as a 'present moment' vibrates, so to speak, with the frequency of 'hydrogen 12'. Hydrogen 12, as you remember is a meeting point, or connection of the intellectual part of the emotional centre, which at this moment vibrates with the 'mi 12', sexual centre, which vibrates with the 'ti 12' and 'higher emotional centre', with which the connection is made possible. The first conscious shock of Self-remembering and dividing attention allows for the speeding up of the frequencies of perceptions to the frequencies of 'world 12', making the experience highly emotional (pure love and gratitude) and at the same time 'sexual' (intimacy, interconnectedness and euphoria). To be established in the higher emotional centre is to live life fully centred in Divine Presence.

However, Reality is infinitely deeper than this Divine Presence and the appearances of the pictures within it. The 'Present' is just the surface of the bottomless ocean of infinite reality. Being present still severs the 'now-here' experienced at this particular moment in this particular space from the totality of all moments in all spaces.

As is eloquently said in the great Itihasa 'Tripura Rahasya': 'The casual ignorance is said to be of the nature of absence of knowledge of the wholeness of one's own Self. The Self that is Consciousness should only be whole on account of the exclusion of limitations. For, it is that which brings about time and the rest which are the causes of limitations. That kind of knowledge of the Self which exists as the non-wholeness (of the Self) can alone be the casual ignorance of the nature of "I exist here at this time". That is the embryonic seed from which shoots forth the sprout of the body as the individualised self (growing up into the gigantic tree of the cycle of births and deaths). The cycle of births and deaths does not end unless ignorance is put to an end. This can happen only with a perfect knowledge of the Self, not otherwise.'[13]

For the reason of better understanding of the speed of perceptions and the different frequency fields of infinite reality, we can take it as an example that our ordinary perception of reality is a molecular perception, so to speak, meaning that it is very slow. When the speed of perceptions increases with the practice of expanded cognition (divided attention), one makes connection with higher forms of intelligence – namely the higher emotional centre – in which one is miraculously established in the all-embracing presence. We can call this shift in the cognition a shift into atomic perception. If, however, the speed of perceptions further increases, one's consciousness-awareness can destroy or break through the screen of space-time projection, vibrating with the hydrogen 12 into the subatomic and quantum realms of infinite reality – the domain of the higher intellectual centre (world 6).

Together with the practices of Self-observation, separation from the 'machine' and establishment in the witnessing consciousness, 'Self-remembering', refinement of inner and outer alchemy, education of an uneducated essence and other working tools, I was working on the development of willpower. As stated by Gurdgieff, one of the highest achievements possible for a man is to become a 'master of himself'!

---

[13] "Tripura Rahasya: The Mystery Beyond Trinity" translated by Swami Sri Ramanananda Saraswathi

Working With the 'Fourth Way' Ideas

According to the Fourth Way system, the increased efficiency of a human chemical factory allows one to create an additional amount of 'higher hydrogens', which then saturate the whole body. If there is enough of these higher substances, these 'higher hydrogens' can 'crystallise' into a 'higher body'. Often, for this crystallization to take place one needs to add to one's spiritual practice an intentional struggle. One must create friction, which can generate 'spiritual heat' and endure these almost unbearable conditions in order to allow for the 'fusion' of higher hydrogens into a 'body of will'.

One of my best friends, Constantin, asked Robert Taylor on some occasion how to create willpower. Robert gave him exercise. Once daily he was to stand on his toes with outstretched arms for half an hour. I began to practice this exercise daily. After my first five minutes standing on my toes with my arms stretched out on both sides, I realised that half an hour in such a position is simply impossible. My shoulders began to feel that they were made of lead. It seemed to me that, like the titan Atlas bearing the whole world on his shoulders, I was carrying this almost unbearable heavy weight, and yet I continued to endure this 'torture'. Time stretched dramatically. Ten minutes... fifteen minutes... twenty minutes... and I am still able to endure this. What seemed to be impossible became possible because of endurance.

I am not sure how much willpower these exercises created in me, but they gave me a better understanding of the value of sincere effort and created a more intimate connection with the higher forces. As Robert Taylor often pointed out (although he was often criticised by the other 'old students' for being very 'instinctive' in his teaching), sincere efforts made in any centre (instinctive, moving, emotional, intellectual, or sexual), if done for the connection with the Divine, affects and opens up the emotional centre – the Heart.

Sometime later I discovered the descriptions of these sorts of endurance efforts, which in Sanskrit language are called 'Tapas', translated as 'heat', in some of the Yogic Scriptures. We will be returning to these spiritual practices and the benefits of such sacrifices later, when we plunge deeper into the main subject of this book – Yoga.

Working With the 'Fourth Way' Ideas

One thing, however, I would like to say here: these sorts of effort should not turn into a form of lunacy, for if the 'inner battle' takes place for the wrong reasons, there is the possibility of crystallisation of the wrong hydrogens. Gurdjieff had a special name for such unfortunate individuals – 'Hasnamuss'. In this respect, there are three types of individuals: 'tramps', 'lunatics' and 'good householders'. Tramps are those who don't properly value of correct efforts and are therefore unable to clearly discriminate between right and wrong. They therefore cannot make the situation 'profitable' for themselves. Everything seems to be on the same scale to them. Lunatics are those who put extreme amounts of energy and effort to something that is not very important, or to a very particular thing, often for wrong reasons. They are therefore unable to give energy to more wholesome aims or see the wider picture. Good householders on the other hand are those, who have the right values. They use their intelligence and energy wisely, knowing that, to achieve a certain aim, they must put in a certain amount of effort.

Having spoken about making a situation 'profitable', I should give some more clarity to this statement. As written in the gospels, Jesus said: 'Do not store up for yourselves treasures on earth, where moths and vermin destroy, and where thieves break in and steal. But store up for yourselves treasures in heaven, where moths and vermin do not destroy, and where thieves do not break and steal. For where your treasure is, there your heart will be also.'[14] Do not gather treasure for yourself but become richer into God.

To understand what it means to be profitable, we first must understand who we really are. To whom is this profit? The question 'Who am I?' is possibly the most important question of all, for this sincere question is the beginning of true wisdom and Self-discovery. This most important question is the beginning of the process known as 'Self-inquiry' (atma-vichara), which we will discuss further in great detail, for Self-inquiry is one of the most essential parts of Kumbhaka Prana Yoga – the main reason and subject for this book.

---

[14] Matthew 6:19-21

All Haqq (I am the Truth)

A fter I had been in the Fourth Way school for an about a year, I became highly impressed with a book I found in a stall on the street of Moscow: *The Sufi Path of Love – the Spiritual Teachings of Rumi* by William C. Chittick. I was specifically taken with the chapter called 'Naughting the Self'. The seventh paragraph of this chapter called 'I Am God' impressed me the most.

"'With God, two I's cannot find room, says Rumi. You say "I" and He say "I." Either you die before Him or let Him die before you; then duality will not remain. But it is impossible for Him to die, either subjectively or objectively, since He is the "Living God, the Undying". He possesses such Gentleness that were it possible, He would die for you so that duality may vanish. But since it is impossible for Him to die, you die, so that He may manifest Himself to you and duality may vanish. (F 24-25/36). What is our "we" when Thou sayest "I?" What is our copper before the elixir? Before the sun can a handful of snow do anything but become annihilated in radiance and light? (D 35349-50). When Hallaj's love for God reached its utmost limit, he became his own enemy and naughted himself. He said, "I am God," that is, "I have been annihilated; God remains, nothing else." This is extreme humility and the utmost limit of servanthood. It means, "He alone is." To make a false claim and to be proud is to say, "Thou art God and I am the servant." For in this way you are affirming your own existence, and duality is the necessary result. If you say, "He is God," that too is duality, for there cannot be a "He" without an "I." Hence God said, "I am God." Other than He, nothing else existed.

All Haqq (I am the Truth)
Hallaj had been annihilated, so those were the words of God.' (F
193/202)[9"15]

These words of highest wisdom made a very deep impression
on me. I immediately realised the immensity and importance of this
highest truth. I understood completely and irreversibly that my Real
Self, my Real 'I' is God-Absolute, apart from which nothing else
exists!

Now, in the light of this realisation, we can ask ourselves: what
is the greatest 'reward', what is the highest 'profit'? Isn't it the
regaining of Godhood, by losing the false appearance of the
separate 'I'? Isn't it melting in the Beloved's love?

So, when we intellectually realise that our true self is God-
Absolute, the next step is to regain the actual experience of this
sublime Truth!

To fully experience God as our true Self, we first must
understand the nature of God – the Reality, and His/Her attributes.
One of the most obvious quality of God is His/Her abundance.
Everything comes from God, emanates from God, radiates from
God. He/She is the exhaustless reservoir. He/She is the perennial
flood of giving. He/She is limitless sufficiency.

Would such a 'Being', who is the very source of everything,
want something for Him/Her Self? And so, to be God we must
possess God's qualities i.e. radiance, shining, giving. And again,
now, the highest profit does not come to us because we are trying
to recover something that we lack or do not possess, but on the
contrary; through the realisation that we ourselves are the
overflowing fullness, showered from head to toe with Divine gifts!

We should let this love out, we must learn to be open and allow
God's loving energy to flow through us, and not seek profit for our
limited nature which we consider to be our selves. The best course
here is to seek God's will, attune to it and make it our own. 'Thy
Will be done'!

In connection to this, I would like to bring your attention to the
biblical story of the expulsion of Adam and Eve from Eden, which
so beautifully was captured in John Milton's *Paradise Lost*. In the
higher sense, Adam and Eve were in paradise having none but one

---

[15] "The Sufi Path of Love: The Spiritual Teaching of Rumi" William
C. Chittick

All Haqq (I am the Truth)

God's command or will: 'do not eat the fruits from the tree of knowledge (of good and evil).'

Satan, who assumed the form of a snake and began to sing hymns to Eve (the last and the most perfect part of creation), praising her beauty and superiority over everything that was created before, introduced doubt into her consciousness about the unfairness of God's law, and tempted her to eat a beautiful apple. When she took a bite, Eve felt that her eyes had opened to something that she had never experienced before. Excited, she called for Adam. Praising the wise snake and the magic fruit, she offered the apple to Adam. It is said that Adam in an instance saw that she had already fallen from grace, but because she was his wife, he had accepted and eaten the apple.

Suddenly, their eyes were open, and they saw each other in a new light, seeing the tempting beauty of their bodies and their union. With their sexual union they experienced the ecstasy of absolute freedom, for at this moment, even a single God's law was broken and not applicable here. After this amazing sexual union, they got tired and fell asleep. After awakening however, looking into each other eyes, they saw the consequences of breaking of God's law. And the process of the differentiation, duality, shame, and blame began. They start to blame each other for what they had done. They began to be ashamed of their bodies and covered their intimate parts with fig leaves (the beginning of differentiation).

A similar story is that of Lucifer, who, allured by the growing pride in him began to doubt God's authority and imagined himself to be higher than God. And again, by freeing himself from God's law for a moment, he fell into the precipices of hell.

From these narratives, I understood then, that true happiness, joy and freedom lies not in breaking God's law, but in finding it, understanding it, channelling it, and become one with it. 'Thy will be done!'.

In the Fourth Way, progress towards great liberation lies in gradual liberation from the 'mechanical laws', 'false personality' and later 'true personality' and even the 'essence', which is still considered to be part of the 'functions' and not pure consciousness. The man-machine doesn't possess 'will', but only 'self-will' or 'wilfulness', says Gurdjieff. To become liberated from wilfulness

All Haqq (I am the Truth)

and regain 'will', man must submit his wilfulness to the one who has a true will, i.e. to a guru, or spiritual teacher.

This idea, however, is like a double-edge sword, for one must find an original, honest, true teacher, otherwise he can be misled, tricked, used. I am sure that you've heard of many such cases of dishonest teachers. Nevertheless, on the positive side, it is said in some teachings that it is often the disciple who makes the teacher.

In other words, if the disciple trusts his guru openheartedly, follows obediently the guru's teaching, makes sincere efforts for his own purification and education, then it sometimes happens that even, though his guru was dishonest, the honesty, efforts and sacrifices of the sincere disciple, not only open his (disciples) mind and heart to a greater understanding and realisation of Higher Reality, but also forced the teacher to evolve.

Unfortunately, it is not always the case, for in some gurus, who betray their students' openness, the ego grows stronger, and the ability to easily manipulate their obedient disciples, blinds them and blocks their conscience.

Meeting Teacher

Despite being a member of the Fourth Way school for about a year and a half, I was yet to meet the founder and head teacher of the school. Of course, I had heard many stories, told by the other members of the school, about his 'crystallisation'. I had been told that he is what is called in the Fourth Way as a 'man number seven'.

Here is a brief explanation about the meaning of this number: man number one, two and three are those whose centre of gravity, so to speak, lies in the moving-instinctive, emotional, or intellectual centres respectively. Man number four is the one whose centre of gravity lies in the 'work on himself' and in whom flashes of the higher emotional centres begin to appear. Man number five is the one in whom the crystallisation of higher hydrogens takes place, and so, he has established permanent contact with the higher emotional centres. Man number six is the one in whom the higher intellectual centres begin functioning and man number seven is the one who is fully 'crystallised' in the higher centres and has achieved the 'marriage of the higher centres'. In short, this is a man who has accomplished everything that can be accomplished, a man who has a single 'I', 'will' and a fully blossomed Consciousness. As you can see, it seems like a very profound accomplishment and a very serious claim.

Although I thoroughly enjoyed my time in the school and could undeniably feel the big changes that its knowledge and the work on myself created in me, I began also to see the limitations of Gurdjieff's teachings. In fact, from my present understanding, based on many of my direct experiences of the Higher Realms of Infinite Reality, I see now with great clarity, that Gurdjieff's teaching is full of limitations, and also very naïve statements. Nevertheless, I was given this role to play and sought the Truth in such a way in this 'life-game'. And as I mentioned before, the most important thing on our way towards the Ultimate Truth is utmost honesty with oneself, openness of mind and heart to our Beloved, efforts of self-exploration, development of intuitive knowledge and the sharpness of the intellect discriminating with great precision between what is based on sweet beliefs, and what is based on uncompromising Truth.

Sometime in the summer of 1997 we heard the news that the head teacher was coming to Moscow and Sankt Petersburg for a few days, and he was going to give some 'formal dinners' (a form of education). Having been in the school for so long, following his teaching and hearing the stories about him, I was looking forward with great anticipation to see him. My close friend, Genya, somehow figured out that the teacher was going to see the ballet at the Bolshoi Theatre. That's where I meet him for a first time. Tall, with dark-grey eyes, big even teeth, a neatly trimmed grey beard, wearing expensive suit and gold-framed glasses, holding in his hands small notebook and gold-plated pen, he was standing in the foyer of the Bolshoi with a small group of young men when my friend and I approached him. Genya, who already knew the teacher, introduced me to him.

Teacher, looking at me, said: 'Some of my friends were just telling me that the fountain in front of the Bolshoi Theatre is one of the oldest fountains in Moscow.' Then he threw his notepad, which he was holding in his hands, into the air, followed by the pen, that he was also holding. Both landed on the floor. 'That is the oldest fountain' he said, 'that is self-remembering'.

This was his way of teaching: to create an unexpected 'shock', which produces 'moments of memory', that cannot be destroyed by time. Later, we went to the restaurant that had been specially prepared for this occasion. Around forty students from the Moscow centre gathered there. I wouldn't say that I was highly impressed with the questions and answers and the whole atmosphere and energy of this gathering. After the dinner, it happened that I was the one who ran to get a taxi for Teacher. Seeing this, he asked me to jump into the taxi with him. With the small group of young men accompanying us, along with my friend Genya, we ended up in a small café at the Metropolitan Hotel, where Teacher – Robert Burton – was staying. While having a coffee, he asked me, if I had any questions. With the help of my friend's translation, I asked him: 'How can I get rid of "wilfulness" and find and surrender to the will of Higher Forces?' (In the Fourth Way this is called 'C-influence', meaning the influence that comes from the outside of 'life' from 'conscious beings or angels'.)

He said something, about me being a gentle sun (another Fourth Way idea about different body types) and said that I rightly understood that I needed help. Then, pointing towards the door on which the gold-plated handle appeared as a cross, he said that he was a conscious being and that he could see more then we normally see, and that this handle represented Jesus on the cross, and that the horizontal line was 'time', and the vertical line was 'present' and that was how man escapes from time.

Returning home after these events, I was in a state of confusion. My intuition was not in agreement with the statement that he was a 'conscious being' – a 'man number seven', but somehow, I forcefully convinced myself of it.

Life continued. It was full and adventurous. Many positive activities were taking place in Moscow and other Russian centres. We were educating our uneducated essences by studying the works of 'Conscious Beings', which Teacher said were directly working with him.

Here is the list of these 'beings': Leonardo da Vinci, Geoffrey Chaucer, William Shakespeare, Johann Sebastian Bach, Antonio Vivaldi, Meher Baba, Michel de Montaigne, Lewis Carol, George Gurdjieff, Peter Ouspensky, Rodney Collin, Josef (son of Jacob), Moses, Ezekiel, Lao-Tzu, Buddha, Socrates, Plato, Aristotle, Virgil, Horace, Jesus Christ, Peter, Paul, Epictetus, Marcus Aurelius, Omar Khayyam, Dante Alighieri, Francesco Petrarca, Hafiz, Fra Angelico, Elizabeth I, Miguel de Cervantes, Rembrandt van Rijn, John Milton, Benjamin Franklin, Johann Wolfgang von Goethe, William Blake, Hans Christian Andersen, Abraham Lincoln, Walt Whitman, Rainer Maria Rilke, Solon.

Regardless of whether it was true or not, that these 'beings' were working with Teacher, studying of works of these 'beings' expanded the horizons of general knowledge and gave essence a better education. In our Moscow centre, we were also engaged in

91

the production of theatrical plays, organisation, service and participation in "formal dinners", attending concerts of classical music and ballet performances, visiting museums, arranging balls, and sometimes 'symposiums' – specially arranged evenings centred around a certain philosophical subject, accompanied by excessive amounts of wine, etc.... We were also working with the small exercises, which were changing every week and were designed as reminders (alarm clocks) to observe and to remember ourselves. I began to lead small gatherings in my studio apartment, where with the intimacy of just a few students we could further explore our understandings and specifically concentrate our attention on the expansion of consciousness.

At certain times, specifically, when Robert Taylor, who was such an inspiration to us all, left Moscow, I could clearly observe how the energy of the formal 'meetings' were plummeting. The obvious conclusion of my observations was that, when too much formality, or form begins to dominate, the essence becomes suppressed.

Although Love-God is the creator of all forms, being Herself formless and limitless, to show Her transcendental beauty, She begins to strip Herself off all Her beautiful clothing, revealing Her astonishing majestic nakedness. Two major aspects of Love-Truth – Boundless Freedom and Infinite Energy begin to destroy every form, destroying everything that appears as boundaries and limitations, breaking all cups and holy grails, for the Love-Reality is limitless and nothing can hold Her. And so, She ever springs, ever surges, ever flows.

At these times, I felt like the revolutionary Kazimir Malevich – the artist of the 'Black Square' painting – calling 'Arise Comrades, and free yourselves from the tyranny of objects'.

I would like to disclaim here all false imagination, if such may appear, and say with uncompromising honesty that I am not a saint, and far less of a saint was I in the period I am describing now. Neither was I established in perfect clarity and wisdom. All forms of negative states (jealousy, pride, laziness, calculativeness, avoidance of pain and seeking pleasure, etc.) surged to the surface of my being, when triggered by a certain stimulus.

Also, I was quite naïve, which is in my opinion double-sided. One side of naivety is that it is easy to deceive a naïve person, but another side is a greater openness which brings the possibility of faster learning. And so, I was more and more open and willing to learn from the lessons that life was presenting. Acceptance of what is presented to us, moment by moment, without judgment, or desire to escape, change or deny these 'presents', and the ability to learn and be grateful for whatever comes, brings us greater appreciation of life events. We begin to realise that every moment, regardless how pleasant or painful it may be, is a gift, or a lesson from our Beloved and it is our choice to reject this gift-lesson or learn something profound about ourselves from the given moment. Learning from these lessons, we grow stronger into gratitude and love.

Inner Jesus Prayer, Zikr and Mantra-Japa

Around this time, I came across the book titled *Candid Narratives of a Pilgrim to His Spiritual Father*, known in English as *The Way of a Pilgrim* written by a simple-minded Russian peasant, whose heart was longing for the knowledge of an 'inner Jesus prayer'. After an intense period of searching for the spiritual teacher who could instruct him in a practice of the inner Jesus prayer, he received initiation into it. His practice was to repeat the Jesus prayer – 'Lord Jesus Christ son of God have mercy on me' – continuously throughout the day, increasing the numbers of repetitions in the following days. It was very hard at the beginning, but with practice our Pilgrim became so united with the inner Jesus prayer, that it became second nature. His heart picked the prayer and carried it with him day and night. The book is full of the most fascinating stories of his pilgrimage throughout the country, engaged in inner Jesus prayer, with the unfolding of the true miracles this prayer brought about. In later stages, he began to practice this inner prayer by plunging his mind into his heart on each inhalation with the words 'Lord Jesus Christ son of God' and on each exhalation with the words 'have mercy on me'. The book moved me deeply and I began to practice the inner Jesus prayer as often and for as long as I could.

Around the same time, I was also drawn to Sufism, following the teachings of Rumi, the poetry of Hafiz and Omar Khayyam, and also the teachings of the Naqshbandi and Nimatullahi Sufi orders, particularly the teachings of Javad Nurbakhsh. And again, I found Zikr, or Dhikr at the heart of Sufi teachings. Zikr, it is said

Inner Jesus Prayer, Zikr and Mantra-Japa

by the Sufis, has stages. As Imam Ghazali said, "'You must know that Allah removed all the veils of ignorance and brought people to the state of vision through their continuous Zikr'.

The first stage of Zikr is the Zikr of the Tongue. In this stage, sadhakas make zealous efforts to repeat Dhikr – to dwell in the presence of God's name, but the Heart is not yet ready for Dhikr and rejects it.

Then is the Zikr of the Heart. In this stage the Heart of a sadhaka fully accepts Dhikr and repeats sacred words, even without the mind's effort. This is followed by the appearance of the Divine Presence in the reciter of Dhikr, making him no longer need to do Dhikr."[16] In this stage, Dhikr has completed its purpose and culminated in the vision and perpetual Presence of the Beloved. (The Name itself translates into 'Beloved'.) Zikr can be seen as the unique name encompassing all attributes: 'Allah', and also the negation and affirmation 'La Ilaha Illallah' – there is no other reality than Allah (God Absolute).

And so, I adopted the practice of Zikr also, often combining it with the inner Jesus prayer. A few years later I discovered similar ways to draw oneself nearer and nearer to God by repeating His/Her Holy names and, with the help of these sacred formulas, dwell in God's Presence, known in Hindu traditions as Mantra-japa. Later in this book we will return to this important subject and will talk not only about japa, but about the whole 'mantra' science and its significance more extensively.

---

[16] "Classical Islam and the Naqshbandi Sufi Tradition" Muhammad Hisham Kabbani.

Growing Intimacy with The Beloved

As time passed, I became more and more open to connection and communication with the higher forces, feeling any suggestion of the given situation as a gift that must be accepted with gratitude. Of course, such openness brought with it not only 'easiness', but also a lot of complications. Despite of these complications, however, I felt a growing connection with God. I felt His presence around me, as though my Beloved liked to keep a very close eye on me, follow my every step, and didn't like to leave me for even a moment. This intimacy with the Beloved filled me with overwhelming gratitude and a natural desire to pay him back for the joy of his proximity. I asked myself how I could repay this gift of joyful intimacy. The answer to this overflowing gratitude was in the sharing of this surging love and joy with other people; being an empty flute for the Beloved's breath and rhythm, letting this wonderful love flow through me to the whole of creation.

I noticed that the greatest suffering and dissatisfaction with myself I found at those times, when I was unable to transmit this Divine Love due to certain impurities, for example after periods of heavy drinking. These impurities blocked the passage of God's love, and I felt ashamed and unable to talk in these states about higher planes, for it felt that to talk about such pure things from the lower place would be a lie. However, through these painful lessons, I found a great solution to the eternal question of destiny and free will. Not that this solution answers unequivocally this paradoxical question in any definitive way, such as: 'free will is an illusion and

Growing Intimacy with The Beloved

everything is predestined', or 'everything depends on the choices that one makes'. Both statements are not very useful for practical application.

When man learns from the scriptures or scientific conclusions, that free will is an illusion and everything is already predestined and predetermined, he begins to dismiss the necessity of 'spiritual effort', for, if everything is already predestined, then choice is an illusion. In this case, there is no difference between choosing one option over the other, let's say sitting in meditation, or going to a pub and getting drunk. The outcome will be the same. This idea of super-predetermination has a positive side, and also a negative one. The positive side is that man is throwing himself totally to the grace of God, realising that he himself is not a 'doer' of any action and has no power to change anything and that everything is done by God alone. The negative side, however, is that, convinced of predetermination, he dismisses the value of 'self-effort' and of the right choice. In this case, the right choice and the effort to know and unite with the Ultimate Truth has no value.

In our human condition, however, regardless of if we believe in free will or predetermination, we cannot avoid choices, we are forced to choose. Of course, one can practice openness to whatever comes unsought, practice full, choiceless acceptance of anything that is presented in the moment, and that is a very good practice that will lead to a greater intimacy with the Higher Power, but still, at certain times one simply has no choice but to make a choice.

And so, the practical (profitable) application to this paradoxical situation in my view is firstly to consider that every outcome depends greatly on the one's applied effort and the choice one makes, and secondly, and this is almost inescapable: that when one makes the wrong choice, and sees the consequences of this wrong choice, one should immediately realise that one didn't have a choice, because it was already predestined. In this case, instead of going into self-judgement, self-hatred, or self-pity, one immediately forgives oneself, for it wasn't one's fault, but it was destiny, and one quickly let go of all matter. We spend so much time attached to negative judgmental states that suck slowly at our energy. Learning to instantaneously forgive and forget is a way to liberation.

Growing Intimacy with The Beloved

If one however, expects to receive only the bestowal of pleasures and happiness in exchange for one's total trust, openness and acceptance of whatever is presented, one could be greatly disappointed that this is not always the case. On the contrary, one could be presented with increasing difficulties and harder lessons to learn. The roots of the lotus are in the mud. The deeper the mud the more beautiful the flower. The iridescent pearl is produced by the oyster, when it gets irritated by a grain of sand. Suffering is food for the awakening soul.

Confusing Sexual Games with Teacher

And so, my situation then became more chaotic and problematic, and filled with the gifts of hard lessons to learn. It began in the summer of 1997 with the invitation from Teacher to join him in his travels around Italy. I met him again, this time in Venice, from where we travelled in two minivans with a few other young men to Rome and later down south to Napoli, and further to Ravello, built on a picturesque hill on the Amalfi coast. The aim of travelling with Teacher was education: studying art, visiting fascinating places filled with beauty, dining in fine restaurants etc. Of course, there would also be time for questions and answers, however Teacher would usually say that he was not teaching at the time of travelling.

We travelled from Venice to Rome, from Rome to Napoli and then to the Amalfi coast. The breath-taking views of shimmering sparkles of reflected sunlight playing on the surface of a clear blue Mediterranean Sea, stretching seemingly into infinity, when viewed from a cliff in gorgeous Ravello filled me to the brim with gratitude for such beauty. I felt that it was possible to be awakened simply through the sheer power of the majestic beauty of nature.

After such overwhelming impressions, on the evening of our first day in Ravello, Teacher asked me if I would stay the night with him in his room…

How could I, soaked in gratitude and longing for the surrender of self-will, possibly say no? And so, I stayed that night with Teacher, who told me that he was neither male nor female, but rather a 'conscious being' – an angel, who had achieved the

99

marriage of the higher centres, and that 'making love' to him was a rare privilege.

I, in response, said that I was extremely happy and grateful... In the end, I felt that it was not a big deal, or a tremendous sacrifice, to allow someone, especially your teacher, to give you oral sex. I didn't feel being abused, or damaged, I just took it very lightly, as in the saying: 'Angels fly because they take themselves lightly'. After this night, I became the temporary 'teacher's favourite', which was slightly uncomfortable. I received a few gifts of clothing and a pretty heavy golden chain.

After about ten days of travelling around Italy, I returned home to discover that my business, which I had left in the hands of my friend, had suffered a great deal. I was working as a middle-man between the supplying sea-food company and shops and supermarkets. The company would lend me their products, for which shops and supermarkets would pay a few weeks later. It was always risky business during these unsettled times, when mafia ruled, to supply products to certain shops from whom it was almost impossible to get your money back. And step by step I was not only losing money but plunging deeper and deeper into debt. Sometimes I would wake up in a cold sweat in the middle of the night, filled with panic and the instinctive fear of survival.

I had a great desire to move to 'Apollo' – the teacher's property in northern California, populated by hundreds of Fourth Way school students, most of whom were working on a vineyard and vinery, making 'Renaissance' wine. My imagination drew Apollo as a little paradise, a community of friends non-expressing negativity and working on the betterment of themselves and their surroundings. A big number of students from all around the world were coming to Apollo at the beginning of autumn, to help with the harvest of grapes. Teacher called me, offering to take care of all my needs, if I moved to his property and lived in the 'academy' – his luxurious home. For some reason, I was denied an American visa, and had no choice but to stay in Russia, often joining Teacher on his travels around Italy, Greece, France and Spain.

The more time however, I spent with Teacher, the less I trusted him. I could see from the summit of my spiritual mountain that his teachings were quite limited and naïve in comparison to the expanded visions of Reality I received as the direct revelations

100

from the Grace of the Almighty. I could see with the growing clarity that he was not the man he wanted us to believe he was. Not only was he not 'the man number seven' but was not even 'the man number five'. Often his explanations triggered nothing but irritation in me. I began to see how he used people for his own gains and sometimes my rebellious spirit revolted. On one occasion, while Teacher was resting in his apartment in Rome, me and my constant companion, Genya, after having dinner in Piazza Navona, accompanied by an excessive amount of alcohol, returned to the apartment quite late and drunk. Teacher was woken up by our return, and released by alcohol, my rebellious spirit lost its fear and confronted him. I told him I didn't believe him, and that all students who travelled with him were just afraid of him, afraid that the next time he would not take them to travel with him, afraid to be thrown out of school, etc. As a sign of a protest, after Teacher retired to his room, I smoked a cigarette sitting on the windowsill of our room, which was quite a daring and unwise thing to do.

The next morning, however, I regretted the explosion of my suppressed feelings. I wasn't yet ready to leave the school, for it was such an important part of my life. There was nothing, as it seemed to me, in this world to retreat to. I asked Robert for forgiveness, blaming everything on the excessive amount of alcohol I had consumed. Teacher did forgive me, saying his usual stuff in these sorts of scenarios: that my instinctive centre was trying to escape conscious control... Looking honestly at this period of travelling with Teacher, I see us (all the students, but particularly me and Genya) as naughty boys playing with 'teacher' and around 'teacher', hiding to smoke, or drink etc.

Teacher's sexual games also broadened. He began to introduce into his little orgies' new Russian young male students and friends. And so, we were forced to break taboos. It all was quite unnatural, but I learnt to take it all easy, as though it was a game. Often, observing Teacher during these distorted sexual activities, I saw clearly a man in possession of demon – lust.

I am not going to write here about all his monstrous perverted sexual fantasies and games, for it could sound disgusting, and it is also not the point of these writings.

I remember when I came back from one of my travels and was leading a meeting in Moscow, where students were eager to know

Confusing Sexual Games with Teacher

what it was like to be with the teacher. Someone asked if I truly considered him as my teacher. After a long pause, I said, to the astonishment of everyone, 'no'.

Nevertheless, I was asked by Teacher to travel around to few Russian centres as a 'travelling teacher' and lead meetings there. Trained and inspired by my first mentor Robert Taylor, desiring more than anything else to bring people into the highest state of consciousness, brave enough to talk about the most intimate relationship with God, and with the courage to invite gathered friends to rip off all lies and pretence and uncover the most beautiful Truth, I led meetings resulting in very intense sparkling energy and high states of consciousness that many remember. A couple of my friends even admitted to me that they were still staying in the school because of me and my meetings. I travelled from Karelian town Petrozavodsk down south to Odessa, leading meetings in Petrozavodsk, St Petersburg, Moscow, Kiev and Odessa. My experience of the higher states of consciousness gave me the courage to transmit the Highest Truth. In a way, it was some sort of 'Shaktipat' – the transmission of Shakti energy, although I didn't know this term back then.

One girl from Odessa told me a few hours after our meeting finished, while we were walking with all the students from the Odessa centre towards the observatory, where they had invited me to look at the moon, stars and galaxies at night, that she was so blown away by the energy of this meeting, that she was delaying to come back home, afraid that her mother would notice her 'non-ordinary' state of consciousness.

Seeing my positive changes, after my being in the school for couple of years, my wife decided to join it too. After being in the school for about half a year she decided to try to get an American visa and go to Apollo for the harvest. She got a visa without any problem and in the late summer of 1998, leaving me with our nine-year old son, she went, supposedly for a couple of months to Apollo. She soon got a job at the French bistro situated on the teacher's property. She seemed to be very happy and extended the period of her stay firstly for six months and then for a whole year.

False Prophesy and Cancellation of the 'Sex Exercise'

Teacher had predicted that in the summer of 1998 there would be a great earthquake in California, and because of which, California will fall beneath the Pacific Ocean.

Before this prediction, he announced that, if 'California's fall' didn't happen, he would cancel the 'sexual exercise'. (For many years there was a rule within the 'Fellowship of Friends' that forbade having sex outside of marriage). So, when the prophecy didn't happen, students of the school, mostly young people between the ages of 20 and 40, didn't pay much attention to the fact that prediction was false, but rather were looking forward to tasting the fruits of the cancellation of the 'sexual exercise'.

I must say that most people had taken the rules seriously, because without which, there wasn't much point of staying in the school. There had been one accident some time earlier, of which I am not so proud now, but which clearly shows my deep involvement in the school. There was a rule that after one year of joining the school, students must stop smoking. On one occasion some older students gathered for a party in someone's garden. As party went on, some of my friends started smoking. I couldn't accept it and urged them to stop smoking to no avail. I felt very distressed at this breaking of the rule. I felt that a crime has been committed against the teacher's will. I had no choice but to report

103

False Prophesy and Cancellation of the 'Sex Exercise'
this crime to our centre director. My dear friends were asked to pay
penalties for breaking this rule.

Almost immediately after the sexual exercise was cancelled, I
found myself in multiple sexual relationships with fellow students.
Love, I felt then, must be shared. The intimacy of sexual union is
one of her highest expressions. Not lust for pleasure, but rather lust
for union and intimacy, a desire to give, to make a lover happy by
giving my affection, love, kisses, soul, self, were guiding my
spontaneous actions, leading to new sexual relations. While my
wife was having a great time in Apollo, one young girl from our
school entered my life.

Only about four weeks had passed since our first sexual union.
I was sitting in a kitchen and reading *Discourses* by Meher Baba.
The chapter I was reading was titled 'Children must be welcomed'.
My girlfriend entered the kitchen and said: 'I think I am pregnant.'
I had not the slightest doubt that it was another gift from the higher
forces, which I had to accept without any resistance or hesitation.

When my wife return home (obviously, I had told her about
everything), my girlfriend and I began to search for a new place to
live so we could move out of the apartment I was renting. My
business wasn't flourishing, and I found myself plunging deeper
and deeper into debt. Towards the end of November 1999 our baby
was already couple of weeks overdue. On the 28th of November
1999, in one of Moscow's small studio apartments, my second son
Andrey was born.

Me and one self-taught, but experienced midwife, with couple
of her small kids hanging around, helped Lena deliver the baby into
the warm waters of a blow-up swimming pool. This birth process
truly was balancing on a razor-edge between life and death. The
chief new-age he-midwife, responsible for the baby's delivery,
slightly miscalculated the time of delivery and was absent,
attending some of his workshops. The remaining midwife and I
were swapping our positions, trying to help Lena to deliver. After
long time of pushing without success, Lena began to panic, asking
midwife crazy questions about the possibility of somehow being
transported to hospital. 'There is no time for it, either you deliver
now, or your baby will die' – the midwife said sharply! After lots
of 'push', finally, a squashed and almost purple head came out, but
the wide shoulders and the rest of the body were stuck in the birth

104

canal trapped tightly around the neck. Frightening déjà vu stroked me. Yes, I had experienced this shocking moment before and already knew exactly what was going to happen (the baby dies)!

We swapped positions again. I was delivering. The midwife told me to try to catch the baby's left shoulder and get it out. I no longer cared about harming Lena but was solely concentrated on urgently getting the baby out. Somehow, I pulled left shoulder out and to all our great relief the whole body came out. Phew...

But the baby wasn't breathing and didn't have a pulse either for about a minute or so. Undoubtedly, he didn't want to be born again. The midwife in a panic was pumping the umbilical cord and commanded me to throw the bucket of prepared beforehand ice-cold water on the baby. Only after this cold shock, the miracle happened. He opened his eyes and began weeping piously. This extreme experience was so pure, unpretentious, emotional and rewarding, that I felt like I wanted to learn to be a midwife. That was what I want to do with my life: help babies to be born.

In the following couple of months our financial situation worsened dramatically. I owed quite a big amount of money to a company from which I was borrowing goods and the director of this company was planning to send some mafia boys to track me down. Intensified by this great financial pressure, the relationship between me and Lena became very tense.

One day, my wife Inna, to whom I had been married for twelve years, and whom I had left for Lena, invited me to visit her. Being with her, our love was rekindled, for I saw her love and her willingness to sacrifice anything to help me. It was so different from the strenuous demanding relationship with my girlfriend, that I decided to stay with my wife. Finding blindly reasonable excuses for my cowardly behaviour, I left Lena in quite a difficult situation. Fortunately, Lena's mother helped arrange for our son to stay with her in Ural.

New Adventures

Just a couple of days later I was invited again by Teacher to travel with him around Europe. This journey became the longest one yet. Teacher was now making a new prediction, based on a few, as it seemed to me, very silly observations; a prediction for the new date of California's fall. He advised me and my friends and companions, Genya and Vasily, not to go to Russia. He insisted that, in the case of California's fall, there would be lots of crime around the globe and it would be practically impossible for us to go to U.S. if we lived in Russia. On my suggestion to try to apply for another American visa, he replied that I had tried it already, another attempt wouldn't work. He was entertaining some crazy, criminal and very dangerous plans; the first of which was to smuggle us onto a boat to the U.S.A. from Cuba. And so, while we were staying in Paris, we went to the Cuban embassy to apply for visas. Fortunately for us, the Cuban embassy refused to give us visas. Teacher's next move was to ask one of our Italian students from Napoli to get for us fake Italian passports. We sent Pasquale our passport photos and he began his negotiations with the Italian mafia. Meanwhile, after our teacher went back to California, we were left to ourselves in Paris. We travelled in Teacher's MPV, which he left for us to use, around France and Europe, seeing famous works of arts and visiting cathedrals and castles, following Teacher's advice.

On Genya's request, we picked up his girlfriend Tina in Amsterdam so she could travel with us. Waiting for her at the airport, Genya went to search for her. I was looking through the big airport window when my eyes meet Tina's sparkling eyes, and recognised her, even though we had never meet before. Apparently, the company with whom she had been travelling had lost her luggage, but despite of it, Tina looked extremely happy, although she just won the lottery.

When we travelled back to France, we stayed at the little hotel next to actress Maria's (I don't want to mention her second name for privacy reasons) villa in Fontainebleau. Maria was very close to Teacher and was helping him find and purchase of items of antiquity in Paris.

I cannot describe with certainty the motivations of my friend Genya, but it was with his encouragement that we became involved in a threesome with Tina. She was a very light-hearted, adventurous, and fun girl with cheeky sparkles in her eyes. A couple of days later at one of the 'FOF' gatherings in Paris, another girl, Martha, joined our journey. The five of us travelled through Lyon and Avignon to Cannes and Nice and further down to Italy, visiting towns such as Siena, Mantua, Venice and Florence. I had a brief crush on Martha, which led only to one sweet kiss in a beautiful villa garden in the French town of Grasse, where one of our 'FOF' friends was working as a gardener. Tina and Genya accidentally witnessed this kiss, and I noticed how it made Tina very jealous. Well, three young men and two girls in one car travelling through the beautiful places at the summertime; obviously, there was some intense vibes. Our journey was filled with sexual and emotional energy, jealousy and beauty. The best way however, to describe the emotional roller-coaster of this journey would be to share with you a little bit of my first clumsy but unpretentious poetry, which was freely pouring like streams out of my swollen heart onto the pages of my notebook....

'I want to share my love with you, I want to share with you my wonderful state.

Please take my sacred fire, eat and drink me.

What can I do for you? Only share the best I have.

In the proximity of Death, I am hurrying to say sacred words to you: I love you.

This moment is filled with God's love!

Let's drink this wonderful nectar.

No more Venice, no dining table, we are in a new dimension and we are free.

New Adventures

Now we can truly meet each other, now we can truly touch each other.

We are unbelievably beautiful.

Our souls are sweet innocent children.

We are in Love with each other, because there are no more separate individuals.

We are one. We are Love. We are Infinity.

These are the most intimate relationships.

In this majestic moment, our souls making love.

They are blending in love-ecstasy and trembling with a thousand orgasms.

We are at home. We have no need to go anywhere. Love is our home!

Our Beloved is here!

Love made us free.

We are the happiest and the most fortunate beings on Earth.

We know the greatest secret of Love.

We've tasted the elixir of Heaven.

Please don't leave this majestic house, we have nowhere to go.

In every moment is hidden paradise.

My soul is the life-water.

Please drink it while it's springing.

Honesty is in the sharing with our friends the radiance of our soul, our beautiful state, our Love.

O! How I want to die in this unbelievably beautiful moment.

To die from love means to stay alive.

I know many divine mysteries and I know many secret paths to God.

I've been already His guest.

He is unbelievably beautiful, but to meet Him we must say goodbye to ourselves.

To disappear, to burn out like a candle on the way to Love means to become free.

First step towards God is the step out of oneself.

O! How can I transmit to you what happiness to be free in God's embrace?

Why do I so often speak of God? Because he is my True Beloved.

How can I keep silent about him?

You saying: of what God, do you speak, have you seen Him?

Yes, I am acquainted with Him. God is the only reality.

Everything else disappears and therefore are only forms.

God is the essence. Love is the essence. We are Love.

Our names and individualities are given to us only for we become our Self – Love.

Love is the highest dimension.

I am suffering only because I cannot give you more,

But I believe that at certain moment I will shine like a Sun and fill you up with Love.

I am repeating it again and again: I am the happiest man, for I know it.

I am the happiest man for I've met God.

If you meet Him, you will immediately fall in love with Him.

He is in love with me and doesn't leave me even for a second.

I see Him everywhere. He fills me to the brim with Love.

I cannot describe you what happiness it is to be God's lover,

And every moment to rejoice in His presence.

Truly, we are the doors for God's Love.

Our individualities are only the doors.

We are the radiant light.

Open your door and I will burst in and daze you with my beauty.

A thousand orgasms would shake you with my stunning vibrations.

Awakening is the returning Home.

Awakening is the opening of the door.

Awakening is the disappearance.

Awakening is the leap into death.

Awakening is the plunge into Love.

Playing games of our lives, we inevitably move towards death.

Where are we going? What do we want?

We are longing for our Home. We are thirsty for our True Freedom.

Here is our Home!

Our Beloved is always with us!

He is the fire and blinding light.

Open your windows.

Throw away your morals and other taboos and laws.

New Adventures

Love is the universal law.

Love is freedom.

We are not our roles. We are eternal fire.

Our job, o, what a beautiful job, is love!

I am not trying to achieve anything in this life.

All I want is to regain Freedom.

All I want is to surrender to the fiery Divine hurricane.

God filling my lungs with the blaze of love.

When I am listening or looking, I am breathing in love.

When I am speaking or writing poetry, I am breathing out God.

To open the doors of perception – this is my job.

I am a flute of Divine music.

With his sweet breath, God blowing dust out of me.

Soon there will be nothing left of me, except God's fiery gale.

Love is excruciating, for she is too hot.

To see God is agonizing, for our eyes are not accustomed to such blinding light.

Trust me, all I write is not only imaginary words.

It is the Truth.

I do not care about my life.

I gave my body to my teacher and I am offering my soul to God.

I am a whore, ready to give myself for free to anyone who asks.

I am freeing myself from all laws, commandments and exercises.

Love is my only law!

Step into the present and you will become free.

Present is the road to paradise.

Dive into the unknown, it's the only way home.

I know, it's terrifying to leap into a place where you've never been before,

But I assure you that at the very last moment wings will grow in place of your shoulders.

You will be flying above time in stunningly beautiful places.

You will see that life is only an ancient theatrical play.

I am saying this to you with such certainty because I already have been in paradise.

The sphere of the universal knowledge will be shimmering with majestic beauty above you.

Touch it, and you will know more than is written in all intelligent books.

Knowledge reveals itself by the touch.

To truly know you don't need thinking.

The road to Knowledge is the Present.

The Present is eternity.

The Present is Love.

The Present is paradise.

The Present is freedom.

Do not wait for death to find this out.

Death comes so suddenly.

Your chance is always now, remember only now.

Come to me and I will show you the path to God.

Poetry is more than facts.

If I was operating by the facts only, how dry and flat would be my speech.

If I was operating by the facts only, I wouldn't have left a free space for a miracle.

The essence of our work – is to leave a free space for a miracle.

Every instance is an opportunity for sacrifice.

Sacrifice, and the miracle will fill this space.

Give space and God will make everything for you.

Listen and look attentively!

Your Beloved is here!

He is waiting for a free space in you to show Himself.

He is waiting for your ears, eyes, your nostrils, tongue, and fingers.

Maybe you forgot what it means to be alive?

Listen and watch!

Give all your attention to these two things, and you will come back to life.

Your Beloved is here!

In this car that you are driving, on this field, in this bar, in the sky and beneath your feet...

He is waiting for your attention!

Try to see Him, try to hear Him.

Sacrifice your intrusive I's, sacrifice, and you will be showered with gratitude.

Invite God to be your guest.

He is such a sweet companion.

Prepare space for Him.

Wash your dishes, sweep the floor.

God loves clean things.

He doesn't like when your house is full of old rubbish.

Free yourself from your accumulated knowledge.

I haven't seen anything more useless than this old garbage.

Be new-born, listening, looking!

Drink this magic moment, drink this water of life.

Be thirsty for this life-water and water itself will find your dry lips.

Pray, ask, knock, search for your Self in new dimensions.

Hack the road to heaven.

Search for yourself in love.

Do not be afraid, stride towards the flame.

Enter your house of fire.

Fire is not an attribute of hell.

Fire is the symbol of paradise.

Hell is eternally cold.

Deceive Death!

Die before She kisses you with Her cold lips.

Do not be afraid of Her.

She is charming. Don't let Her out of your site.

Ask Her. She will teach you Love!

Death is a muse. She is kindling the flames of Love. She inspires poetry.

It's difficult to speak prose in Her company.

Death creates angels from our souls.

She gives us wings in place of shoulders.

If you become Her lover, She'll give you freedom.

Die, disappear, dissolve…

Only then, you will be born, only then, you shall become your Self.

God is Life.

Awakening is returning to Life.

In the quantum world, everything happens differently.

You cannot meet God until you become him.

I am the love of the moth, who throws itself into the flame of the candle.

New Adventures

If I won't be burnt by this inviting flame, the pain of separation will burn my wings.

Give to Caesar that which belong to Caesar.

We are God's!

We are primordial light!

Let go of this golden vessel.

Step into the light from your shadow.

Become the light.

Open your rusty gate.

I am here at the threshold of your door.

I am thirsty for your death.

I will burn you to ashes.

There will be nothing left of you.

I will give you freedom.

You will lose your consciousness from such blinding beauty.

Everyone who sees God losing consciousness.

There is not a slightest possibility to see him and retain our ordinary consciousness.

Different consciousness will appear: Divine consciousness.

The only way to God is Death.

Love is the beginning of the road; Death is its end.

Death is the beginning of the road; Love is its end.

Love is the beginning and is the end.

Rejoice! Every moment of your life is a gift from God.

Look at these beautiful flowers, these magnificent trees.

Look at these bottomless skies, this gentle sun full of love.

Look at these beautiful faces of boys and girls and even more beautiful faces of old people.

Plunge into these bottomless eyes, into this cosmos.

Breathe in the fragrances of grass.

Hear birds' songs, chirping of grasshoppers, gurgling of water.

All this is a crazy gift from God, and all this is for you.

Awake!

Every moment is filled with His Love.

Life is the unbelievable Gift.

We are the most fortunate beings in the universe.

We are showered from toes to head with Divine Gifts.

O, God!

How magnificent is this road towards death, called life!

Absorb it with your eyes, like a hot sand absorbs moisture from the sky.

Beauty needs your cognition.

As a child, she is waiting for your precious attention.

Music needs your grateful ears,

Flowers are searching for your eyes,

Fragrances are searching for your nostrils,

Tastes are searching for your lips and tongue,

Skin is thirsty for your touch.

Be a grateful receiver.

Do not reject.

Open your doors and breathe in Love.

Let every cell of your body be filled with Love.

When I am filled with Love I cry with Gratitude.

I am a crier of God.

I am a crier of Love.

How can I keep silence about my Beloved?

I am like a downpipe.

It was raining and I cannot keep even a drop of water.

Love is pouring out.

Love is bursting out with the flood of tears.'

After our travelling, leaving Genya, Vasily and me in Paris, Tina left for her parents' in England. The next day she called us in our Paris 'teaching house'. I picked up the phone and asked her if she would like to talk to Genya, but she replied that she wanted to talk to me... Genya temporarily felt heartbroken.

Teacher flew from California back to Paris and together we travelled down to Napoli where Pasquale was waiting for us with the fake Italian passports. Apparently, Teacher had paid five thousand dollars for each passport. We returned to Paris and went shopping in some posh shops as teacher had an idea that we should look smart at the airport. Teacher decided to use the UEFA Euro Cup final between France and Italy, played in Rotterdam, as a good timing to send Genya from Amsterdam airport to Newark, USA, thinking there would be lots of Italians in Holland attending the final and it would draw less attention to him at passport control. Genya went through Amsterdam airport security without visible problems. Teacher flew back to California. Vasily and I stayed in

Amsterdam and were waiting for the good or bad news. We received call from Teacher saying that Genya had been stopped at passport control in Newark, but after some considerable time, the authorities allowed him to pass. Teacher decided that it was risky to send us the same way and he asked us to go back to Paris until he came up with a new plan. The Schengen visas on our Russian passports had already expired, so we decided to travel back to France with our new fake Italian passports. Foolishly, we packed our Russian passports into our suitcases with the stash of five thousand dollars which teacher had left for us.

Russian Mafia in a French Prison

At the border between Belgium and France, police stopped our van, looked suspiciously at our Italian passports and decided to search our vehicle. They found our Russian passports with expired visas and five thousand dollars cash. Wearing heavy golden chains, posh clothing, driving a French car, having fake Italian passports together with our Russian passports and the big stash of cash in our suitcases, we must surely have looked to the French police like Russian Mafia. We were taken to prison in the town of Lille in the north of France...

Teacher had told us a few times, that in case of such an incident (i.e. being stopped by police and taken to prison for criminal investigation), we were under no circumstances to mention him or the name of our school, Fellowship of Friends!

This condition brought a great deal of complication into our explanations to the court of how we had gotten fake Italian passports, to whom the car we were travelling in belonged, why we had a stash of money and many other details with which we had to improvise unsuccessfully. And although Teacher sent to court one of his French students, who was an attorney, and also Maria, a famous actress in France, our half-baked explanations didn't sound genuine. We received a sentence of four months in Lille's prison!

Later, however, there were two amnesties, which shortened our sentence to two and half months. As it appears to me, this forced pause in my life was yet another gift from the Beloved. I consider my time in prison as one of the most precious and productive. This sudden stop in our race of travelling, excitement and a

116

kaleidoscope of quickly-changing events created a wonderful space to reflect, to ponder, to awaken to a higher degree. While being in prison I wrote a diary, fragments of which I would like to share with you.

Excerpts from my prison diary:

21.08.00. Tonight, I was woken up by pricks of my conscience. Conscience poured the light on those parts of me which had been sleeping inside for a very long time. I suddenly saw with utmost clarity, that I had been enmeshed in a web of lies, imagination and self-deceit. I've lost the aim. I will start to write a diary in which I will try to see myself objectively, justly, with greater clarity, without hiding my bad or good sides. Today I was thinking of my son Anton. I feel ashamed that I have given him so little. He needs my love and attention. This feeling within me is not weakness, but sober view on reality. It is the light of conscience!

I am so grateful to God and for the conscience for I can see myself with greater clarity. Conscience touched me and I will try to hold on to it. In this diary, I will try to shine the light on all dark parts of me. It could possibly help me with my awakening. I also thought today about my parents. I haven't seen them in around eight or nine months, and I am not even writing to them. I thought that they could die, and I would never see them again. They gave me so much love. I feel ashamed for I so rarely see them and never try to help them. I feel ashamed for being dishonest with them. I looked at my conscious 'work' of this last period, and I could see that practically no real 'work' was being done. I am not trying to help anyone. Love, about which I so often speak, seems to me now as only imaginary. I am only imagining that I love and believe in this imagination. My love is only empty words. I continue smoking. This is my weakness. I don't feel a responsibility towards Robert for breaking his exercise, but I have a responsibility before God. Every day I promise him that I will quit smoking, but nevertheless, I easily break this promise. This weakness takes away my power and purity.

I have decided to look deeply into what triggered this change that plunged my best parts into sleep. Possibly, partially it happened on my last journey with Genya and Vasily. Our conversations weren't refined but rather vulgar and often negative. Possibly this plunge into sleep happened even before this, during my travels with Robert. To be honest with you, it's very easy to become steeped in slumber with Robert. From my observations, he does not so often call on our best parts, such as honesty, conscience and purity, but often triggers lies, pretence, a desire for profit etc. Being here in prison, I feel more awake, more honest with myself. I don't want to leave the school. So many beautiful people are in the school.

My position is very difficult at the present moment. I have no sources of income and I must support two families. I am dependent on Robert's money. This dependence gives birth to lies. But now I feel that I must be honest with Robert, regardless of where it would lead. I am noticing parts of me which would've liked to move to Apollo only for the comfort and of course, being around teacher brings me lots of attention. Many people would like that. All this sounds like I am blaming Robert for everything. In truth, however, it all depends on ourselves, on our power to be honest, and not being afraid that next time you will not be invited to travel with Teacher, even not being afraid that you would be asked to leave the school. Honesty is soberness. If we try to support sobriety, support purity, follow conscience, regardless of how painful these decisions might seem, we can come to awakening. More than that, only in this way we can come to awakening.

I do not believe that Robert is awakened being. His behaviour, his answers and points of view do not resonate with my experience and my understanding. Because I do not believe in his awakened state, the question presents itself to me: why does he deceive us? My machine produces a responsive reaction: okay, if he lies to us, I will play his game. I will pretend that I believe him. Based on my intuition that Robert is not man number seven, six, or even five, I also do not believe in his predictions. More than that, I do not believe in C-influence in forms of forty-four conscious beings. I used to believe in all of this, and my faith helped me a great deal in making intelligent efforts that led to higher states of consciousness.

Now, having no faith, I am beginning to rebuild everything. I need to rebuild everything having as foundation my personal verifications, my personal experience. I believe in God. I believe that my real 'I' is a part of God. I can come to Him by being honest with myself, other people and God, by following the voice of conscience, by sharing my understanding, experience, prayers, sacrifices, love and all the best that I've got with other people.

I have an idea to organise my own group. I think that it is quite possible. I am sure that I could give so much of the good that is in me. I have plenty to share. At the same time, I need the 'third force' in my personal work and I see nothing better for it than the responsibility for my honesty and my efforts before other people. I feel that this work could be very successful.

22. 08. 00.

Today I received letters from Robert and my beautiful Tina. Both letters are very emotional. Robert gives us lots of attention and love. He says I cannot disappoint him. I am very grateful. Tina is a real poet. Her love letter forced my heart to beat faster. I am looking at people as poets and not-poets. I think it's a quality of soul. Tina is a poet. I love her very much. What can we do for each other? Only share the best we have. Tina's letter awakened my love. It gave me higher state. This is a gift.

24.08.00.

Letter to Robert.

'Dearest Robert,

We received your letter and were deeply touched by your love and attention. Our time in jail is filled with deep meaning and self-remembering. This little pause in the endless rhythm of life creates a space for a new vision. It is a time for rediscovering the truth of ourselves. Difficulties are tests of our being. We have something very solid in ourselves that cannot be changed by any external circumstances. I think with self-remembering we would feel at home in any situations. Our home is Love. Our Beloved is always with us. Suffering is a necessity for the birth of Love. I think that the work of the conscious being is a transmutation of coarse materials into gold. It is a transformation of suffering into Love. I remember you saying that the Absolute is in a perpetual process of transformation of suffering and "external consideration" (thinking and taking care of others). The Sun is constantly giving out itself. It scoops Love from its own pain. I strive towards Love with all my might. To become Love is my biggest desire. I refuse to profit but long only for unselfishness. What aims can Slava pursue if they are not connected with God's aims? When I am looking at one of Rembrandt's last self-portraits, I see in his eyes the infinite pain

119

transformed into the infinite Love. I remember your saying that "to understand real art, one must go through suffering". To really understand Christ's teaching, one must go through Christ's sufferings. And there is no higher art than the creation of one's own soul. External circumstances are not causing a great deal of pain for me. Everywhere, I feel myself saved in God's embrace. I know that my path is right – it is the path of Love, and therefore I have nothing to be afraid of. I suffer only from my limitations. I suffer that I cannot give more. If I was limitless I would of drown everyone in my Love. I know that big things begin with small steps. So, what can I do now? Give away everything that I possess and keep asking God for more Love. Love does not know fear. I am not afraid of any circumstances. I know that I can transform sufferings into Love and that is precisely what I want. I remember you saying that if you had three wishes they would be "Thy will be done! Thy will be done! Thy will be done!".'

25.08.00.

Postcard to Monica (a friend of mine from Paris, who sent me a postcard).

'Dear Monica,

Thank you for your Love. Do not be afraid of falling in love. Do not be afraid of breaking your heart. Put down your armour. Appear naked. Ascend the sacrificial bonfire. Let the Universal firestorm burn you to ashes. Only the blaze of Love can save us from death. Cry thank you for pain, suffering and injury. Ask for fire and share fire. Pain will nurture your Love. Unbearable pain gives birth to light. Your true nature is Love. You are not only your beautiful body. Separate from your Monica, be Light, be God. Nothing exists but God. Trust Him. Refuse being profitable. Refuse being fearful. Refuse selfishness. Refuse aim. God will do everything for you. If you are Love, there is nothing to be afraid of. Disappear as Monica and appear as God. When Al Hallaj noughted himself, he realised that "he" did not exist, but only God. He realised himself as God and shouted in ecstasy: "Al-Haqq – I am Truth, I am God." Nothing exists but You. You have no limitations, you are infinite. These are not just lofty words, it is Reality. Your real "I" is Light and Love.'

26.08.00.

Saturday. Maria came to visit us. I love her very much. She is very emotional, and she gives us so much love and attention. She was telling us about Apollo from where she returned just a day ago. She spoke of it like a little paradise. I was almost there in this little paradise with her. Yesterday we received her letter which she sent us from Apollo. There was such concentrated energy in her letter, as though she was writing this letter in heaven. It seems to me that Vasily wrote to Robert to tell him I am smoking. Robert sent a letter with Maria asking me not to smoke any more, and that he forgives me for breaking the exercise. We had a long chat with Maria about it. She asked me why I started smoking. I replied to her that I had started to smoke because I had lost my faith in Robert.

I received letters also from Genya and Martha. They seemed to just be ordinary letters, but some low vibe was there, which created a sense of alienation. I felt such deep, infinite loneliness. My soul rushed to my friend Rita. I cried to her in a letter. The whole evening tears were running down my cheeks, tears of helplessness and loneliness.

I decided to write letter to Robert, in which I honestly will say that I do not believe that he is an awakened being. More than that, I am refusing to have sex with him, which means that I am intentionally choosing empty pockets and difficulties. I am also refusing to accept his gifts and his money. I want to be honest with him, with myself and with God. I am observing lots of lies in my relationship with Robert. I know that I could be happy and secure in Apollo. But it is my machine who is interested in all these. My conscience tells me to choose another, more difficult path, possibly to say farewell to Apollo. This decision could also lead to leaving the school. I will try to be honest to the end. I realise that I might look stupid in the eyes of many people. Rich people have more advantageous position. And of course, a street person with pure conscience still may look just like a pitiful loser. But who knows what fortune is? Maybe no one will understand you. Maybe people will despise you. Only God would remain. It is difficult of course to feel independent from 'not being understood', especially if you are not understood by those whom you counted as your best friends.

Russian Mafia in a French Prison

Many 'I's' were crowding in my head today. Again, and again I was weighing up my decision to write to Robert. Possibly it is a very stupid decision, and I will regret it, but now my soul tells me to choose honesty, which also means difficulties. I thought also about Inna and Lena and decided that it would be more honest to live separate from them, even if it means going back to my hometown of Luchovitcy.

31.08.00.

After an intense inner struggle, I finally sent a letter to Robert in which I said that I did not believe him, refused to have sex with him or accept his gifts and money. I feel slightly relieved after this. I feel liberated from many 'I's'. I can imagine what Robert would say to this letter. He would possibly say that man number four is unstable and it's only a group of 'I's'. He might also say that this happened as a responsive reaction to my breaking of the exercise, and that my instinctive centre wants to get rid of conscious control, and also that August is a time of meteorite showers, which triggers the expression of the extreme 'I's' .... I notice that every new day in prison my King of Hearts appears more often. Yesterday we had a soul-to-soul conversation with Vasily, whereas before, I couldn't talk to him about anything deep.

02.09.00

Today Maria came to visit us again. I am so grateful for her efforts and her love. She was ill, but despite it, drove from Fontainebleau to Lille to see us. She brought some letters from Robert. I can feel how much love Robert is giving us. I cannot be an ungrateful person when I see that unwell Maria, putting aside her own business and spending her Saturday having a little chat with us in not-so-pleasant surroundings. I cannot be an ungrateful person, seeing how much love and attention Robert gives us. I felt a little bit ashamed for the letter that I sent to Robert. He sent me such warm, loving and hopeful letter, and I sent him such a prickly letter. He received my previous letter and replied that he really liked it and that writing is in my essence and maybe I should try to write a book about our experience. Well, I will write another warmer letter to him to heal the wounds.

10.09.00.

Happiness does not depend on money, success, fortune or fame. Happiness is the direct recognition of one's own perfect state. Happiness is the recognition that every moment of one's life is a gift from God. Happiness is being more awake. Happiness is being in love and gratitude. Happiness is remembering one's Self, feeling oneself in Gods loving embrace, seeing God everywhere. An awakened man is showered with God's gifts. Diamonds, rubies and emeralds are scattered around him. An awakened man basks in God's Love...

Today was a beautiful sunny day. Truly the Sun changes the quality of our blood. It gives us joy and makes us happy. In the evening, I was sitting on our barred window seal, looking at the swaying trees, at the enchanting, pregnant moon, breathing in the delightful fragrances of the evening, looking at my life, and falling in love with it. How strange. Some people can teach us how to live, not seeing their own helpless situation. I do not teach how to live. I teach how to rejoice. I teach happiness.

11.09.00.

Another beautiful day. The fragrance of autumn, or rather Indian summer in the air. I am so sensitive to fragrances. This magical molecular state can easily transport me into childhood, to an enchanted forest, to a playful river. Lille is not that far from the sea and the wind brings sea fragrances to our nostrils. How can I be ungrateful for such lovely gifts from the Beloved? Today I received a postcard with my favourite Rembrandt self-portrait from our friend Francoise from Paris. Francoise is wonderful. She has sent us more postcards than anyone else. It is work and it is the expression of Love. I am always waiting for letters and postcards and feel very happy receiving them. Receiving attention is so dear to us. We need to encourage and support attention, for it is the beginning of Love. Together with this diary I am writing a philosophical essay (about time, space, divided attention, higher centres, love, conscience, consciousness, etc.). I am not very successful at it, for it requires prose and I am more attracted to poetry. Nevertheless, I will continue to make notes. I have a vast array of material which I would like to share. Possibly, the writings of all these ideas will take a long time (more than a year). Goethe recommended making little notes every day, to accomplish, in the end, a big work.

15.09.00.

Only five days left until our liberation. I can observe a blend of different emotions in my machine. From one point of view I forefeel an intoxication by freedom, from another, the heavy load of freedom. Freedom means that you must take responsibility for your life. I have no idea of what is waiting for me in my life. There is only one big question behind everything!

I don't need much in life. I care about money, mostly to support Inna with Anton and Lena with Andrey. Of course, it is slightly humiliating not to have money, but so far, I am short of ideas how to make money. Funnily enough, this prison institution in my view is a place where people, mostly drug smugglers from Algeria, Morocco and Turkey come to build some muscles in the gym and share experiences and ideas for future unlawful activities...

Last night I watched Thelma and Louise. *Such a breath-taking and touching moment, when they are cornered on the edge of the Great Canyon. On one side, the army of policemen, on the other the precipice of a Great Canyon. For half a minute they are thinking what to do, and then one, innocent, naïve and extremely beautiful soul, says to the other: "Just keep going!"*

"What?"

"Go!"

"Are you sure?"

"Yeah!"

With the eyes, full of tears, wonder, the unknown, hopelessness, love and self-pity they hit the gas pedal... O, how unbelievably emotional these moments before death are! If we can feel death every moment, if we can live by death, how entrancing life becomes! A miraculous, magical, crazy gift from God! Everywhere is God!

I have been noticing lately the overflow of my emotional centre, possibly my queen. Tears are flooding with reason and without. Tears are running at the slightest sentimentality. Phrases that visit me often lately are 'Socrates, my master, is my friend, but the Truth is dearer to me', and 'Even if you are in a minority of one, the truth is the truth'.

To summarise my experience and my lessons of prison, I must say that being there I was asking myself: what if for some mistake or unjust reasons, I was given a life sentence in prison? Friends and relatives would visit me, but less and less with the passage of time. What would be the point of my life then? It would not be really a life, but some sort of sad, lonely existence, the uneventful proceeding towards the final destination. I found only two obvious answers as the solution to such a condition. The first was to take my own life – to commit suicide. The second was to find and befriend God. And so, although sometimes I experienced loneliness, more and more I felt happy in my True Eternal Beloved's company.

Now, many years later, I can see with far greater clarity how immature I was back then. Now, I would prefer 'solitary confinement' to the eventful life, for there is less distraction in such solitude. Little did I know back then the joy of the real adventure: adventure into the bliss of Self. And to be absolutely honest with you, there is nothing in this entire world and beyond, more satisfactory, purposeful, rewarding and joyful than knowledge and union with God, who is none other but your very Self. Those who plunge deeper and deeper into the depths of the inner dimensions, into the bottomless ocean of Self-mystery, discovering that there is nothing more beautiful in the seven worlds than the naked Truth! Only the real joy of Self-abidance can never be taken away, for the True Self is the Eternal Reality. True Self is the perpetual flood of excessive joy, love, wonder and creativity.

For now, however, let us return to our story, for I hope you agree with me, this story nicely binds everything together and also gives an extra dimension to these writings.

In the morning of 21.09.00. we finally were taken to Charles de Gaulle airport to be deported to Russia. Policemen passed us to the aircrew, and we were sat at the back of the plane. We dove into the magazines and suddenly were shocked by the words: *privet lyubimyie* ('hello beloveds' in Russian). Robert was the first man to enter the plane. A group of boys followed him. Of course, it was very emotional, to meet our friends and teacher right after leaving prison. Robert bought us many gifts. The airhostesses were probably very surprised and possibly had some thoughts about the unbeatable Russian Mafia. Robert asked me where I was planning to stay, and I said that I would be staying with Inna. My friend Sasha, who was giving me a lift from the airport, nevertheless, forgot to drop me off at my tube station and instead took me to the teaching house. Of course, I received the very nice surprise of seeing so many friends, among whom was Martha. After about half an hour in the teaching house I went to Inna's place. Seeing Inna was a great contrast to a friendly atmosphere of the "teaching house". She was drunk and her behaviour and words were rather unpleasant. I wanted to leave, but she persuaded me to stay...

I am sorry to disappoint you my dear reader, but I was seduced again to travel with Teacher. Somehow, I was deeply impressed by his seemingly utmost sincerity when he was answering rather tricky questions at a formal dinner in the Moscow teaching house. Then I was invited to accompany him to Saint Petersburg, where he also was giving some talks and formal dinners.

Spending this autumn in Russia and having frequent telephone conversations with Tina, a new plan slowly emerged, this time on my initiative. I had some friends in Moscow, who had some relatives in the Czech Republic, who had some connections to the Czech police department. All I needed to do was give my passport photos and money to my Moscow friend and he could apparently arrange an very good Czech passport for me. I thought if I ask my school friends in the Czech Republic to send my fake Czech passport through the traveling agency to the American embassy in Prague, then I had a chance to get an American visa. And it happened. I got a ten-year multiple-entrance tourist visa on my new Czech passport!

Somewhere before Christmas I travelled to Budapest in Hungary. It was decided that to fly from Budapest to New York would be safer than flying from Prague. I stayed in Budapest for a couple of days, expecting a school friend from the Prague centre to deliver my new passport. On my departure, there were some doubts at the checkpoint about the authenticity of my passport, but somehow, they let me on a plane. The passport control in John F. Kennedy airport in New York let me in without any problems. From New York, I flew to San Francisco, where Tina was expecting me.

Russian Mafia in a French Prison

After spending the night with Tina in one of the San Francisco hotels, we went downtown to meet Robert at the opera house. After watching the *Cinderella* ballet, we drove to Apollo. I must admit that it looked much smaller and not as grand as I was imagining it to be. While being in Apollo I was staying with Tina, who was renting and sharing a house in the woods, about twenty minutes' drive away, with her good friend Karina. Occasionally though, I stayed at 'Academy' – Robert's posh home. It happened that while I was in Russia, Tina had a romance with a new young boyfriend, and so I had no choice, but to accept this condition without any moaning. I must admit that it was painful to spend some nights in Academy, knowing that Tina was having sex with her boyfriend. One of these nights I wrote: 'Love has many different states and names. Tonight, I call her an unbearable pain, tomorrow melting sugar.'

Here is another interesting lesson for you, my dear reader. I had never blamed Tina or put any pressure on her for spending time with her new boyfriend, whereas he began to demand she make up her mind and make a choice. And so, she chose me. My life in Apollo was mostly easy, filled to the brim with beauty, love, adventures and mischief. As always, I increasingly felt the Beloved's presence whenever I went. At a certain point, Robert decided to make me his secretary. And so, I practically always travelled with him around California, answering his phone.

The Magic Mushroom Portal

A most fascinating event happened in January when there was a sudden snowstorm. One evening, Tina, her German friend Thomas, Karina with her boyfriend Nick, and I were in our house when there was a power cut. Thomas suggested we have some magic mushrooms, which he possessed.

'I'd like to bring some portals,' he said smilingly. I had never tried magic mushrooms before, so I had no idea of what to expect. We ate two 'golden teachers' each, and waited...

At some point, Tina exclaimed: 'Wow! I am going from one extreme to the other, first I couldn't stop moving, now I am not able to move at all.' I said that I was going into even more profound extreme: I hated anyone who was moving. It felt like every moment was a majestic crystal palace, in which our Beloved was always waiting for us. To enter this magnificent palace, we must leave ourselves on the patio. This unbelievable palace was so beautiful, but also it very fragile. Even the slightest movement of thought could easily destroy it.

After some time, I went to the bathroom. Spellbound, I stopped in front of the mirror and my gaze was glued to my reflection. I was gazing into the eyes of my reflection, and also, through the eyes of my reflection, back to the space from where I was looking. I was realising with increasing clarity and growing love that the one whom I see in a mirror is my dearest friend. He loves me, for he knows me very well. He is the witness of all my highs and lows, all my victories and all my miseries, all my proud moments and all my shame, he is with me at every moment, and because of that, he knows the beauty and the goodness of my soul. I kept gazing into the reflection until all separating us layers dropped off and the one in the mirror revealed himself as God. I realised that it was God looking at me!

The next instant, a real miracle occurred: the mirror dividing us disappeared! I was standing face to face with God, when even the walls of bathroom, together with the sensations of the space-time continuum began to fade away. This was my first acquaintance with these sacred plant-teachers, who, as you will see from the further unfolding of this story, became my most powerful gurus, surpassing, with their unique way of teaching, the teachings of all external gurus. We will be returning again and again to the magical and the miraculous, to the unique language of chemistry and to the ability to unlock the doors of perceptions with the help of these incredible and very direct teachers.

Three Weeks in Oakland Jail

I stayed at Apollo for about four months. Robert began planning his travels in Europe. Although I really liked Apollo, I didn't want to be stuck there forever. I was pretty confident now, after having been allowed into U.S., that my new passport was okay, and I could try to go to Europe. We arranged our tickets and flew from San Francisco to Paris. I was stopped, however, at French passport control. After about one hour of checking and re-checking, I was taken to the airport's holding cell. The French authorities decided to deport me back to San Francisco.

When I arrived in San Francisco, I was taken into the custody of local police. Their behaviour and jargon were precisely as you can see in Hollywood movies. They looked at the passport and couldn't find any faults with it. 'Well, it's the stupid French,' they said, 'we think that we can send you back to Paris.' Unfortunately, one of these police officers had recently visited Prague and learnt a few simple Czech words. I, on the other hand, did not know any. He asked me how Czech people pronounce 'Prague', and what they call a bus. I knew neither of these. I had no choice but to tell the truth; that I was Russian, and this passport was fake.

I was sent to Oakland jail. Spending the night with one of the other inmates, in a very small, dark and uncomfortable cell, in which it wasn't possible to lie down, or even to sit, the next morning I was sent into a big cell containing around thirty inmates, most of whom were Mexicans. I would say that this American jail was a bit tougher than the jail in Lille. At four o'clock in the morning we had quite disgusting breakfasts, and dinners was served at four p.m. It wasn't a real jail, but a place where people were awaiting a court decision either for deportation, or a transfer

130

to another prison. Some days later, Tina paid me a visit. Her car broke halfway to Oakland, she just left it there and hired a taxi. We sat on either side of the scratched plastic window, talking through the phone, gazing into each other eyes and making window dividing us miraculously disappear.

Every morning police officers announced the list of people to be taken to court in San Francisco. Every day I was expecting to be taken to court and deported to Russia. Once, I was taken to the building in San Francisco with a group of other prisoners. I was called by the police officer and surprisingly they put me in handcuffs with the chain connected to leg-irons. I was taken in the lift to a room on the upper floor.

'My name is Barbara, I am a secret service agent,' said a woman. 'Whatever you do, please don't try to jump out of the window, we're on the eighteenth floor,' she said alarmingly. I was asked to sit down at the desk, on the other side of which there was a young male stenographer. The secret service agent began questioning me about my fake Czech passport and American visa. As I understood later, it was the first time in their practice, that someone in American Embassy in Prague had put a real American visa into a fake passport. Their suspicion was that there was someone inside the American Embassy who would do such a thing. I told my story, most of which was true, with a few lies and some withholding of information about names and places. The young stenographer quickly wrote down everything I said. They even asked me to draw a map of the Moscow street where I had supposedly received the passport from my Russian friend.

Towards the end of our conversation I began to feel that they trusted me, and I decided to play a game a bit further. I asked what was going to happen to me, and whether I would be able to come back to the States again. The woman said that I would be deported, and I would possibly be prohibited from entering the U.S. I told her how much I liked California, and that my only reason for buying a fake passport was to come here, for I was unjustly denied an American visa on my Russian passport.

'Is there any chance of making this restriction smaller?' I asked. She then told me that it might be possible if I agreed to work for them in the secret service. She gave me a name of a person in the American embassy in Moscow, with whom I had to make contact

131

with after I was deported. Frankly speaking, they were inviting me to be their spy! I thanked her profoundly. Of course, I wasn't planning to contact anyone in the American embassy, but I just thought it would help me to be deported quicker.

However, days were passing, and I still was waiting for deportation. I learnt from one Russian guy, who had been bailed out of jail, that I could also be easily bailed out, but I was sure Robert didn't want any exposure of my connection with him and the F.O.F.

While being Robert's secretary and using his phone regularly, I had memorised the code, which I could use from any phone to call abroad. I called Robert from San Francisco's court building and asked him if he could bail me out of jail, but I didn't get an answer. Robert was traveling around Europe with his new toy – a lover, one of my friends, Vladimir. I knew that just a couple of weeks ago, Vladimir, who lived in Amsterdam, had had some difficulties with his girlfriend Anna. It seemed to me that he felt temporarily cornered. So now, he was travelling with Robert. I could clearly see how Robert preyed on young man in difficult situations. Predator psychology. Works every time.

I spent three weeks in Oakland's jail, after which I was deported on KLM to Amsterdam, from where I caught a plane to Moscow.

Farewell Wife, Friends, School, and Welcome the Unknown

I rented an apartment in Moscow from my school friends. A few days later, Tina, who had dropped all her business in California, came to Russia to stay with me. In June in Saint Petersburg there was a little scandal at one of the big meetings with Robert. The wife of a young man, who had had sexual relationships with Teacher asked Robert directly how he could justify 'having sex with our husbands'? The next question also was harsh. A young man pointed out that Robert always was saying that our school was a 'conscious school' in which forty-four conscious beings worked directly, but why did this 'conscious school' not produce any conscious beings? These two people were expelled from school the next day.

Sometime in July I went for a little holiday to Crimea with Tina. We also visited our friends in Odessa and led a meeting there. Towards autumn, with great difficulties we found a new apartment in Moscow. Tina had gotten a job as a substitute art teacher for an American diplomat's children. She had a reasonable salary. I started my business of selling hats in a wholesale Luzhniki market in Moscow. Unfortunately, my partner and I made a big mistake in December by switching to another product. Expecting a big profit, we bought five thousand dollars' worth of fireworks for New Year's parties. There were difficulties with the legality of selling it, as well as a lot of competition, so we were stuck with lots of it. My

133

Farewell Wife, Friends, School, and Welcome the Unknown partner Sasha later transferred everything into his garage. My situation and my relationship with Tina became a bit tense.

Tina decided that we needed to leave everything and go to her parents in England for Christmas. It was a lovely Christmas, after which we returned to Moscow for the celebration of the New Year. In the middle of January, we decided to move to England for good.

Staying at our school friend's apartment in Belsize Park, I started work, helping our friends in Crouch End rebuild a café called 'Bistro Aix'. A few months later, Tina and I decided to get married. At some point, Tina was chosen to be London's centre director. We moved to London's teaching house in Crouch End.

I felt a growing dissatisfaction at being within the frame of the Fourth Way school's limitations. One of the lines of work that was bringing me joy, was my 'octave' of meetings for new students. Here, where the minds of young people weren't yet too contaminated with the school dogmas, I felt I could give my best. We had some amazing small meetings, saturated with high-octane conscious energy. Sometimes new students would sit and bask in this mesmerising energy for another three to five minutes after the meeting was over. One girl, Linda, remarked, that this amazing state could be so addictive.

Somewhere in July of 2003 I had an interesting conversation with the mum of one of our students, my good friend Natasha. She was staying for a few days in the teaching house. Apparently, she was studying so-called astro-psychology. Having heard from me that I was born on 06.08.66., she got very excited, saying that it was a very important year for me. It was the end of the thirty-seven years of Saturn's cycle. Some big changes were about to happen, I could be reborn again, and I could make direct contact with the Sun on my birthday, she said.

At the end of July, I was again with Robert in Saint Petersburg. Robert and co were making plans to fly to Amsterdam on the fifth of August. Tina went to Amsterdam too, for we were planning to meet there and celebrate my birthday. Somehow, the young men travelling with Robert forgot to buy me tickets. Robert and the other guys left without me. Someone was trying to help me with new arrangements.

On my birthday, I flew from Saint Petersburg to Moscow, from where, after couple of hours waiting in Sheremetyevo airport, I

Farewell Wife, Friends, School, and Welcome the Unknown changed my plane and flew to Amsterdam. While on a plane, I was reading Osho's *Death: The Greatest Fiction* and was very impressed by it.

At Amsterdam airport, I was stopped again at passport control. Apparently, I was not allowed to enter Schengen countries for a certain period, after my being in French prison. I was brought into a separate room at the airport, to wait for a decision. Tina got permission to see me. Filled with tears and laughter, she kissed me happy birthday and gave me a birthday card with Sean Connery as a James Bond on the front and the words: 'From Russia with love' written on it. When I opened it, there was a sound greeting saying 'by the way, have a nice day'. And so, it was. Another crazy gift from the Beloved!

Amsterdam's airport administration decided to send me to England. Phew… a big relief that they didn't decide to send me back to Russia. When the plane took off, the sun was just kissing the horizon and reflecting its magnificent light on the countless lakes and ponds which seemed to be ablaze with the unearthly fire. I was sitting next to the window and absorbing this majestic show. Overwhelmed with gentle love, tears rolled down my cheeks. I was filled to the brim with gratitude and realised that the connection with the Sun, about which I had received predictions was happening right now and I truly felt reborn!

As you will see, in just one month later, my life took an utterly new course.

At 11.30pm that night, I crossed the threshold of my friends Rita and Ivan's house in Muswell Hill. At five to midnight, we had a toast for my birthday.

For some reason, in August 2003, Tina became very close to Robert. She almost devotedly followed him on his trips to Europe, as well as paying lots of money for the formal dinners with him. I, on the other hand, felt on the verge of leaving school.

There was a new requirement for Russian citizens; all of them must renew their internal passports if they didn't want to lose their citizenship. I decided to call Robert and tell him that I was planning to go to Russia to renew my Russian passport. Robert, who was encouraging me to be a 'new man', as he put it, had told me a few times that, when I was in Russia, my 'old man' with his drinking habits woke up. So, when I decided to call Robert and tell him, that

Farewell Wife, Friends, School, and Welcome the Unknown
I needed to go to Russia to renew my passport in order not to lose
Russian citizenship, he replied: 'No, you are not going to Russia
my dear.' I said I was going to Russia, to which he replied: 'If you
go to Russia, you are out school, and if you go to Russia, Tina will
leave you!'

Shocked, not knowing how to reply to these words, I put the
phone down. For a couple of days, I weighed up the situation; made
a couple of phone calls to my friends, who suggested not to hurry
with the decision. I asked Tina if she would leave me, if I left the
school. She was in a state of confusion, not knowing what to say to
me. I called Robert and told him that I was leaving the school, to
which he replied: 'The doors of the school will always be open for
you, my dear.' I bought a ticket to Moscow, had a farewell dinner
with some of the students, and flew to Russia next morning.

Farewell the life that I knew for eight and half years, goodbye
beloved wife and dear friends, I am grateful for your lessons, your
love and friendship. Now the time has come for me to depart. I am
choosing the long-forgotten, insecure and slightly frightening, but
freeing unknown!

Before my departure to Russia I bought two books:
Adyashanti's *The Impact of Awakening* and *Be as You Are* by
Ramana Maharshi. Impressed by both books, especially by Ramana
Maharshi, I experienced a high state of consciousness by simply
reading it. There is undeniable truth in the words of Ramana
Maharshi, which resonates so loudly and harmoniously within my
heart.

After a short stop in Moscow, I left alone for a wonderful
picturesque place in Crimea called Novy Svet (New Light), just to
simply sit on the mountains, to meditate, to be consumed by Self-
contemplation. My desire for Self-realisation was so intense. I was
ready to die for it. I was using the wisdom of Ramana Maharshi,
who says, that the mind originates from the Self, which is the
Reality – Satchitananda (being-consciousness-bliss), but ordinarily
goes out to its lovers – external objects. Through Self-inquiry, one
must bring the mind back to its source. Self-inquiry (who am I?),
destroys all other thoughts, and will itself be destroyed like the
stick used for stirring the funeral pyre.

I had a very productive time in Crimea and met some beautiful
people outside the school. When I came back to Moscow to stay in

Farewell Wife, Friends, School, and Welcome the Unknown

one of my school friends' apartment, I met my beautiful young friend Maya, whom I liked very much. The easiest way to describe her would be using Fourth Way terminology that describes different body types, based on planetary influences on personality through the endocrine glands and the hormones they produce. From my observations throughout the years in the F.O.F., I would say that this system of classification of body types was pretty accurate. Maya could be described as a Solar type; whose chief feature is a naivety. As I mentioned once before, naivety can be also described as openness and trust. Very often these types of people die young, for life becomes too unbearable for their fragile nature. Having short red hair and delicate features, the energy of a gentle sun radiated through her beautiful eyes. Once before, while I was still living with my girlfriend Lena after the birth of my second son, Maya came to visit us and when we were saying goodbye to each other, our gentle kiss lasted possibly a second longer than it supposed to be. Only one extra second of this sweet and unexpected kiss was enough to reveal our mutual attraction. Maya told me that she had also recently left the school. She had just returned from the southern region of Russia, Abkhazia, where she had fallen in love with someone. Her behaviour was rather strange and slightly worrying. We decided to keep in touch via email.

The First Lesson of Magic Mushrooms - Pranayama

S omewhere towards the end of October I returned to London, where my friend Natasha was waiting for me. She still was a member of F.O.F. but was filled with doubts about Robert and his teaching. We had a plan beforehand, that she would meet me with L.S.D., and we would have some psychedelic experiences together. After my plane landed at Heathrow Airport, she met me in London that evening, and we drove to her house. She hadn't managed to get L.S.D., but instead bought a box of Mexican magic mushrooms. I, filled with the energy and new understanding based on Ramana Maharshi's teachings, suggested having a small 'meeting' (satsang), before the mushrooms began to work.

After a little talk, we were sharing and eating the mushrooms. Natasha suggested going for a little walk. We stepped outside and walked along the almost empty street. Natasha got very excited about the explosion of colours and the changing of space perceptions. We came back home, put on Indian music, and sat in her room in front of each other... Natasha began to laugh, for she could see that my face was transforming. I suggested going into different rooms to continue meditation alone. I went downstairs, settled down on a sofa, closed my eyes, and plunged deeper and deeper into meditation – self inquiry.

'What am I?' Total acceptance of what would be revealed, surrendering to what is, full trust and holding attention – awareness of the sense of 'I' are the only things that occupied my mind. I relaxed and allowed myself to be taken, without any resistance, wherever the mushroom teachers would take me, whichever lesson

The First Lesson of Magic Mushrooms - Pranayama
they would teach me. 'Do not think, plunge deeper and deeper into the unknown…'

After a bewildering kaleidoscope of intense and fast visuals, reshaping of the complex geometrical patterns, dancing mandalas and yantras, I started to feel strong pressure on my third eye. It seemed that my eyes were turning 180 degrees in search of the perceiver, the source, the 'I'.

The next instant, my consciousness separated from body, and with great amazement I saw my body lying down on an operating table. Some benevolent alien 'being of light' performed an operation on my cranium. I felt an intense pressure on the top of my head, and the angel opened it up with a laser-light scalpel. Suddenly the pressure was released, and dark clouds of thought escaped through the hole in my head into the either. My mind (brain), at this point turned upside down, and looked in the direction of my chest. The gravity of awareness moved down from my head into my body in the direction of the Spiritual Heart on the right side of my chest. I was penetrating the inner realms of the body and discovering the infinite cosmos within. The totality of my awareness concentrated on the region of my upper lungs. All sensations of the external world were switched off. Instead in the absolute silence of my mind, in inflating wonder, I was seeing the Angels realm! I was hearing the most captivating divine music of celestial musicians!

Concentrating on the source, my attention continued to move down my chest and then slightly (two finger-widths) to the right side. I felt a very powerful electromagnetic field there and the strong pull of my attention from this place. The totality of my attention merged into the Spiritual Heart – the source of light, the source of 'me', and there, in this paradoxical singularity, I recognised my Eternal Home, as also I recognise that I have never ever left this wonderful Home.

I am ever Present! Here is the realisation – the real experience of what it means to be Present. Realisation and the direct experience of Pure Being. Realisation that the only reality is 'I' – the Self! Realisation that time and space do not exist, but they are only the manifestation of my Real 'I'. 'I' always was, always am, and always will be.

139

The First Lesson of Magic Mushrooms - Pranayama

Unfortunately, I have no choice, but to use such words as 'was', 'am', and 'will', and also 'here' and 'everywhere' which are related to space and time, but which cannot express the Reality. In Reality, space and time does not exist.

With no sleep whatsoever that night, the next morning I shared my Divine revelations with Natasha, who for some reason forgot about the spiritual practice of Self-inquiry. Feeling my extremely heightened state, and fascinated and inspired by my accounts, she proposed to buy some more magic mushrooms, and take another journey.

I was pleasantly surprised that magic mushrooms were legal at that time. One could freely buy them in several shops around London. During our journey to the shop and back, my heightened state didn't dissipate. It seems I was established in witnessing consciousness. After we bought the mushrooms and returned to Natasha's house, we waited for her friend Kallet to join us. After his arrival, we ate the mushrooms (Kallet had only one) and we began our conversation on psychedelic, spiritual subjects. At a certain moment, I felt that I needed to be alone. Natasha and Kallet went for a walk.

I went to the living room, sat on a chair and plunged into meditation – Self-surrender – Self-inquiry. For the first twenty minutes I couldn't enter the desired state. The question 'who am I?' was just empty words, unable to penetrate my being. I decided to go to the room which Natasha had kindly allocated for me and lay down on the bed. I continued my Self-inquiry.

After few minutes my attention began to plunge into the depths of my being. My attention, which I viewed as a mass of light, was standing still at the threshold of my Spiritual Heart. During the next couple of hours, I registered only around ten thoughts. I was abiding in the beauty of thought-free awareness, emptiness and silence, filled with consciousness. My breathing became very shallow and even. It became almost immovable. It seemed that all I needed to sustain life, was a quarter of an inch of inhalation and a quarter of an inch of exhalation. I can say that my breathing almost stopped.

Thought and Prana have one and the same source – the Spiritual Heart, in Sanskrit 'Hrt', or 'Hrdaya', which can be

The First Lesson of Magic Mushrooms - Pranayama translated as 'This is the centre'. In the absence of thought, breathing slows down.

Suddenly, without any volition on my part, absolutely spontaneously, my body began to breathe very vigorously, rapidly and deeply; a full breath in and without stopping, an equally powerful breath out, again and again and again, becoming faster and more intense, filling my body with buzzing oxygen, producing the sensations of electric discharge on the tips of my fingers and toes. All my body was tingling and buzzing as though filled with the tiny ping pong balls bumping into each other, as though my body was water saturated with bubbling gas. At the same time, there was not a single thought, only expanding awareness-consciousness. Sensations of my body became replaced with the sensations of dancing energy.

Last breath in and the last breath out... I am merging into the Heart – Home – the Source of Light... Time has stopped... There is no desire to breathe any longer... Deeper and deeper the mind is plunging into the Heart, its very source... Last thought after approximately four minutes: 'This is Death and I am ready'! I am disappearing into the Heart of Reality!

But my body and thoughts gradually began their struggle for survival. My body began to breathe. This process of intense breathing with long periods of plunging into the depths of breathlessness continued for another three hours. I opened my eyes. The ceiling at this moment was not solid, but rather had a floating, liquid energy state. Divine light was pouring into my third eye and further into my heart. Without usual emotions, tears came gushing out...

I decided to stand up and walk around the house. Impressions simply flowed through my empty head. I went to the window. Majestic light was pouring on a beautiful tree in the garden. Bright flashes of vivid images of all my lovers and relatives appeared and disappeared before my eyes. The image of Robert appeared last. I did not feel any judgment, only love towards him. I decided to go to the mirror and to look at what was happening in the world behind the glass. I continued the Self-inquiry. I gazed into the mirror and asked myself: 'Who, what am I?' Images began to appear, to change, to disappear and to metamorphose. I saw bearded men, Mongolian women and children in my reflection... I

The First Lesson of Magic Mushrooms - Pranayama
decided to lie down on the floor in the living room. I gazed into one spot on the ceiling and continued my meditation – Self-inquiry – Self-surrender. I am! I! Am! The waves of joy at feeling the Reality submerged me and I disappeared into the Heart.

The wave: I am! The wave: I! The wave: Am!...

I was so close to awakening. I desperately wanted to wake up. With the deepest joy, I would die into the unknown, I would sink into the Source...

However, I was getting tired of the struggle. I felt that I had lost my battle today. It was evening and I decided to eat something. I hadn't eaten anything for couple of days. Sometime later, Natasha and Kallet came back. I shared with them my unbelievable trip. Our conversation gently moved towards science. We talked about the idea that we do not see the real colours of an object, but only the reflection of light. And then we wondered whether, if we could move with the speed of light, the only thing we would see would be our own Self.

This unbelievable journey within the seed-mystery of Reality, I consider as my turning point and the beginning of what later developed into Kumbhaka Prana Yoga – my spiritual practice, my teaching and gift to humanity. Although I was equipped with my previous practices of dividing attention, Self-remembering and recently with Ramana Maharshi's Self-inquiry, it was the blessing of the sacred plant gurus – the magic mushrooms – that radically opened the doors of perception and let me into magnificent inner dimensions. It was this ancient wisdom of magic mushrooms that, with their unique chemical language, temporarily removed the space-time constrictions from my consciousness. It was the sacred plant gurus who showed me the power and role of Prana (life force) in liberation!

I recollected from this experience that I had already had an encounter with the power of Prana when I was just thirteen years old. I grew up in a village called Aksenovo, which was in the Luchovitcy region, somewhere around one hundred and forty kilometres south of Moscow. In the summertime, all the schools from the region sent some chosen pupils (about eight from each school) for a pioneer (Scout-like) gathering with camping and sports competitions. These gatherings also included topography in a beautiful location in nature.

The First Lesson of Magic Mushrooms - Pranayama

It was there that it somehow became popular among the boys to experiment with breathing. It was just fun back then. I will try to describe this procedure. One should breathe very intensely for about twenty-one exhalations and twenty-one inhalations. With each exhalation, one should bend forward, and slightly bend the knees, and with each inhalation one should straighten up. When the last inhalation finishes, a person from behind should tightly squeeze the chest of the breather and keep it squeezed. The breather then often goes into a state of involuntary convulsions, shaking, or a state of deep relaxation. It was a very peculiar state, in which the stable picture of the world-appearance was shattered, and one's consciousness lost hold of the world and the body. Often then, the body went into convulsions, for it was trying to hold on to 'solid reality'.

Once at home, I decided to do it on my own. After the intense breathing, I squeezed my chest with my arms. I lost consciousness. My body collapsed. I felt flat on my back. My consciousness returned to normal after just a few seconds, but within these few seconds I re-lived in a full measure a complete parallel life!

Truly, time is purely subjective. We are all familiar with the idea that one big thing can contain within itself countless small things, but rarely do we realise that every little thing can contain within itself countless big things. We can see that there are uncountable quantities of atoms within the universe, but it is equally true that within the single atom there can be countless universes. So is with time. Within the single moment of Now there can be countless lifetimes. Logic is not applicable for the comprehension of the Absolute. The Absolute is a storehouse of paradoxes. From a logical point of view, the Absolute is impossible. But there is nothing that is impossible for the Absolute. For the unborn, uncreated, ever-existing Reality, the essence of which is Infinite Supreme Intelligence-Energy, everything is possible, even if it appears as a contradiction.

The next day Natasha gave me a lift to Crouch End, to my friend Shams, who agreed to give me temporary accommodation on his veranda. Shams was still in the school but was very fond of me and very suspicious of Robert. He asked me about my intimate relations with Robert and was stunned by my stories about his orgies and his perverted sexuality. Shams periodically attended

143

The First Lesson of Magic Mushrooms - Pranayama
Sufi gatherings in a mosque located near Seven Sisters tube station.
He took me there a couple of times. It was a Naqshbandi Sufi
order. I was very impressed by their ecstatic chants and whirling.
They also were very friendly. I purchased a book from their library,
which I had had in Russian language before, and which I highly
valued. I mentioned this book earlier. It was Rumi's *The Sufi Path
of Love*, translated by William Chittick.

I also bought the classic Advaita book *I Am That* by
Nisargadatta Maharaj in Watkins bookstore. My money had almost
run out. I was living mostly on baked beans, sleeping on a mattress
on Shams's veranda, which was getting increasingly colder, and
without a great deal of enthusiasm I was slowly looking for a job.
Meanwhile, in practically all my free time I was immersed in Self-
inquiry and Nisargadatta's 'I am' meditation.

I found the Ramana Maharshi Foundation in London and
became a regular visitor of their satsangs in Hampstead. I made
many new friends there. I liked their gatherings, especially the ten
or fifteen minutes of silence in the middle of it. I wrote back then:
*'Meditation is the plunging into the unknown. In the beginning of
meditation, we control our attention. We are trying to hold our
attention on the 'I', or 'I am' thought only. But who controls
attention? Until there is a control of attention, there is a false 'I'
who controls this attention. In meditation, there is a point at which
the false 'I' which controls attention, disappears. This is the
moment of miracle! In this moment, we are leaving everything
familiar behind and stepping into the unknown! Not to know
anything means to be free of all concepts and be our Self – pure
happiness!'*

I became a very good friend of the chairman of the Ramana
Maharshi Foundation, Alan Jacobs. He invited me to lunch at his
apartment, where we discussed Self-inquiry, and many other topics,
including my magic mushroom journey. He was very impressed
with my description of Self-inquiry on this journey. He told me that
before he had discovered the teachings of Ramana Maharshi, he
also was a student of a Gurdjieff group in London. He
recommended I attend Richard Lang and Douglas Harding's
classes on the 'Headless Way', which I very soon attended and
found very practical. Being impressed and deeply touched by the
Bhagavan Ramana Maharshi's 'Promises and Declarations', in

The First Lesson of Magic Mushrooms - Pranayama
which Ramana urges us to give all our problems to him, for he has
the power to deal with them, and instead to seek the Self within,
which is identical with his 'Svarupa' (real nature, real form). I am
giving all my troubles and worries to him and depend on grace
only.

Occasionally I met Tina, and often returned to Shams upset
after meeting with her. I could not understand how our love could
have died simply because I had left the school. One evening, while
having dinner with her in an Indian restaurant, I received a call
from the Loch Fyne restaurant in Covent Garden. They had
accepted me as a waiter. Thank you, Ramana.

I began to work in the restaurant. It was difficult at the
beginning, but due to my perception of the world as an illusion and
my concentration on 'I am' only, I accepted everything with ease.
'Angels fly, because they take themselves lightly'. Sometime in
December I moved from Shams's, to my friend Aya's in Belsize
Park. It had become very cold on the veranda.

Before Christmas I became friends again with Tina, and we
decided to spend Christmas in Kent with her parents. It was our last
Christmas together. When we came back to London our
relationship fell apart again. She said that she was leaving and that
she was not sure if she wanted to be with me any longer. I, who
often thought in extremes, did not want to live with someone who
was not sure. I wanted to live with someone who was ready to die
for me and I for her.

The Second Lesson of the Magic Mushrooms - Hell

I continued my experiments with magic mushrooms. Camden Town, where I could legally buy them, was just the next stop from where I lived. At that time, however, I didn't yet know much about the importance of 'set and settings'; information I discovered later in *The Psychedelic Experience: A Manual Based on the Tibetan Book of Dead* by Ralph Metzner, Ram Dass, and Timothy Leary.

The end of December and the beginning of January was a very hectic time. Lots of alcohol was consumed. On one of these days, the 'teachers' (magic mushrooms) showed me the dark side of Reality!

Me and my Argentinian friend Juan were already slightly drunk. We had a litre of whisky with us. Passing Camden Town, we decided to pay a visit to a secret dancing party in one of the Turkish kebab stores. Before going there, we decided to pop up to the flat I was renting in Belsize Park, to consume few magic mushrooms and have a little drink. The mushrooms appeared to be very strong ones. After about twenty minutes, Juan was sitting with his eyes wild, not believing what he was experiencing. He kept repeating that he had never experienced anything like it. Kaleidoscopes of dancing geometrical patterns were displayed before his eyes. There was lots of laughter at the beginning. We kept drinking whisky...

At a certain point, however, our trip turned negative and progressed into a nightmare. At the beginning of this turning point, Juan kept interrupting my silent state of meditation with the

146

The Second Lesson of the Magic Mushrooms - Hell
phrases: 'What are you doing? Everything is here. Why do you
need to meditate?'

'Juan, there are certain things that you can discover only in
stillness and silence,' said I. Then, something happened that I
wasn't expecting. Juan came closer to me and, looking into my
eyes, began to stroke my chest with his hand, repeating with a
smile on his face: 'Slava, do not lie to me.' I registered this as a
sexual gesture, not really knowing what he meant by these strange
words. At the same time, I was repelled by the idea of being
intimate with Juan.

Immediately, despite the fact that the external world hadn't
changed yet, I recognised that we had entered a different dimension
– grey, cold, full of suspiciousness, fear and paranoia – a dimension
of hell. There was no doubt that Juan recognised this terrifying
alien plane of reality where Satan rules, too. For some reason I
became afraid to enter the kitchen. I felt some sinister presence
there. It could have been triggered by the fact that the window was
slightly open there and with the open window it became cold. I had
always associated cold with something alien, ominous, eerie. More
appropriate however, would be to say that it is not the cold itself
that draws these associations in my mind, but rather the lack of
cosy elements such as fire, warmth, love, light and compassion.
Our mutual mind was creating this hopeless, frightening, but
somehow also long-forgotten reality.

Regardless through which portal one enters hell, one does not
get surprised, or discovers anything that one has not seen before,
but on the contrary, recognises this menacing spooky cold dark
plane of reality, for it is very ancient, and one has been here a few
times before. The most frightening realisation here is that this plane
of existence is real and eternal! One has no doubt, when one is
there, that regardless of how long one will be saved, if one escapes
it, regardless of how long one can avoid it, the time will come
when dark forces will claim one back into this petrifying kingdom.
Despite of all one's previous knowledge, heart-beliefs and even
utmost conviction that Reality is Divine Love and Light, it doesn't
help one escape hell when one is in it! Hell destroys these
convictions; it shows that they were untrue. Hell is very real. This
plane of reality is as real as the life you are experiencing now. I
even could say that it is more real, than this cosy earth realm, for

The Second Lesson of the Magic Mushrooms - Hell
the despair of the situation and the intensity of fear and attention to
frightening details is far more pronounced, far more real in
experience.

I knew all Juan's thoughts and feelings, knowing that he
equally knew all my thoughts and feelings. After I put my arm on
his shoulder and looked into his eyes, I saw that he understood that
he is in a mental asylum. Through my gesture, Satan said to him:
'Yes, my dear, you are in my hell right now, and this is forever'. I
had the same thoughts regarding Juan. I was in his demonic side. I
entered the toilet and while there, some ancient hazy memories
gave me a new fright: there was some sense of recollection in my
murky memory that I had signed some dodgy pact with the Devil.

When I came out of the toilet, I breathed a sigh of relief, for
Juan had escaped. 'Satan has left me,' I thought for a second, but
the reality I were in didn't change into anything more positive. On
the contrary, with each instant it was becoming more frightening.
Switching the heater on full blast, which I had never done before, I
was trembling from cold, hugging the radiator. The cold, it seemed,
had penetrated the marrow of my bones, my heart, and held my
whole being in its grip. Strong winds were shaking the blackened
windows. I felt like the whole flat was going down underground
and taking me to Satan himself. One thought came to my mind: a
week ago, I was serving food to a Russian priest in the restaurant I
was working in. Realising that I was Russian, he gave me a little
icon with Mary and Jesus. At the end of his meal he asked me to
make donation to the church. I didn't want to have a connection
with the church and priests, especially having observed the
consumption of a very expensive dinner by this young and
seemingly vain priest. I refused to give him a donation and returned
his icon. He looked at me and said, 'This comes from the deceiver
– the devil.' So, the thought that came to my mind was that this
priest had cursed me. Being in this Christian hell, my mind was
desperately looking for salvation. I remembered my Christian
friend Kirill in Russia and wondered if he could somehow help me.
I tried to call him, then Genya and even Tina, but everything was
against me. The telephone, for some reason refused to work.
Everything was an evil plot against me. Joni Mitchel was singing
from her *Court and Spark*: 'because you lost your heart', 'fallen
angel', and 'you can complete me, and I complete you'. And I

The Second Lesson of the Magic Mushrooms - Hell

deeply felt that I had lost my heart, I was a fallen angel, who had been moving towards love, but was falling to hell, where I was going to become one with Satan. The next realisation was exactly that; I was Satan! This was the last destination.

Yes, I am Satan. But what can I do with it? It is who I am. It is my true nature.

At this moment, I accepted myself and I accepted the situation. I calmed down and sometime later, managed to go to sleep.

The whole next week, as I continued working in the restaurant, I felt that I was living between the two worlds. I saw that the reality of the earthly plane is as unreal as the reality of hell. I realised that there are thousands of 'unrealities', which we can call 'realities' and all of them are eternal and stretching towards the infinity. All of them are as real as the world that we see in our ordinary life. But if life is as unreal as hell, then what is real? I had no ground beneath my feet. Everything was unreal.

Somewhere at the end of the week I seriously began to worry if I had lost my mind completely. I had this sense that I was actually living not in the real world, but in a lunatic-asylum. I felt that maybe I needed some medical help. The next thought, which seemed the only right one, was that by any means, I must earn enough money for tickets to India and go to Ramana Maharshi, to the sacred Arunachala mountain and stay there in meditation and prayers until Self-realisation dawned. But then next thought presented itself saying: 'Where is India? Where is Ramana and Arunachala? Do you think that they really exist? The whole world is in your mind only. Where can you go? Everything is a projection of your mind.

The Flood of Happiness

I lay down and plunged into a meditation of self-inquiry. Who am I? The thoughts and disturbing feelings gradually subsided. My attention kept focus on the sense of 'I', brushing off everything that was not 'I'. Gradually, my attention fixed its unwavering gaze on the 'I', merging with it into One, and here; in this timelessness and spacelessness, devoid of thoughts, the direct realisation, the direct experience of True Being – the Eternal Infinite 'I' presents itself. This I-consciousness/I-reality is the very ground of everything. I am the Reality, unborn, unsurpassable, the infinite fullness of Happiness and Bliss! There are no ways exist to destroy this 'I'. I am that being which allows all illusions to exist, all space-time tunnels, all parallel and perpendicular realities!

A week later, at a meeting with C.C., a lady from a movement called 'Waking Down in Mutuality', whom I met at the Ramana Maharshi foundation, I met a girl named Lynne. She had come specifically to this meeting all the way from Liverpool. After the meeting, I invited her to dinner at a Belsize Park pizzeria. We had a very interesting talk about mushroom journeys, about fear, and the esoteric. After dinner, I walked her to a bus station from where she went back to Liverpool. A couple of days later I bought Hawaiian magic mushrooms in Camden Town. Returning home, I ate half a portion, for these unusual mushrooms had unusually bitter taste and I had a slight concern about being poisoned. Before the mushrooms began their magic work, I decided to call Lynne. She picked up the phone and we had a very emotional, sweet, love-conversation. At the end of the conversation, in a very uplifted state, I swallowed the rest of the mushrooms, and laughing at the strange, funny words and letters that appeared on my phone while I tried to input the text, I sent her a message: *'You are very beautiful soul'*.

'*And so are you,*' she replied.

I sent another: *'It looks like I am falling in love with you'*.

I stepped outside to have a puff of cigarette and received another message: *'I would never let myself to fall in love with someone as beautiful as you are'*. This message of love under the influence of magic mushrooms sent me into a very heightened state of consciousness. Full of love, but unable to send any more messages, I went to bed and plunged into deep meditation.

The mushrooms appeared to be the strongest that I had ever tried. I could feel Kundalini energy rising from 'muladhara' up my spinal cord (sushumna channel), reaching my cranium and flowing through the soft palate down into my spiritual heart. I was spinning with the increasing vortex of energies. Familiar life zoomed out into a microscopic point, and flew far away, devoid of any interest from my awareness. No thoughts. My breathing stopped completely. Death... I was experiencing myself as Buddha, Jesus, Ramana Maharshi, Meher Baba, and Hafiz.

I was Buddha, sitting under the banyan tree in meditation, I saw Maru, demon of illusion. Being Buddha, I experienced the shattering of illusions and the disappearance of Mara, but at the same time I was dying as Buddha: that was the moment when the ego of Buddha died and there was the realisation, that there never had been Buddha, but only a shadow in the luminosity of Self-reality.

I died... The world stopped... Time froze... There was nothing separate from me. There was no movement, for there was no time and no space for the movement to happen. Dead, (my ego-self had temporarily died), I rose from the bed. Tears of all-permeating, overwhelming happiness flooded like rivers down my cheeks. Clothed in pearls of tears, I asked myself: 'What can I do now with this flood of happiness?' I realised that if anyone was here in this room now, they would be immediately healed simply by the power of the radiance and the flood of happiness. I went down to bathroom, but there were no movements in my conscious presence. Every step of my body was happening within the immovable consciousness that I am. Every step was not taking me away from the experience of the immovable Being. Sometime later, still in full repose, I realised that the crystallisation, about which Gurdjieff spoke, had happened. I would not be thrown back into the body's consciousness any longer. Completion... Nevertheless, somewhere towards the morning, this Cosmic consciousness faded away and my ordinary body consciousness returned.

Sometime at the beginning of February I moved out of Aya's flat to a small room in Finsbury Park. Working at the restaurant, I could afford now to rent my own room in the house of a nice Indian family. I continued my experiments with magic mushrooms practically every week. I discovered that I could buy mushroom growing kits and grow my own mushrooms in my room, which was much cheaper. Each new psychedelic journey brought me new insights, new Self-discoveries. I was grateful to my sacred plant gurus for their most valuable lessons. I enjoyed being alone now. The most fascinating adventures were the adventures within the inner dimensions! I was coming to conclusion, that going out to visit someone, to be engaged in conversations was just a waste of precious time...

Nevertheless, occasionally I paid visits to my friends who lived just five minutes from me. My new group of friends, who also lived in Finsbury Park, were Russians. There were four of them: Eduard, Eugene, Michael, and Slava. Three of them rented the same one-bedroom apartment. They were usually very happy to see me. From Michael, I discovered a book by Rick Strassman: *DMT: The Spirit Molecule*. We will return to subject of DMT later in this book. For now, I would just like to say that if science really have wanted to understand the workings of Reality, they should have concentrated their efforts on studying DMT, for this 'Spirit Molecule' can teach us more about the true nature of consciousness, which is the very foundation of Reality, than any other studies.

I also decided to investigate the nature and the mechanics of shamanic trance. It was interesting to notice that shamans also have the 'Goal' – a point of entrance, or a portal, which could be external, such as a flame, or inside, as a spiritual heart. Shamanism, however, regardless of the descriptions of many different planes of reality, seemed to me incomplete in comparison with, let's say, the teaching of Ramana Maharshi.

Sometimes I had mushroom journeys in my new friends' apartment, where they assisted me, introducing psychedelic trance music into my journey, along with the sounds of the Yakutian Khomus ('Vargan' in Russian) as also commonly known as a jaw-harp. I found that the incorporation of certain sounds and rhythms into the psychedelic journey could serve as very powerful allies, guiding me deeper into the inner dimensions. Occasionally, I still had bad trips. In one, Michael's face began shapeshifting, and I could see devilish horns growing from his head. A few moments later I was stuck in a time-loop; some thirty seconds of an insignificant event was repeating itself again and again continuously; this could easily make one paranoid and mad.

On one occasion, my best friend Eduard decided to try magic mushrooms with me. We ate not a very big portion, for I didn't want to introduce a shocking amount for his first trip. We lay down; Eduard on a bed and me on the floor next to it, and we went into silent meditation. After about forty minutes I could feel that Eduard was approaching some disturbing space of consciousness. His body was shaking, and it felt like he needed some help, but I felt that if I start talking, it wouldn't help him at all. I decided the best help I could give him was to go deeper and deeper into death.

I had already learnt through many experiments that the beginning of a mushroom trip could often be filled with great anxiety and the moving shadows of demons and evil forces. One must dare to face these inner demons and worries, accept them, and move on to the next levels of the inner dimensions. I often felt that around one hour after the ingesting of mushrooms, after passing the turbulence of these intense visuals, I reached the state of symbolical death, after which the enlightening and liberating journey unfolded. Often, after the most intense couple of hours of psychedelic journeying, people come out of it and begin conversations with others. I found that these couple of hours were only a prelude for the real journey, which often required additional efforts of pranayama and Self-inquiry. My mushroom journeys normally lasted around six hours. The mushrooms help one to unlock the doors of perception, but to really walk deeper into these open doors, Sadhana (spiritual effort) is required!

Approximately three hours after we took our mushrooms, our friend Eugene walked into the apartment. He had a little chihuahua with him. Some of his friends had asked Eugene to look after their dog while they were on holiday. When this little doggie entered our room, something unexpected happened. It was knocked down by the energy permeating our room. The poor fellow began to cough and roll on the floor like it was crazy. Eduard immediately recognised what had happened. He asked Eugene: 'Do you know why is it behaving like this? It was knocked down by our energy.' He was right. In my further encounters with animals, while under the influence of mushrooms, it became obvious that animals are far more sensitive to energy beings than humans. Dogs and cats were dancing, rolling and behaving as though they had lost the plot around me during my mushroom journeys. I have also noticed that, not only are animals so sensitively connected to this energy, but even such things as fire and air respond to this amazing energy.

I swore I could breathe the oxygen into the fire and make it roar, not by the means of breathing into it, but by pouring love and intention from my spiritual heart. I swore I could move the air with the love and intention radiating from my heart!

At the end of winter, through spring, and into the beginning of summer, I often stayed with my new polish girlfriend Marishka. My experiments with mushrooms continued uninterrupted. However, it seemed that I hadn't yet learned the best possible way to have them, and occasionally visited dark hellish planes of existence. Once Marishka invited me to have a dinner at a Thai restaurant nearby. Foolishly, I ate couple of mushrooms before we went. We ordered food and, while waiting for its arrival, I began to notice the spine-chilling metamorphoses with the space. In everything, the music, the waiters, the room, I felt the presence of evil. I asked Maria if we could just go home, for I didn't feel very good there. She understood and asked the waiters to arrange a take-away for us. I was desperate to leave this restaurant and impatiently, with growing fear endured our 'eternal' waiting for the take-away. When we finally walked out of the door, the situation didn't resolve. It was cold and the street was desolated and dirty with lots of plastic rubbish around – this spooky dimension again!

This moment of crossing the threshold between the two worlds, the moment of passing through the thin veil separating these two worlds is sometimes captured with great accuracy in horror movies. It seems that nothing has changed externally, except for the growing suspicion in the eyes of a film character, and then visible

The Flood of Happiness

breath comes out of their mouth with the exhalation, which shows that the character is already in a different, dark, cold world.

When we approached her house, Maria decided to kiss me, and while doing so, she transformed into a lizard being. Sometime later the nightmare was gone and turned into joy with Joni Mitchel singing 'California I'm coming home'. I felt that I had returned home...

The Headless Way

A t one point, Maria and I travelled to Ipswich to pay a visit to Douglas Harding, the founder of the Headless Way. I had previously attended a few Headless Way workshops with Richard Lang in London. I found the Headless Way very practical. Through a series of simple experiments, the Headless Way directs one's attention towards the seer. "Douglas Harding, the founder, realised that his identity depended on the range of the observer. From several metres he was human, but at closer range he was cells, molecules, atoms, particles... and from further away he was absorbed into the rest of society, life, the planet, the galaxy... Like an onion, he had many layers. Clearly, he needed every one of these layers to exist. But what was at the centre of all these layers? Who was he really? So, what are you at zero distance? In other words, what are you really? Others cannot tell you because they always remain distant from you. But you are at your own centre, so you are well-placed to look and see what you are there."[17] Do you really believe that you are looking through the chinks of your eyes from the meatball above your shoulders? When I look at the place from where I am looking, I see transparent emptiness – the space for the world. At the very centre of where I am, I have no head!

Directly seeing who you really are, as in the Headless Way, is very similar to 'Self-remembering', or as Ouspensky sometimes called it, 'divided attention' (one vector of awareness is directed to the objects of perception, and the other is pointed at the perceiver-experiencer). Ordinarily, the totality of our awareness dwells on

---

[17] "The Headless Way" Richard Lang

objects of perception. In the Headless Way, and also in Self-remembering, one is aware of oneself being aware and being awareness itself. All these practices also very close to Nisargadatta Maharaj's practice of 'I am-ness' and Ramana Maharshi's 'Self-inquiry'.

A few weeks earlier, Richard Lang had invited me to visit Douglas Harding's house in Ipswich. We drove there with a couple of Richard's friends. Douglas, who at that time was already ninety-five years old, led a wonderful workshop for a company of his headless friends. Now, Maria and me, were coming to visit him and his charming wife Catherine. When he found out, that we were both ex-Fourth Way school members, he quoted a passage from *In Search of the Miraculous* and said that he really liked Ouspensky's teaching. He said then, that nowadays, he read only *Sherlock Holmes* and he quoted: 'Look Watson, we both are seeing the same things, but only I am noticing them'. When he found out that I was Ramana Maharshi's devotee, he asked me if I considered Ramana Maharshi superior to myself in any way? Surely not, as Ramana Maharshi stresses himself: 'There is no difference between me and you, I am your Self,' so I and Ramana are one and the same, said I. We had a lovely walk around the woods and creek with Catherine, whom I found to be a very sweet lady. We had some more lovely chatting with Douglas, had some lunch which we brought with us, and with warm hugs departed to London. Two and a half years later, Douglas died. I am very happy to have known him.

The Hell of Oneness

Somewhere in summer I had a little holiday from work in which I decided to go back to Crimea for a week. Bringing with me my dry mushrooms and even a few buttons of peyote cactus, I flew to Russia and then to Sevastopol, where my friends were waiting for me. My friend Oleg had bought a little holiday cottage there. There, in sunny Crimea, yet another episode with mushrooms took place. While we were sitting in the midday sun on the shores of the Black Sea, about twenty minutes' walk from Oleg's cottage, I asked Masha, Oleg's wife, if she would like to try some mushrooms. She was very curious and agreed. The mushrooms were very small – they were those that hadn't fully formed in my growing kit. I didn't expect them to be strong. But on the contrary; they let their presence to be known just fifteen minutes after ingesting. We hurried home. While walking, Masha kept telling me about the magical transformation of the objects of perception. Look! With a sense of unbelievable wonder, she pointed to the pieces of little stones on the road: 'Wow, they are turning into the beams of light!' When we finally approached the cottage, she seemed to be a little nervous. I asked her if she would like to lie down in the grass next to me in the empty field next door. But she decided to stay in Oleg's garden. I went into the empty field next door to Oleg's cottage, lay down on a grass and went into Self-inquiry. After a few minutes, all my attention, like a powerful magnetic field infused with light, was standing at the threshold of my spiritual heart....

'Slava! Can you come here; Masha is not feeling very well.' I heard Oleg's voice from his garden. I came out of meditation and rushed towards Oleg's garden. Masha was looking at me. I took a few steps toward her, but she sprang back. I realised that she didn't trust me and was seeing in me some evil force. She asked me: 'Can we call an ambulance? Can I somehow get rid of the mushrooms?' I told her that to call an ambulance would be the most unintelligent thing to do.

'Look, you are already almost at the height of the experience now. Please endure another twenty minutes and then you will calm down,' I assured her. I went back to meditation. After a couple of hours, I went back to Oleg's cottage. Masha was sitting there in utter disbelief. Tears were pouring like rivers out of her eyes. She had calmed down greatly and could speak more or less adequately. She was saying that she had seen the Matrix! She had realised that everything, without exception was made of the same staff. Everything was One!

Interestingly, this Oneness was hell for her. Reference to this statement we can find in *The Tibetan Book of The Dead*. The primordial light of Luminosity for some departing souls may appear as the most terrifying thing. There is no place for individuality, which means separation, or any points of references in this all-consuming, all-permeating Luminosity. Only those ripe souls who are ready to lose their individuality and are looking forward to self-annihilation by the Supreme One, can truly die as something separate from the Reality and recognise their true nature as Luminosity – The Dharmakaya.

Masha and Oleg were very grateful for the powerful lesson of our magical plant teachers. Sometime later, Masha asked me if we could have another session with the magic mushrooms, for it was the greatest revelation of her entire life.

One evening, me and my friend Philipp, who was staying with us at Oleg's cottage, went to the Balaclava hills for a shamanic trip with peyote. While in Moscow, I had bought a masterfully crafted Yakutian Khomus made by a shaman master from the Yakutian republic, Sakha. I practiced playing it and had already made significant progress. We found a quiet spot among the trees, gathered wood for the fire, ate a couple of buttons of peyote each, lit the fire and waited for the peyote to start working. We waited for about three and half hours and realised that it was not going to work. Slightly disappointed, we made our way back to cottage in the growing darkness, tearing our clothes, passing through spiky bushes, hills and ravines. Sometime later though, when we had dropped into our beds, I felt a gentle, but at the same time powerful and overwhelming tide of energy. I regretted that we had left our shamanic spot.

The teachings of Ramana Maharshi were at the core of my understanding about the true nature of reality and were in harmony with my direct experiences of higher states of consciousness. I was especially impressed by his personal story – the story of his temporary death in which he realised that he was immortal spirit, the story of his leaving home and finding Arunachala, the story of the absorption in the Bliss of Samadhi that obliterated his body consciousness (insects chewed portions of his legs, while his consciousness was fixed in Supreme Bliss), the story of his years of silence, his teachings and his simple exemplary life as a realised being. I had no doubt that the Self is already and always realised, and there is no need to doubt whether one can gain or lose one's Self.

Maya

I returned to London and continued working in the restaurant. All this time I was kept in touch with my beautiful solar friend Maya. We often communicated via email. She divorced her husband, who had also left the school and joined a Russian esoteric movement called 'The Path'.

I wrote in one of my emails to her:

'Hey Mayechka.

Hey, my gentle radiant sun. Where did you disappear to? It's been so long since I've heard a word from you. I know that you moved to a different apartment. I would be happy to get your new phone number. I tried to call the phone number at your workplace that you gave me. I got a reply that they didn't know Maya. I am as always, abiding in a state of happiness and bliss. I am gazing into myself in a state of childlike wonder and amazement. I am almost always in a state of joyful wonder. I am continuing my experiments with magic mushrooms. Every time I am making new discoveries. I am shooting my notebook with bullets of Love, and not only the notebook, but everything that is in the field of my awareness. I am kindling the fire of Love. I am forcing dogs and cats to lose their minds and dance waltzes of Love. I am becoming an experienced shaman. I live in the parallel dimension – the dimension of Love. I am shot away by Love, I am murdered by Love, I am choked by Light, I am drowned in Love, I have lost myself in All. I am almost awakened and maybe already awakened. I remember your words at Genya's apartment, that everyone is so unbelievably beautiful, however, some people do not know it. But if one can touch their very hearts, to warm up their depth, to awaken their soul, they begin to spill themselves like paper streamers and bloom like

flowers. Everyone is unbelievably beautiful, and you, my sunshine
even more beautiful. Mystery-beauty. Distance is an illusion. I have
verified it. I am You. Wherever you are, wherever you turn your
gaze, I am around you, laughing as the Sun, blooming as flowers,
perfuming as fragrances, singing as birds. I am You. Love.'

As our intimacy through the emails and long phone
conversations grew and grew, I invited Maya to travel with me to
Crimea for a week in the middle of October; a golden time of
'Indian summer'. To go with me to Crimea was a very big, brave
step for her to take, for as I understood later, the people
surrounding her – her parents and closest friends – were trying to
bring her and her ex-husband Oleg back together. She also needed
to take a break from work, and leave her five-year-old son with her
mother.

I met Maya at Kursk train station in Moscow. Love kindled our
hearts with a new powerful blaze. A bottle of vodka, take-away
food, and we were on a train carrying us together towards the
beautiful destination. We had an amazing, full-of-Love time in
Crimea. One day, we gathered some branches of cade juniper to
purify our space, and climbed a mountain, where we took our
shamanic mushroom journey together. We lit the fire and ate
mushrooms. Just before the mushrooms began to work, a deep fog
enveloped us. We couldn't see further than couple of metres. I gave
Maya some last words of guidance: 'If fear troubles you, give your
full trust, concentrate and pray to your beloved gurus, be it Jesus,
Buddha, or Ramana Maharshi.' I played a little bit of my khomus,
and we plunged into the depths of meditation. When I opened my
eyes, sun was pouring its golden light on a majestic meadow far
below. It seemed that we had landed on a different planet. It was an
almost unearthly landscape. I looked at Maya. Her radiant eyes
were wide open, looking at me. She said: 'Slava, you know
everything, don't you?'

I smiled and said yes.

The sun was setting, and we hurried back to our room, realising
that in the near-darkness we could lose our way home. We went
down the mountain, but paradoxically, after fifteen minutes or so of
going down, we found ourselves at the very top. The mushrooms
and the mountain were playing tricks with space. Suddenly Maya
acquired a very interesting vision of reality. She calmly said, as

though separate from her body and looking from above on our bodies: 'Relax, she (the Earth) holds them (our bodies). Look,' she said, 'everything you see now is a landscape of your mind. It's all within you.' Surprisingly, her walk was firm and easy. I, on the other hand could hardly stand, and was often sliding and falling. The darkness surrounded us.

We lost our way, but it didn't matter at all, for we were in love, and this love was growing by the second. After climbing an almost-vertical wall at some point, and following some distant voices, we finally made it home and had many more beautiful and crazy days and nights in Novy Svet and Sevastopol.

On one night in Sevastopol, possibly inspired by Jim Morrison and Patricia Kennealy from *The Doors* movie, we performed a secret marriage ceremony, cutting our veins with razorblades, and mixing and drinking our blood.

Returning to Moscow, I stayed a couple more nights with Maya and her son in her flat, but then I had no choice but to leave, for I had to continue my work in the restaurant, which was my only source of income. I didn't know yet how it was going to work, but I was hoping somehow to settle in London and later bring Maya there.

Christmas time was very intense in our restaurant. We had been fully booked for Christmas dinners since the end of November. I was moved from my position of waiter to a position of bartender. I had to serve not only all the orders that were coming from waiters, but also serve drinks and cocktails to those customers who had just walked in and were waiting at the bar, which at Christmas time was more than plenty. Our restaurant had about thirty tables on two floors. Not only did I have to serve the drinks, but also had to make friendly conversation, mix cocktails, run down to the cellar to deliver some more wine, and sometimes even run across the road to the pub next door with the bucket and ask if they could give me some ice, which we had run out of. Well, in the end it seemed that it all worth it, for I had enough money to buy tickets to India with a stop for a few days in Moscow for New Year. The hard work in the restaurant, where I had been lifting lots of boxes of wine, triggered my sciatica. I had had some problems and very painful moments with the sciatic nerve many times before. Now it began to let me know about the pain again.

Maya

Just a day before New Year's Eve, my plane landed in Moscow. My friend Alexander met me at the airport and gave me a ride to Maya's place. We had a lovely, lively evening together. The next day, the celebration of a new year, there was lots of delicious food and obviously, lots of vodka.

When, after a few days, the time arrived for me to go to the airport and catch my plane to India, I was still under the influence of alcohol and managed to miss my plane. After spending one night at the airport, I finally caught a plane to Delhi.

The directions on how to get to Tiruvannamalai and Ramanasramam I only vaguely knew. All the information I had was from the first Russian book about Ramana Maharshi *Shree Ramana Maharshi: Message of Truth and the Direct Path to Self* by Oleg Mogilever, which Alan Jacobs, who had received it from Oleg, gave me as a gift. All I knew was that I had to catch the train from Delhi to Chennai, from where I should take bus to Tiruvannamalai. Alan Jacobs also sent an email to Ramanasramam, saying that I was a devotee of Ramana Maharshi and asking if they could accommodate me. Upon landing in Delhi, for some reasons I ignored the prepaid taxis and instead jumped into a rickshaw, asking the rickshaw driver to take me to Delhi's train station…

I was kidnapped! Instead of taking me to the train station, the rickshaw driver took me to a travel agency somewhere on the outskirts of Delhi. It was late evening. Cows were walking in streets, bonfires were burning on pavements, and the whole Indian atmosphere created the most powerful cultural shock for me. Never in my life had I seen anything like India! Sly tourist agents were trying to rearrange my entire plans. After they heard about my wish to go to Tiruvannamalai, they started lying, frightening me with the stories that after the tsunami on the 26th of December in Tamil Nadu, there were still lots of places covered with rotting corpses and great diseases were spreading. They offered to take me to any other guru at other places instead. I had no need or the slightest desire to go anywhere else. To go to Arunachala, to Ramana Maharshi was the sole purpose of my coming to India. These cunning agents also lied to me that there were no available seats on any train to Chennai for next four days. They proposed to take me via taxi to Agra, so I could catch the train to Chennai from there after couple of days. Being new to such a situation, I didn't know what to do, or how to get away from these guys, so I agreed. Obviously, it cost me a substantial amount of money. We drove through the interesting 'India at night' with chai stalls and bonfires on the sides of the road. Early in the morning, we arrived in Agra. I used my time in Agra as best I could, visiting the Taj Mahal and the other palaces around. I became good friends with my taxi driver, who obviously was taking me to some posh shops to get his commission. After couple of days in Agra, I finally boarded my train to Chennai and next day I was there. With some minor difficulties, I found a bus to Tiru. People on the bus were very friendly, and the surrounding nature was awe inspiring.

Arunachala – Shiva. The Heart of The Universe

Now, finally, I felt with the all fibres of my being: 'I am in the real India and this is so wonderful. A totally different world.' I could feel the joy all around and in my heart. 'Yes! I am here in the wonderland! A new chapter of my life begins here.' Impatiently my eyes were searching for the sight of majestic Arunachala. And there she was, rising high from the relatively flat landscape surrounding her: the centre of the Universe! The concentrated into the Sacred Hill Shiva-Consciousness! Awe! Magnificent Arunachala! I was here, where I had always wanted to be. Waves of joy welcomed me to this unique place.

While on the bus, I made friends with some young boys, and when we arrived in Tiru, they helped me to find a rickshaw to Ramanasramam. I am still in touch with my first rickshaw driver, Kumar. The rickshaw brought me to Ramanasramam. Entering the main hall, I prostrated to my satguru, Ramana. I felt the thrill of joy and a deep silence penetrated my being. After a few formalities, Doctor Murthy allocated me a room opposite the main ashram. The room was very basic, but I didn't care in the least, for I was so happy to be here.

I loved the morning routine in the ashram. I was deeply impressed by the chanting of Vedas by Brahmins. Sitting in meditation and listening to the chants was a very powerful practice. The chants washed away all my thoughts, leaving me empty and radiant. The evening devotional singing in the main hall also filled my heart with overflowing joy and gratitude. I felt my heart

166

Arunachala – Shiva. The Heart of The Universe blossoming. I felt a very special powerful presence in the old hall, sitting next to the couch of Ramana Maharshi. Magic was in the air all around Arunachala. The ashram was very clean and filled with the sweetest fragrance of frankincense. I did many Pradakshinas – circumambulation – (as explained by the Ramana letter 'Pra', which stands for removal of all kind of sins; 'da' which stands for fulfilling the desires; 'kshi' which stands for freedom from further births; and 'na' which stands for giving deliverance through Jnana), around Bhagavan's Maha-Samadhi. With each circle I felt that all my worries and unhappiness were melting away.

Soon, I met a few friends from London's Ramana Maharshi foundation. My friend Sean told me his story of the bliss that had descended on him. For two months, he didn't have a single thought in his head. He was drowned in silence. In the Sahashrara, petal by petal, the thousand-petal lotus flower was opening. Sometimes he would walk the shop to buy something to eat, but being there, forgot why he came, and would walk out without buying anything. Soon, he began to worry about his health, and the silence gradually disappeared. Now he was functioning normally but was longing for his lost blissful silence.

Meeting Tarananda

At my very first dining experience in Ramana Maharshi's dining hall, I sat next to a very beautiful, unique, English lady from the Isle of Wight, named Tarananda. She had dark hair down to her knees (the object of envy of many women) and was dressed in a saree. Immediately we became very good friends. Tarananda means 'the blissful compassionate one, who carries you across the ocean of samsara'! She was enigmatic and full of bliss. She had been a devotee of Ramana's, since she was fourteen years old. She was also a mantra-yogini. We spent lots of time together. Somewhere in the middle of January was a full moon. Thousands of Ramana's devotees were circumambulating around Arunachala. The endless stream of devotees was walking, many barefoot, clockwise for fourteen kilometres around the holy mountain. Tara and I decided to do 'Pradakshina' by the inner circle, further from the crowd, but closer to the heart of Arunachala. It was a truly magical journey. By the mystical light of the moon, almost as bright as the daylight, Arunachala, hugged us from all sides, while almost fairy-tale like stories about some mysterious episodes of her adventurous life were narrated by Tarananda, along with poetry, songs and the chanting of mantras. It was miraculous!

O, Arunachala! Undoubtedly you are Shiva! You are Dakshinamurti (aspect of Shiva), dispelling the doubts of your devotees with the power of your mighty silence. You are the mass of Shiva consciousness. You are the Shiva lingam. You are the centre of the universe around which everything rotates. You are the spiritual centre, drawing like a magnet those who long for Truth and Liberation, to yourself.

168

Meeting Tarananda

A few days later I went for a day trip to Pondicherry to see the Indian ocean, and to visit Sri Aurobindo Ashram... O, how happy I was, when I returned to Arunachala. O, Arunachala! You are Hrt Hrdayam (this is the centre), you are the spiritual heart. O Arunachala! The ocean of bliss, the 'I'- consciousness, swallow this bubble (me) into the unalloyed happiness of Thy silence.

I spent lots of time with Tarananda, a blessed, insane (in the positive meaning of its word), woman. She told me some very fascinating stories from her life; her decision, when she was only sixteen, to become a sanyasi, to give away all her possessions and travel overland from England to India. She told me incredible stories about her paintings that she had left in England, mysteriously appearing on the wall of a Turkish hotel, about her awakening as a different, male person, about the disappearance of a whole building in front of her eyes, about the crossing, and sleeping in an Iranian desert, about living temporarily in a mud-house in Afghanistan, where she got very sick, and couldn't make her way to India.

Tara and I attended a satsang with Arunachala Ramana – the founder of Aham ashram. I had met him before in London and was quite impressed with his way of teaching. The whole satsang revolved around my question: How do you trace the 'I' thought back to its source? 'Can you feel this "I"?' asked Ramana. 'Feel this 'I'. Be it always. There is clear difference between the 'I'-thought and the' I'- consciousness. Although they stand very close to each other, one is in space and time, and the other is outside of space and time. You are consciousness, limitless and timeless.'

Often, I woke up at six o clock in the morning and walked to Arunachala to meet sunrise in meditation. The very presence on Arunachala takes you deep into the inner silence.

Muz Murray, known also as Ramana Baba, Tarananda's mantra yoga teacher arrived at the ashram with the group of his English followers. I attended a little session of chanting with Muz, Tarananda and small group of mantra-yogis in the main hall of Ramanasramam. They started with chants to Ganesh, the elephant-headed god, son of Shiva and Parvati - the removal of obstacles. *Om Gum Ganapataye Namaha.* I was very impressed with the chanting. I could feel the power within these vibrations.

169

Meeting Tarananda

I am writing down below a few sentences from my diary of my last days at Arunachala in the winter of 2005, to share my state and feelings back then:

' *31.01.05.*

The weekend was filled with quiet bliss. Sunday I was chanting with Tara. Chanting purifies the mind. As soon as you stop chanting, you penetrate the undisturbed silence. This evening was the last evening with Tara. Many beautiful stories were told on this charming evening at Ramana's ashram. This beautiful evening was soaked in love. Stars, no directions, no up, no down, no inside, no outside, no me, no you..., only pure uninterrupted bliss-consciousness. This morning I said goodbye to Tara. She went back to England. I have a strange feeling that I might see her again. Later, I went to the satsang with Radha at Kanapa temple. We were sitting in silence. After the satsang, Alan Jacobs, who arrived recently from London, invited me to lunch, at which we had conversations about his new translation of the 'Gospel of Thomas' and about Self-inquiry, of course.

03.02.05

A couple of days ago, I met a few interesting Russian guys from the town of Ufa and a Russian girl from Novosibirsk. These guys were telling very interesting stories of teleportation, clairvoyance and telepathies. We played khomus. In the morning, they left for Sai Baba ashram.

I went for meditation to Arunachala. Arunachala is the quietest place. Simply being here takes you deep within the Self. I am everything. I am talking to myself. I am everywhere. The world-pictures are floating in the immovable consciousness, that I am. Here there is no coming, no going, no journeying. I am the present state, always here. Undisturbed by any activities...

Yesterday, after devotional singing in the ashram, I ended up at a dancing party on someone's roof-top terrace. Shy at the beginning, the party developed into ecstatic psychedelic dancing. Now I am going back to mountain for the enlightenment. There is no one to get enlightened though, for there is nothing but enlightenment. Satchitananda – being-consciousness-bliss.

04.02.05.

Everything is so crystal clear and simple. Do you want to be happy? Be happy. Do not try to be happy, but simply be happy. What else could you wish for? Enlightenment? Peace? Why? Be happy and that's all. You are the source of happiness. You are happiness itself. To be happy is so easy. It is our natural state. Nothing can cloud your happiness, because it is who you really are. Happiness is the absence of a non-existent imaginary unhappiness. There is nothing else but happiness. Everything else is just passing thoughts, which do not need to be identified. Stay in happiness. Be happiness. It is very simple and natural. Ramana says that man himself is illumination. He illumines others. This is the best help. What else can you desire? Maybe to be even happier? Very well, be happier. Illumine your world with your happiness. Feed it with the love of your happiness. You are the creator. Blow away clouds, and shine like a sun. Love thy world. Love thy Self.'

Negative Shock on My Return from India

W hen I returned to Moscow in mid-February, I found Maya in a very worrying state. I picked her up at Gdanovskaya metro station. She was in a very poor condition and could barely speak. I thought at first that she was very drunk, but there was something more to it. I almost carried her through the metro stations, for she couldn't even walk properly. Finally, I managed to bring her to my friend's Oleg apartment, which he kindly let me stay in for a week. I took great care of Maya and in a couple of days she got a bit better, but her mental condition was worrying me. I could describe it only as a sort of mental exhaustion or mental apathy. Her state visibly got worse when she was having conversation on the phone with her mum. At the end, I was asked by her mum to bring Maya home to her parents.

At her parents', I told them that I loved Maya and would like to marry her and take care of her and her child, but I also needed some time to somehow arrange my life in London, so that I could afford to bring her there. I stayed at her parents for one night and the next day somehow managed again to miss my flight to London. When I was trying to rearrange my tickets for the next flight, the lady at the airport, seeing that I had also previously missed my flight to India, looked at me and asked with the smile: 'Are you sure you want to leave Russia?'

I managed to get new tickets, but my flight was leaving only in a couple of days. I returned to Maya's parents and found that they had called an ambulance and Maya was being taken into a mental

172

asylum. It was all wrong. I managed to get her out of there, for I noticed the heavy depressing atmosphere of this place and that Maya was going completely berserk there. The situation at her parents wasn't much better. Her older brother was drinking medicinal spirits and I felt a very strong dominance and abuse from him directed towards Maya. I felt that this distressing atmosphere was greatly damaging Maya, but I couldn't figure out at that moment what could I possibly do to help her. The only thought I had was that I needed to quickly get her out of this depressing place.

When I returned to London, my sciatica worsened dramatically. I went to the emergency room. After the examination, I was awarded income support; not much, but it kept me afloat. Maya's parents cut off my communication with Maya, changing her phone number and not answering the landline.

Letter to Maya:

'Mayka, my love! My beautiful girl with the most enchanting smile I have ever seen. My goddess with the radiant sun in your chest. My magician, every moment giving birth to the miracle of being. I miss you so much. I so long to see you, to be with you. It's springtime. The sun is shining. The world is filled with so many people, but without you, it's like I am in the desert. I need you. Mayka, my darling, everywhere, everywhere you. When I am thinking of you, the fire begins to roar in my heart. I am losing my mind from the remembrance of your smile, your laughter. I remember the touch of your lips, your joy, your gentleness, your limitless love. I love you with all my soul. The beam of light is pulsating from my heart in search of you at the same moment I am living in. You and I live in the same moment. You entered my heart. When I want to see you, I look within my heart. A tunnel of light stretches between our hearts. You entered me with all your soul, with all your being. I am You. You and I are One – Love.'

The Power of Mantra

While trying to organise my life on benefits in London, I received a phone call from Tarananda. She invited me to visit her on the Isle of Wight. Soon, I received many beautiful spiritual poems from her. Having not much to do in London, I went to the Isle of Wight to see Tara.

Her bungalow was full of colours and the sweet aromas of incense. Pictures and batiks of Ganesha, Kali, Lakshmi, Shiva and Ramana Maharshi hung on the walls. We feasted on the vegetarian Indian carry and towards the evening she initiated me into mantra yoga!

Tarananda is a mantra yogini. She leads chants in the Kashmir Shaivism tradition. I followed her instructions, repeating the chants after her, accompanied by dynamic breathing. We were not singing these mantras but intoning the sounds and sending it into our very being, to vibrate in the whole body, to let these sacred sounds reverberate within the marrow of our bones. The chanting was very intense, and my head started spinning. We took breath in...

'Relax your body and feel the quality of your inner space,' says she. The effect of chanting was very powerful, almost psychedelic. It was the closest thing to a fully psychedelic experience with magic mushrooms. We chanted the Bija (seed) mantras: Lam, Vam, Ram, Yam, Ham, A, Aum, quietly and gently at the beginning, but growing in intensity, until finally we chanted with full power, and I felt that my whole being was the vibration!

There are couple of possible interpretations for the word 'mantra'. The first is that the root – 'man' – means to think, and also 'manas' = mind. And the suffix – 'tra' – means the tool of protection. And so, man-tra in this sense is the tool which protects one from thoughts. Swami Lakshmanjoo gives a slightly different interpretation. He says that 'man', from the word 'manana' means 'cause you to reside in your own God consciousness.' 'Tra', from the word 'trana' means 'protects you from all the evils of the world.' So, when you focus your mind towards the God consciousness, you are protected from all the horrors of the world. Mantras are not just any words, or sounds, but the vibrations of sounds chosen with mathematical precision, following a certain metre, rhythm and sequence. Mantric science says that the whole body and every organ in it, as well as everything else, is composed of sound, or vibrations of different frequencies. When we look deeply at the very essence of creation, within the quantum field, we will find that at the very core it is a pure rhythm and dance, it is Shiva Damaru's (two-headed drum) beat, it is 'Spanda' (vibration), the origin of creation, it is the Anahata – the un-struck sound.

Although the chanting of mantras is undoubtedly a great and powerful spiritual practice that reharmonizes the body and takes one into the inner dimensions of consciousness, into the inner silence, the real meaning of mantra can only be directly experienced on a very high level of reality. The speech itself, according to tantric scriptures, has four distinct levels: Para Vak, Pashyanti Vak, Madhyama Vak, and Vaikhari Vak, so mantra on a gross level appears only as the vibrations of sound, but on higher levels, mantras are no longer just sounds, but living forces (Sakties) creating world manifestations.

As said in the Bible; 'In the beginning was the Word and the Word was with God, and the Word was God'. This is mirrored in the teachings of Kashmir Shaivaism tradition, as well as Shree Vidya, and many others, stressing that Para Vak – the Highest Speech, the Creative Word, or the Divine Language is the same as Svatantrya Sakti – the very freedom of Shiva's creativity!

It is Vak (Word) which has created all the worlds. Saying though, that the vibration of sound is the origin of creation, would not be entirely correct and it would undermine the Truth. For on a highest level there are no differences between sound, visions, phonemes, or a thing in itself. The best description I can offer is that language on this highest level is the spontaneous movement, the spontaneous play of conscious energy. This energy – Shakti – the Shiva's freedom, expresses itself as the unfolding of the Divine

Alphabet. The phonemes and the sequences of Divine 'speech' are the creatrix of all that exists!

It is said in the Malini-Vijayottara tantra, which was considered by Abhinavagupta, as the highest tantra – the heart of Trika system of Kashmir Shaivism – that Shiva at the beginning of creation produces seventy crores of mantras (Malini Sakti) out of his own body of consciousness, which impregnates Maya (illusion). The phonemes are also known as 'matrikas'. 'Matrika' could be translated as 'misunderstood, pregnant mother', or 'the Mother who is unknown to the universe'. She is the creative cause of all mantras and all knowledge. It is through the emergence of language that the appearance of limited knowledge is triggered and formed. Matrikas (the letters) give birth to all objective knowledge, but to consider matrikas as just letters would be wrong, for each matrika is a living force – Sakti!

As we have seen in the Apocryphon of John, and also in Gurdjieff's Ray of Creation, at a certain stage of creation a deviation takes place. It is said also in tantras, that not all sakties are friendly and some of them are working in the opposite directions. It is said that through the power of incorrect knowledge imbedded in language, some matrikas can drown 'jivas' (individuals, souls) in the sea of Samsara (repetitive existence). If matrikas and the power of mantras are rightly understood and applied, however, they can lead one to liberation.

This right application of mantras forms the basis of the second path of yoga (Shiva-Shakti's Union), known in Shiva-sutras as Saktopaya Marga. When the phonemes are arranged in a certain sequence and directed with the force of intention, they have tremendous power.

In Kabbala, tarot and 'practical magic' based on the knowledge of Hebrew alphabet, letters also correspond to numbers. Hebrew letters constitute a primary expression of the language and mathematics of spirituality. Magic spells are also the incantations of words, verbal formulae, which can have a magical effect, if charged with power and intention. The famous 'abracadabra' incantation is said to be derived from Aramaic and means: 'I create as I speak'.

The Power of Mantra

One of the most remarkable and extremely fascinating stories from Norse mythology about the significance and magical power of Divine language is the story of Odin discovering the runes.

A determent seeker of knowledge and wisdom, the Norse god Odin observed the Norns –three mysterious sagacious maidens who create the fates of all beings by carving runes into the Yggdrasil tree trunk. He ached for their powers and wisdom and decided to undertake the task of coming to know runes.

Runes are not just simple letters but the symbols of some most powerful forces in the cosmos. 'Rune' means both letter and secret/mystery. These letters called the runes allow one to access, interact with and influence the world-shaping forces they symbolise.

Thus, when Odin sought the runes, he wasn't merely attempting to acquire a set of arbitrary representations of human vocal sounds. Rather he was uncovering an extraordinary potent system of magic!

Odin decided to undertake the most severe form of penance or tapas (self-sacrifice) by piercing himself with a spear and hanging upside down on a branch of Yggdrasil (the great tree at the centre of the Norse spiritual cosmos rising from the Well of Urd and holding its branches and roots in the Nine Worlds), staring attentively into the depth of the Well of Urd.

Since the runes' origin is in the Well of Urd with the Norns, and since the runes do not reveal themselves to any but those who prove themselves worthy of such fearful insights and abilities, Odin hung himself from a branch of Yggdrasil and gazed downward into the deep waters below. He forbade any of the gods to grant him the slightest aid, not even a sip of water. And he kept peering downwards and call to the runes.

He survived in this state, teetering on the precipice that separate the living from the dead, for no less than nine days and nine nights. At the end of the ninth night, he perceived shapes in the depths: the runes!

They had accepted his sacrifice and shown themselves to him, revealing to him not only their forms, but also the secrets that lay within them. Having obtained this knowledge, Odin ended his ordeal with the scream of exultation.

The Power of Mantra

Having been initiated into the mysteries of the runes and equipped with the knowledge of how to wield the runes, he became one of the mightiest and most accomplished beings in the cosmos.

Words create reality, not the other way around! Language is an inescapable structuring element of perception. Words don't merely reflect our perception of the world; rather, we perceive and experience the world in the way that our language demands of us. Thinking outside of language is literally unthinkable, because all thought takes place within language itself – hence the inherent, godlike creative power of words. The runes and other letters/secrets such as matrika or the Malini alphabet are meaningful symbols that can facilitate communication between a human being and the invisible powers that animate the visible world, providing the basis for a plethora of magical acts.

There exist many different mantras for different purposes; mantras for removing obstacles, for acquiring wealth, healing mantras, mantras for protection from snakes, mantras for protecting from demons and dark forces, mantras for invoking goddesses, mantras leading to enlightenment, etc.... Of course, there are certain hidden, or secret mantras which can be revealed only at the time of initiation, by the competent guru to a ripe disciple. There are mantras, which can be revealed only by Divinities, Gods and Goddesses, when one gets access to the higher planes of reality. Mantras work as passwords to access the higher planes of reality. There are also Utkilam, or Nishkilam mantras, which serve as keys, or passwords for purification of certain mantras and of befriending them. It is said in Goutamiya, that before any Mantra is made efficacious (siddha), it has to be purified.

It must be understood however, that regardless of how powerful the sequences of phonemes are, if they are not charged with the power of attention and intention, they are just a collection of sacred words, not mantras. As it is said in Tantrasadbhava: 'The life of all mantras is solely the energy of God consciousness. When that energy is absent, all those collections of words are useless, just like a mass of clouds in the rain-less autumn sky'.[18] Mantras are not the combination of dead letters but the living energies – Sakties. All

---

[18] "Shiva Sutras: The Supreme Awakening" Swami Lakshmanjoo

178

mantras get their life from the Divine Mother Kundalini! She is the centre of all mantras!

As said in Tantra Sambhava: 'That Divine Mother, who is filled with supreme light, has pervaded the whole universe up to Brahmaloka. Oh devi, just as all letters are found in the first letter 'A', in the same way, the whole universe is found in that Divine Mother'.[19] Out of the energy of Mother Kundalini, the language in a form of fifty letters arises. Beginning with the letter 'A', each following letter gives birth to other letters. There are five sacred states of the Self that rise from this Kundalini and they are five mouths of Lord Siva: Tatpuruṣa, Aghora, Vamadeva, Sadyajata and Isana. Those mouths have appeared from Mother Kundalini, so that Lord Shiva may emanate Knowledge.

As also said in The Sutras on Creation: 'Welling up out of His pure joy, this entire universe comes into being. Descending in an arc of Light, Spanda becomes the subtlest of the subtle. Then, forming a straight line of pure gold and taking her form of golden Light, the Goddess Spanda Sakti dances back and force in pure delight between two points (visarga), becoming this very creation inside and out. Sound is inherent in Light, and Light in Sound. Springing forth together, the Creation is thus formed out of what already exists in his own being. From the Light that is its own power source (Prakasa), the Supreme Shiva manifests a vibration (Vimarsa). From that vibration comes sound. And from that sound, He causes letters to manifest. This Spanda creates her own reflection in the objects of this world so that Absolute can survey Himself. This vibration takes on the nature of awareness of distinctions. In this way, it manifests as fifty perceptions. These perceptions are phonemes and these phonemes becomes the objects. This is how external objects manifest in the body of supreme consciousness. The illusion of the existence of a world, a universe, is Creation. And Creation is the illusion that a world actually exists. This very illusion, known as Shiva's Maya Sakti, is neither real nor unreal. And yet She appears to be both real and unreal. That is His genius. Out of What exists in His own being, Shiva creates this world through His own Vimarsa (Spanda Sakti)

---

[19] "Shiva Sutras: The Supreme Awakening" Swami Lakshmanjoo

and manifests a universe comprised of this very energy of Light and Sound.'[20]

We will be returning to mantras, matrikas, Malini, and Vak, for I have been blessed by the Grace of Mother Kundalini to have directly experienced her magnificent supreme forces (Garlands of the Divine Alphabet), a become fully united with her.

Although the vibrations of mantric sounds are very powerful keys for the opening of doors to the inner dimensions of reality, I also realised that it is the rhythmic flow of Prana and Apana (inhalation and exhalation) tied to the chanting of mantras that made the psychedelic effect so profound!

On the June 16th, I received the last email from my love - my darling Maya:

'My beautiful Slavka! How are you there? Is everything bright, warm, and magical in your soul? In mine, honestly speaking, it is not. I am so tired. Lost... Lost everything... Lost the meaning of life... and, it seems to me I am not going to regain it. The whole world seems to be so unnecessary, unfair, and demanding, but demanding what, it is unclear. I am completely confused. I cut my veins few days ago..., nothing. No fear, no pity, nothing... I wanted to finally stop this carousel. Now I am in touch with Oleg. Only in touch, nothing more. But it seems everyone is so happy with our reunion. But it is not the truth. From communications with him, everything becomes more and more complicated and difficult, that I want to howl. I am very unhappy. Everything is hopeless. Only you, my bright happy memory. I need to finish now. Tenderly kissing you. Despite everything, life is interesting, and I will try to love it again and again. If you can call me this weekend on landline, my parents will be away. I hope I didn't make you very sad. Just with every passing day I become more and more abnormal. It's pity that I didn't manage to see Rita. I wanted so much to say and ask her. Maybe she can write me couple of sentences. I will be waiting. Kiss. Kiss. Kiss.'

A few days later, while staying in my London flat, I received a phone call from my friend Alexander. Maya was found dead in a Moscow river.

---

[20] "The Sutras on The 5-fold Act of Divine Consciousness" Acharya Kedar.

The Power of Mantra

O God! O, my sweet tender beautiful girl. O, my darling, my love… I could feel it coming. I felt guilty that I had had a chance but didn't save her. I had no doubt that she had drowned herself. She was only thirty years old. I made a phone call to her best friend. She told me that she had seen Maya a few days before it happened, and that she didn't recognise her, as though the life-force had already left her. I called Tara to tell her the devastating news. She suggested I come over to her place to grieve over Maya's death. I went back to the Isle of Wight. A bottle of vodka, tears, grief and sobbing over Maya's death, deep communication with Tara. Tara suggested I write a letter to Maya; ask her forgiveness, give my forgiveness and my blessings on her way to other planes of infinite Reality. The next day we went to the seashore in Compton Bay, where I swam out and offered my letter to Varuna (Lord of Waters). Immediately, big fish started to play with my letter, taking it further into the sea. It was so wonderful and reassuring.

Victor

Maya's death wasn't the first death of someone so dear and close to me. At the age of twenty-four I lost my cousin Victor, who was only twenty-five, to whom I was very close. I consider Victor my first mentor, who formed my view on reality. He was rebellious spirit. At the age of thirteen, he stopped going to school, motivated by his view that education must be a voluntary thing. When my mum was hit by a motorbike and spent almost a year in a hospital, I stayed with Victor in his summer cabin. Victor was the first among my friends to start to listening to short-wave radio: Voice of America, Radio Freedom and the Russian service of the BBC, from where lots of information suppressed by Russia, about Stalin's gulags and other nasty government deeds during the Soviet regime, was revealed. Our favourite program was a half-hour musical program on the Russian service of the BBC led by Seva Novgorodcev.

Friday at midnight, the time this program was on, was our the most awaited time of the week. From Seva we discovered amazing music, information on which we lacked in Russia. The Doors, Led Zeppelin, David Bowie and other musicians gave us much inspiration. Victor wrote and sent a few letters to Seva by the crooked way: through my father, who was working now in East Germany. One Friday we were very excited, for Seva read Victor's letter on his program. A couple of decades later I was delighted to accidentally meet Seva in the restaurant in Covent Garden where I was working as a waiter.

While living in Victor's summer cabin we were reading with great pleasure *The Hobbit*, which Victor found in our village's library. Fascinated with Tolkien's descriptions of the hobbit's shire, his elegant round house with lots of provision and ale, we imagined ourselves as hobbits. We even bought smoking pipes, tobacco and an electric fireplace to recreate the atmosphere.

Victor wasn't a conventional guy. He always had his own unique view on things, regardless of what others thought. He thought of himself as an autistic person, who kept himself to himself, and he was very interested in psychology. He was also the first person who told me that he believed in God!

He didn't attend school for a year and a half, but during the next school term, my teacher came to visit us and had a conversation with Victor, in which she asked if he would consider returning to school with me. Victor agreed.

The next morning, having drunk a shot of moonshine, wearing a red and white stripy t-shirt, jeans, a big heavy cross on his chest, and with hair to his shoulders, Victor came with me to school, where everyone was supposed to wear a uniform. The teacher of physical education, who was checking the uniform at the door, turned Victor away.

To this day, I've got a letter from my teacher to Victor, in which she apologised for the misunderstanding and invited him to attend to school again. Victor made another attempt one day later, and this time the schoolteachers allowed him to attend, but after a few lessons Victor told me, that it was not for him and that he was leaving. It was his last day in school.

Being fourteen, and looking at life and the people in it we felt, that when people got older, they lost their spark, their essence, their joy, and we decided that we preferred to die at the age of twenty-seven – the age at which our favourite people (Jim Morrison, Janis Joplin and Jimmy Hendrix) had left the stage of this world.

At the age of eighteen, when every Russian young man must join the army, if he doesn't have any medical problems, or hasn't secured himself a place in some half-military institution, Victor was called to attend military registration. He went to the enlistment office and obviously, the first thing they said was that he must cut his long hair. He did, but not short enough, so the officers sent him back to cut his hair shorter. Rebelliously, he just left and ignored them. He also ignored the next mobilization notice. After few days, while I was staying in Moscow, a military car arrived at his address and took him to a lunatic asylum. After being there for a week, about which he later told me many interesting stories, they brought him back and gave him a 'white ticket', which enabled him not to go to the army on the grounds of being mentally ill.

I never considered Victor mentally ill, but on the contrary, one of the most intelligent persons I had ever came across. Undoubtedly, he was unusual, but not mentally sick. Doctors prescribed him some strange pills called Cyclodol, the effects of which he was greatly concerned about. Victor told me that they produced a very creepy state of consciousness. I had heard of them recently and asked Victor to try them. One evening, I swallowed three tablets and lay down on a mattress on the floor in Victor's house. When I opened my eyes, I saw that the curtains of his room had opened and an arm with a pointed finger was calling me in. Suspiciously, I assumed that it was Victor inviting me to his room. I entered. Victor was sleeping on his bed. I went to pee. The toilet was located outside the house. Reality was wobbling. It was as though the walls were trying to squash me, and big rats were running around my feet. It was scary. This experience I can describe as an hallucination. And this was so different from the clarity of perception on a DMT trip!

We will be returning to DMT as the book unfolds, for it is a very important key for understanding Reality, and we cannot leave this book without deep inquiry into it.

As time passed, I served two years in the army and got married at the age of twenty-one. Then I left my village and my hometown to live for a couple of years with my wife Inna at her mum's house in a town called Livny, two hundred and fifty miles south of Moscow. All this time I kept in touch with Victor, sharing with him my philosophical discoveries in letters. I read then Bhagavad Gita, but wasn't highly impressed by it, and now I understand why. It was translated and interpreted by Bhaktivedanta Swami Prabhupata and had his personal flavour in it. Now, I've read many other translations of Bhagavad Gita and greatly treasure Krishna's wonderful revelation. I liked Dostoyevsky and, in association with him, came across highly intriguing and inspiring books by Leonid Andreev and through him discovered Nietzsche: *Thus Spoke Zarathustra* and *The Antichrist*. I read major German philosophers such as Immanuel Kant, Hegel and Leibniz, but was highly inspired by the book *The Twilight of Gods*. I fell in love with the existentialism, which was expressed in the works of Sartre, Kierkegaard, Kafka, and especially Albert Camus with his amazing 'feeling of absurdity and riding on the wave of absurdity' in *The Myth of Sisyphus.*

Our search for meaning, for the truth often begins in two ways. Firstly, it is a genuine attraction to goodness and love - a call from the Truth!

Secondly, it is a repulsion to injustice, absurdity, lies, etc… I must admit that my search for truth started with a repulsion to my current situation, repulsion to the ways of society, lies, absurdity and injustice. The first book that created such a deep impression of repulsion on me was Petrus Borel's *Champavert.* 'What is our society? A stinking bog. Only deep down, there can be found something transparent and clear'.

When I heard the news that Victor's and my favourite Russian poet and musician Alexander Bashlachev had ended his life at the age of twenty-seven, flying out of the eighth-floor open window of his Saint Petersburg's flat, tears rushed out. I was so deeply touched by his death, for I felt such an intimate connection to him and his soul-wrenchingly honest poetry.

Truly, the poet is a naked nerve who refuses to close his eyes on death, pain, absurdity and contradictions. The poet transforms suffering into the beauty and love. As described by some of his fellow musicians: 'You see, there is darkness, but he was lighting the bonfires with his songs.'

'He was walking on a razor edge on one side of which was Love, on the other – Death.' The death of Bashlachev created a massive wave of urging for Truth among many people of my generation, for his death was so real. He followed the prophecy of his songs: 'It's time for me to leave, following the song that you believe'.

My first son Anton was born, and soon we moved back to my hometown Luchovitcy. One day, my wife and I went to see Victor at his house in Aksenovo village. We had a dramatic, wonderful, crazy evening and night, reminding me somehow of a very passionate Dostoevsky's *The Brothers Karamazov*, with our hearts wide open, fuelled with vodka and moonshine, with our beautiful, mad, Russian souls dancing. We stayed up until dawn, laughing, weeping, and having very deep conversations.

Victor

Inna and I left in the morning for our town, half an hour ride by bus. In the late afternoon, someone rang the bell to our apartment. I went to open it. It was one of our relatives. 'I am very sorry, I have bad news; Victor hanged himself,' said he.

The words 'hanged himself' bashed me like a sledgehammer.

There was nothing in Victor's behaviour betraying his intention to commit suicide. In disbelief, we rushed back to Aksenovo. Victor's body had already been taken to the morgue. Victor's younger brother Alexander, who had gone to visit his friends when it happened, told us about the last time he'd seen Victor. Alexander said that Victor offered a shot of vodka to his mum and they drunk together. The last thing Alexander recalled before he left was that Victor was listening to Bashlachev's 'Vanyusha' – possibly the most passionate and heart-wrenching Russian song of love and death that has ever been written and sung.

Alexander told us that Victor had hanged himself in his barn standing on his knees. At any moment, he could have lifted himself back to his feet. Victor's death created ripples of chaos in the village. The next day we were searching the forest, for one of his friends had disappeared and there were growing concerns that he was going to hang himself too. Fortunately, we soon found him. It seemed that many friends of Victor had caught a virus of suicide.

Arrogant and vain in my youth, I was angry with the unjust Creator. 'If you offer me the keys of paradise, I will throw it back, for I am not with you, but with my dear cousin, who hanged himself in his barn'.

One day later, I myself was standing on a rooftop of a nine-floor building, ready to jump into death. But I simply didn't have guts to do so. To end one's own life demands tremendous courage!

'To be, or not to be, that is the question:

Whether 'tis nobler in the mind to suffer

The slings and arrows of outrageous fortune,

Or, to take arms against a sea of troubles,

186

Victor

And by opposing, end them. To die, to sleep;

No more; and by sleep to say we end

*The heartache, and the thousand natural
shocks*

That flesh is heir to? 'Tis a consummation

Devoutly to be wish'd. To die, to sleep;

perchance to dream: aye, there's the rub;

*For in that sleep of death what dreams may
come*

When we have shuffled off this mortal coil,

Must give us pause. There's the respect

That makes calamity of so long life,'
inquires Shakespeare's Hamlet.

Now, many years later, I am glad that I didn't end my life back then, for life has given me so many lessons to learn. If I had arrived at death back then, I am sure now that I wouldn't have been able to find the right way. I wasn't ripe for death's gift.

I have not the slightest judgement, but on the contrary, am forever grateful to my dearest ones, who took their own lives, for their deaths took me out of the mindless, trivial enjoyments of life, and focused my attention on the most important questions of purpose and meaning of Life, Death, Love, God and Truth. With their deaths, I could no longer stay the same. Their deaths forced me to search for the Ultimate Truth. If one is willing to learn, then one can extract something very valuable from every moment of one's life, regardless of how joyful, or painful it is. Each time, one can learn something new and profound about oneself. One can harvest the lessons of life and bake the most delicious cakes from those lessons, that will nourish one's soul.

Liberty Caps, a Black Hole and Singularity

Tarananda was not only a great mantra yoga teacher, but also a very talented artist. I had never painted before, so at the beginning she taught me how not to be afraid of starting to paint. We made a few paintings ala Jackson Pollock, splashing and dripping colours, but soon began to do more interesting projects. One of the paintings we did together, I am very proud of. It was a portrait of Ramana Maharshi. We decided to do this painting with short strokes of brushes as 'dancing particles' radiating from Ramana's face to infinity. When the painting was finished, we brought it into the living room for a proper viewing. We were awe-struck; Ramana had come alive! His essence was pulsating and radiating from our painting. We've done many more interesting experimental projects together. Feeling that I was just wasting my time in London, I moved to live with Tara.

In July 2005, the UK Government moved psilocybin mushrooms from class C to class A, making them highly illegal. Shops selling fresh magic mushrooms and mushroom growing kits were closed. It was now only possible to buy Amanita Muscaria on the streets. However, Amanita Muscaria didn't have the same psychedelic properties as psilocybin mushrooms. It certainly had some interesting effects, but it was far below the intensity of the psychedelic states induced by psilocybin mushrooms. Fortunately, the Isle of Wight was famous for its psilocybin mushrooms (*Psilocybe Semilanceata*), commonly known as 'liberty caps'.

Liberty caps are considered one of the most potent psilocybin mushrooms in the world. In conversation with my friends, I learned also that liberty caps from the Isle of Wight were considered the most potent mushrooms in the UK. And so, in the autumn of 2005 we made many journeys to the fields collecting our sacred field gurus.

I remember very well our shared trip that autumn. In the evening, in the very cosy atmosphere of Tara's bungalow, I consumed around fifty fresh liberty caps and Tara had only a homeopathic dosage of around ten. After the initial state of anxiety and the intense visuals, with the help of Self-inquiry, we settled into a very deep stillness. Our bodies were lying on their backs on the floor holding each other's hand. I could feel all Tara's thoughts and knew that she also knew all my thoughts and my inner battles with visions of a demonic nature. It had become natural for me to experience a fearful agitation in the initial stages of a psychedelic journey, knowing this agitation to be only a temporarily barrier through which I would successfully break into the more peaceful, filled with loving light, inner dimensions of Supreme Intelligence, with the help of Self-inquiry and surrender to Divine Grace. In the end, the radiant light of Shiva – the True Self, always shone triumphantly!

In this deep stillness, almost without breathing, my sense of identity was plunging deeper and deeper into my spiritual heart. The whole world and my body consciousness disappeared, leaving only the concentrated light of awareness fixed on my spiritual heart. Within the heart, I began to witness what could only be described as the ecstatic dance of chromosomes. The dancing patterns of two pairs of chromosomes were about to join into one new being at any moment, but as soon as this ecstatic union was about to happen, the electric shock from Tara's brain sent a wave of electricity, which passed through Tara's hand, up my hand into my brain and from there into my heart, causing a dislocation of the pattern. Again, after a few minutes of concentration, this union of dancing chromosomes was about to happen, but in this crucial moment a new electric discharge from Tara's brain shifted the dancing chromosomes from their union. It happened again and again.

On another mushroom occasion, I had the experience of a 'black hole'. With the continuation, of experiments with magic mushrooms, it had become as clear as day for me, that the body itself is a cosmos. Within this cosmos there are hells and heavens, Gods, demons and alien beings, there are countless parallel universes with different inhabitants, there are stars, galaxies, and also black holes.

Black holes present some problems for science. Supermassive black holes, which are said to be located at the centre of every galaxy, have three layers, so to speak. Outer event horizon, inner horizon and the singularity. It is said that nothing, not even light, can escape a black hole if the outer event horizon has been crossed. A tremendous gravitational force sucks everything into the black hole; gas, dust, and the surrounding stars, together with their light. As the matter and light falls into the black hole, they move towards the centre of the black hole, known as the singularity. Singularity is a paradox. It is said to be a one-dimensional point of infinite density and mass. Such description of black holes and specifically the description of singularity goes against our logic. It is the point where all mathematics and science break down, for the infinity is an enemy of science, which can only operate within something calculable, something that has limits and boundaries. When a mathematical equation ends up equal to infinity, science stops there.

In one of my shamanic meditations with magic mushrooms, in which an intense dynamic, breathing developed spontaneously, I discovered that my very centre (Hrt, Hrdayam, or Spiritual Heart) is simultaneously a quasar (the most luminous object, apparently up to 100,000 times brighter than Milky Way galaxy) and a black hole. Some scientists believe that quasars are powered by supermassive black holes. Some even propose that quasars could be the other end of a hypothetical tunnel within the black holes. Quasars are called active galactic nuclei (AGN).

'The above from below, and the below from above – the work of the miracle of the One,'[21] says the Emerald Tablet of Hermes Trismegistus. As in macrocosm, so it is in microcosm.

Within the body cosmos, the Spiritual Heart occupies the central position. Although there are different numbers from different research, they undoubtedly show that the heart has the most powerful electromagnetic field in the body. Some scientific

---

[21] "Emerald Tablet" Hermes Trismegistus.

Liberty Caps, a Black Hole and Singularity

research tell us that the heart is sixty times stronger electrically than the brain, some says that heart is 100,000 times stronger electrically and 5,000 times stronger magnetically than the brain, but despite of such vast differences, all of them agree that the heart has the strongest electromagnetic power. My understanding and my direct experience is that the Spiritual Heart, which is the centre of all creation, emits the pure light of awareness, at the time of the creative process, which passes through the moving slides of the mind, so to speak, projecting the visible universe into cognition. As when white light passes through the prism and gets broken by this prism into the spectrum of the seven colours, similarly the undifferentiated light of consciousness emitted from the Spiritual Heart, passing through the prism of the brain, gets broken, and appears as a visible world to our limited senses.

As Ramana Maharshi pointed out: 'The creation begins with the birth of the 'I thought', or to put it in other words: the apparent world picture appears at the moment of identification of Self-Atman-Brahman with the ego (a separate sense of Self related to the body). In Hindu philosophy, the principle of giving birth to the sense of a separate self is called Ahamkara – the 'I maker'. When consciousness awakens from a state of deep sleep (sushupti), the immediate birth of 'I sense' takes place. With the birth of 'I thought', all 'others' (you, he, she, they), and the whole visible world with all its history is born simultaneously. At the time of deep sleep, the rays of consciousness are said to be withdrawn back into the heart. Ramana Maharshi often used the analogy of the mind and the spider: 'Just as the spider emits the thread [of the web] out of itself and again withdraws it into itself, likewise the mind projects the world out of itself and again resolves it into itself'.[22]

I would like to mention here, for the occasion has arisen, that I totally disagree with those pseudo gurus who compare Awakening to a state of deep sleep in which there is no perception of the limitations of body and the world. As it is rightly said in the great itihasa Tripura Rahasya: 'In the so-called waking state of consciousness (Jagrat), the grand universe is reflected in the unique mirror of consciousness and in the state of deep slumber the

<hr>

[22] "The Spiritual Teaching of Ramana Maharshi" Ramana Maharshi.

reflecting surface can be compared to that which is covered with tar. Although there are no perceptions of limitations, but equally, there are no perceptions of the positive bliss and the True Glory of Supreme Intelligence in such state. The state of deep sleep rather resembles the state of 'non-being' – the absence of any sort of experiences.'

The heart is not only the source of the mind, but also the source of Prana (life-force). As Ramana Maharshi says: 'Either trace your thought back to its origin, or by holding the breath dive into the heart, for the heart is the origin of both; the mind and the Prana.'

'The Self dwells in the lotus of the heart, whence radiate a hundred and one nerves [nadis]. From each of these proceed one hundred others, which are smaller; and from each of these, again seventy-two thousand others, which are smaller still. In all of these moves Vyana, which is the fourth Prana. And then at the moment of death, through the nerve in the centre of the spine, the Udana, which is the fifth Prana, leads the virtuous man upward to higher birth, the sinful man downwards to lower birth, and the man who is both virtuous and sinful to rebirth in the world of men,'[23] says Prasna Upanishad.

The movement of consciousness towards its origin (the Singularity of the Spiritual Heart), is not the movement into the void proposed by many gurus. On the contrary, the movement of consciousness into its source is the movement into the states of greatest density of vibrations, density of energy. The movement towards the Heart's Singularity is also the movement within the very compact relationship between opposites. Good and bad, black and white, hot and cold, male and female, yes and no, and all other pairs of opposites sits side by side in this compact intensity of experience.

The plunge into the Heart of Reality requires unshakable courage, unwavering trust, and unreserved willingness to die, to be squashed and annihilated by the tremendous density of the bliss-energy of Undying Reality. In the dying process, as described in *The Tibetan Book of The Dead* the five gross elements collapse, or getting absorbed into each other, beginning with the element of earth collapsing into the element of water, water collapsing into the

---

[23] "Prasna Upanishad"

element of fire and so on... Consciousness becomes further and further interiorised with each element's dissolution, losing to the corresponding element its sense and withdrawing itself from the prison of matter. With the dissolution of earth into water, the dying person loses the sense of smell, which corresponds to the element of earth. With the collapse of water into the element of fire, one loses the sense of taste. When fire dissolves into the element of air, it takes with itself the sense of sight. The dying person at this stage can relate to the outside world only by means of touch and hearing. When air enters the ether, it withdraws the sense of touch from the perception of the external world. And when finally, ether dissolves into the Singularity, one loses all connections with the outside world.

There is tremendous importance to what is happening at this crucial moment of dying; the massive density of energy of this vital experience, pressing the no-longer-important perceptions of the world and one's body out of its sight. It must be said here that while abandoning the perceptions of the world and the body appearance, awareness is not entering into the blackness of emptiness, but on the contrary, is having extremely intense psychedelic experience, getting involved in the battles of good and evil forces and in the playout of a great fear of losing all sanity and hope for safety. At the culmination of this terrific battle of opposites, one realises that he/she is unable to maintain this struggle any longer, and the emerging sense of carelessness, complete surrender and relaxation allows one to enter its own source.

Awareness then, is totally interiorised and enters its own source; the paradoxical Singularity, which in *The Tibetan Book of The Dead* is referred to as Luminosity. But Luminosity is a no-man's land. It is non-referential. There is nothing to point to here as this, or that, and no possibility to grasp. It is the greatest paradox, the seed in which all is contained, the pregnant-with-infinite-possibilities mystery. Not only objects and space are dissolved here, but time also ceases to exist. Not much can be said about the Singularity, or Luminosity, for it is beyond understanding, beyond logic. Even the wildest imagination cannot imagine it. It is the storehouse of all contradictions.

Liberty Caps, a Black Hole and Singularity

From the point of view of a logical mind or human intelligence, such a state, such reality is simply impossible. It just cannot be. All our understanding is broken down here. From the logical point of view, for the perception of anything we would require a duration of time, for without time there is no experience possible. And yet the highest reality is timeless, and there is no absence of experience, as so many pseudo gurus proclaim, but the fullness of Ecstasy and Bliss. The highest reality is the greatest mystery and it will remain the greatest mystery forever, even for itself. Neither I, nor anyone else, not science, nor philosophy, not even the highest scriptures can describe, or reveal to you the reality, my dear reader. Everything that appears in the field of your cognition at best can point you in the right direction, can show you the portal, but only you can walk through it. Self-realisation is never a finite achievement. The amazement and wonder of comprehending one's Self never stop, for the reality is infinite!

Even Almighty God Absolute Him/Herself cannot fully comprehend itself, for comprehension is an imposition of limitations – putting imaginary restrictions upon Infinite Reality. To comprehend the fullness of reality, intelligence must have an infinite speed. The highest possible speed is 'being everywhere at once'. But 'being everywhere at once' also means 'not moving at all'! Could we conceive such a being that is simultaneously aware of all and is all? The comprehension must be extended not only to the macrocosm and microcosms within it, the space within all celestial spheres, galaxies and stars, the minutest details and the processes of these minutest details, such as the movements of all living creatures, movements of all molecules, atoms and subatomic particles within the space of our visible universe, but it also must be stretched throughout all time and include all countless parallel realities and infinite births of infinite possibilities within all planes and stages of infinite intelligence. If it was possible for the Supreme Intelligence to fully comprehend its own totality, it would immediately limit its own infinite abilities.

The absolute openness of Reality means that one can never know it completely, can never stop wondering, can never stop discovering. To stop wondering is to stop the unfolding, to stop dynamism. The unfolding of Self-apprehension can never be stopped, for reality is infinite in its possibilities and that's why it

Liberty Caps, a Black Hole and Singularity

would be forever a mystery. As reality is infinite, so is its realisation. One cannot just arrive at the full comprehension and stop there. To comprehend it is like to put it in a box, to limit it. The full comprehension of its own totality destroys the element of newness, which is one of the most joyous aspects of Supreme Intelligence. The Absolute is newly born every instance. The never-diminishing, childlike wonder, astonishment and amazement at the fullness of its own abilities is probably one of the most exiting characteristics of Highest Reality. Supreme Intelligence is never without movement. It is the perennial surge of unconditional Love – the eternal fountain of excessive Joy, the inexhaustible source of creativity, always overflowing, always spilling itself out.

As in descriptions of quantum mechanics, the pregnant-with-infinite-possibilities vacuum splits itself into virtual particles of matter and antimatter, and the Absolute splits itself into the observers and the observed, subjects and objects. The surge of excessive joy born out of its own unstoppable, unrestrictable freedom and infinite potency, erupting, bubbling, spilling itself out, creates the numerous vortexes and wormholes of space-time rays – the parallel realities.

One may ask: what is the point of striving for the Truth then, if regardless of choices, the familiar life appearance will terminate at the death crossroad, in which everyone will be absorbed by Luminosity? The answer lies in the accumulated tendencies, attachments, habits and preferences which force the individualised consciousness to move into one or another plane of experience. Vasanas (mental tendencies and predispositions) and accumulated karma play a vital role in the unfolding of further events. Luminosity itself could be recognised by some individualised consciousnesses as the most beautiful, the dearest of all eternal home, and as a terrifying enemy by others. Into which space-time vortex the individualised consciousness flows is determined by many factors; the most pressing of which are the lessons one learnt in their lifetime, how sincerely and passionately one has been longing for the True Self, how far down the rabbit hole one has dived in search of true knowledge, how many efforts and sacrifices one has made to return to Highest Reality. The right judgment, the discrimination between real and unreal, between the important and not important, the willingness to face one's fears, the willingness to

195

be annihilated by the Reality and the unshakable trust in the words of Truth; that I am Brahman the Reality, the spirit of inquiry into the Truth and the spirit of experimentations with different ways of enabling one to know Oneself, the power of Self-recognition and the Grace of the True Self, who is none other but Shiva-Shakti, God Absolute; all of these sacred efforts play a crucial role in the further unfolding of one's destiny!

The Spiritual Heart – the Source – is the absolute paradox. When, like a quasar, agitating nadis and mind, it blazes outside, projecting the world appearance, there appears to be as many hearts as there are bodies. But when the rays of awareness are withdrawn from the external objects into the Heart, which at this moment becomes a supermassive black hole, one enters the Singularity, and the Heart is realised to be the One only. Heart is Thy Name O, Lord!

Back to Beloved Mother India

In the beginning of February of 2006, Tarananda and I arrived at Ramanasramam in Tiruvannamalai, lying at the foot of our beloved Arunachala. This time we decided to stay in the holy land of India for three or four months. I had heard a few stories from some of my friends, that on their first nights in this sacred place, many of them were having nightmares. This time I found these rumours to be true. Here are brief notes from my diary:

'10.02.06.

Tonight, I was woken up from the nightmare. I was dreaming that I was chased by mechanical animals. I tried to run away, but suddenly there was a flood on my path. I jumped on some sort of inflatable mattress, but a mechanical man was trying to catch me. When his mechanical hands were about to grab my feet, I gasped for breath, and woke up. Precisely at the same moment Tara, lying next to me, gasped for breath and awoke from her nightmare. She dreamt that she was driving a van, which fell into a big pit, and she couldn't get out. Regardless of all her efforts, she was hopelessly stuck there and was in great panic. Then, she heard voices from above. Some people, or gods were talking to each other. When she heard, them saying; 'the problem is, she thinks that it is real', she gasped for breath, and woke up at the same moment as I did.

We understandingly looked into each other's eyes. I started to analyse the meaning of my nightmare. Mysterious forces had attacked my astral body from all sides. How naïve I was coming to Arunachala and desiring awakening. Here, in this 'place of power', almighty Gods are able to frighten us to death. But with death,

197

comes the end of sleep. I realised that it was an attack on my ego.
Mighty Gods were attacking it. It is a mortal combat, the great
Mahabharata, in which ego must die. But how cunning is ego. Even
creation of poetry is its act. Even the desire to be nobody and
nothing is a play of ego, for it is 'I' (ego), who wants to be nobody
and nothing. Non-existing, but appearing to exist, ego cannot be
killed by any other means but by a one-pointed search for it.
Consciousness turned inside in search for ego (sense of I), drives
the ego away. With all my being I prayed to Ramana, Ganapati
Muni, Shiva and Arunachala to help me to kill the ego. The totality
of my attention concentrated on my Spiritual Heart. It is not me,
who is trying to kill the ego, but consciousness pouring its light and
the ego runs away and dissolves. Truly, awakening is suicide.
When I was coming back to my physical consciousness, I observed
that my body was breathless and the totality of attention, without
thought constructs, was drilling my heart. I know with utmost
crystal clarity, that everything around me is awake. Everything is
the awakened consciousness, and this awakened consciousness is
only waiting for my awakening, or rather waiting for me to lose my
sleeping 'I'.'

At the bookstore across the Ramanasramam, Tara was drawn to
buy a book of Ram Alexander, based on the diaries of Atmananda:
Death must Die. Atmananda is a western seeker of truth, who spent
many years with the great Indian sage, the Self/God-realised master
Sri Anandamayi Ma. In the evening, when I returned from a
gathering with a couple of Russian friends whom we met at
Arunachala, at which we smoked good quality charas from the
Manali valley and I played the Yakutian khomus, we decided to
look at the book to which Tara was so drawn. We looked at one
photo of Anandamayi Ma at the first pages of this book. We looked
and we kept looking. Some miraculous metamorphosis was
happening with this very powerful and beautiful photo. For at least
ten minutes, we just kept gazing at the photo. Anandamayi Ma's
face was transforming into the face of Ramana Maharshi and then
into the face of Shiva and Kali. This amazing photo was alive, and
it was radiating pure Love. Stunned by it, we decided to include a
visit to Anandamayi Ma ashram and her mahasamadhi in Kankhal,
Haridwar.

Back to Beloved Mother India

I had a few interesting conversations among my new Russian friends about the significance of one's own name and why many people who enter the spiritual path receive from their gurus their new spiritual name. There were lots of jokes, and attempts to wear certain names, for example, one of these Russians decided to call himself simply 'God'.

I brought around three hundred dried liberty caps with me to Arunachala. And so, one night I decided to take 108 (the sacred number of 101 nadis plus seven chakras), mushrooms at the feet of holy Arunachala. Tara and I had chosen a spot on the stone plateau, about halfway around the giripradakshina (circumbulation around the mountain), by the inner path. Tara decided not to take mushrooms this time but be an assistant and a carer for me. When the mushrooms began to stir their magic, I heard the threatening sounds of approaching baboons, which gave me a little bit of fright. But as I mentioned before, fear is the reservoir of concentrated energy and if one can tap into this energy, transform and direct this energy into the appropriate channel, this immense energy can be used as a fuel for expansion, or even an explosion of intelligence. And so, I embraced fear. Gazing into the standing rock of Arunachala, I turned fear into love.

The wall of Shiva's concentrated consciousness, radiating from the mighty Arunachala in front of me, hit through my body as fast as an approaching tsunami, and scattered my consciousness and my entire being across the cosmos. I became the Universe.

The sky is the top of my head. The stars are my ornaments. I am Shiva. My body is standing at the feet of mighty Arunachala and trembling. The flood of Love gushing as rivers of tears through my eyes, and I know that this is Ganga Ma descending from the heavens through my matted locks and flooding through my eyes, cleansing and purifying my sight. I see that matter does not exist and everything is made of purest Love. I see that everything is Love. I see nothing but Love. I could never ever imagine that Love of such intensity is possible. Arunachala is transparent now like a crystal. I see the celestial cities of perfected siddhas and sages within her. I am gazing into her Heart. One mighty heart is beating. Arunachala – the Self! No space, no time, no directions, not even here and now. Only Thou – I – Arunachala – Shiva! I arrived! O, Arunachala! I am Shiva!

Back to Beloved Mother India

After this tremendous revelation, I simply couldn't call myself anything other than Shiva. Arunachala gave me that name.

A few days later we went for a darshan (auspicious sight) of Aum Amma, who, as the story is told, have been meditating in Arunachala's Ali cave, which is now known also as Aum Amma's cave. Blessed Amma, shaking in her exalted state was throwing flowers and giving hugs to the gathered devotees. Tara and I decided later to spend three nights, in Aum Amma's cave, immersed in chanting, beginning on the moonless night of Mahashivratri (the great night of Shiva). We delivered a few canisters of fresh water to cave beforehand. Unfortunately, a little misunderstanding happened with our preparations and our last meal, because of which, Tara had partially uncooked and badly prepared unhygienic food, which led later to her poisoning. In the evening, while most of the people were marching around Arunachala on the external path of giripradakshina, we went to a place next to our cave. We were chanting all night, but towards the morning, Tara began to feel unwell. I should have dropped my plans to stay in the cave for three nights and take care of Tara, but my initial resolve was very strong, and so I just helped her to the road, where she took a rickshaw to our new apartment, which we hadn't had a chance to see properly yet.

I stayed in the cave for another couple of nights. On the first of which I took the remaining mushrooms. I made the mistake of covering the opening of the cave with a mosquito net. As the mushrooms began to work, there were lots of bats flying in and out of the cave. Following their usual routes, they seemed not to be registered the net, bumping into it and falling, which created unnecessary panic. After a few minutes of this chaos I took the net down. I began to hear the warning cries of baboons nearby and so, I decided to chant very loudly to scare them off. I hardly slept that night. The next day I was immersed in constant chanting accompanied by rhythmic breathing. Towards the night, the skies burst open with powerful rain. Drunk with ecstasy, I danced naked on top of the cave, receiving the purifying blessings of Mother Ganga. Arunachala became transparent again. I felt that if I jumped into it, I would not hit the rocks, but would go straight through it.

On the third day of constant chanting and rhythmic breathing accompanied by Self-inquiry, the totality of my awareness plunged

200

into my Spiritual Heart, with which I felt identical, I realised and became one with the Aham-Sphurana (The throb of the Self – the I-pulsating light of consciousness). Sometime later, couple of people from Arunachala's forest protection turned up at the cave and asked me to leave. My perception of reality was temporarily altered after these three days of intense Sadhana. While walking back to our apartment, I perceived the three-dimensional world as sort of two-dimensional. The people I met appeared to me as two-dimensional pieces of paper.

Walking into our new apartment I didn't find Tara. After some time, I found out that she had moved to the Athithi ashram. When a stranger comes without announcing the date and time of his arrival for a short stay, he is an Athithi (without date and time). It was a lovely, clean and very peaceful ashram, not very far from Ramanasramam. My thanks go to our rickshaw driver Kumar, who took care of Tara in my absence, taking her to hospital and helping her to find this beautiful healing place.

In March, it became much hotter in Tiru and many visitors moved up north to more comfortable weather. Very often, people left Tiru in March to go to Goa for a few weeks of rest and then further north to Haridwar and Rishikesh. We decided to travel the same route. Tarananda had stayed in Goa some years before and had friends there who owned a small hotel at the beach in between two expensive Taj hotels. I found Goa the most uninteresting place in the whole of India. One can easily have almost identical experiences on the beaches of Mallorca, or Ibiza. Although we stayed in a beautifully luxurious, spacious and fresh room, although we had tasty dinners on the shore of Arabian sea, Goa didn't impress me at all. I didn't see even one sadhu (holy man) here, nor any authentic Hindu temples. Most conversation circled around business opportunities. I do not want to belittle Goa. It's certainly not a bad place and many people enjoy its offerings, specifically young hippie-ish westerners, looking for fun at the psychedelic Goa trance parties. It's just too westernised for my taste and lacking the authentic spirituality.

Tara's food poisoning let itself be known more dramatically here. We had no choice but to take her to hospital, where she spent a few days on a drip. After couple of weeks of the warm Arabian sea, we headed towards the cool, refreshing holy Ganga. We made a big mistake however, deciding to take a taxi from Delhi to Haridwar, instead of the train. Firstly, it cost us extra money, but more importantly, the driving was so dangerous and took so long. We were stuck at twilight in a massive traffic jam somewhere in the middle of the forest. There was no possibility of moving neither forward, nor backwards for miles. By some miracle, after some hours in this traffic jam we broke through and continued our journey. We arrived in Haridwar around two o'clock in the morning and went to a small hut-hotel advertised in the *Lonely Planet* guide just on the banks of the Ganges, but after about fifteen minutes of inspecting our room, we left. The room was infested with fleas, and we noticed a few rat traps around. Desperate for sleep, we found a rickshaw driver who took us to a very expensive hotel. We had no choice but to pay this price.

The next morning, we went straight to Anandamayi Ma ashram and her mahasamadhi in Kankhal. The perpetual intense fragrance of roses is a very special feature of Anandamayi Ma mahasamadhi. After the full namaskaram (prostration) at Ma's holy feet and a few minutes of silent meditation, we went into the ashram's bookstore, where, after a brief conversation with the bookstore manager, without us asking anything, or even considering the possibilities of it, we were invited to stay at the Anandamayi Ma's guesthouse, next door to Ma's Mahasamadhi Shrine. Surely Ma wanted us to stay near her and arranged this surprising invitation. We were exceedingly happy, honoured and blessed to stay at Ma's guesthouse. We were spellbound by the breath-taking picture of Ma with the Sri Yantra radiating from her heart and the most beautiful words of prayer, written by Rabindranath Tagore, printed on it:

'Let me not pray to be sheltered from dangers, but to be fearless in facing them.

Let me not beg for the stilling of my pain, but for the heart to conquer it.

Let me not look for allies in Life's battlefield, but to my own strength.

Let me not crave in anxious fear to be saved, but hope for the patience to win my freedom.

Grant that I may not be a coward, feeling your mercy in my success alone;

But let me find the grasp of Your hand in my failure.'

Peace, beauty, reassurance and Divine Grace were emanating from this amazing picture.

Doctor Gosh – the caretaker of Ma's guesthouse was also an amazing Ayurvedic cook. His unusual recipes were probably the most delicious meals we ever tried. Ma's guesthouse also had a very extensive spiritual library. Two books immediately attracted my attention: *Shiva Sutras* and *Spanda Karikas* with commentaries and a translation by Jaideva Singh. As soon as I started reading them, I immediately recognised their significance. These two books, alongside the *Vijnana Bhairava, Pratyabhijna Hrdayam* and *Paratrisika-Vivarana* to this day I consider as the most sacred, most esoteric, and the most accurate in their descriptions of Highest Reality and the methods of realising it, through systems of knowledge known as yoga and tantra.

In the late afternoon, very friendly rickshaw driver, who had gotten his rickshaw as a gift from Anandamayi Ma's ashram, took us to Hardwar's Ganga Ghats.

O! Ganga Ma! May your holy waters wash away all accumulated impurities and sins, may your soma-like liquid purify my mind, heart, and my entire being with your refreshing balm. Jai Ganga Ma!

O! What a contrast with the warm Arabian sea were the cool, refreshing, powerful streams of Ganga. The current was so strong, that if I hadn't been holding onto a chain, I would have been swept away by it. At the twilight, we went to Har Ki Pauri – a magical place of pilgrimage. It is believed that Har Ki Pauri is the place where a drop of Amrit (Divine nectar) fell from the celestial Kumbh (pot) carried by Vishnu, and thus the Maha Kumbh mela (festival) is held here every 12 years.

Doctor Gosh, who became our friend, invited us to attend next Maha Kumbh mela. He was telling fascinating stories about the activities during Kumbh mela, saying that the whole city of Haridwar transforms into one big festival for a couple of months. All ashrams and many volunteers cook food for anyone who is hungry.

I loved India for its charity, its Prasad, its care for their holy men. We bought baskets of flowers, lighted incense sticks and lamp shades and sent our offerings with our prayers and chanting down the Ganga's streams. We attended the aarati (fire ceremony) and basked in the streams of the Ganga with hundredths of devotees from all around India.

Ah! What a blessing to be here and bask ourselves in this atmosphere of Joy and Ecstasy. Our hearts swell with Divine Gratitude. Thank you, Lord! Thank you, Hari (Vishnu)! Thank you, Hara (Shiva)! Thank you, Shakti! We are prostrating at Thy lotus feet.

Haridwar can be written also as Hardwar, for both Shiva and Vishnu are worshipped here. We fell in love with Hardwar. Hardwar is full of ashrams, temples, sincere sadhus and holy men.

The next morning, we went for puja at the Anandamayi Ma Mahasamadhi shrine. Beginning slowly, the ceremony gradually developed into ecstatic chanting building into a crescendo of loudly ringing bells at the finale. Ah! What a beautiful and powerful way to wake up. In the shrine, we were happy to again see one of our friends from Belgium, whom we had met at Ramana Maharshi ashram and with whom we had a chat about Anandamayi Ma.

After few days in Haridwar filled with love, joy and gratitude, we moved to Rishikesh. Rishikesh is a charming town situated in picturesque nature, where the Ganga is wide and peaceful. A few sandy beaches along the Ganga add to Rishikesh's sense of relaxation and tranquillity. Unfortunately, due to its popularity among spiritually inclined westerners, Rishikesh has become a major tourist attraction, transforming into some sort of westernised marketplace, where the spirituality is on sale. We visited the major aarati on our first evening and was greatly disappointed by the big show they performed. We could feel the lack of essence and naturalness of this event, which had been so evident in Hardwar. For some reason, this aarati triggered in Tara the most agonising and unbearable migraine that lasted for hours. Local fake sadhus rearranged themselves into sellers of yoga practices, spiritual teachings, guidance, or simply 'duplicates' of charas (bad quality charas) for westerners. Rishikesh was packed with young Jewish boys and girls escaping the army.

The highlight of our stay in Rishikesh was visit to Vasishta Guha (a cave) situated about twenty kilometres from Rishikesh. A relatively long tunnel leads to a wider cave opening. The energy within the heart of this massive rock is intense. The story says that one hundred of the sage Vasishta's children were killed by the rituals of black magic performed by Vasishta's rival, the sage Viswamitra. In grief, Vasishta decided to commit suicide in the Ganga river, but was refused by Goddess Ganga, who carried him safely unharmed and deposited him on the other bank where his wife Arundhati was waiting for her husband. They decided to go on a pilgrimage to south India, away from the tormenting memories of their killed sons, but on the way, they found the Guha in its peaceful location, and they stayed for a very long time, meditating and performing austerities.

Another sacred site worth visiting while in Rishikesh is Neelkanth Mahadev Temple situated on a hill, thirty-two kilometres from Rishikesh. According to Hindu mythology, the place where the Neelkanth Mahadev Temple currently stands is the sacred location where Lord Shiva, in order to save the living beings, consumed the poison that originated from the sea when Devas (Gods) and Asuras (Demons) churned the ocean to obtain Amrita (Divine Nectar). This poison that emanated during the churning of the ocean made Shiva's throat blue in colour. Thus, Lord Shiva is also known as Neelkanth, literally meaning 'The Blue Throated One'. We spent a day in this powerful place.

Soon, we decided to leave Rishikesh and go further north to the spiritual source of the Holy Ganga, the place of pilgrimage of many sadhus – Gangotri. But first we decided to stay in Uttarkashi (North Kashi). Kashi is another name for Varanasi or Benares. After five hours' drive, we arrived at this holy town. We immediately fell in love with Uttarkashi. The Ganga, which at this point is called the Bhagirathi, is very pure and mighty here. There are a few ancient temples in Uttarkashi. One of the temples; the Shakti temple, dedicated to Goddess Parvati is situated opposite the Vishwanath temple and has a giant trishul or trident six metres in height, which said to be thrown at the devils by Goddess Durga. This trishul is estimated to be one thousand five hundred years old. One of the amazing features of the trishul is that it cannot be moved with one's entire body force, but it vibrates the moment one applies pressure with one finger. It is also said that no one has been able to identify the metals from which the stambh is made though its globular base was created out of asht dhatu (eight metals). Wandering on the banks of the Ganga we met an Italian girl, Durgai Nath, with her

Italian companion Francesco. Durgai was initiated into the Nath Sampradaya tradition.

The Naths consider Adinatha (primal Nath), or Shiva, as their first guru with varying lists of additional gurus, starting with Matsyendranath and Gorakshnath. The legends say that Matsyendranath was born under an inauspicious star. His parents threw him into the ocean, where he was swallowed by a fish, in whose belly he lived for many years. One day the fish swam to the bottom of the ocean, where Shiva was imparting the secrets of yoga to His consort Parvati. Upon overhearing the teachings, Matsyendra began to practice yoga sadhana inside the fish's belly. After twelve years, he finally emerged as enlightened Siddha. Matsyendranath means 'lord of the fish'. Matsyendranath is considered to be the founder of hatha yoga. He is also related to the Kashmir Shaivism Kaula tradition and is credited with composing hatha and tantric works such as *Kaulajnananirnaya* (Discussion of the Knowledge pertaining to Kaula Tradition). Gorakshnath is believed to be the first disciple of Matsyendranath. He is also the founder of Nath Sampradaya and it is stated that the nine Naths and eighty-four Siddhas are all human forms created as yogic manifestations to spread the message of yoga and meditation to the world. It is they who reveal Samadhi to mankind. Gorakshnath is the author of *Goraksha Samhita* and *Siddha Siddhantha Paddhati*, which are considered to be one of the earliest scriptures on hatha yoga. *Siddha Siddhantha Paddhati* contains many verses which describe the avadhuta (liberated yogi). *Siddha Siddhantha Paddhati*, as I see it, is interconnected with the teachings of Kashmir Shaivism tradition. It includes quotes from various tantric texts, including *Lalita Svacchanda*, *Pratyabhijna*, and *Vamakeshvara Tantra*. Abhinavagupta of the Trika system of the Kashmir Shaivism tradition hails Matsyendranath as his guru in his epic work *Tantraloka*. The teachings of Gorakshnath harmoniously resonate with the teachings of Abhinavagupta.

Durgai introduced us to a small group of Nath yogis, who were gathering on the banks of the Ganga next to a small Shiva temple. I immediately felt an attraction and respect towards these Sadhus. I could feel the energy of wisdom, calmness and experience radiating from some of them. As one walks into a Sadhus' gathering, it is almost certain that one will be invited to participate in the smoking of a chillum. And there it was. Boom Shankar! A nice inhale of a good charas and I immediately went into Kumbhaka and Samadhi. A few minutes later I took a few steps towards Ganga Ma, to splash her Holy waters on my body, and then... I stopped...

My mind opened wide in the absence of thought, and became like an infinite, boundless, calm lake, permeating all and everything without any agitation whatsoever. I lost my ordinary particularised, focused vision, and discovered new panoramic vision without centre or periphery.

I am the embodiment of the totality. Ramana Maharshi says of 'Mauna' – the absolute inner silence, that it is not an effortless state of indolence. 'All mundane activities which are ordinarily called effort are performed with the aid of a portion of the mind and with frequent breaks. But the act of communion with the Self (atma vyavahara) or remaining still inwardly is an intense activity which is performed with the entire mind and without break. Maya (delusion or ignorance) which cannot be destroyed by any other act is completely destroyed by this intense activity which is called "silence" (Mauna)'[24].

This expanse of consciousness could be also called 'sattva' (clarity). In this state, one feels oneself as being all, containing all within one's own body of consciousness. It is not the final stage of realisation however, for the perception of the world appearance can be experienced only at certain frequencies. If the frequency of cognition accelerates and expands, the habitual world appearance gets shattered by the explosion of intelligence, firstly into the perception of abstraction, until consciousness leaps into a higher frequency domain. This expansion of consciousness, and beholding all at once (the surface, the reflection and the depth of the lake of mind) is very closely connected with the idea of expansive Vyana (fourth Prana) permeating all and gleaming with consciousness. The quantum leap into a new frequency domain (parallel reality), in which the habitual world is not perceived, could be associated with the Udana (fifth Prana), which according to Upanishads, at the moment of Death, following the Sushumna channel, takes a virtuous man into higher realms of infinite reality, a sinful one into lower realms, and both a virtuous and sinful one into rebirth on the

---

[24] "Collected Works of Ramana Maharshi" edited by Arthur Osborne.

Earthly plane. Udana abandons the lower senses one by one, withdraws itself from the object of perceptions, radically interiorises and enters the mysterious Singularity point (Bindu) in the centre of the black hole of one's Spiritual Heart.

After a few minutes of omnipresence, I returned to the sadhus' gathering. One of them asked me if I had been inside the temple yet. Tara and I enter the Temple. A natural Shiva lingam is located here, around which this temple was built, and it emanates Divine Energy of such tremendous power that we simply cannot stand. We fall to the floor in a humble prostration.

Namaskaram. Pranam. Om Nama Shivaya. Har Har Mahadev.

Rhythmic chanting of mantras with a full inhalation/exhalation cycle, followed by intense dynamic breathing leading to prolong repose in Kumbhaka (retention of breath) became my main practice in Uttarkashi. Deeper and deeper I was penetrating the mysteries of Prana with my practices of spontaneous pranayamas on the shores of Mother Ganga. Every evening we gathered with sadhus, where, after smoking chillum, I was sent into spontaneous Kumbhaka and Samadhi.

After Tara's birthday on 26th of April, which we celebrated with sadhus, we decided finally to go to the spiritual source of the Ganga – Gangotri. A very gentle and sweet one-legged sadhu, Santoshnath, asked to accompany us to Gangotri. A very dangerous road on the cliff edges finally brought us to Gangotri, after one stop at Gangnani, where we took a relaxing, warming dip in hot springs. Although I grew up in Russia and had experienced many times weather as cold as -30 Celsius, the cold in Gangotri was of a different sort. Due to a great humidity at -2 Celsius in Gangotri, the cold was penetrating the marrow of our bones. The main temple wasn't open yet and masses of pilgrims were expected only in the beginning of May. Three of us stayed one freezing night in a room with no windows. Tara was shocked by the dense cloud of steam from her urine when she went for a wee. Yes, it was bloody freezing, but at the same time the roar of the Ganga, the raw power of this magical place was immense and transformative. Somewhere around five o'clock in the morning it started snowing. The roaring Ganga, mountains, softly falling snowflakes; it was breathtakingly beautiful.

Back to Beloved Mother India

Abandoning the idea to go further to the actual source of Ganga – the glacier called Gomukh (Cow's Mouth) – we decided to return to Uttarkashi. Even our sadhu friend Santoshnath thought that it would be a wise decision to go back to Uttarkashi and return to Gangotri sometime later together with the other pilgrims. Although it was very cold, I couldn't miss the chance to take a dip in the freezing roaring waters of the Ganga at Her spiritual source.

Oh, Ganga Ma! May your holy waters cleanse my entire being, may your holy waters wash away all my sins, may your holy waters return me to my primal purity.

Fully clothed, wearing a woolly hat and gloves, Santoshnath was astonished to see me (the crazy Russian) jumping naked into the Ganga's waters. Tarananda had already gotten used to my swims in the cold winter sea of the Isle of Wight. So, she just kept smiling. After traveling back to Uttarkashi, Haridwar and Delhi, in the beginning of May we returned to England.

Somewhere at the end of summer, while staying with Tara in her 'Aruna' cottage on the Isle of Wight, I received an unpleasant surprise from London. Our landlord, without notifying me, had forcefully evicted us from his flat. My London flatmate informed me that all our belongings had been removed from the flat and piled under the stairs near the front door. I urgently went to London to save some of my belongings. I brought the most valuable things and documents with me back to Tarananda. Another friend of mine suggested to me that I immediately claim that I was homeless. The government had to provide me with temporary accommodation. I still had genuine sciatica problems, and although most of the time the pain was under control, occasionally after an unusual body movement, or after lifting something, or simply after loud sneezing, I could be almost paralysed for a day or two. I also went to the orthopaedic hospital to make a scan of my vertebral column. The result of the scan was that one of my intervertebral discs was damaged and was occasionally pressing on my sciatic nerve. And so, now I was claiming income support and incapacity benefits. Spending a day in an office dealing with homelessness, I was granted temporary accommodation, a room on Holloway Road. Being a recipient of the incapacity and income support benefits, helped my prospects for re-housing, when I began to live in temporary accommodation in London. Most people who live in temporary accommodation are waiting for rehousing. When suitable properties become vacant, people living in temporary accommodation will be invited to move in, depending on how many points they have got on a points system. Obviously, living in a temporary accommodation requires one to be present there. One must be visible.

Margarita

y story would not be complete if I didn't mention yet another girl whom I admired and desired for nearly twelve years. Her name was Margarita. I met her when I joined the Fellowship of Friends in 1995. From my very first meeting with her, she charmed me with her delicate beauty, and her enigmatic, mysterious, poetic, sophisticated flirtation. She was always a bright star at the gatherings, around whom, like around the sun, other planets (admirers) were circling. To me, she seemed to be out of my league. She had graduated from a prestigious university and hung out with famous counter-culture writers and musicians. What the heck she would do with simple village folk like me? The more we began to know each other however, the more our attraction to each other grew. I felt deeply connected not only to her body, or personality, but to her very soul. It seemed to me that in her presence, my sensitivity heightened to a degree in which I could touch and blend with her gentle soul. Specifically, I could feel this gentle touch of her soul love, when I was reading poetry or speaking words of truth from the heart. The more she allowed me, the more I was falling in love with her. But she kept her distance, and I didn't dare advance. Our love and passion began to fully blossom when my girlfriend Lena was already a few months pregnant. I remember one evening when I invited a few friends for an evening of poetry at our little flat. After a few glasses of red wine, I read my first honest poetry, which I had written that day, to my friends. Everyone was deeply touched, especially Margarita.

Through feeling poetry, one can look into the very heart of a poet, connect with the poet's soul, and through the heart and soul of a real poet one feels one's own heart, one awakes to one's Love, which is always glowing within one's beautiful heart. Real poetry, that touches and awakens souls, comes from utmost honesty with oneself. It comes from those, who know, or are in suffering, pain and contradiction, but who don't moan and complain, but instead, turn this unbearable pain into love and gratitude. The lover is always searching for ways to undress Love, to strip all clothes and fig leaves from his/her beautiful Soul, for his nakedness is Beauty and the precious Gift. He searches for the most beautiful garland of letters to express his beauty. It often happens, that when he cannot find the appropriate words, unable to express his Love, he dresses himself in tears. These sweet tears are the messengers of his beautiful Soul, they are the pearls of Love.

'The Soul is unbelievably beautiful. We cannot see its beauty with our gross vision, but we can feel its touch upon our own Soul in rare moments of utmost openness and nakedness. And when these two naked Souls meet and touch, it takes our breath away. Has anyone seen how Souls experiencing orgasms, how quiver in love ecstasy these extremely sensitive beings? I know it only in you. I want to pour on you streams of my love, make you drunk with my happiness. With you I am drunk on Love. And if I am drunk, you will get drunk also. My wine is my Soul, my Soul is your Soul. I got drunk on Love again today by thinking of you. My Soul is a drunkard addicted to your wine,' I wrote after this poetry evening. The next evening, we kissed. *'My teasing goddess let me taste the nectar from her lips and drink love-light from her eyes. All roads disappeared except heaven. I became her slave, wishing nothing but her love.'* Well, I was hopelessly in love. Hopelessly, because she got engaged to a F.O.F. student from London and was soon leaving for Chicago, where Ivan was temporarily working and where they were planning to get married and live.

When Rita left for the U.S., I was reflecting thus: this is love, and it's beautiful, but with the passing of time, as we live apart, this beautiful love will calm down and gradually disappear. What can I do to feed my love? I don't want this love to die. It's too precious. I can keep writing poetry, I thought, it will feed the burning fire of my love. But what if I don't have a talent for poetry?

I know! I can wake up every morning half an hour earlier than I usually do, and run; run for my Love, run with only one aim in mind and heart to fuel Love. And every day for the next two or three months I ran for my Love. A little sacrifice of our comfort for some higher aim is a wonderful and very practical idea.

In yoga, the sacrifice of one's comfort for the sake of union (Yoga) with the Beloved can take an extreme degree and one's sadhana (spiritual practice) can turn into an intense Tapas, which could be translated as 'spiritual heat'. Many yogic and tantric scriptures would say that there is nothing that cannot be achieved through intense Tapas. Any boons are granted by Gods to those who perform Tapas in devotion to them.

I can now say that my 'running for love' somehow gently reshaped the unfolding of my life story. Almost whenever I went, Rita was there. I was traveling in Italy with Teacher and attended evening meeting with students in Florence – Rita was there. We had a sweet love-walk-talk-kiss on the night streets of Florence. When I was serving my time in the French prison, we were writing letters to each other. I went to California to see Tina, and Rita was there. I moved to London and Rita was living there with Ivan just forty minutes away from our place. So, we often saw each other in various places in London. Me and Tina often stayed overnight at Ivan and Rita's apartment in Muswell Hill. When I left the Fourth Way school and fell in love with Maya, we had a dinner in our Moscow apartment kindly rented to us by our friend. Rita was in Moscow and was invited for dinner. Maya loved and respected Rita and looked to her as at a woman of wisdom and was eager to talk to her or seek advice. After splitting with Ivan, Rita came with her new boyfriend, to visit Tara and me on the Isle of Wight for couple of days. I had a couple of mushroom journeys with her and her boyfriend, while being in London, and so on....

Now that I was living in temporary accommodation for the homeless, Rita returned to London from Russia without a husband or boyfriend. After ten years of our loving friendly playful relationship, she finally was free, and our love was rekindled with new force. Love like a magnet forced us into each other's arms. Love has so many epithets and states. She can be sweet, or painful. She can be blind and unfair. She can hurt deeply. She can make one forget morals and taboos. She can make one her hopeless slave. She can invoke painful jealousy or make one angry. I caused so much pain and suffering to Tara by my decision to stay with Rita.

Margarita

My search for the perfect woman hadn't ended yet and now that Rita was available and loving, after so many years of desiring her, I thought that my search was over. I had finally come together with my soulmate. We lived together for a couple of months. With the passage of time it became more evident to me however, that although she loved me, she was still searching for someone with money. She longed for security, which I couldn't offer, living as homeless in a temporary accommodation. Meanwhile, I was regularly receiving beautiful letters from Tara with copies of pages from *Yoga Vasishta*, which I regarded as very deep and profound teachings on the true nature of Reality. A couple of days before St. Valentine's day, Rita told me that she was going on a date with a rich and handsome guy whom she had found through a dating agency. And that was the end of our brief sweet life together. On the 14th of February – the 'day of lovers', begging for forgiveness, I returned to Tara. Of course, I had caused her great pain, but with her beautiful loving heart she forgave me and took me back.

Satsang

After further medical examination in London, I was granted incapacity and housing benefits. I found a suitable one-bedroom flat not far from Finsbury Park tube station, the rent for which was paid by the government.

The next summer Tarananda invited Muz Murray (Ramana baba) to stay with us and to lead three days of mantra yoga workshops on the Isle of Wight. Chanting mantras accompanied by pranayamas for three days in a row, without a doubt, purifies the space of consciousness from the contamination of thought and doubt, and Nadi's system (subtle energy channels) from toxins, clogs and emotional blockages. The light of Consciousness shines and the energy of Prana flows freely and harmoniously after this amazing purification. Without offence, I must say that while I enjoyed Muz's mantra yoga enormously, I wasn't very fond of his satsangs. I had attended a few in Tiruvannamalai before and wasn't impressed back then either. There was nothing wrong with his satsangs, but they were in a format of questions and answers and for me the satsang is not about getting answers, but solely about the transmission and awakening of conscious energy – the real teacher.

Being a student of Robert Taylor, I knew how powerful and revelational satsangs could be. I had realised a long time ago that there is not much benefit in intellectual answers to intellectual questions. However profound these questions and answers might be, they can only be labels, or pointers at best. They do not reveal the Truth but create an illusion of understanding. The information received through intellectual answers stays on the same intellectual level only. Satsang, which could be translated as 'association with Truth' or 'abidance in Truth' or 'being together in Truth', requires utmost honesty, total openness and courage not only to talk about God and Truth, but to allow God –Truth – to speak through one's mouth, and radiate God from one's heart, to be God, to be the Truth. Satsang requires courage to rise above the illusion of separateness, see and feel everyone and all as oneself. Satsang is an open invitation to leave behind comforting but limiting objective knowledge and plunge into the intense and often frightening energy of the unknown. More than anything else, satsang is the release of spiritual energy from the clutches of fear, ignorance and sleep. It is heart-to-heart talk. Satsang is the gentle touch and encouragement to open and to blossom the lotuses of everyone's hearts – the thrones of True Knowledge.

Spiritual Energy (Shakti) is the Guru here, not the words. The real answers are not the words, but the revelations. The best satsang could be described as Shaktipat – the transmission of Shakti (spiritual energy) from the teacher and awakening of Shakti in aspirants. Jnana (True knowledge) cannot be brought from somewhere outside, for it abides in everyone's Spiritual Heart (Hrt, Hrdayam – the centre). The leader of a Satsang must awaken himself first to the abidance in Truth and God's Presence. To be able to transmit the energy, he/she must raise his/her own vibrations and state of consciousness. To speak of God and Truth from the lower state of consciousness is a lie. At best it can be done only from memory. But the real satsang is the shaking off of conceptual reality, leaving behind the past with its memory and future with its imagination, stripping off the tight clothes of objective knowledge and abiding in the thought free Nowness full of God, Truth and Love. 'When you are in love, where do you want to be? I want to be with my Beloved. Your Beloved is Here!' The leader of the satsang needs to ask all gathered to help him/her with their attention, efforts and trust. The satsang is not about words, but about energy. Shakti (Supreme Energy) is the surest guide to Shiva (Supreme Intelligence).

It became Tara and my daily routine to read a few pages of *Yoga Vasishta* every morning. What makes *Yoga Vasishta* so fascinating are the countless incredible stories within the stories, worlds within worlds, manifestations of infinite possibilities of infinite consciousness, which would seem highly improbable for the rational mind. *Yoga Vasishta* points again and again to the fact that Supreme Intelligence – Infinite Consciousness is the inexhaustible flood of creativity. The nature of Reality is Infinity. There is nothing impossible for Infinite Consciousness. Everything is possible, regardless of the opinions of the finite rational mind. As the nature of Reality is Infinity, so is its realisation. The illusion that one can arrive at Self-Realisation and just stop there in peace and repose contradicts the infinite nature of Reality. Self-realisation is a never-ending journey from ecstasy to far greater depths of ecstasy.

1.21 Gigawatts into a Flux Capacitor

E very autumn on the Isle of Wight I looked forward to mushroom season. What new lessons would I receive from these amazing gurus? My shamanic journeys that autumn included one in which Tom York from 'Radiohead', guided me into the higher dimensions while I was meditating to his solo album 'Eraser', and another one under the influence of a staggering 30g of dry liberty caps' (around 800-900 medium sized mushrooms) (For reference; Terence Mckenna speaks of 5g of dry psilocybin as a 'heroic dose'.) At the end of this, all the pieces of the jigsaw fell into place, and I lost the world and experienced pure intelligence prior to the world appearance.

One journey I would like to describe in greater detail. After ingesting around seven hundred dry magic mushrooms (approximately 25g), I resolved not to close my eyes throughout the entire duration of the journey. Instead I fixed my gaze on one spot and actively engaged my peripheral vision. This practice, quite similar to the Fourth Way practice of dividing attention' is named 'Bhairava Mudra' in yoga treatises.

Bhairava mudra was regarded in the tantras as the ultimate mudra. It is that inner comportment through which, by simultaneous identification with outer and inner spaces of awareness, one comes to experience awareness itself as one singular space of awareness – a unified field of awareness embracing everything we can experience within it, both inwardly and outwardly, including both thoughts and things, emotions and

218

material bodies, sensual qualities of awareness and the sensory qualities of objects.

'As taught in the sacred tradition, he enters the Bhairava mudra in which all his senses are widely open simultaneously, but the attention is turned within as described in the following verse: Attention should be turned inwards; the gaze should be turned outwards, without the twinkling of the eyes. This is the mudra pertaining to Bhairava, kept secret in all the tantras. He sees the totality of objects appearing and disappearing in the ether of his consciousness like a series of reflections appearing and disappearing in a mirror. Instantly all his thought constructs are split asunder by the recognition, after a thousand lives, of his essential nature surpassing common experience and full of unprecedented bliss. He is struck with amazement, as though entering the mudra of amazement. As he obtains the experience of vast expansion, suddenly his proper, essential nature comes to the fore.'[25]

'If you project the vision and all the other powers [of the senses] simultaneously, everywhere... by the power of awareness, whilst remaining firmly established in the centre like a pillar of gold, you shine as the One, the foundation of the universe'[26]

As soon as the mushrooms began to do their magic, our cat Merry entered the room. I immediately realised that I could not exclude her from my consciousness, and with all my will, expanded awareness and intelligence, I embraced her as being part of my Self. This sort of conscious effort opened my awareness to the possibility of inclusion of the totality of existence in my being. I started to feel responsible for everything that was ever created, for at this moment of expanded awareness, I realised myself with utmost clarity as the Creator of all apparent manifestations. Rapidly and deeply breathing, I was embracing all in its totality, including the horrendous suffering of war, wounded soldiers, raped women, tortured prisoners etc. As the Creator I felt totally responsible for all the suffering in my creation.

At that time, a few volcanoes were erupting and sending clouds of ash into the atmosphere, making it impossible to fly between

---

[25] "Spanda Karikas" Ksemaraja.
[26] "Kaksyasotra"

1.21 Gigawatts into a Flux Capacitor

England and Europe. Many people were stranded. Somehow, I felt great pity for those people who were unable to see their loved ones. In my vision I connected with the core of Planet Earth, the Heart of Mother Gaya. At the same time, I connected to the countless spiritual centres around the globe with a silent call and the intention to send collective harmonious energy to calm the volcanoes.

Highly intense unstoppable spontaneous pranayama enhanced by compassion and empathy for all my creation and the desire to release all humanity from suffering, created uneasiness and pains in the organs of my body. My body was begging me to stop, or slow down the breathing, but my will was strong enough to continue. Visuals appeared before me from the comedy I had recently watched, starring Simon Pegg; *Run Fatboy Run*. In the marathon Simon Pegg 'hits the wall' – the expression meaning the athlete gets out of breath and loses the will to proceed any further. In this funny comedy an actual wall of bricks appears before Simon Pegg. In flashbacks, he sees the episodes of his past failures, in which he was always running away from his fears, problems and difficulties. Somehow, however, he finds the willpower to break through the wall. This was also my experience at this moment. I 'hit the wall'! Feeling immense pain and suffering, my body was crying to me to stop this torture.

Another episode from a recently-watched movie appeared to my inner vision. Now, it was *Back to the Future*. Just before their first departure into the future, Doc explains that he needs plutonium to trigger a nuclear reaction to generate 1.21 gigawatts in his flux capacitor. And I also felt that I needed the energy of nuclear power to break through the wall. This power was extracted from the pain and suffering I was experiencing at that moment, as also from my willpower to proceed with the intense breathing. I broke through this imaginary wall and found great ease and fun.

The next episode from *Back to the Future* appeared to my inner vision: Doc returns from the future in a modified car with the new flux capacitor that no longer requires plutonium but uses rubbish as energy, including a half-drunk beer and a beer can. I now felt that, while just a few minutes ago I had needed nuclear power to break through the wall, I was now capable of turning all rubbish into energy. And the suffering and the pain of my creation turned into a source of energy, joy and love. The centre of gravity of my

1.21 Gigawatts into a Flux Capacitor

consciousness zoomed to the outskirts of our solar system from where I could observe Planet Earth floating in space. She appeared to me very fragile, on the brink of great catastrophe. It was clear to me that humanity must awaken now from their carelessness and greed to save our beautiful planet and itself.

Without closing my eyes, established in Bhairava mudra, I proceeded with the intense pranayama without any rest whatsoever for six hours straight. If you've done any practice of pranayama, my dear friend, you probably can imagine my expanded state after six hours of non-stop intense dynamic breathing, fuelled by the energy of seven hundred liberty caps!

My body and mind melted in the ecstasy of Truth. I become the pure energy. My breathing itself transformed into streams of liquid Love – Divine Amrit. As Pranic energy, which at this point became a flow of liquid Love, was moving through the channels of my body, purifying all Nadi's system and the space of my consciousness, she also forced my fingers move in certain patterns forming what is known in yoga as 'mudras' (seals). Together with the formation of mudras, my whole body went into the spontaneous formation of unbelievable yogic 'asanas' (postures). At one point this awakened Prana-Kundalini energy brought my body into the very unusual but extremely comfortable posture, which I can only compare to a sort of a rocking chair. I tried to recreate this asana next day without success. This shamanic trance with the spontaneous movements of my body and its parts forming yogic asanas and mudras, became a major feature of my mushroom journeys.

Tara, who occasionally came to check on me during these shamanic journeys, told me later that she thought I did not need mushrooms any longer, for now I had developed a shamanic trance technique which could take me into the highest realms, even without the need of psilocybin.

Out of many other shamanic experimentations of this autumn, I remember one journey in a 'cartoon universe' just like in a computer-simulated reality. The lesson I learned in this trip is that life is not only a dream, but a game also. I was playing a character like the one of Mario in the *Super Mario* games. I was collecting points (good deeds, right choices) and by reaching certain amounts, was plunging into different parallel realities with new possibilities.

221

1.21 Gigawatts into a Flux Capacitor

By losing points (doing bad deeds, making wrong choices, or not learning lessons) I had to run extra miles of circles as a penalty, just like how in a biathlon, the athlete who misses the target must run an extra circle. On yet another journey I had visions, possibly from my previous lives. In this journey I was a rower on some sort of boat. My body was completely covered in intricate tattoos, seemingly Mayan in nature.

The Mysterious Language of Chemistry

From our ordinary macroscopic point of view, we have a body with a pair of eyes and ears, we have a nose and mouth, pair of hands and legs, we have one heart, two hemispheres of brain and few other inner organs. But if we zoom within, we will see that on the next inner level we have 37.2 trillion cells, all operating by their own laws and having their own likes and dislikes, their own games, and their own lifespans. Virtually every cell in the body is covered with thousands of receptors. The function of a receptor is to pick up signals coming from surrounding space. Once the receptor received signal it initiates cells interior into action. Cell division and growth, cell migration for attacking the enemies and making repairs and cell metabolism to preserve or release energy are just a few of the receptor-activated functions. The signals from the other cells carried to receptors by the streams of informational substance. The streams of information substance from brain, gut, sexual organs, heart and all other organs of body-cosmos communicate cell to cell having a "conversation" within the body-mind. These information juices known to us as hormones, neurotransmitters and peptides are also known as "ligands", which means "to bind". Each receptor, just like a lock and a key is specifically shaped to receive only one particular ligand. Information carrying ligands perform ninety eight percent of all data transfer in our psychosomatic inner universe. Remaining two percent of communication takes place at the synapse between brain cells. Such ligands as peptides consisting of the chain of amino acids trigger complex emotional cords such as

223

bliss, anger, joy, hunger, apathy, relaxation or satiety when their signal is received by the cell. Receptors covering the cell are not sitting there immovably, but constantly changing from one configuration to the other, creating by their movements a vibratory field for ligands to find them. This dance of receptors creates a cellular resonance attracting ligands which vibrates on the same frequency.

At the next level within, we find that cells consist of seven billion billion billion (seven with twenty-seven zeros) atoms combining themselves into the structures which we call molecules. From this perspective, our body is truly a universe.

Regardless of whether we like it or not, chemistry or biochemistry is of great importance if we are trying to understand Reality. Chemistry is the language of molecules and atoms in a constant dance of exchange and transactions. Chemistry is intimately connected with electricity. Chemistry triggers our emotions. Chemistry is the inner language that defines our perceptions. If we are searching for Truth, we should not close our eyes on the subject of chemistry, part of which is commonly known as 'drugs'. We should not shut down our openness and willingness to experiment with it, just because we are frightened, uncomfortable, or embarrassed to see people 'out of their heads', or because we have been brainwashed by those with 'power' to whom the explosion of intelligence, and therefore liberation from the clutches of fear, could appear as a real threat.

The body itself is a chemical and alchemical factory, receiving food, air and impressions, separating gross and subtle elements, and transforming them into more refined substances and energies, even into those subtle structures, which could be a building blocks of a new life. Chemistry is a psychosomatic organic language, far more intimate than our verbal language. Even falling in love, or the experience of ecstasy, or greater clarity is the work of this 'chemical language'. Chemical substances can swing our mood, make us ill, or healthy, make us happy, sad, euphoric or paranoid, purify our spiritual vision, or make it dim and unclear, sharpen our intellect, or plunge it into dullness and darkness, make us slaves, kill, or liberate us.

Words cannot make such an impression and connection between two people, as chemistry can. One glance into the eyes of

The Mysterious Language of Chemistry

a very special person can trigger a huge chemical process, which can leave one unable to sleep. Some substances can open gates to overwhelming intimacy that one could never have imagined was possible. The knowledge we receive by the means of words cannot compare even an iota with the direct experience, which we can receive through the grace of sacred plants, and 'spirit molecules'. The chemical language could be a key to unlocking the 'doors of perception' to the realms of reality far more real than our so ironically called 'waking state'. According to some scientific speculations and propositions, even our perceptions of reality itself depends on the level of DMT in our pineal gland, bloodstream, or brain. The additional amount of DMT can take our consciousness into the different realms of Infinite Reality, often far more intense and real than our usual perception of the 'human channel'.

Even ancient Vedas gives us whole chapters, hymns and mandalas praising 'Soma' – the nectar of gods. One could meditate for years, and then have all one's previous understanding of reality be thrown upside down within a matter of minutes under the influence of these extremely powerful teachers. Not that meditation should be abandoned in favour of the wisdom of sacred plants, but they should be made companions in the quest for Self-exploration and Self-knowledge. Most shamans plunge themselves into the inner realms of reality and bring healing energy to people around them with the help of sacred plants. Experimenting with sacred plants, one begins to experience and know directly the inner dimensions of Prana. Plants teach one how to breathe and take one into the 'possession' (Samavesha) by Goddess Shakti Herself, who is none other than Supreme Intelligence Energy or The Highest Reality. If we are truly wholeheartedly longing for the Beloved Truth, then we must open ourselves to the teachings of this incredible chemical language.

Unfortunately, many different substances, with different (sometimes opposite) effects on our wellbeing are called by the same name in our society: 'drugs'. By the gift of our intelligence we must carefully discriminate between the substances which can bring us into their slavery and substances which can help to break our addictions – substances which can liberate us, or at least show us the possibility of liberation.

The Mysterious Language of Chemistry

I have known people with heroin addictions. The depth of their slavery to this substance was shocking. Heroin robbed them of the qualities which make us truly human, such as courage, honesty, care, love. It seemed as though their very light was stolen from them. I have seen nothing uglier and more pitiful than the lies of a heroin addict born out of fear of being find out - a cowardice afraid to face the truth. Heroin robbed them of moral values. Hiding from the light of truth, they used any excuse, to avoid pain. The combination of the euphoria and deep relaxation of heroin makes people feel on top of the world and provides a lucrative escape from the emotional pain and stress of everyday life. Using heroin on a consistent basis is thought to change the functioning of the opioid receptors so that when a person stops using it, they experience anxiety, muscle spasms, insomnia, and general sickness. And so, often they get trapped in this vicious circle of heroin slavery. If a person attempts to get off heroin, or other strong opiates, he could be prescribed methadone for replacement therapy. Many people visit methadone clinics and get relief from the drug but end up becoming nearly as addicted to methadone as they did to the original opioid that caused them problems. Heroin, amphetamines, benzodiazepines, GHB, cocaine and crack cocaine, crystal meth, OxyContin, alcohol and nicotine are considered to be the most addictive drugs.

MDMA (ecstasy), which can be very useful and beneficial in many aspects, such as shedding the crust of personality and opening the heart and senses to the experience of far greater intimacy, or as a healing tool for post-traumatic stress disorder, if taken often on a regular basis for a long period of time can also become addictive. Cannabis (marijuana), which can also be very useful for spiritual insights, meditation and even yoga, can in some cases trigger paranoia and loss of short-term memory and also become an addiction if smoked (not for a spiritual purpose) often for a long period of time.

Psychedelic substances, specifically psilocybin mushrooms, DMT, mescaline/peyote, ayahuasca and ibogaine, which ironically are known by the same name 'drugs', on the contrary, are not only non-addictive, but can often be the only means of breaking an addiction to heavy drugs. In recent years, ayahuasca retreats have become a very popular means of looking deeply within one's psyche and bringing psychological and emotional healing by purging oneself of accumulated psychological impurities. Mother Ayahuasca, which is known among shamans as 'medicine', together with the psilocybin mushrooms have at their core N, N-dimethyltryptamine (DMT), which Rick Strassman coined as the 'Spirit Molecule'. Rick Strassman also said that he likes to think of psilocybin, whose molecular structure is very close to the structure of DMT, as 'oral DMT'. Of course, it would be hugely beneficial to look in great detail into the exact mechanics of the molecular dance, that triggers non-ordinary states of consciousness, but as I mentioned earlier, I do not have sufficient education in this department. Therefore, I don't want to speculate on this subject, which requires precision, nor do I want to reproduce quotes from 'Wikipedia' on this subject. And so, I would rather stick to what I know through my own experiences and the revelations received from these incredible molecular teachers.

The time arrived this autumn to have my first experiments with DMT!

Astonishing DMT World

Just like Dorothy, picked up by the magical tornado, leaves behind a colourless world and finds herself in dazzlingly colourful Oz, filled with the bizarre elf-like munchkins, flying monkeys, witches, and unbelievable adventures, so it was with the inhalation of DMT vapour. The dim light of the so familiar world was switched off in a matter of seconds and a new brilliant psychedelic light of inner intelligence was turned on instead.

Regardless of how masterfully and artistically one tries to describe this DMT world, our bleak human imagination in its ordinary condition is simply unable to transmit or grasp the true magnitude of this miracle.

Wow!

Who could ever imagine that such things are possible?

What I am experiencing now is simply beyond belief and imagination!

And all this is not projected from any external sources, but is a marvellous display of my own consciousness, the magnificent ability of my own, hidden 'til this point, higher level of intelligence.

'Hallucinations'- a sceptic would dismiss this experience in one 'explanatory' word.

However, in comparison with the dim light of our familiar human world, the bright, astonishing, shocking DMT world is surely far more real.

Those who have experienced it would never dismiss it as hallucination.

Astonishing DMT World

The astonishment of the DMT experience gives one a new perspective on the world in which we seem to be living; one of the low-frequency domains of Infinite Reality, practically unreal.

The effect of DMT is almost instantaneous. It's a very short-lived experience in human measures of time, lasting only around ten to fifteen minutes, but is one which might alter our complete ontology. As soon as you start to inhale your first vapours of DMT, you already begin to feel very peculiar and suspicious. It seems although all the air gets pumped out of the room and you start to feel a strange anaesthesia. One must be courageous enough at this point to take a second drag. It is always good to have someone nearby to assist you, for it often happens that one is not able even to put one's pipe down after the second or third drag. I have heard many people are unable to proceed at this point, and although they might have an interesting, fascinating, colourful trip, they don't fully break through the psychedelic threshold. To fully break through, one needs to take a third and, if possible, a fourth good drag. Accompanied with a rustling, crackling sound, sort of like the crumbling of a plastic bread wrapper, one gets propelled into a chrysanthemum mandala, at the end of which there is a sensation of bursting through some sort of membrane. On the other side of which, there are astonishing three-dimensional computer-like animations, but at the same time there is a solid three-dimensional world, in which you perceive a thousand details per second. Everyone, of course, has their own unique experience on DMT, but there are also features, which those who have been there can surely relate to, and which cannot be understood or visualised otherwise. As it is almost impossible to bring all the memories of such an immensely rich experience to our 'normal waking' state, one needs to experience it again and again to be able to describe it, or at least capture the essence of it. My first experience of DMT is almost identical with the wonderful description of Terence McKenna's DMT trip. I wouldn't be able to describe it better, and I can relate to everything he is describing here.

Terence Mckenna masterfully describes quintessence of his thirty or forty DMT trips. He stresses that his DMT world was not a some sort of a 'state of mind', but a real place (a rounded room) which seemed to be located somewhere underground, filled with self-transforming-machine-language elves, self-transforming jewel-basketball-like things, who were very excited to greet him upon his arrival, pounding forward like badly-trained dogs, cheering, dribbling, rolling, jumping up and down, jumping into his chest, and then jumping back out. "They possessed an astonishing array of language, which is completely alien to us. They produced language that you could see. They could condense meaning before your very eyes. For them, syntax was not made up of acoustical rules, but rather pictorial rules. Via language they created objects into existence, which they offered as gifts. They jumped excitedly, saying, 'Look at this! Look at this!' And as your attention went into these things, your emotions were indescribable. These objects were made of gold, ivory, smaragdite, chalcedonies, beryllium, flesh, blood, tears, and it was all-changing, morphing, transforming itself as you looked at it. And as you looked at these things, you had not an iota of doubt that if you could bring these things across, it would end human history. Arguments would cease if you could just say, 'Look! Look at this!' And they were pushing each other away, saying: 'Look at this one, look at this one.' These objects themselves were in mid-sound and made other objects. The whole thing was going on in an atmosphere of hilarity and confusion.

It's now been one minute, since you left your friends in that badly furnished apartment. Naturally, the fact that you are having this experience, raises certain fundamental questions, such as: am I dead now? Is that what happened? And the entities say: don't give way to amazement. Don't flip out about how you cannot believe it and that it is impossible, and so forth. Don't do that. Just pay attention. Pay attention to what we are doing, and what we are showing to you. And what they preach is a new dispensation of language – language that can be beheld. As you sit there, you feel like a bubble is forming in your stomach and beginning to make its way to your mouth. And when it comes out as a kind of a glossolalia, you discover that in that space you too can make jewelled objects with spinning interiors, reflexively rotating subthemes and so for. All driven by the kind of glossolalia that is very spontaneous and indescribable, but fortunately doable. And when the time nears to leave this incredible world, they all wave goodbye and the last thing you hear is the word 'Deja vu'".[27]

---

[27] Terence McKenna (The DMT Experience. YouTube)

Astonishing DMT World

On my first DMT trip, I experienced almost exactly what Terence McKenna described. Somewhere in the middle of this mind-blowing adventure however, my previous practice of Self-inquiry let itself known to me. I found that, even in the midst of such unbelievable things, it is possible to inquire into the Self. So long as there are any sorts of appearances of any sort of objective reality there must be a perceiver. Who, or what is it? What am I, who is cognising these appearances? Self-inquiry is not just a question of 'who am I?'. The question 'who am I?' serves as the starting point, which gives direction for attention to follow. As this question was raised and my awareness turned towards its source, the sense of identity, the sense of 'I' – the seer – began to drift somewhere to the left in this space and gradually evaporated. And now, there was just is-ness without any I-ness. Pure experiencing – knowing without the 'me' – the knower. In the next instance though, I felt my Spiritual Heart. I am The Heart – Hrt – Hrdayam – the Centre. And I felt as though red carpets were thrown into my Spiritual Heart and I as Shiva – the Lord of all existence, was walking on this carpet towards the centre – the Source. The air was filled with Divine music played by gandharvas and other angelic beings. All sorts of celestial creatures were gathering for the biggest celebration. The atmosphere was one of utter joy. After countless reincarnations, after a long time of self-imposed exile, after all deeply-rooted beliefs in life stories, I – Shiva – God Absolute, was marching within, towards the most beautiful Beloved Truth – the Real Self. What can be higher than that? What can be more rewarding than that? This is the ultimate joy! Bliss! Happiness! The Unborn One, temporarily under the spell of Maya Shakti was experiencing one's self as being born, shaking off this spell, and coming to the ultimate realisation! The return of the Sovereign ruler Shiva to his incomparable Kingdom of Ultimate Freedom, Bliss, Love and Beauty is the quintessence of search, the quintessence of purpose and meaning, the quintessence of joy. The whole cosmos rejoiced! The return of Shiva to his unparalleled kingdom of ecstasy propelled the whole cosmos into the wildest, maddest, outrageous party ever!

On returning from the dazzling DMT dimension to our familiar world, seeing the faces of Tara and my friend Eduard spinning and flashing at the beginning and then gradually coming into focus, there was a strange sensation of returning to the insignificant and long-forgotten world of shadows.

On my next journey, which happened just a couple of hours later, I had encounters with an alien intelligence in the form of silver bees. Three of them were hovering above the region of my Spiritual Heart. It was difficult to say if they were friendly or evil. I would say that they were rather indifferent to me, but they were undoubtedly interested in what was happening within the nucleus of my Spiritual Heart. When I was reaching the point, which can only be described as the death of the ego, they reached the greatest proximity to my Spiritual Heart nucleus. I realised they were waiting for the moment of my death.

There exist many reports of encounters with the alien insectoid type of intelligence during DMT trips. Ants, praying mantises, bees and so on. Some individuals have even been taken into the alien beehives.

On another occasion I was stuck in a place where I was surrounded by the letters of an unknown alphabet, symbols and numbers. I don't think I fully broke through the psychedelic threshold this time. These letters, numbers and symbols occupied the entire space of consciousness, preventing any of my attempts to move further or out. I called them 'tathagatas', for they reminded me the description of tathagatas' from the *Tibetan Book of The Dead*. They just were sitting there, very hostile, preventing any sort of escape. And just as the tathagatas from the *Bardo Thodol* are described as a 'peaceful', or 'wrathful' blood-drinking deities, I felt the same suspiciousness about these letters and symbols. Although I had the realisation that all these letters and symbols were essentially the projection of my mind and as such were not different from myself, yet there was something frightening in their nature and they also seemed to be independent of me. They were teasing and playing games with my mind. I stayed for a long time in the retention of breath, but now, in order to shift my attention, I began to breathe rapidly. I came to the realisation that the only way to break through this screen of symbols was death – the ultimate and complete annihilation of the sense of 'me'.

I must mention here that what I also discovered during these astonishing adventures into different realms of Infinite Reality, is that how breathing affects the state of your consciousness, even if you seem to be out of your 'normal' mind and separate from your body. My regular practice of pranayama and especially Kumbhaka (retention of breath) gave me a great advantage in the investigation of parallel realities. It happened automatically, that after inhaling the last vapours of DMT, I immediately went into a very firm Kumbhaka and stayed there for a good three to four minutes. I noticed later that regardless how far out your consciousness is, the movements of prana drag the attention back from the incredible DMT world to the sensations of the body.

Despite the unbelievable, astounding nature of all my previous DMT ventures, a thousand-fold magnitude of amazement in comparison to all my previous experiences happened to me a few weeks later. This time I decided to prepare myself better for the sacred journey into the higher realms. I did three days of complete fasting, accompanied by continuous meditation with dynamic intuitive pranayama. Although it is believed by some that fasting and other preliminary spiritual practices are not essential for the quality of the DMT trips, I found this opinion false. I am absolutely sure that sincere efforts and sacrifices towards the Beloved Truth set a favourable ground for the actual DMT experience. And so, even before smoking DMT, I already felt extremely high and thoroughly purified.

I took three deep drags, breathed in, locked my bandhas, and got established in a firm immovable Kumbhaka, just like my favourite personage, Sage Uddalaka, from *Yoga Vasishta*. The outside world and my inner being – consciousness – mind, with one stupendous 'Big Bang' exploded as a grand, majestic firework of numbers and symbols, gradually solidifying into what can be only described as a multidimensional geometrical crystal. It was some sort of a gigantic rotating Rubik's Cube, occupying the totality of space of consciousness with the numbers and the symbols on each side of multiple compartments. I was this 'mathematical universe' of Higher Intelligence in the form of a multidimensional rotating crystal, as well as the numbers and the symbols, and also the movement of consciousness-intelligence within it. It was immediately obvious that I had to make very rapid choices to proceed in one or the other direction of this magnificent maze. My choices weren't quick intellectual decisions, (thought is far too slow and heavy to operate in such fast-moving display of intelligence), but rather the direction of my attention. I was within the glowing cube, which itself was within a bigger network of rotating cubes. The symbols and numbers were glowing on the walls of the cube on all sides of me. If my attention was directed towards a symbol on the left, then immediately the left panel opened, and I was moving into a new compartment with new symbols, or numbers. I noticed very quickly that the most rewarding choices were those in which my attention turned within to the panel at my back, so to speak, and I was moving deeper within myself. I realised very quickly that the level of my intelligence was expanding very rapidly with arithmetical, or even geometrical progression. Not that it was expanding in volume as space, but it was expanding in quality and in the ability to comprehend the most mysterious and the most secret Divine laws of the origin of Reality. My intelligence abandoned human limitations and became truly Divine. I realised how the Supreme Intelligence of the Absolute can be regained in a matter of seconds in favourable situations, such as with adequate amounts of DMT, or when approaching the moment of death. Now, it is very difficult for me to put the crumbs of the memories of my experience into vague words of description. It's like squeezing enormous elephant into a tiny ant hole. I just remember that in this mind-blowing trip I saved one of the universes of our multi–universal reality.

From somewhere, which seemed to be a different universe, some shouting reached my attention: 'Shiva Breathe!!!'. I cannot say for sure how long I wasn't breathing, possibly six, or seven minutes. I had no desire to breathe. When the battling forces of 'prana' (exhalation) and 'apana' (inhalation) cancel each other, the yogi is said to achieve 'Kevala Kumbhaka' (permanent cessation of breath). In Vasishta Samhita it is said: 'when after giving up inhalation and exhalation, one holds his breath with ease, it is absolute Kumbhaka (Kevala).'

When we are talking about enlightenment, Self-realisation, moksha (liberation) and so on, I personally like the term 'Kaivalya' derived from 'Kevala' (alone, isolated). Although from the first impression 'isolation' may suggest a not very happy state of being in some sort of isolation from wholeness, with the right analysis and understanding, it points towards the highest state of reality. Kaivalya in this context means the isolation of Purusha (Spirit –

Universal Self) from Prakriti (Nature – the material part of reality). Kaivalya is the isolation from unhappiness and limiting conditions, it is isolation from Gunas (rajas, tamas, and sattva), isolation from the changing moods of Prakriti. Kaivalya is the very nature of the Self; unblemished, pure, without attachments, absolutely free.

Shiva, whose very nature is Svatantrya Shakti, does not have any restriction in any aspect of being knowledge and action due to his absolute freedom and sufficiency. In other words, the Absolute Being is eternal and infinite, the magnitude of its intelligence is unfathomable, and the irresistible will manifesting as activity has no deficiency in its infinite potency. Nothing is impossible for the Absolute. Everything is possible. Although many 'gurus' would eagerly point out that the world-appearance is also a visible part of Shiva-Shakti's intelligence and must be realised as a part of blissful Universal Consciousness, (not excluding, but including all), I would argue that it is impossible to experience the limitations of the world's duality and be free at the same time.

If Heaven and Hell could coexist, it would not be 'coexisting Heaven and Hell', but Hell only. The Divine Ecstasy of Shiva-Shakti is so dense that it presses all 'secondary worlds', with all their impurities, misery, unhappiness and evil forces, out of its perfect existence. Kaivalya is the liberation from the illusory, but nevertheless appearing real, prison of 'secondary worlds' and the returning to the pristine, unblemished bliss of Highest Reality – Absolute Freedom. When the 'Hrt-granthi' (Heart-knot), which bonds the spirit, lifeforce and body together, gets severed or untied, Kaivalya (liberation/isolation) is the result.

We must also understand that consciousness, mind and Prana are closely interrelated. With the expansion of consciousness, the dual nature of Prana-Apana changes into the expanded homogenous Vyana. In other words, when consciousness rapidly expands, breathing naturally stops. It is breath-taking! Going a little bit deeper into the subject, extracted from my own experiences, I would say; that Prana (lifeforce) only appears to be different from the mind and with the practice of Prana-Yoga is realised as identical to the mind and consciousness. With the acceleration of Pranic Energy and the simultaneous expansion of cognition, Prana-Apana transmutes itself into the gleaming, throbbing-with-intelligent-energy, all-permeating Vyana, which in turn changes the nature of the mind by purifying it, stretching, expanding and energising it, until the point in which not the slightest difference between the two remains. 'Prana-Mind' becomes stable and omni-present. Ego (the false sense of a separate identity) merges into this blissful state of Oneness.

The dying process, and also the yogic process of ascendance to the state of Parama-Shiva through the 'dissolution of Tattvas' (conquest of the elements): earth into water, water into fire, fire into air, air into ether and ether into the sushumna channel and Bindu – singularity, is also sometimes described as the dissolution of pranas. In particular, the dissolution of Prana-Apana into homogenous Vyana, and then, the shrinking, so to speak, of expanded Vyana into the fifth prana – Udana – which totally introverts consciousness into the sushumna channel (the middle channel in the spinal cord), and further into the Spiritual Heart with the mysterious singularity point at its centre. In these ways, Upanishads say, Prana takes with itself the individual souls to a new rebirth on lower, higher, or other planes of infinite reality, according to accumulated karmas, mental predispositions, habits, boons and curses.

I would also like to illustrate the reverse process of development of Pranic Energy. It is said in the Bible that Adam (red) (Adamah = red earth/clay) became alive because God breathed his breath into him. 'Then the Lord God formed the man from the dust of the ground. He breathed the breath of life into the man's nostrils, and the man became a living person.'[28] From the mysterious Singularity, as the movement of God's Energy (God's breath), Udana comes into manifestation. She is expanding into the Universal Consciousness as Vyana, gets maintained (preserved) as Samana and then splits into the duality of Prana and Apana, as well splitting the unified Consciousness of the Prana-Mind into the unequal branches of mind and Prana. Through the battling forces of Prana and Apana, the lake of the mind gets agitated and produces all sorts of cognitive phenomena. From the Prana-Indra (Lord of the senses) senses (Indriyas) spring forth.

If through prana yoga, after prolonged dynamic breathing, one enters Kumbhaka and attempts to stay there as long as possible, one

---

[28] Genesis 2:7

finds at a certain point, that it is practically impossible to retain breathlessness. As unbelievable as it sounds, it is possible however, to stop breathing completely by the sheer willpower, but such willpower must be considered superhuman. What one may observe however, if one holds one's breath with all one's might, is that Prana and Apana are like two magnets with the same polarity. The closer one brings Prana and Apana together, the stronger the force is that pushes them apart. What one also may observe in such yogic practice (staying firm in breathlessness) is that some sort of relief and ease of the tension begins to present itself gradually, through which the uncomfortable knots get gradually loosened. Prana and Apana, when held by the willpower of firm Kumbhaka for a considerable amount of time, gradually become fused together.

Sometime later when I lived as a sadhu in a Himalayan cave, I heard from one Nath yogi, who stayed with us for a couple of days, that Adi yogi Gorakhnath achieved 'the impossible'. He fused his Pranas!

'Shiva breathe!!!!' I heard the voice of Tara for the second time somewhere in the deep background. And I resumed breathing, gradually landing on 'Earth' from the unbelievable heights of Supreme Intelligence. I knew that I had saved the Universe, so I felt like a real hero, filled with joy, gratitude and satisfaction. My lower lip was bruised and slightly bleeding, for I had been holding it tightly between my teeth, while staying for ages in this magnificent Kumbhaka.

No amount of meditation or imagination can prepare one for the astonishing revelations of DMT Reality. One will be saying to oneself: 'Wow! I could never, ever have imagined that such things are possible'. The DMT world is not a hallucination, but existing dimensions of multidimensional reality. After the experience of DMT, one's view of the reality of the 'world' we are living in is likely to change.

New Darshan of Mother India

In February 2008, Tara and I returned to our beloved Mother India. This time we planned to travel extensively throughout India, and also pay a visit to Nepal. We landed in Chennai airport. The air outside was warm, in contrast to the cold English weather, and it smelled like India. I prostrated on the ground and kissed this holy land.

O, Mother India! We are so blessed to have your Darshan (Holy Sight).

Our first destination was obviously the Sacred Arunachala with Ramana Maharshi ashram at its foot. Pretty soon we were engaged in the activities of the local spiritual community. Muz Murray was also there, so we attended his mantra yoga workshops a few times. We also discovered a beautiful gathering of mostly western people, singing heart-opening 'kirtans' (devotional chanting). As it often happens when you are among many different people, there is always someone sweet and bright, who captures your attention the most. We became friends with a twenty-three-year-old American Israeli-Palestinian man named Randi. He often joined the kirtans gatherings, and played guitar, which he had brought with him from Thailand, where he had stayed recently with his sister. He was open, intelligent and receptive. He was often seeking our company. In a very short time, we became good friends. I saw him once in quite a melancholic state, so I decided to share with him the wisdom of the *Song of Ribhu* – the Tamil transliteration of the holy *Ribhu Gita*.

238

Tara had introduced me to *Ribhu Gita* not long ago, and I considered this amazing book as one of the best and a very powerful exposition on the true nature of Reality. The sage Ribhu returns from the holy mountain Kailash (the abode of Shiva), on which he received 'Upadesha' (spiritual teaching) directly from Lord Shiva. *Ribhu Gita* is the exposition of teaching and instructions received by the sage Ribhu from Shiva, to the assembly of revered sages. It specifically imparts 'Jnana' (true knowledge) to a young sage, Nidagha – disciple of Ribhu. Ramana Maharshi praised this book highly. He said that reading *Ribhu Gita* is as good as Samadhi (absorption in Reality) itself. This book may appear boring and insignificant to those who are not ready to receive its message, to those who haven't investigated Truth. Only those whose minds and hearts are open, are fit to receive its powerful knowledge.

At the heart of these teachings is 'Bhavana', which can be translated as 'creative contemplation, certitude, conviction'. This liberating Bhavana is of two sorts:

negation of the world, body and everything else

affirmation of Brahman – who is the Real Self as the only existing Reality.

The best way to receive the power of these words is if someone reads them to you, while you are in contemplative meditation. Bhavana, specifically in the Kashmir Shaivism tradition is considered one of the highest yogic practices. As your conviction that you are Brahman – the unsurpassable mass of Bliss of Reality – grows, so you gradually become thus. As your conviction that the world does not exist in Reality gets rooted within your consciousness, so you become free of world appearance. Creative contemplation leads to conviction, and this conviction in turn brings one into unshakable certitude: 'Aham Brahmasmi' – I am Brahman, the only Reality beyond all appearances. This creative contemplation, conviction, certitude, which obviously must be applied in practice, leads one to the experience of new higher levels of Reality, to the direct verification of the Truth contained within these words. The direct experience of the higher realms of Reality leads to an even stronger conviction of 'I am Brahman – God Absolute'. And so, Bhavana leads to the experience of higher states

239

of consciousness, and verification of higher states leads to adamant certitude.

I read one chapter from the *Song of Ribhu* to my new young friend. He listened very attentively, and as I finished, I saw his face glowing with joy and relief. I learned from the Fourth Way school to use 'scale and relativity' for curing negative states triggered by recent negative events or worries. When one is immersed in a negative state, the whole world seems unfair and life itself seems filled with misery. Negativity is an optical lens which makes small things much bigger, occupying the whole consciousness with misery and judgment. When we bring the right scale into the picture, negativity shrinks and becomes insignificant in comparison with the enormous picture of Reality.

I had brought with me to India about twenty grams of dry liberty caps, and so, one night my new young friend and I decided to have a mushroom journey at the foot of Arunachala. We walked on the inner Giri Pradakshina path of Arunachala until we reached my favourite plateau. Giving my friend all necessary guidelines for a safe journey, specifically those for how to face Death, we consumed 108 liberty caps each (the sacred number), and before the mushrooms began their magic work, I read one of my favourite chapters from the *Song of Ribhu* – chapter fifteen, 'The Means for the Conquest of the Mind'. Half-way through this reading, I already felt very high on mushrooms. The reading from this amazing book magnified the experience of the psychedelic expansion by the Truth contained in the words of *Ribhu*, which was penetrating our essence and shattering our ordinary perceptions. This time I didn't go into the shamanic movements but lay like a corpse in breathless shavasana.

From my numerous experiences with magic mushrooms, I would say that the best way to take them is to take them alone. As Kilindi Iyi, whom I highly respect, would say: 'There is much fuss around ayahuasca these days. A group of people attending a ceremony with shaman, singing, purging, healing. Ayahuasca is a 'medicine'. Mushrooms are magic! I wouldn't advise you to take thirty grams of psilocybin in company. The magic mushroom is the way of the lone warrior.'[29]

As the aim of all spiritual practices is the realisation of Oneness, when psilocybin unlocks the doors of perception, everything that appears as 'other' than Self must be reduced to 'sameness', otherwise the perception of dual nature will not allow the full experience of the Ultimate Truth. When two people share one mushroom journey, it may often be experienced as a battle of two egos. For Reality to reveal itself, one or the other must die! If I want the Truth to triumph, I must either die myself, or totally consume everything that appears different than my True Self with the power of Love, which reduces everything to Sameness – Oneness.

My young friend had a very hard time. He rolled among the spiky bushes, and when I finally looked at him, trying to feel that he and I were one, he had the expression of pleading with me: 'Shiva, I beg you, don't kill me'. After four or five hours of our journey, he calmed down and started to gently sing *Lord of the Dance*. I looked at him again and now, everything about him (his posture, face, hair, clothes) appeared to me as attributes of the Tamil saint Seshadri Swami, who took care of Ramana Maharshi. And I felt identical to the young Ramana Maharshi under the protection of Seshadri Swami. We started singing together, transforming our experience and becoming more and more ecstatic. We were enraptured.

When Tara and couple of our new lovely friends went for a pradakshina in the early morning they found us immersed in ecstatic singing. They laughed with us and basked in the waves of our joy. Leaving the rest of mushrooms with our new friends, Tara and I walked back to our cheaply rented apartment, not far from the post office. Our new friends went in the opposite direction, continuing their circumbulation around Arunachala. My young friend, who decided to call himself 'Nataraja' (Dancing Shiva) from this moment on, was still standing on the plateau, and as a prophet, full of joy, was singing beautiful poetry which was flooding through him spontaneously.

---

[29] Kilindi Iyi (High-Dose Mushrooms Beyond the Threshold) YouTube.

New Darshan of Mother India

Nataraja and I had a good time together in Tiru, sometimes sharing our views on Reality, sometimes immersed in spiritual practices, such as eye-gazing, sometimes playing guitar and jaw harp in tandem, not far from Ramanasramam. Soon, Tara and I were planning to go to Varanasi via Delhi. Nataraja had plans to go north to Dharamshala. We said goodbye for now, promising to keep in touch.

From Chennai we took a train to Delhi, and after spending one night in Delhi, we took the train to Holy Kashi – Benares or Varanasi. My first impression of this ancient holy city was that I had never ever seen so much traffic. If you've been there, you will understand what I am talking about.

'To see Chidambaram, to be born in Thiruvarur, to die in Varanasi, or to remember Arunachala, all of this alone will confer Liberation' says Skanda Purana. Well, Arunachala always lives in my heart as Shiva and as the very Self. And now, we were in the city that, dying in which is supposed to break the cycle of deaths and rebirths. Funeral pyres never stop burning on the Ghats of the Holy Ganga. The temples, in which the original fire was lit some thousands of years ago, never stop burning. When my body dies, I would like to be cremated like this; on the shore of Holy Ganga with the pandits chanting sacred mantras and the body being offered back to the five elements; earth, water, fire, air, and ether.

After a few attempts by some crooks, which Varanasi seemed to be full of, to get from us a rip-off price for a miserable apartment, we took the initiative and found very lovely place to stay at quite a reasonable price. This place was called Ganapati Guest House and was situated just above the stony shore of the Ganga, practically next to the main burning Ghat. It had a lovely courtyard, where we could comfortably enjoy the local cuisine. They had also a music store and a studio. Varanasi is famous for its concerts of classical Indian music. We quickly become friends with some musicians and other guests.

Sunrises in Varanasi are the best. If nothing else, you must come here to see the spectacular sun rising over the Ganga. Of course, we also took a boat ride, and although the Ganga is very polluted here, filled with the floating corpses, I couldn't allow myself to miss the opportunity of taking holy bath in the sacred waters of Mother Ganga. To the great surprise of our boat-rower, I plunged headfirst from our boat into her holy waters.

Tara, with her very long black hair and I with a considerable beard, wearing saffron robes, and most importantly, with our natural Indian essence, and with the great respect to this Divine Land, looked like native Indians by this time, and were allowed in every temple. This included the Golden Temple; entrance to which is normally forbidden to foreigners. For one day, by some miracle, we squeezed through the mass of traffic in hectic Varanasi to visit the very tranquil Sarnath, a place where Gautama Buddha first taught the Dharma.

With the approaching of Holi, Varanasi had already turned into an explosion of colour. Mischievous children and teenagers were throwing not only colourful powder at us, but all sorts of coloured liquids. Imagining what was going to happen on the actual day of Holi in Varanasi, we decided to leave for Nepal the day before the celebration. It was the wrong decision!

A Brief Visit to Nepal

In the evening, we boarded a train heading to Gorakhpur situated on the border of Nepal. We were rudely awakened in the early morning by something hitting our faces, the sounds of explosions and a shock of flying balls of mud coming through our open window. Local boys, who couldn't afford colourful powder, were celebrating Holi by throwing mud balls through the windows of our train. But this was just a beginning of our unfortunate adventure on this Holi day. Taxis refused to go on this day to the Nepalese border, suspecting some mischievous interruptions on the road. The only van driver willing to go asked us to pay double price and I don't know how, but about twelve people squeezed in the back of this relatively small car. Our van was stopped in the middle of the road by a big group of young loud boys who were intoxicated by alcohol and bhang and were throwing coloured powder and liquids through the windows. They began to rock our van from side to side. Finally, after lots of pleading with them, they let us go, but it wasn't the end of our Holi adventure. Another group of intoxicated men 'attacked' us, while we were making our last bit of journey towards the border on a bicycle rickshaw. It was futile to plead with them. We were covered from head to toe, including our luggage, in smudged colours. As these powders had certain chemicals in them, Tara began to feel very unwell and unable to think properly. She exchanged a big sum of money at the border at a rip-off rate. Paying lots of money to our new taxi driver, just to leave this chaotic place, we finally crossed the border and zigzagged through the hillside towards the Nepalese town of Pokhara. After a few

A Brief Visit to Nepal

hours of driving we finally arrived. Opening the taxi door, Tara vomited.

We rented a clean spacious room with a magnificent view of the snowy peaks of the Annapurna mountains. After a very long washing of each other, we went to investigate our surroundings. Nepal was much cleaner than India, the air full of the sweet fragrance of some sort of woody incense. Pokhara appeared very westernised in comparison with the rural raw beauty of Indian towns. It was nice comfortable time of relaxation, indulged in the tasting of local cuisine and Tibetan hot beer made out of fermented millet. We spent a few days in Pokhara, visiting grand caves, rowing boats on big beautiful lakes, dining in restaurants and enjoying the majestic view of the Annapurna mountains. I bought the highest quality charas here, and also compressed marijuana pollen, which I liked to smoke and immediately go into samadhi, after reading an inspiring chapter of *Shiva Sutras*. After few days we left Pokhara for Kathmandu on a tiny Nepalese Airlines plane, which was delayed for about seven hours.

We rented a room in a hotel next to Boudhanath Stupa. I must say that although I enjoyed the rich Buddhist culture, it wasn't my cup of tea. My heart was longing for the rawness, unpretentiousness, madness and authenticity of Mother India. Our visit to the Hindu Pashupatinath Temple for me was the highlight of our visit of Kathmandu. Ironically, it was the only Hindu temple into which we were not allowed. However, we had a great time sitting with local sadhus around dhuna (fire pit) and passing chillum with my Pokhara charas as a gift to the sadhus in their small building next to the Pashupatinath Temple. I felt great sympathy with them and had a great inclination to become a sadhu myself. 'Shiva! Shiva! Shiva!' one of them started to shout, enraptured with joy.

A Growing Desire to Become a Sadhu

After few days in Kathmandu, we flew back to Delhi where, upon visiting a musical instruments shop, I bought a bamboo flute with a great voice. We met a lovely couple in a Delhi café. They were leaving India next day, and kindly left with me their Indian mobile phone.

Our next destination was our favourite place in Haridwar, Anandamayi Ma's guest house.

Doctor Gosh greeted us as best precious friends and cooked something very delicious for us. I sent a message to our young friend Nataraja, saying that we had returned to India and were staying in Ma's guest house, and if he was still in India and would like to join us, we would be very happy to have his company. Meanwhile, in Ma's ashram there happened to be chanting of the complete Ramayana text for three days and nights in a row, without a break, but periodically replacing musicians. The music and ecstatic chants like divine nectar flooded over me, sending my consciousness into blissful trance. I also participated with the musicians, adding my jaw harp's voice, to which they were very grateful.

On the evening of a second day, stepping outside of the ashram, I was surprised and delighted to see smiling face of Nataraja. We spent the evening smoking chillum and playing some songs with the red-robe-wearing Shakta Sadhus, who gathered outside Anandamayi Ma's ashram.

A Growing Desire to Become a Sadhu

On our way to Uttarkashi, we stopped for couple of days in Rishikesh. This time, we decided to stay on the less crowded western side of the Ganga.

The idea of becoming a sadhu and devoting the remaining span of my lifetime solely to the sacred efforts of union (Sadhana, Tapas) with Shiva – the Ultimate Reality, discarding all remaining attachments to worldly pleasures, was growing deeply within me. I simply stopped being attracted to anything but God. I wanted nothing, but union (yoga) with the Beloved. Only in knowing God and being consumed by God I saw fulfilment and satisfaction. Nothing else; not Earthly life with its fake values, nor delightful paradises could satisfy me, but only merging into the ecstasy of the Absolute Truth. What is there in this world that we haven't experienced yet? Day after day, things just keep repeating themselves, with a degree of deviation, in some small and large circles.

'Tomorrow, and tomorrow, and tomorrow,

Creeps in this petty pace from day to day,

To the last syllable of recorded time;

And all our yesterdays have lighted fools

The way to dusty death. Out, out, brief candle!

Life's but a walking shadow, a poor player,

That struts and frets his hour upon the stage,

And then is heard no more. It is a tale

Told by an idiot, full of sound and fury,

Signifying nothing.'

(from Macbeth by William Shakespeare)

Even if I fulfil all my earthly dreams, (get rich, healthy, famous, adored, loved, wise, pampered in luxuries and comfort) I would not

A Growing Desire to Become a Sadhu

find absolute satisfaction. I am not attracted to earthly pleasures in the least. Even more than that: I feel a repulsion to the luxuries of life. I am finding that happiness does not depend on wealth. I've seen many rich, miserable people in my life. Simple village folks enjoying Mother Nature, appear far happier to me. And of course, the devoid-of-any-possession sage basks in the ecstasy of the True Self and drinks thirst-quenching all-satisfying Amrita (nectar of gods) even amid a desert.

Some time ago, reading *Talks with Sri Ramana Maharshi*, I came across the question from one of the truth-seeking sadhakas: 'Is it true,' asked he, 'that after forty days of complete fasting, man can become enlightened?' Ramana's surprising answer encouraged me on my next spiritual experiment. 'Yes, it is true' answered Ramana, 'providing that during all these forty days of complete fasting, one is constantly engaged in 'Atma-Vichara' (self-inquiry)'.

Many of us experience mini-enlightenments at different moments in our lives, but we always return from these non-ordinary states to our 'normal' perceptions of our life-stories. But, without an iota of doubt, there must be a point of no return to our ordinary perceptions. There is a point when, the hrt-granthi (heart-knot) gets severed, a point where the gravity of accumulated habits is no longer capable of holding consciousness within its orbit. If death of the physical body is inevitable, why there should be a grief over the loss of a body? 'Unreal has no real existence. Reality never ceases to be' say the Upanishads.

If we ignore Death, it doesn't mean that Death won't find us. On the contrary, Death is the greatest teacher. Nachiketa learnt the highest wisdom from the Lord of Death. We must become acquainted with Death, approach Death, learn the most valuable lessons from Her. We must become Her lovers. Death teaches us Love and self-sacrifice. Through Love of Truth and Self-sacrifice, Death gives us freedom from the cycles of samsara (repetitive history). Self-realisation is very similar to Death; it is the crumbling away of all that is false. But Death alone doesn't grant Self-realisation. She only gives us possibilities.

Longing for Truth no matter what, a willingness to die for Truth, the offering of the mind and soul into the all-consuming fire of Absolute Truth, humble endurance of the total annihilation of ego, are the ways to great liberation. I was ready to go beyond the point of no-return. As Papaji says: 'If you go to a guru (spiritual teacher), you should not buy a return ticket.' So was my resolve: to plunge all the way into the bottomless ocean of Divine mysteries, without reserve, burning all the bridges behind me. Scary, but the only way to the Beloved. What can a heap of snow do, but melt and evaporate in the presence of the luminous Sun?

The Rewards of the Fasting Tapas

T he plan of doing forty days of complete fasting including mauna (silence) was slowly brewing in my mind, seeking its actualisation. Those beautiful souls who are not satisfied with the natural course of evolution, and whose longing for the Absolute Truth, longing for union with the Beloved, whose longing for Reality forces them to find new ways towards this all-satisfying Unity, may add the Spiritual Heat – Tapas – to their usual Sadhana. It has been said in many holy scriptures that there is nothing that cannot be achieved through intense Tapas, that Gods are greatly pleased with these intense efforts of self-sacrifice, and can grant any boon to those brave souls who subject themselves to the sacrifice of comfort and desires and transform their pain and suffering into the Love of God. Suffering is a form of food for the awakening soul, generating the spiritual heat that is needed for the transmutation of chemical and alchemical substances into the higher refined substances. It is the transmutation of copper into gold, the transmutation of the individualised being-consciousness into God.

One of such practices is a long-term complete fasting. Legend says that our beloved poet Hafiz went twice in his life for a complete forty days of fasting. At the end of the first fast, Archangel Gabriel appeared to him. Amazed at Gabriel's sublime beauty, Hafiz completely forgot about the girl whose heart he was aiming to win through his effort of fasting. He said: 'I want God'. And so, Gabriel led Hafiz to his guru, Attar. Years later, Hafiz, unsatisfied with his spiritual progress undertook another forty days

The Rewards of the Fasting Tapas

of fasting. At the end, Archangel Gabriel appeared again and asked Hafiz of his wishes. Surprisingly, Hafiz realised that all desires at that moment had left him. He returned to his guru Attar, who offered Hafiz a glass of a very special vintage wine. After drinking it, Hafiz became intoxicated with God, seeing and hearing God everywhere.

'Running

Through the streets

Screaming,

Throwing rocks through windows,

Using my own head to ring

Great bells,

Pulling out my hair,

Tearing off my clothes,

Tying everything I own

To a stick,

And setting in on

Fire.

What else can Hafiz do tonight

To celebrate the madness,

The joy,

Of seeing God

Everywhere!'

(Hafiz)

The Rewards of the Fasting Tapas

Although Buddha is known as a founder of the 'middle way', his previous severe Tapas, among which was prolonged fasting, surely cleared the obstacles to his enlightenment. Needless to say, great spiritual transformation happened for Jesus when he went for forty days of fasting in the desert. As a rule, at the end of Tapas, one gets tempted. One could be offered siddhis (supernatural powers) or can be frightened by the powerful forces. One's resolve to the Union with the Absolute Truth only, rejecting anything else, must be unshakable.

I shared with Tara my thoughts and my wishes to become a sadhu, to find a cave, or an isolated room, where I would not be disturbed for forty days of fasting and spiritual practices. Obviously, without a great deal of enthusiasm for this prospect, she accepted it and supported me in preparation for it. She made for me the most beautiful sadhu's bag, with a big sign of OM on it. She spent a large amount of time creating this OM with small stiches of wool, chanting mantras with each stich. In Rishikesh we bought couple of Ayurvedic herbal jeevanprash tonics in case I needed some extra energy during my fasting.

When we arrived in Uttarkashi, we ordered some typical Sadhu clothing from a local tailor and some saffron dye in my preparation to become a sadhu.

At our favourite spot next to the Shiva temple with the natural Shiva Lingam, we were delighted to see among the other sadhus our Italian friend Durgai Nath with her companion Gangai Nath. We spent most of our time in the company of sadhus, smoking chillums, playing kirtans and having conversations on spiritual matters and the true nature of Reality. I also began to learn to play my flute.

One of the gathered people dressed as a sadhu, named Muku Baba, who was providing us with high quality charas from Kullu Valley, after hearing my wish to do a forty-day fasting retreat in a cave, told me that he knew an empty cave near the village where he lived in Himachal Pradesh. He gave me his email and phone number. With regards to how to find this cave, I only wrote a little note in my notebook: '*Delhi to Solan, from Solan to Mangarh, village Khasla Dinger, 5km. Look for Rajendra Puri Maharaj*'.

Tara and I also went to investigate a quieter place on the opposite side of the Ganga, where I expressed my wish for a forty-days fast and a silent retreat to a sadhu living in a small room. He eagerly agreed to share his accommodation with me. There is always encouragement and respect among sadhus for those desiring to be engaged in Tapas.

After about a week in Uttarkashi, Tara received a phone call from England from her son Adam. It wasn't good news. Adam had lost custody of his daughter, India. Now, India was only allowed to visit her dad at certain hours on the weekend and a few hours midweek. Tara was quite distressed by this bad news. She loved India very much, as knew very well the wickedness, violence, abusing behaviour and trickery of her mother. Tara decided immediately to go back to England and try to sort things out. Her relationship with our young friend Nataraj, who was very fond of me, also became a bit tense these last few days.

I asked Nataraj if he would like to join me in search of a cave for a forty-day fasting retreat. He eagerly agreed, and without telling Tara, we agreed that after her departure I would find him in Rishikesh. From there we would proceed to Himachal Pradesh in search of the above-mentioned cave. We said goodbye and I made my way back to Delhi with Tara. Spending one night in a Delhi hotel, I accompanied Tara to the airport next morning, where, after sweet goodbye kisses she departed for England.

A Magical Journey into the Land of Shiva

I received an email from Nataraj, which I write below:
'Beloved Supreme Shiva,
All of creation dancing within you!
There is no doubt of this.
I never really understood half of Rumi's poems... but now I do...

The poems that were dead to me, you have brought to life.

That I could meet God in human form, and human form that knows,

That is doubtless, that he is the supreme bliss of Brahman...

A friend that lets me know that I, indeed, I am the immortal Sultan.

I bow to your feet my Guru, and then I lift my face and am startled to see my own eyes

Looking back.

Sometimes my rational mind has given thought to leaving India before our retreat.

Then I heard God, and my Heart laughs hysterically.

Even if I have to cross the Siberian wilderness to join you I would.

Even if the most seductive female form offered herself to me without condition,

I would throw her off like a piece of sour candy.

If poverty would assail me and the thorns of Arunachala cut me apart, I would still rejoice

At the promise of seeing the silence in your eyes once more.

254

A Magical Journey into the Land of Shiva

The sweetness you bestow is the sweetness of Brahman.
And once it has been tasted nothing less will satisfy.
Indeed, indeed, we are the undivided ocean of consciousness…
The ocean of utterly indescribable beauty and mystery.
If I was a waterfall of blessings,
Your river has washed over me
And flooded me completely.
What is I? What are words?
What is that infinitely vast expanse I keep catching clearer
glimpses of?
Oh, Supreme Shiva, God of Gods, Allah, Pure Brahman, Oh
indescribable all pervasive
Consciousness bliss… silence
I AM
Let us melt brother… Let us drink and be drunk… until we are
absolutely lost in the purity
Of our very own wine.
If my blood were to be the wine… still I would wait for you…
such is this thirst… this
Unquenchable thirst for Silence and Union'.

Leaving my luggage in a hotel storage room for an indefinite period and taking with me only my sadhu bag with couple of books and the most essential stuff, I popped into a music store, where I bought an inexpensive guitar and a pungi (the snake-charming music instrument), the magical sound of which I really liked. With all this, I travelled back to Rishikesh, where I found Nataraj in the quiet, non-pretentious Phool Chatti ashram, situated on the bank of the Ganga, just outside of Rishikesh. We spent three days there, psychologically preparing for our search for the cave and our silent, fasting retreat. In the evenings and nights, we usually walked to the shores of the Ganga, where we played kirtans, songs, flute and jaw harp. We felt real joy and became very good in playing ecstatic music together. After three relaxing days in the Phool Chatti ashram, we went back to Haridwar to catch the bus to Solan on the road to Shimla. Spending the early afternoon in the Anandamayi Ma guest house, we caught the five o'clock bus to Shimla, and our magical adventure into the unknown began.

Somewhere around one o'clock in the morning, we left the bus in Solan. Not knowing where to go exactly, we just stayed in

255

darkness at the bus station. After about half an hour, a police car stopped in front of us. An officer, who appeared to be drunk and stoned, commanded us to jump in the car, and the other policemen put our bags and guitars in the trunk. We arrived at the police station.

The chief police officer was most definitely drunk and very arrogant. Apparently, his father was the chief of police of all the Shimla region. It seemed to me that, while representing the law itself, father and son were standing above all laws. The other policemen didn't even dare to argue or question his commands. Making fun of us, he was playfully hinting that because he was the law, he could hold us in the police station for as long as he liked, possibly for week, or a month. My young friend was very tired and was drifting away into sleep, while I was listening to this buffoon, or answering his questions. He was surely delighted to have us to entertain himself. Noticing our guitars, he asked me to play something. I took my guitar and slowly began the most passionate and heart-wrenching, twelve-minute-long 'Vanyusha' by Bashlachev. He listened attentively, and when this song began to go into the most exciting crescendo, he became bizarrely exuberant, prostrating before me, and banging his fists on a floor. He kept repeating: 'You are the fucking genius; you are the fucking genius!'.

After I finished this song, his whole attitude towards us changed dramatically. He sent his inferiors to find some charas for us. A nice turn of events. In the morning he was very helpful, giving us a lift to the bus station, and explaining which bus we had to take to bring us closer to our destination. I am not exactly sure which town we arrived in next, but the bus from there to Khalsa Dinger village was not leaving for another eight hours. Having not much money to spend, we played some kirtans on the street, and were invited to have a free meal in a local café. After having a delicious lentil-based meal, we climbed a big hill nearby, where we found a nice little ashram with two sadhus living there. After smoking chillum with them and having a little chat, they asked us to drop the idea of the cave and stay with them. But we were determent to find this cave, so saying thank you for their hospitality, we descended from the hill.

256

Shiva's Messenger

A polite young man approached us and asked: 'Are you looking for Rajendra Puri Maharaj?' Our jaws dropped in amazement! What? How on Earth? It was beginning of miracles! We had told no-one that we were looking for that person, and the town we were in now was apparently a good twenty to thirty miles away from our destination. 'How can you possibly know that we were looking for him?' we exclaimed in absolute astonishment.

'Shiva sent me' he replied, pointing his finger towards the sky! And the pure magic, where the unseen Gods and Divine forces roam, began to be visible, and their orchestration of our fantastical play of incredible synchronicity, had begun!

O, Himachal Pradesh – Shiva-Shakti's land, where one who is open and ready begins to feel a very tangible presence of Gods!

'I would like to give you a lift to Rajendra Puri ashram,' said Dave. I agree, a strange English name for an Indian Pundit. It turns out that Dave was a learned scholar, well versed in Vedas, knowing mantras and rituals. Thanking Shiva for giving us sign and help, we jumped into Dave's van, which he drove through the lovely pine forest. We stopped in a forest, where four sadhus lived and were now gathered around the fire. We had a good chillum with them, after smoking which and feeling highly inspired, we played some music. Nataraj played guitar and sang and I played flute with absolute spontaneity. We were really good! Love was flooding freely from our hearts as beautiful sounds and vibrations penetrating the hearts of the gathered sadhus. Dave confessed that he was planning to charge us for petrol, but hearing us play music made his heart blossom, so he decided to give us a ride for free.

Shiva's Messenger

Towards the evening, we arrived at the place where Rajendra Puri was building a little Shiva temple. After a little bit of search, we realised that Rajendra Puri was away. Dave took us to a local family nearby. The mother of this family was a caretaker of another Shiva temple. After offering us a delicious meal, the whole family gathered in the living room, and we sang our hearts out in a joyful kirtan, to everyone's delight. They offered us a room to sleep in, and in the morning, after feeding us breakfast and giving us forty rupees (such kind souls), Dave drove us to Shringi Rishi Gufa, after a stop at the Shiva temple, where we prostrated before Shiva Lingam, which was adorned with Ganja leaves.

The Life and Sadhana of Sadhus in a Himalayan Cave

bout four hundred steps up from the little village road led us to our place of retreat. According to Hindu Puranas, the great saint Shringi Rishi (of sage Kashyapa's lineage), stayed in this cave, meditating and performing yagnas (Vedic devotional sacrifices, worship, offering oblations and libations into the sacred fire 'Agni'). Legend has it that Shringi Rishi cursed King Parakshit for his sinful conduct against Rishi Lomash. The boons and curse uttered by him were proved to be absolutely true. Rishi Shringi was a distinguished expert of the super science of mantras. Rishi Shringi is credited in Indian mythology as the inventor of 'Putrakameshti Yagna', the Vedic sacrifice for begetting a male progeny. This first ever Putrakameshti Yagna was performed by Rishi Shringi for the Suryawanshi Emperor Dashrath of Ayodhya (of Ikshavaku lineage) and the outcome of this yagna was the birth of Lord Rama, the great Indian God-king and revered 'Avatar' (incarnation) of Lord Vishnu, the powerful god in the Holy Trinity of Brahma-Vishnu-Shiva.

Local schoolboys, who later came to visit us almost daily, told us that Lord Rama himself had stayed in this cave and that the monkey-god Hanuman (the reincarnation of Shiva) made the entrance into this cave with his powerful fist. At the entrance of this cave there is a bas-relief painted sculpture of Hanuman. We entered the main entrance of the cave, followed by a few schoolboys, who were very excited to have couple of new western sadhus coming to live in their sacred cave. We washed the floor of

The Life and Sadhana of Sadhus in a Himalayan Cave
the cave. Dave, who was a learned Vedas pundit performed Puja (a sacred ritual of washing the Shiva Lingam in water, coconut milk, etc... and offering to the Shiva Lingam fragrances of sweet incense, the light of fire, mantras, and food). He blessed us and our cave, we lit the fire in our dhuna and our life as sadhus in this holy place began.

Very soon our first impression that this cave consisted of only one hall with the Shiva Lingam in it, gave way to the amazement of how big this cave actually was. Just behind the Shiva Lingam there was a small opening, through which we could just about squeeze through. As soon as we passed this narrow channel, there was a big opening with further narrow passages straight down, and one very narrow passage leading up. First, we investigated the way down. The narrow passage about five metres long led us to a massive opening, which we could call now a real cave. On one of the sides of this cave there was a massive natural Shiva Lingam, to which some of the rare pilgrims paid homage and gave special respect and adoration. At the bottom of this cave there was a little lake, filled with fresh water. A few days later we managed to squeeze through the narrow passage leading into an upper cave which had a name of Ganesha Gufa. We were surprised to see a vast open space there also. The whole cave was about the size of a four-floor building. And so, sometimes we were together in the upper or lower cave, and occasionally we would split up and meditate or chant in solitude.

Our resolve to maintain silence was broken after couple of days. We realised that it would be very sad not to communicate at all, especially in these most difficult days of the beginning of the fast, when our bodies felt very weak and psychologically, we felt down. We decided to keep the necessary amount of conversations, read each other chapters from great *Ribhu Gita* and sing ecstatic kirtans together. Our spiritual practice consisted of a continuous 'I am Brahman' Bhavana, Bhairava Mudra (expansion of awareness), chanting of mantras accompanied by intense pranayamas, meditation, self-inquiry and generally keeping our minds free from thought, not giving the power of attention to thought, but actively engaging our attention to reverse its direction towards its source, and also to its expansion with the effort of comprehension of the totality of all impressions simultaneously.

The Life and Sadhana of Sadhus in a Himalayan Cave

Every thought craves attention, for precious attention is food and the very life for a thought. If a thought does not receive the energy of attention, it either dies, or retreats for an indefinite time. Every thought says: 'give me your attention, I am important'. The most fundamental aspect of man's 'free will' is the choice of what he allows his attention to dwell upon. We must be on alert and very selective of what we are giving our attention to, for what we give our attention to, will grow. So, for example if you do not want to continuously dwell in negative states, do not feed them with your precious attention. It is beneficial, however, to cultivate and feed with our attention such thoughts and feelings as 'I am Brahman', 'I am Energy', 'I am Intelligence', 'I am Love', 'I am God-Absolute', 'I am Truth', 'I am imperishable Reality'. Such thoughts are the essence of Bhavana itself, i.e., conviction, creative contemplation. These thoughts, nevertheless, are only pointers towards the Truth. The Truth within these thoughts must not only be thought of but must lead to direct experience. The attention directed towards the meaning of these words of Truth, will eventually face its own source – the I-Consciousness. These positive affirmations – thoughts, and also the thoughts negating illusion, lead to 'Savikalpa Samadhi' (holding to Reality with thought).

The 'Nirvikalpa Samadhi' (unqualified samadhi, abidance in Reality without support of mind) sounds far more profound and far more an advanced experience than 'Savikalpa Samadhi'. However, due to the very nature of mind to restlessly move, to conceptualise, to idealise, to imagine, to cling to the objects of perceptions, Nirvikalpa Samadhi is not an easy achievement. From my spiritual practices and experiences, I would say that it is much easier to come to Nirvikalpa Samadhi with the help of Savikalpa, which is sometimes termed 'Savichara'. More than that, I agree with the statement, at which I came across later in the teaching of Great Avadhuta Datatreya in the book *Tripura Rahasya*. Datatreya says: 'Ignorance is dispelled by pure intelligence, which is Samadhi. Ignorance cannot be dispelled by the mere experience of an unqualified expanse of intelligence as in Nirvikalpa Samadhi. For such expanse is in harmony with everything (including ignorance). Nirvikalpa Samadhi clearly will never eradicate ignorance.

The Life and Sadhana of Sadhus in a Himalayan Cave
Therefore, in order to destroy it Savikalpa Samadhi must be sought. This alone can do it'[30]

When the mind has no control and no directions, it easily slips into a dream state, or imagination. I've heard a few lectures by transcendental meditation (T.M.) teachers and Maharishi Mahesh Yogi himself, that propose that the nature of the mind is bliss itself, and if one stops to control the mind and lets it just go wherever it pleases, it will return to its source – bliss. Fortunately, the T.M. teachers also give you a mantra, so one can tie the mind to mantra, which can help one navigate. I observed later in my life though, during satsangs and meditation sessions, that most T.M. practitioners drop their heads during meditation and even begin to snore.

It is said in many yogic and tantric scriptures that the path to Shiva is Shakti! In other words: the way to Supreme Intelligence is through the expansion of energy. The growing of energy is the surest guide towards the explosion of Supreme Intelligence. The expanding energy itself becomes Supreme and as such is no different from Supreme Intelligence. Energy and intelligence are interrelated, and with the expansion of one, the other expands too. Therefore, to encourage energy towards expansion, we also can use our intelligence.

As Swami Lakshmanjoo points out in the comments to Shiva Sutras in the book "Shiva Sutras: The Supreme Awakening": 'The Goddess can only be awakened by (Nada) Supreme I-Consciousness filled with Supreme Awareness. To awaken her, the yogi has to churn his point of one-pointedness in the heart without break, again and again. He must churn it by inserting sparks of Awareness, one after another, again and again in unbroken continuation. The process is to insert one spark of Awareness. Let that one spark fade. Again, insert fresh Awareness. This process must continue over and over again in continuity'.[31]

In other words, one must continuously wake oneself up from the previous half-sleep state to reach the next more dynamic level of energy and intelligence, and then the next, and the next. Simply closing one's eyes, letting go of control, and drifting wherever

---

[30] Tripura Rahasya: The Mystery beyond the Trinity. Munagala S. Venkataramiah

[31] Swami Lakshmanjoo "Shiva Sutras: The Supreme Awakening" 2.3

one's mind takes one, will undoubtedly bring one into a state of deep slumber, or to a new dream. By giving the mind directions to follow, such as the affirmation: 'I am the field of energy' we then must experience this statement as truth. We must feel the identity to the field of energy with the totality of our being. In such a way, one's spark of awareness inserted, and this spark churns energy into its expansion and awakening. 'I am the Supreme Intelligence' – another spark inserted into the heart of your being to churn your energy – Shakti. 'I am the imperishable incorruptible ultimate Truth, I am Brahman, I am Shiva, I am Shakti, I, AM..,' many new sparks of Awareness inserted to churn energy. Now, with this expanded Awareness and a new level of awakened energy, stay thoughtless and feel identity to the field of shimmering energy. Let it fade away into the Nirvikalpa (undifferentiated) state.

Next, negation: This does not exist! This, which I am temporarily experiencing, does not exist. Feel it with the totality of your being. It's only appearance, temporarily blinding my real vision, it's only a veil drawn over my luminous nature, it's only a superimposition on my unblemished consciousness. Space, time, distance, gravity, direction, temperature… all these limitations do not exist! I am the fullness, the totality, weightlessness, direction-lessness, timelessness… Reality! Feel and Know with every fibre, every atom of your being these words to be the Truth. Let it all fade away into the Nirvikalpa Samadhi.

The surest sign of progress towards the realisation of Truth is rapidly increasing, expanding energy. In the process of awakening, your eyes are opening wide, your pupils open to the maximum, your jaw drops, opening your mouth, the skin on top of your skull might begin to shiver, the hairs begin to tremble, to move, to stand on their ends, for you begin to see and experience the greatest miracle to which you were blind before. You start to sense the arrival of your True Beloved, who easily can destroy 'you' and 'your world' with the mighty vibrations of Her incomparable terrific beauty and overwhelming Love. You are in a state of childlike wonder and astonishment at what you are seeing and experiencing. Some great metamorphosis begins with your visual perceptions. So-called 'objective reality' gradually loses its objectivity and turns into a glowing, shimmering abstraction. The false sense of distance fades away and you begin to feel that there

The Life and Sadhana of Sadhus in a Himalayan Cave
is nothing separate, or distant from you. You permeate everything with your being-consciousness-energy. The sense of solidity gives way to a sense of liquidity. You begin to experience yourself as liquid light, liquid energy, fluid-like consciousness – Divine Nectar, Ambrosia, Soma – and nothing is separate from you. Everything is connected and permeated. Any sense of direction and gravity fades away, and you feel the butterflies flapping their wings within your heart, because the ground beneath your feet is gone and you are falling or floating now into the bottomless unknown. You are wide awake!

But this is only the beginning of the infinite mystery and ecstasy of awakening. Malini-Vijayottara tantra, which was considered by Abhinavagupta as the highest Tantra and the heart of the Trika System of Kashmir Shaivism speaks of seven levels of percievers. On the way to the apex of Intelligence – Parama Shiva – one passes through the stages of lucidity, or the states of the hierarchical ladder of intelligence, with each succeeding level becoming a super-perceiver of new inner higher levels of Infinite Reality; Pralayakala, Vijnanakala, Mantra, Mantresha, Mantramaheshvara, Shakti and Shiva! There is no end to the wonder and amazement on this magnificent journey of Self-discovery! The unborn, undying, forever-existing infinite Absolute Intelligence is sufficient to always amuse and astonish itself!

I hope you can feel the energy of this description of the beginning of awakening, my dear reader, and I do not need to convince you any longer that simply closing your eyes and drifting into the thoughtlessness, peacefulness and relaxation, which most people consider as meditation, has nothing to do with awakening. Some fake gurus and prophets even draw comparison between awakening and the deep sleep state. How silly it is to compare the highest ecstasy of the Shiva-Shakti union to the dullness of slumber.

Although the world and the body, with all their sorrows, imperfections and limitations, do not appear in the state of deep sleep, at the same time there is no positive bliss and ecstasy of Divine wakefulness. The mirror of consciousness, which was reflecting the world appearance on its surface, has now become covered with tar and is reflecting only darkness.

The Life and Sadhana of Sadhus in a Himalayan Cave
The absence of any experience is simply insentience, a characteristic of inanimate objects.

Bhavana, Bhairava Mudra, Atma-vichara and most importantly, pranayama are the major tools for ascending the levels towards the Higher Reality, and in themselves could be sufficient for liberation from the limiting conditions, if practiced continuously with great zeal and an unquenchable longing for the Absolute Truth. But if your longing for Truth is overwhelming and you desperate to find shortcuts, to arrive at your Beloved quicker, then I would advise you to incorporate into your sadhana the wisdom of sacred plants and add the spiritual heat of Tapas.

With the passage of time, immersed in this continuous practice, we felt lighter and happier than ever before. Our minds were almost wiped out with the continuous dynamic pranayamas and now were pure and radiant. Our hearts were cleansed of negativity and ready to receive our Beloved. When the light of awareness turned within constantly shines on the sense of 'I', all long accumulated Vasanas (mental tendencies and predispositions) melt away in its radiance just like a picture exposed to the sunlight for a prolonged time loses its pigments and becomes white. As often as we could, we experimented with different types of breathing patterns, my most favourite of which was fast 'kapalbhati'' (shining skull) pranayama, in which you rapidly and actively expel air through your nostrils, by contracting muscles of your stomach and then, let your stomach and lungs passively return to their primal position. The duration of this, and other pranayamas, in our spontaneous experiments depended on the state of our consciousness. The best advice here for beginners is to breathe until you begin to feel dizziness, or faintness. At this moment, breathe in or out and enter into the firm retention of breath (Kumbhaka). With regular practice, you shall intuitively begin to feel that the approaching moment is just perfect for entering into Divine 'Kumbhaka' (retention of breath).

For beginners of Kumbhaka Pranayama I would not recommend, after the intense dynamic breathing, going into 'Bahya Kumbhaka' (retention of breath after the exhalation), but rather to start with 'Antar Kumbhaka' (retention of breath after completing inhalation). Practicing Bahya Kumbhaka is better to do after practicing 'Antar Kumbhaka' for a prolonged period of time. In this manner, your body-cosmos becomes filled with invigorating oxygen and it is much easier to become firmly established in 'Bahya Kumbhaka', without the desire to breathe in. After intense dynamic breathing, when you feel the moment is right, you should breathe in slightly more air than usual, lock your throat by lowering and pulling your chin slightly back in 'Jalandhara Bandha'. As an experiment you could also occasionally add 'Mula Bandha' (the contracting and lifting muscles on the pelvic flor, between the anus and genitals). You could also occasionally play with contracting and releasing the pelvic muscles, simultaneously visualising and feeling how the dormant sleeping Kundalini Shakti who was coiled within your Muladhara Chakra begins to wake up and uncoil. You can also visualise, or better to say 'experialise' (to imagine experiencing the tactile and energetic sensations) how the pranic electric Kundalini energy flows up your spine through the middle sushumna channel, rising from the Muladhara towards the crown of your head (Sahashrara Chakra).

However, there cannot be strict rules when practicing yoga. Yoga is not stiff and formal, but fluid and flexible. It is born out of experiments which trigger intuition and lead to a greater degree of spontaneity. Some yogis teach you to count the periods of inhalation, exhalation and retention of breath, all giving different ratios, such as to inhale for one count, hold your breath for three counts and exhale for two counts, for example. I personally consider such pranayamas dangerous. The body has its own innate intelligence. When we try to change such an important bodily function as the distribution of prana by controlling it with our mind, it can be dangerous to health.

Any attempts to control the flow of life energy (prana) with the aid of the mind is like teaching lovers to move in a certain restricted way to reach orgasm. Lovers are moved by Love herself! It is an extremely heightened sensitivity, alertness to every minute sensation, to every tiny detail (experiencing myriad dancing universes in just one tiny corner of the beloved's lips), immediate recognition of the most subtle intentions of a lover, and more than anything else, sacrifice of the sense of separation between two, and complete surrender to 'Love that moves'… brings lovers into the highest state of Divine union. Lovers recognise that they are not two separate persons making love, but they are One Love herself,

The Life and Sadhana of Sadhus in a Himalayan Cave blossoming with sweet kisses, love-bites, and gracious movements into the ecstatic freedom of Truth – pure Love expression. Love is not stiff, but fluid and flexible. She flows as streams of liquid energy – Divine Ambrosia, creating majestic patterns. She dances. When one tries to control the flow of prana by counting periods and lengths of inhalation, exhalation and retention, it is the stiff mind trying to control fluid prana. And so, the two (mind and prana) remain separate. The aim of Kumbhaka Prana Yoga, which spontaneously emerged as a result of my longing for the ultimate Truth and the revelations of plant teachers, and about which I will be writing later in this book, is to encourage the innate intelligence of the body-cosmos to fully blossom.

The practice of Kumbhaka Prana Yoga leads to the fusion of mind and prana into one intelligence-energy: prana-mind. Just as lovers lose themselves in each other, lose themselves in the spontaneity of 'One Love that moves', so the practitioner of Kumbhaka Prana Yoga is in love-affair with prana and loses oneself to become One with prana. When one is absorbed in the inner dimensions of Supreme Intelligence-Energy (the inner dimensions of prana), one loses the limitations and restrictions of the body appearance.

I will write a detailed description of Kumbhaka Prana Yoga in a separate chapter towards the end of this book, my dear reader. Now, I would like to take you back to our magical story.

Seduced by the schoolboys who regularly paid us visits and brought with them some food, my friend Nataraj broke his fast and decided to start eating. One lovely young local woman, who regularly paid her respects to this holy place, also brought food for us. I remained strong in my fasting resolve and was delighted to see Nataraj happy. Near the entrance to the cave there were couple of small concrete buildings; one served as a kitchen, having some pots, knives and few other utensils in it, the other had a raised concrete platform for a bed and dhuna (a square fireplace) in the middle of it. Early every morning the milkman stopped at the bottom of the stairs on the road below. He would pour milk into Nataraja's pot as his humble offering. The boys brought rice, onions, potatoes and chili peppers. One day they even cooked a sweet halva for Nataraj.

The Life and Sadhana of Sadhus in a Himalayan Cave

Our friend Dave came to see us after a week or so. He brought his cousin and children with him and asked us to give them our blessings. I had become accustomed to performing puja rituals and at that time looked like a real sadhu, completely covered in ash. Waving light and incense and chanting the 'Mahamrityunjaya' (great freedom from death) mantra, I blessed them, putting three strands of ash on their foreheads and giving them my Rudraksha beads as a gift. Dave brought the most potent charas with him as a gift. With the continuation of fasting and our intense sadhana I became lightheaded and, after smoking a chillum with wonderful charas, I lost sensations of body and world. After regaining 'normal consciousness' I found my body collapsed on the floor.

It became a permanent feature of my experience, that after intense pranayama, as soon as I was entering Kumbhaka, the immense energy would shatter the habitual picture of the world, and my body would go into shaking and convulsing mode, as though the very electrons within the stable atomic structure of my body were becoming unstable and were leaping out into the next high velocity orbits. My shaking hands were desperately trying to find some support to prevent my body from falling, often successfully, but occasionally they lost their grip, after which, my body collapsed and entered a very peculiar early childhood-like perception. In this state, the tension of 'being human' wasn't prominent yet, and complete relaxation prevailed. However, in a matter of five or ten seconds, consciousness rapidly reconstructed a 'normal' picture of reality.

After couple of weeks in Shringi Rishi Gufa, to our surprise Muku Baba (the one who had given us information about the location of this cave) came to visit us. He said that he had heard some rumours in a village about two sadhus staying in a cave, and he thought that it must be us. Of course, we all were very happy to see each other and have some chillums and spiritual discourses.

My fasting lasted for two weeks. While in a very jolly spiritual state, I was tempted by the delicious looking plums, and plum wine, which our new friend Amish brought for us. After conversation with Amish, who visited us often, sometimes providing us with charas, the strange decision to buy a camcorder emerged. I must say that since the time we had met Dave, who told us that Shiva had sent him to help us, we were in a state of absolute

The Life and Sadhana of Sadhus in a Himalayan Cave
surrender, only following signs, or the decisions of the people
surrounding us. We never made active decisions ourselves. The
white flag of surrender was waving at the entrance to our cave. Thy
Will be done. Thy Will be done. Thy Will be done.

The idea came from Amish, who also organised to take us to
Solan to buy the video camera. We just agreed that it could be
useful to record our spiritual practices and our life as sadhus on
camera.

We had spent twenty-five days in Shringi Rishi Gufa, and our
being was pure and radiant. Happiness and gratitude were exuding
through our eyes, hearts and pores, as though Shiva himself had
been established in our bodies. Amish's friends, Ram Kumar and
his brother, arrived in their car to take us up to Solan. It was a very
strange feeling as you probably can imagine; after twenty-five days
of living in a cave to suddenly see a big town, just like a beehive,
filled with lots of busy people. It was absolutely obvious to me that
I was experiencing the Matrix!

Unfortunately, we couldn't find an affordable camcorder in
Solan and our new friends insisted on taking us to Chandigarh,
where we finally found a camera we could just about afford. In the
darkness of late evening they delivered us back to our beloved cave
but offered to pick us up the next morning and give us a tour of
Holy Renuka Ji lake. As I mentioned, we were free of our stiff
decisions and were flowing gently wherever Shiva and his
messengers wanted to take us.

After prostrating to our holy cave in which we were spending
such an amazing precious time, Ram Kumar, his brother
(unfortunately I forgot his name), Amish (who charged our camera
and decided to be our cameraman), my young friend who had now
become known as Nataraj Baba and I jumped into the car early in
the morning, with tears of gratitude streaming down our cheeks,
and departed for Renuka Ji. To be honest, we had no idea where
and why we were going, or for how long, but simply obeyed the
power that was guiding us.

Fairies of Renuka – Rivendell

R enuka Ji (lake) is a very special, magical place. After Renuka Ji heard that her husband Jamdagni Rishi had been killed by the sons of King Sahashtrabahu, she took her own life by drowning herself in a lake, Ram Sarovar. Puranas narrate that Ram Sarovar immediately took the shape of a lady and since then it has been known as Renuka Ji Lake. After killing Sahashtrabahu and his sons in a fierce battle, Parashurama, who is the sixth incarnation (avatar) of Lord Vishnu, and the youngest son of Renuka and Jamdagni Rishi, gave a new life to his father with his Divine powers. He came to the bank of the lake and prayed for his mother come out of the waters. His mother responded to his prayers and Lord Parashurama vowed at her feet. She said that she would permanently live in the lake, but she would come out of the lake on Dev Prabodhini Ekadashi every year to meet her son. Bhagwati Renuka also promised that people gracing this pious occasion of mother's affection and son's devotion, would be showered with Divine blessings. On the day of celebration of Dashami (usually in October/ November) the palanquin of Lord Parashuram is brought to Renuka Ji from the ancient Parashuram temple in Jamu Koti village in a traditional procession known as 'Shobha Yantra'. It is attended by thousands of devotees.

It was the first day of July, when we arrived at Renuka Ji. A place of a natural beauty, it was tranquil, charming and inspiring. Except for a few sadhus, there were only a handful of people around the lake. Ram Kumar and Amish guided us to the furthest side of the lake towards Renuka's head, where a little chai shop

270

was located. We passed through the musk deer sanctuary, remembering the saying: 'A musk deer searches for the source of intoxicating fragrance here and there, but is not able to find it, because the fragrance comes from within itself.' So, it is with Bliss! It is not to be found outside of us; it exists within us.

We were introduced to couple of sadhus, who were experts in ayurvedic medicine. They gave us some drops for the eyes, to purify our vision. It was a very interesting experience: at the beginning there was a strongly buzzing sensation in the retinas, then it gradually dissolved and clarified the vision. The owner of the chai shop, Bindu, served us coffee and prepared the most potent chillum I've ever tried. After chillum, spontaneous Kapalbhati pranayama and Kumbhaka, which sent me into the bliss of Samadhi, we played some kirtans, and improvised: garlands of words were flooding spontaneously out of our hearts that were swollen with joy. Bindu became very fond of us. He felt the pure energy of happiness radiating from our hearts. We were singing in ecstasy our devotion to Shiva, and Himachal Pradesh is undoubtedly Shiva's land. We could feel Shiva's presence everywhere around and within us.

We walked a full circle around the lake. On one side was a tiger sanctuary and one of our new young friends, whom we just met at Renuka Ji, and who lived in a local ashram, played a tag game with the tigers. When the darkness settled in, our hearts were gladdened to see thousands of light-beings (glow worms) dancing in the summer air. It was truly magical, and we had a feeling that we had arrived at Elrond's Rivendell, or it was Christmas in the middle of summer, with thousands of fairy-lights dancing among the trees. We had no need for torches, for it was bright enough to see the path. We slept on the roof of the chai shop. Bindu gave us a couple of blankets.

The next morning Ram Kumar with his brother and Amish took us for another adventure up the mountain road to Maa Bhangayani Temple in Haripurdar. The very beautiful temple with a breath-taking panoramic view filled us once more with drunken joy and happiness. We were singing and dancing, igniting sparks of joy in the temple-carers and visitors, who joined us in adding their voices, movements and smiles to our ecstatic kirtans, while Amish recorded it all on camera.

Fairies of Renuka – Rivendell

Ram Kumar brought us back to Renuka Ji. We picked up Bindu and drove back to our Shringi Rishi Gufa. Bindu stayed with us that night in the small building with the dhuna next to the cave. He had a tough night, for this space was tiny and the room was filled with smoke, because we couldn't find any dry wood. When it began to rain, we had found that our cave leaked quite dramatically, so it wasn't easy to find a dry spot to sleep on. The next morning, Bindu, who was horrified that we lived in such tough conditions, invited us to stay in his room at Jamdagni Rishi ashram on a Jammu Peak.

Ram Kumar kindly took us back to Renuka Ji. Bindu arranged for us to temporarily stay in the 1008 Shri Nirwan ashram on the bank of Renuka Ji, while he was making necessary preparations to the room at Jamdagni Rishi. We spent couple of nights in the ashram, former home to a silent saint, Sundaram Muni. I must say that living among sadhus, I found that sadly, not all of them are engaged in spiritual practices and the quest for moksha (liberation). Some were drinking alcohol, some used opium, some were just watching TV, like the guy who oversaw Shri Nirwan ashram these days. Fortunately, the local people could see through it all. They felt our sincerity and treated us very respectfully.

On the third day, Bindu and couple of his friends guided us to the top of Jamu Peak, which stands about three thousand feet above the sea level. After a couple of hours' climbing, which seemed to be never-ending, we reached the top just before nightfall. How great was our surprise and marvel at the Divine play which was orchestrated for us by the living Gods in this holy land, when we saw at the top of Jamu Peak, Sitaram Baba, our sadhu friend whom we had met in Uttarkashi couple of months ago. How on Earth, except through Divine intervention, was it possible in the vastness of Northern India, to meet a sadhu friend, on the top of a high hill, whom we had met a hundred miles away in a different Indian State? It was simply unbelievable! It was Divine Providence!

He and his friend, the young sannyasin Harigiri Baba were staying in one room of this small ashram. Tilak Raj, who for some reason had come here from the neighbouring Haryana state, wasn't a sadhu, but temporarily lived here, serving sadhus by cooking food, cleaning dishes, bringing water and taking care of the needs of the ashram. All three were lovely and easily approachable guys with whom we became very good friends. In fact, we soon began to call ourselves a happy family. Bindu placed us in one very basic, but clean, vacated room. After an evening of smoking chillums, sharing stories, and talking about spirituality and filming, we went to sleep in our new room.

When we woke up, Bindu and his friends had already left and only us five remained. The sun had risen, pouring its gentle light onto the hills and valleys below. The majestic view from the top of Jamdagni Rishi Peak stretching for miles and miles in all directions took our breath away. Just beneath we could see Renuka Ji lying on her side. Legend has it that Jamdagni Rishi meditated on this spot for eight hundred years. A beautiful silence, away from all sources of noise pollution, penetrated our very being with its calming vibrations. This beautiful little ashram consisted of a statue of meditating Jamdagni Rishi, a small temple with a Shiva Lingam and temple bell, and a big round dhuna in the middle of a round tiled courtyard surrounded by a wide, low wall, on which one could comfortably sit. There was one building with dhuna in a middle of it, where we would all gather for a chillum, or a meal and couple of rooms where we slept. The locals, as they had been doing for a long time ago already, called us Shiv Baba and Nataraj Baba.

Our Indian visas were due to expire in the next twenty-three days. We didn't have an exact plan for the future but had in mind the possibility of going to Nepal to renew our visas. Now we concentrated all our efforts on transcending mind and achieving Self-realisation! We were quite optimistic that it was undoubtedly possible. When I spoke to Arunachala Ramana some time ago, asking him the question about crossing the point of no return by means of a forty-day fast, accompanied with intense sadhana at the heart of which was Self-inquiry, he replied: 'The point of no return (Self-realisation) may happen in even as early as twenty-one days in such intense conditions.' And so, we decided that, no matter what, but we were staying here for at least twenty-one days.

The Conquest of Mind or Twenty-one Days to Nirvana

We called our retreat 'The conquest of mind, or twenty-one days to Nirvana'. Our spiritual practice continued as before: Bhavana, Bhairava Mudra, Atma Vichara, practically constant pranayama, smoking chillums, gazing into each other's eyes while breathing dynamically, chanting mantras in the Kashmir Shaivism tradition inside the Shiva temple, which had wonderful acoustics, and for joy and relaxation, singing our hearts out in ecstatic kirtans. Every day we recorded the episodes of our lives as sadhus. I began fasting again, making excuses only for the 'Bhang' pakoras (deep-fried Ganja leaves) and 'Bhang' juice, which I found to be the most refreshing tonic. Shiva in His iconography is often depicted as having pot with him in which he keeps his 'Bhang' juice.

It was the middle of July and the marijuana plants, which were abundant across of the whole Himachal Pradesh, including Jamdagni Rishi Peak, began to flower and pollinate. We were delighted to collect our own charas. With every passing day our minds and hearts were getting purer and purer, free of thought and negative emotions. They shone with joy and happiness, like a sun on a cloudless day. Many times, entering the majestic Kumbhaka after intense pranayama, I would lose consciousness of my body and the world around, and entered the inner fields of dense energy-intelligence, almost immediately noticing how consciousness quickly reconstructs the habitual image of reality (almost like putting mosaic tiles together), with my body lying on the floor after its collapse.

The Conquest of Mind or Twenty-one Days to Nirvana

If you love Truth more than anything else, if you thoroughly understand with the might of your intellect and the totality of your being that Absolute Truth is imperishable, indestructible, unbreakable, undying, eternal, and that your True Self is this Absolute Truth, you are getting ready to let go of that which is impermanent and perishable. You are getting ready to enter the mystery beyond the point of no return. When by the grace of your Sadhana you have been brought face-to-face with Death, who is the destroyer of the false and impermanent, and who is about to annihilate 'you', you have the power to humbly offer yourself to Death for annihilation, knowing that the Real can never be destroyed. If death is inevitable, why cling hopelessly to life, why not find the way to meet Death and ask her to teach you the Truth, which cannot be found only on one 'earthly-life' side of eternal Reality, before your time is up and it's too late to learn? Obviously, learning from Death requires utmost courage. You must be ready for the seemingly impossible to happen! Not only your relatives and friends, not only the whole world and everything you know within it, not only your precious body, but your mind, your very sanity and your 'self', or at least what you took yourself to be, are at stake.

When I was reaching these crucial moments in my spiritual practice, in which there was the realisation: one more step forward and I shall never return, one more movement towards the expansion of energy and my mind ('me', my body and the whole world within it) will be shattered, exploded, annihilated, despite my desperate desire to fully plunge into it, consciousness always retreated, preserving life. When we are facing Death, it's almost impossible to proceed further, for a retreat happens often even before we can make any decision. The totality of habitual consciousness clings to what it knows with all its might, frightened by the terrifying unknown. If you nevertheless have the courage to go further, to your great surprise, you will not die, you will not be annihilated, but you will find that you have entered a new level of the highly dense field of intelligence-energy. Knowing this, you can proceed further into the next level of higher frequency, into the ever-expanding and ever-intensifying higher levels of reality, into higher levels of lucidity, ascending towards the higher levels of super-perception, towards the summit (of the ultimate beatitude, of

The Conquest of Mind or Twenty-one Days to Nirvana

the infinite might, of hair-rising wonder, of the utter joy, of the sweetest tears of gentleness and gratitude, of the greatest fun ever, of the complete absence of any tension), to the astounding ride on a rollercoaster of incomparable ecstasy.

On beautiful sunny days, after smoking chillum, I loved to stand on a cliff, deeply breathing, with my eyes wide open, fixing my gaze on one spot far below, but opening wide my peripheral vision and embodying the totality of the majestic panorama, including all sounds and fragrances.

I am God Absolute! I am That! Undoubtedly, God – the True Self – is forever present in the eternal now. To seek Him-Her in a past, or future, or in the sky, or far-away galaxies is foolish indeed. God can be found only deep within the nucleus of one's Spiritual Heart in the eternal Now, prior to any appearances. We are longsighted creatures with the focus of our attention dwelling on the objects of perception. To see God, to feel God, to realise oneself as God, we must bring the focus of our attention-awareness nearer and nearer and nearer… to the very core of our being. Perceive, feel and be all at once, drawing the world picture closer and closer towards the experiencer.

With the practice of dynamic pranayama, prana provides us with the additional energy necessary for the expansion of our capacity to behold the True Glory of the Beloved. The increasing energy – Shakti – is the vehicle and the path towards the explosion of Intelligence – Shiva. We begin to feel, that with the breathing, the whole field of cognition is entering the closest proximity of our innermost Self. An overwhelming sense of intimacy with our Self/God/Love/Reality awakens. The conscious energy is ever increasing, expanding, sparkling and glowing. And the world picture is no longer perceived as an uninteresting neutral foreground, but as a totally magical, miraculous, glowing background with the pinnacle of light of awareness turned within and reaching God – I-Consciousness – at the very centre, the very source, the very heart of our being. The senses of differentiation between within and without, I or this, up or down, left or right, as well as the sense of gravity and all objective boundaries, melt in the ecstasy of flowing soma and become homogenous. Thus, we begin to directly experience Reality – the True Miraculous Self – God Absolute, who is forever present. But obviously, it is only the

The Conquest of Mind or Twenty-one Days to Nirvana beginning of the inner journey towards the bottomless ocean of the rapture and ecstasy of the Shiva-Shakti Miracle, for Reality is infinite and so is the degree and magnitude of its realisation.

Our hearts and empty minds were exuding happiness in this magical place. I remember recording on camera a dung beetle rolling a ball of dung with his hind legs. 'Tired of carrying the bullshit of your life? Join us in Jamdagni Paradise!' was the moto for our 'Conquest of Mind, twenty-one days to Nirvana' video recordings.

Our mini discs for the camcorder were running out and we needed to go to the nearest town of Nahan to buy some more. On the way down, somewhere in between Jamu Peak and Renuka Ji lake there is the small village of Jamu Koti with the Parashuram Temple in it. The local people greeted us and offered us lunch which they cooked for the whole village as though they were one big family. The local villagers were very respectful towards us, always bowing and touching our feet. I became accustomed to such respect and always put my hand over their heads in a gesture of blessing. Such ceremony didn't inflate our egos but was just very polite gesture, filling our hearts with love and gratitude. Some locals took me to be the reincarnation of Lord Parashuram. They showed me the image of Parashurama, and I found great similarities between our faces.

While waiting for a bus to Nahan, we went for a little walk outside the bus station, where another local brought us as a gift a very beautifully made chillum and quite a big chunk of good quality charas. I will be forever grateful to all these kind local villagers in Himachal Pradesh. They have so much respect for those who decide to commit themselves to spiritual disciplines, regardless if they are Hindu, or European. In all the time we had been in Himachal Pradesh, we had only seen one European couple on a motorbike. The rest of the time we communicated only with Indians. We made the mistake of buying a bottle of whisky in Nahan. We thought it would be a funky gift and might cheer up our friends at Jamdagni. Sitaram Baba, Harigiri Baba and Tilak Raj refused to drink it, saying that in the history of this place there was a story of one sadhu, who got mad when he drank. This was a place of power and must be greatly respected. Nevertheless, me and Nataraj Baba drunk, but to be honest, didn't enjoy it much. In this

The Conquest of Mind or Twenty-one Days to Nirvana
sacred place it was the clarity of perception that was giving us joy
and happiness, not the fog of drunkenness.

Sacred to Shiva, Ganja is far superior to alcohol. We found also
a few psilocybin mushrooms growing out of cow dung. Holy cows
were providing us with holy plant teachers. Unfortunately, we
couldn't find enough for a good trip. We made a tea, but the effect
was minimal. Somehow one of Nataraja's friend sent him a book to
a Nahan postal address, with supposedly LSD stamps put in
between the pages. And so, Nataraja Baba disappeared for three
days to Nahan. While he was running down the hill, he fell and
injured his knee. The open wounds became infected and covered in
pus, so he needed to buy some antibiotics.

My daily routine of spiritual sadhana continued as usual. In the
mornings, as a rule, we went to the water spring about a mile from
the ashram. We bathed and collected water to store for later. It was
wonderful walking through the pine woods, with absolutely breath-
taking views of the landscape far below. I often made a very deeply
penetrating eye connection with the few very still and wise water
buffalos grazing there. Water buffalos are truly amazing in their
energy. We basked in the loving energy of Oneness.

Sometimes clouds descended on the peak, and this was also
magical, especially when it happened during meditation. Suddenly
the whole world was obliterated, and then, without any objects in
view, it was so easy for attention-awareness just to be established
in its own source.

I was so glad that I had bought and carried with me my flute. I
discovered that I could incorporate flute-playing into my Sadhana.
Playing flute in a certain way was a subtle method of pranayama. I
often combined these two and with their help was flying to ever-
expanding heights. I thought that the majority of wind instrument
musicians must feel very high at the ends of their performances.
Pranayama accompanied by beautiful music; what can be better?

Nataraj Baba returned after three days. He brought *The Book of
Mirdad* with him, but for some reason the LSD stamps weren't
there. Nataraj Baba, who often was shouting 'Hallelujah!' in
ecstasy, was soon christened by locals as Hallelujah Baba, which
he found just perfect. Sita-Ram Baba asked us to donate a bit of
money for the arrangement of the Guru Purnima festival, which
coincided with the festival for the beginning of the rain season. Big

The Conquest of Mind or Twenty-one Days to Nirvana
cauldrons were brought from the villages below and masses of
cooking began. More and more people were coming to our ashram,
and within a couple of days there were around a thousand people
scattered across the place. Bindu introduced us to his wife and kids
and asked us to play kirtans for all the people gathered there. And
so, we played and sung our hearts out to the cheers and joy of a
massive crowd, while Bindu made video recordings. I almost lost
my voice from singing too much and too loudly. It was relief to
return to silence the next day.

The days were passing, and it became clearer that our
miraculous awakening was not going to happen this time.
Nevertheless, these fifty days living as sadhus in Shringi Rishi
Gufa, at Renuka Ji Lake and in Jamdagni Rishi ashram were the
best and happiest days of my entire life.

There cannot be arguments any longer, for it is of utmost clarity
now: happiness does not increase with the accumulation of wealth
and material possessions! Only the True Self is all-satisfying
happiness! Fools seek happiness outside themselves. Accumulating
more and more objects, giving temporary pleasures, they are never
fully satisfied. Like hungry ghosts, craving more and more, but
never able to appease their hunger, they are perpetually circling in
the illusive 'samsara' (repetitive cyclic existence). I have seen rich
people dying of boredom in the midst of luxury and entertainment,
and I have seen poor simple village folks filled with joy and I have
seen sadhus (holy men) soaked in Soma (Divine nectar), radiating
peace, contentment and bliss. True unalloyed happiness and
absolute satisfaction can only be found within oneself. The True
Self is overflowing abundance. Lacking nothing, everything
emanates from it. The True Self filled with excessive joy is the
everlasting source of perennial giving. Wanting nothing for itself,
because of its fullness, it pours itself out as a flood of love and joy.
Even in the scorching heat of a desert, the Self-immersed one,
basks in the refreshing streams of Divine ambrosia. Only within
One's True Self is everlasting happiness and absolute satisfaction.
Happiness belongs to the Self-sufficient!

Solar Eclipse and a Brief Visit to Hell

With only a few days left until our six-month visas expired, and the possibility of travelling to Nepal to renew them seeming highly complicated, we were faced with the dilemma of either staying, no matter what, as sadhus in Jamdagni Rishi Ashram, or to going back to our home countries with the hope of coming back and continuing our lives as sadhus. The thought of being caught without a visa and being deported from India, unable to return to this magical land, seemed unacceptable. And so, we began making our plans to go home, making phone calls to Ramkumar and Amish to pick us up from the foot of Jamu Peak. Saying our last goodbyes to our happy family: Sitaram Baba, Harigiri Baba, Bindu, Tilak Raj, who invited us to stay in his ashram in Haryana if we came back, and to couple of the local boys who were always around, we made our way down the hill.

All in all, we made about thirty hours of recordings on thirty mini discs. I hope one day we can edit our material and put it together into a documentary film, who knows, maybe with your help, dear reader. Unfortunately, we didn't make any recordings of Shringi Rishi Gufa, where we spent half of our time as sadhus, and was such an essential part of our spiritual journey. I asked Ramkumar if he could give me a lift to Muku Baba's village, from where I was planning to make a brief visit to our cave, at least to include the vision of this cave to incorporate it into our film.

Amish was leaving for Delhi on a big truck delivering tomatoes to the Indian capital. He agreed to give Hallelujah Baba a lift to

Delhi. Last hugs, sweet words for the road, Om Namah Shivaya! Off he went, my dear companion.

I found Muku Baba, who finally introduced me to Rajendra Puri Maharaj. I had a lovely chat and a cup of chai in his ashram, then dinner at Muku Baba's place, where I left my guitar. The next morning, we made a quick trip to Shringi Rishi Gufa, which appeared to have become scruffy and abandoned after we left it. I made a quick recording, for I was afraid of missing my bus, and off we went. Muku kindly decided to give me company and came to Delhi with me.

When, after picking my luggage up from the hotel, I arrived at the airport to board my plane to London, I wasn't allowed to plane, for my Indian visa had expired one day ago. I had to go to the Indian embassy to give them my reason for overstaying and apply for a new one-day extension visa. There was lots of hustle trying to rearrange tickets for a new flight the next day, going to a busy embassy and after permission was granted, driving in search of a different embassy building, where they would put a visa extension stamp in my passport. They took a quick photo for the visa. The department was about to close for the weekend. I begged them to give me the visa and when they finally did, I found that I had no money to pay for it. Saying that I would be back just in a few minutes, I rushed with my rickshaw driver to a cash withdrawal machine nearby, and Delhi went very dark! It was the 1st of August 2008 – I was witnessing a complete solar eclipse! A massive omen! I got my visa extension just before the embassy closed, but it has been ten years now since I left Mother India, and I haven't yet had a chance to return. My heart is aching to come back to my motherland, where I feel truly at home!

Without further complications, I returned to the Isle of Wight, where my darling Tara was waiting for me. A few days later we were celebrating my forty-second birthday, and life returned to its habitual rhythm.

In September, after feeling so high for a very long time, while living as a sadhu, I lapsed into a low state – a bad trip. At the popular 'Bestival' (the Isle of Wight music festival), I got quite drunk on strong gin and tonic. Later, in the twilight, my friend offered me a cube of sugar with a few drops of liquid acid on it, and when the night enveloped Earth in her darkness, I topped it up with ketamine offered by some dodgy people who had gathered in an abandoned marquee. Suddenly I returned to the already-so-familiar dark and cold dimension of hell.

As the troubled mathematical genius John Forbes Nash Jr. from the movie *A Beautiful Mind* keeps relapsing into paranoid schizophrenia, seeing Charles, Marcee and Parcher again and again in his persistent gloomy dimension, so did I immediately recognise all the hell-players whom I had seen many times before in this shadowy realm, gathered there in the abandoned marquee, where we snorted ketamine. Leaving the marquee, I stood for a long time on the side of the campsite, not risking going to sleep, but waiting for the sunrise to end this murky plane of reality. Two very suspicious people approached me and offered me a half-filled plastic cup of wine and a rolled cigarette. The way they tempted me to accept their offer immediately made me think of the story of Jesus tempted by Satan. I felt something bad would happen if I allowed this transaction.

'Who are you?' I asked.

'We are the old spirits of the festivals,' they replied, although mocking me. I, nevertheless, accepted wine and cigarette. Nothing dramatic happened and they went away. In the middle of the night, after finding our tent, I finally went to sleep, but woke up with all these dark memories alive, not trusting anyone. It took me weeks to fully recover from this suspicious state.

Guy Finley helped me dramatically, with his stories of going through 'the dark night of the soul'. We ordered the whole collection of his CDs on this and similar subjects. I would recommend anyone who is temporarily experiencing going through darkness listen to Guy Finley. He is very helpful.

Tara and her friend Uddhava meanwhile, were very excited about the new spiritual technology called 'Holosync'. Uddhava had already ordered the first series of discs featuring the first level of 'brainwave entrainment' and he kindly offered to copy and share it with Tara.

(To read the most important points on how Holosync neurotechnology works according to Bill Harris, the director of Centerpointe Research Institute, see Appendix 3.)

Bill Harris's explanations and the ideas of Ilya Prigogine about self-reorganisation, or the 'escape' of open living systems into a higher order of complexity out of increasing 'chaos', or 'entropy', resonated harmoniously with me. I could see a great similarity between these ideas and my own view of Reality as a hierarchy of intelligence. The additional input into the neuron activities reminded me somehow of the increasing intensity of psychedelic journeys with the possibility to either escape the 'chaos' of intense visual and emotional input into a higher order of reorganised intelligence, or due to the low threshold of coping with such intense input, resist it and therefore build the road into the lower realms (bad trip).

Throughout all my life I have been learning to courageously and gracefully accept the changes, challenges, offerings and suggestions life presents me with, as gifts of lessons to learn something more profound about myself. Of course, one must not be naïve when accepting things or accept suggestion that go against one's conscience and appear harmful to oneself, others, and the whole way of dharma. The important aspect of our intellect, which in Hindu Scriptures is known as Viveka, the discrimination between good and bad, right and wrong, temporary and eternal, important and trivial, must be one's constant companion.

Tara and I decided to commit ourselves to daily meditation with Holosync. For the first month it was just half-hour meditations, which then changed into hour-long meditations, usually before we were going to bed. I really liked the effect the Holosync sounds induced, as also I could clearly feel the difference between each new level of Holosync programme. As I was giving way to spontaneity during meditation, my breathing naturally intensified, turning into a very dynamic intense pranayama, filling my 'Kumbh' (the Sanskrit word for a pot, meaning a body) with buzzing, sparkling, electric prana-energy, and stopping at the appropriate moments for rest and the expansion of the prana-mind in majestic Kumbhaka.

Epiphany and Marriage

The busy family period of Christmas and New Year passed, giving way to more gentle, contemplative and magical times. On the night between the sixth and seventh of January, Tara and I were celebrating Orthodox Russian Christmas; Christmas without noise, crackers, crowds and fireworks, but with the intimacy of just the two of us, on a soft rug in front of a gently burning wood-stove, illuminated by playful candlelight, with champagne, delicious snacks and wine. There is always, as we discovered during the following years, something very special, mystical, magical and mysterious about that night. The weather is usually bright and crisp and there is an abundance of brilliant stars. This day is also known as 'Epiphany', which means 'Striking Realisation'. And a striking realisation it was! The veils covering Reality, which is none other than pure Love herself, were torn apart. The fog in the retina of my eyes and heart was washed away by the sacred waters of this epiphany, revealing the most beautiful undeniable Truth. All previous worries, fears, doubts and tension dissolved in the pristine clarity of direct perception. My old world collapsed, turned to dust and was blown away by the refreshing breeze of change. I was reborn that night and baptised in its holy waters!

Looking into the radiant eyes of my beloved Tara, after the Divine Ecstasy of Love-making, in which we reached the utmost intimacy in which it wasn't possible any longer to differentiate who was who, but only to feel One Love that moved our bodies in a most tender ecstatic dance, I saw the bottomless ocean of utmost trust and openness with the waves of pure love and light radiating tenderly from its greatest depths. The universe with countless

284

'others' no longer existed for us, for we had entered the majestic Universe of Love. The two of us became a complete whole universe. The waves of love exuding from my beloved's eyes, her radiant heart and every pore of her beautiful body washed away the remaining haze of uncertainties. We saw each other with the eyes of our naked souls in our utmost purity and the beauty of our innocence.

My continuous search for my woman, my companion, my playmate, my soulmate was finally over now! She is the One! She is the One with whom I would like to spend the rest of my life. She is the One with whom I would like to spend eternity. She loves me unconditionally! I love her unconditionally! 'Will you marry me, my love?' Tears of Love streaming out of the corners of her shining eyes. 'Yes! Yes! I will! Of course!'

I no longer have any doubts that of the many paths to the summit of Self-realisation, one of the most beautiful is the path of the intense unconditional love of a couple. When the relationship is ripe and pregnant with the energy of mature love, the very act of love-making, which in its intensity and magnitude is far beyond adolescent, immature sex, can take a couple by the potency of their utmost trust in each other and their surrender to 'Love that Moves', through the ecstasy of the spontaneous Love-dance, into the utmost intimacy. In such a state, there are no longer two individuals making love, but One Love that ecstatically moves their beautiful passionate bodies through an amazing sexual play of tender kisses, caresses, licks, touches, heightened breathing, moans of pleasure and love-bites accompanied by the intricate movements of the sensual lingam within the highly sensual yoni, heightens all senses and consciousness itself, and on the waves of awakening and rising Kundalini sexual energy, takes them into the dissolution of all boundaries and limitations, into the full possession of two individuals by Goddess Love into Divine Ecstasy; the absolute freedom of the Shiva-Shakti Union!

In such love-making, a couple experiences super-heightened sensitivity (experiencing a myriad of dancing universes only in one little touch of a tiny corner of the beloved's lips). Every pore exudes the sweetest intoxicating aromas. The skin, lips, tongue, yoni fluid tastes like Divine Amrit. The awakened bodily intuition anticipates the slightest desire and intentions of a lover. The thinking mind gets replaced by love spontaneity. The lover and beloved realise that they are making love not to each other, but to themselves. In such a heightened state, the spontaneous knowledge and mastery of perfect love-making arises naturally. The intensity of the couple's love for each other and especially their love for the ultimate Truth provides them with the unshakable courage to surrender to the movements of Love and go beyond the boundaries of physical bodies. In the utmost intimacy of their love-making, their nuclei become so close to each other that a nuclear reaction takes place, causing two beautiful hearts to become fused into one. The tremendous energy of such fusion explodes and blows away all restrictions of space and time. They are awake as one Shiva-Shakti, and experience ecstatic Reality in their absolute freedom! They have found Oneness! They have become One – Shiva-Shakti!

In the Kaula Tantric tradition, such a couple is called 'Yamala'. As great tantric sage Abhinavagupta puts it: 'The couple (Yamala) is considered itself, the unifying emission and the stable abode. It is the Absolute, the noble cosmic bliss consisting of both Shiva and Shakti. It is the supreme secret of 'Kula'; neither quiescent nor emergent, it is the flowing font of both quiescence and emergence'.

The sexual practices of the Kaula schools, also known as 'the secret ritual', are performed with a so-called 'external Shakti' (sexual partner) as opposed to the purely meditative practices which involve only one's own spiritual energies (the interior Shakti). The role of the sexual 'Kaula' ritual is to unite the couple; a 'yogini' (initiated women) and 'siddha' (initiated man) and have one induce in the other a state of permanent awakening. This achievement is made possible by the intensity of their love.

In their exalted state, the two become absorbed into the consciousness of the Self. Becoming united on all levels; physical, astral, mental and even in their consciousness, they reconstitute the supreme couple of Shiva and Shakti.

The Kaula sacrifice is reserved for the few, the elite who can maintain a state of Bhairava (spiritual illumination) in sexual union. If couples do not attain Bhairava consciousness, even if they reproduce the ritual to the letter (as perceived from the outside), they are merely engaging in a sexual act.

'Initiation by the mouth of the yogini' (yogini vakrta), is a method by which the adept unites with a purified yogini and receives the unique experience of illuminated consciousness. He is to see her as both his lover and his guru.

The energy generated during the tantric sexual act is considered a form of a 'subtle emission', while the act of ejaculation is considered a form of physical emission. In Kashmir Shaivism, the energy of emission (visarga shakti) is considered to be a form of ananda (bliss).

Depending on the orientation of one's consciousness, introverted or extroverted, emission can be of two kinds: rested and risen. In Shanta, the rested form of emission, the focus is absorbed just in one's own Self in an act of transcendence. In Udita, the risen form, the focus is projected on the Self (atman) of one's lover, a state associated with immanency.

Shantodita (beyond udita and shanta) is the uniting form, the cause of both shanta and udita emissions. Shantodita is described as universal bliss (chidananda), undivided consciousness, kaula (the group of two as one) and as an outflow of the pulsation of Shiva and Shakti. This kind of transition from the physical act to the mental and to consciousness itself is characteristic of the tantric world view."[32]

Even one of the main objects of worship – the Shiva Lingam rising from the Shakti's Yoni, itself represents the mystical seed of creation. Penetrating Shakti's Yoni, the Shiva Lingam tells us about the origin of creation. Leaving aside all taboos and negative projections on this delicate subject, we must admit that the sexual union based on love must be considered one of the most pleasurable and desirable acts, as lovers strip off not only their clothes, but also their personalities and their 'egos', reaching an incredibly pure and innocent intimacy. If the very Nature of God Absolute is love and bliss, then, there's no doubt that the ecstasy of the super-sexual union, the highest multiple orgasms of Shiva-Shakti's Love-making must be at the very core of such a being. God could be worshiped through all: act and speech, pain and pleasure. Lovemaking is one of the most pleasurable ways to worship God. Creation itself originates from the orgasmic movements (throbbing, pulsation, rhythm, vibration, trembling,

---

[32] Abhinavagupta "Tantraloka" chapter 29

tremor, contraction and release of energy) of Shiva and Shakti's Divine union.

Although worldly pleasures, which are but reflections of real pleasures, can trap individualised consciousness within their nets, the energy of such pleasures can be directed as offerings of gratitude to the Beloved Creator. Such pleasure-energies can uplift one to the super-pleasures of the Absolute itself.

After this magical night, which happened to be on Tuesday, we decided to celebrate each Tuesday as a special day of Love. Often sitting in front of each other, we would gaze lovingly into each other's eyes, transcending the illusion of difference, until the point when it was no longer possible to keep any distance between our bodies. Then, like two magnets emanating irresistible attraction and exuding love-energy through our open eyes, pores, we entwined ourselves into each other's gentle arms and covered each other's body with tender kisses, surrendering to the sexual delights of pulsating Love.

The next five months we spent in preparation for our wedding, using our limited budget but rich imagination and talent to create a very special day for us and our dearest friends.

On a summer day of the 13th of June, while the gentle sun was shining its lovely blessings on us, we married in the most beautiful official ceremony, after which my beloved wife, and our dearest bridesmaid; our darling granddaughter India, and I departed in our beautiful white limousine for a vegetarian breakfast in our local pub with a gorgeous sea-view. After a series of toasts, champagne, wine and food, we and our guests returned to our beautifully decorated garden, where the second part of our wedding took place. We had a proper Hindu wedding with decorated mandap, fire, and priests (dear friends of Tara), who had made a remarkable effort to memorise the whole Hindu wedding chanting in Sanskrit. We all chanted mantras, for almost all Tara's friends were mantra yogis. Tara, wearing a beautiful wedding dress and exquisite Indian silk shawl, her hands covered in intricate henna tattoos and her wrists adorned with colourful bangles, and I in a long golden suit, silky short and golden moccasins, with long hair and a beard, wearing Rudraksha mala beads, waked around the fire and took seven steps, making our promises to each other on every step. After the last of which, we were pronounced husband and wife! Jai Jai Jai Shiva – Shakti!!!

Truly, it was very special, very beautiful day. Sometime later, Tara, encouraged by the great success of our wedding wrote a small book under the pen-name Stella Bloom: *How to Create a Beautiful Wedding on a Small Budget.*

Instead of quantity of sexual relationships, I have discovered the quality and depth of our bottomless love. Our beautiful journey into the endless mystery of love never diminishes but is ever blossoming. We never stop discovering new dimensions of love-possibilities. Our love and respect for each other, along with our longing for the Highest Reality has made our hearts and characters soft and tender. We nurture our love with our attention, forgiveness and sweet kisses, often getting surprised to discover new aspects, new blossoms of beauty of our souls. One can never get satiated with such love, for it is ever fresh, ever new. Our Spiritual Hearts melt, releasing soma when we see the new, grown up, aspects of our love, truth and beauty, which are but the different names for One Reality. And although we are a complete cosmos ourselves, living in this apparent manifestation, our love, wisdom and harmony also spreads its waves towards our neighbours, our nearest and dearest and the whole of creation.

Forty Days of Fasting

S omewhere at the end of January of 2010 with the consent, help and care of my beautiful Tara, I began my new attempt at forty days of fasting. I wasn't fully satisfied with my two weeks of fasting while I was living in the Himalayan cave and I had a longing to fast for the total forty days. This time I decided not only to not eat food, but to completely isolate myself from any sources of information: no TV, no radio, no chats with friends and relatives, no phone conversations, or texts, or Facebook; only meditation in absolute silence. We decided however, that each day Tarananda would read me a paragraph from great *Ribhu Gita*, which is so helpful for the achievement of samadhi (absorption into Reality). Tara also offered to read me one chapter each evening before going to sleep from another book, which we hadn't read yet, but which she greatly admired. This book was the sacred Itihasa (source of actual history), *Tripura Rahasya*, through which I rediscovered a great connection with the events that took place while I was living as a sadhu on Jamu Peak.

Tripura Rahasya is the spiritual instruction of Guru Dattatreya, who is one of the Lords of Yoga, the reincarnation of Trimurti (Brahma, Vishnu and Shiva – in other texts the reincarnation of Vishnu), who is revered as Adi-Guru (First Teacher) of the Adinath Sampradaya of the Nathas. *Tripura Rahasya*, which gives such a brilliant exposition on the true nature of Reality, that no science can come close, is a spiritual science itself. The text of *Tripura Rahasya* was striking the chords of my memories of living as a sadhu, and my heart-connection to places where actual events (the imparting of Guru Datta's spiritual knowledge to Parashurama) happened.

290

Forty Days of Fasting

The routine of my fasting Tapas was as follows: after waking sometime around eight o'clock in the morning, I sat in a specially prepared space in the corner of our living room and had a rejuvenating ginseng tea. I had a big variety of herbal teas in my specially arranged meditation corner. After tea, I sat in silent meditation, often established in Bhairava Mudra with my eyes wide open, embracing the totality of outer impressions and inner bodily sensations at once, with my unblinking gaze fixed on the radiant eyes of Shri Ramana Maharshi's portrait, through which, as beautifully described by Frank Humphreys (one of the first western disciples of Ramana Maharshi), God was radiating terrifically. During such devotional meditation, profuse purifying tears of gratitude were flooding through my eyes. After a while, Tara would get out of bed and performed the morning puja, an offering to Gods and saints in the form of idols and images, the fragrance of sweet incense, and a lighted gee lamp. She would ring a bell and chant Gayatri and Mahamrityunjaya mantras, at the crescendo of which I would loudly blow through a conch.

In the next phase, I established myself in a 'riding horse' asana (sitting on three or four small cushions with legs bent on each side of them 'just like riding a horse'). I chanted out loud the sequences of mantras in the Kashmir Shaivism tradition, which I had learnt throughout the years from Tara and Muz Ji, accompanied with intense pranayama, slightly bending forward during chanting out, and exhaling the remaining air after finishing one round of chant, This was followed by rapidly filling my lungs and simultaneously straightening my back, getting ready for the next round of chant with the exhalation. Sometimes, when I felt that the moment was right, I would abandon chanting for a while, instead doing just intense pranayama with the majestic Kumbhaka at the end. Such practice inevitably leads to the expansion of one's capacity to behold the magnificence and glory of the Beloved. Such intense chanting, which usually took one, or one and a half hours, made my body sweat profusely, which was so helpful for moving accumulated toxins out of my body.

Followed by another cup of herbal tea of my choice, I would sit in my meditation corner with my headphones on, listening to variations of soundscapes such as Holosync sounds and other binaural beats, Vedic chants, Khomus compositions of Yakutian

291

master Spiridon Shishigin, chanting of Tibetan Nans, and other, usually non-verbal tribal music. I would breathe intuitively and vigorously, triggering the awakening of Prana-Kundalini Shakti – the inner guru. Goddess Prana-Kundalini-Shakti, evoked by efforts and longing for union with her, possesses the individual, taking his efforts in her Divine hands, and unfolds her Divine revelations to such a soul.

Truly, beloved Shakti is a gentle Divine Mother, who, when you touch her heart with your unquenchable longing for Truth and your beautiful courageous efforts, self-sacrifice and wholehearted devotion towards her, begins to wash you in the ambrosia of Love. When riding on a powerful current of prana, you will dive into the very depths of your being, she will pick you up and bathe you in a refreshing delightful soma. She will gently rub off the dirt of your wrong knowledge. She will pull off the sticky cobwebs of illusion which cover your radiant purity. She will blow off the dust of your sleep. She will lovingly shake off all the nonsense about the world and your life stories. She will wave sweet incense with the aroma of pure freshness. She will cleanse your entire being, massaging you with the garlands of her Divine letters, relieving you from all accumulated tension. She will carefully untangle countless knots, freeing you from limiting objective knowledge. She will purify your being from all these silly notions of 'others'. She will astonish you with her unbelievable beauty. She will bring you to a hysterical laughter through the potency of her funniest Divine jokes. She is the greatest joy and fun ever.

Somewhere around afternoon, my darling Tara would read me a chapter from the great *Song of Ribhu,* pregnant with the liberating 'I am Brahman' bhavana. Later, with my headphones on, listening to Pandit Jasraj's 'Shiva Shambho' CD, I would lie on the floor and engage myself in one hour and half of 'holotropic breathing', vigorously breathing through all blockages and pains into a state of undifferentiated light, in which mind melts in the ecstasy of Truth and bodily sensations are replaced with the brilliant radiance of Luminosity.

Holotropic Breathing

Having heard about holotropic breathing for a very long time, I only recently came across Stanislav Grof's book, *The Adventure of Self-Discovery*. Holotropic breathing, which in its essence is very closely related to the revelations that I received by the grace of magic mushrooms and Self-inquiry, got its birth from Stanislav Grof's Self-observation, while under the influence of a large amount of LSD, and also his observation of the breathing patterns of terminally ill patients under the influence of psychedelic substances.

Holotropic breathing does not have a stiff structure or firm instructions on how to breathe. There are only the guiding suggestions that the breathing should be round (without prolonged retention of breath after inhalation or exhalation), continuous, gradually increasing in tempo and amplitude, but ultimately; intuitive and spontaneous. In this sense, holotropic breathing is probably the closest of all other spiritual practices to Kumbhaka Prana Yoga which came to me independently of any other spiritual sources, as a series of spontaneous Divine revelations.

Having obviously a very deep spiritual side, holotropic breathing's main concern, however, is 'healing'. Healing, often at very deep levels, happens naturally and spontaneously when, by means of prolonged intense breathing, individualised consciousness moves away from cognition of so-called 'objective reality' towards the emergence of subconsciousness or super-consciousness, with a powerful catharsis at the end in which healing of deep-rooted emotional and psychological traumas and psycho-spiritual purification takes place.

Holotropic Breathing

'Increase of the rate and of the depth of breathing typically loosens the psychological defences and leads to release and emergence of the unconscious and superconscious material'[33] says Stan Grof.

The individualised consciousness during holotropic breathing often goes through the experience of early childhood emotional traumas, including the first traumatic experience of birth. Stanislav Grof describes, based on his own experience and the feedback of so many practitioners of holotropic breathing, the four stages of birth, which he calls perinatal matrices. These matrices correspond roughly to the different stages of the child's development in the uterus, and its birth through the birth canal.

"The first perinatal matrix corresponds to the time of conception up until the first intrauterine contraction and is often felt as oceanic oneness and peace without boundaries. During these episodes of undisturbed embryonical existence, we typically have experience of vast regions with no boundaries or limits. We can identify with galaxies, interstellar space, or the entire cosmos. A related experience is that of floating in the sea. This seems to reflect the fact that the foetus is essentially an aquatic creature. This experience can be referred to as oceanic bliss. A positive intrauterine experience can also be associated with archetypal visions of Mother Nature – safe, beautiful, and unconditionally nourishing.

The second perinatal matrix lasts from intrauterine contractions until the entering of the birth canal. In the fully developed first stage of biological birth, the uterine contractions periodically constrict the foetus, and the cervix is not yet open. Subjects reliving this part of birth feel caught in a monstrous claustrophobic nightmare; they experience agonising emotional and physical pain and have a sense of utter helplessness and hopelessness. Feelings of loneliness, guilt, a sense of the absurdity of life, and existential despair can reach metaphysical proportions. A person in this predicament often becomes convinced that this situation will never end and that there is absolutely no way out. An experiential triad of characteristics for this state is a sense of dying, going crazy, and

---

[33] Stanislav Grof "The Adventure of Self-Discovery" (New Perspectives in Psychotherapy and Inner Exploration)

never coming back. While under the influence of this matrix, we are selectively blinded and are unable to see anything positive in our life and in human existence in general. The connection to the Divine dimension seems to be irretrievably severed and lost.

In the third perinatal matrix (the propulsion through the birth canal after the cervix opens and the head descends into the pelvis) the individualised consciousness might experience a high degree of anoxia and suffocation. A concomitant of this highly uncomfortable and life-threatening situation is the experience of intense anxiety. The aggressive and sadomasochistic aspects of this matrix reflect the biological fury of the organism whose survival is threatened by suffocation. Facing this aspect of the third matrix, the individual might experience cruelties of astonishing proportions, manifesting in scenes of violent murder and suicide, mutilation and self-mutilation, massacres of various kinds and bloody wars and revolutions. They often take the form of torture, execution, ritual sacrifice and self-sacrifice, bloody man-to-man combats, and sadomasochistic practices.

The fourth perinatal matrix is related to the third clinical stage of delivery, to the final expulsion from the birth canal and the severing of the umbilical cord. Experiencing this matrix, we complete the preceding difficult process of propulsion through the birth canal, achieve explosive liberation, and emerge into light. The reliving of biological birth is not experienced just as a simple mechanical replay of the original biological event, but also as psychospiritual death and rebirth. The 'dying' and the agony during the struggle for rebirth reflect the actual pain and vital threat of the biological birth process. However, the ego death that precedes rebirth is the death of our old concepts of who we are and what the world is like, which we forge by the traumatic imprint of birth and maintain by the memory of this situation that stays alive in our unconscious. As we clear these old programs by letting them emerge into consciousness, they lose their emotional charge and, in a sense, die. As frightening as this process usually is, it is actually very healing and transformative. Following the experience of psychospiritual death and rebirth, we feel redeemed and blessed, experience ecstatic rapture, and have a sense of reclaiming our Divine nature and cosmic status. We are overcome by a surge of positive emotions towards ourselves, other people, nature and existence in general."[34]

Obviously, reliving one's birth process and healing the traumas associated with it, is not the only possible scenario of experiences during holotropic breathing. Participants of holotropic breathing sessions have very wide range of experiences in the depths of their subconsciousness/super-consciousness, such as experiences of the archetypal, Divine, hellish or other realms. Some individuals report the release of 'karmic bonds' of several previous lifetimes, and also experience future events.

One thing I would like to draw your attention to is how powerful dynamic prolonged breathing can be.

Although healing is undoubtedly the desirable outcome of any practice, I personally have never been attracted to the subject of 'healing' as such. Healing has never been my final goal. Although healing through the emergence of unconscious and superconscious materials during holotropic breathing is not limited only to the body but extends to far deeper aspects of psyche and self, nevertheless, it has its limitations. I have always longed only for the Absolute Unlimited Truth of Self-realisation. If you, my dear reader, however, desire to be healed, then I would like to tell you that Kumbhaka Prana Yoga which later I began to teach, will thoroughly purify your entire being from all poisoning obstructions and contaminations and will bring a deep healing as a by-product of this practice.

Often during my fasting sadhana I used the bathroom mirror for a special kind of meditation. Here is my spiritual instruction on this powerful practice:

Fix your steady gaze on the eyes of your reflection. Look through the eyes of your reflection back to the space from where you are looking. Without blinking, or moving your gaze, expand your awareness to embrace the whole field of perceptions. Include in this field all sounds, smells, and bodily sensations. Awaken as best as you can your Love, realising that it is God – the Self – looking at the reflection and through the eyes of the reflection back to the seer. Feel as best as you can that seen, seer and seeing are

---

[34] Stanislav Grof "Psychology of the Future: Lessons from Modern Consciousness Research" (Cartography of the Human Psyche)

one. Breathe gently in the beginning, gradually increasing the amplitude and rate of your breathing. Hold your expanded awareness steady, perceiving all impressions simultaneously. Breathe intuitively, spontaneously, without thought construct, feeling: 'I am the energy, I am the all-permeating prana'. Look through the eyes of your reflection very attentively back into the space from where you are looking. Feel the identity with the reflection in the mirror intently looking in your direction and simultaneously with the space outside of the mirror from where your attention radiates and where you feel the sense of 'I'. Open your eyes wider, open your mind and your heart. Bring yourself into a state of great wonder. Realise that this is the Eternal Moment, prior to time. God is forever here!

Feel that Love is beginning to flood through the eyes of you (in the mirror), basking you (in a room) in Love energy. Know and feel one hundred percent that it is God looking at you, God gazing into His reflection from all directions. Keep breathing dynamically and spontaneously. When you start to feel that you are either losing consciousness, or you feel that the whole world is going to explode, or you feel that you have become liquid energy, or perceptions start to flash in and out in invert colours, or you feel that you are losing all sense of direction, distance, gravity, or all of the above... breathe in, or out, and enter steadily into Kumbhaka (retention of breath). Now, cherish this majestic moment of entering Kumbhaka. It is filled with infinite possibilities. God radiates terrifically in these magical moments. Proceed with the breathing, 'til all and everything is flooded with pure Love, and the world and reflections disappear completely.

As you can probably imagine, such regular practices wash away the dross of doubts regarding one's true nature. No longer can one believe in the idea of the identity of body and Self, nor in the reality of the world appearance. On a contrary, one's conviction that 'I am Brahman – the Reality' strengthens and becomes unshakable through the power of the direct experience of higher states of consciousness. And so, Bhavana, which at the beginning was playing the role of a convincer and helped one achieve of higher states of consciousness, now gets feedback from the direct experience of Truth and becomes a solid, diamantine certainty. It is not yet real Self-realisation, only intellectual clarity, but nevertheless, one's outlook on reality is completely changed. Realising that one's True Self is God Absolute, one comes also to the realisation that, without exception, all cognisable phenomena is not independent of one's own consciousness. Rather, it is only an appearance within one's own consciousness. One also comes to the realisation that the life-story has at its source one's own Supreme Intelligence. The life-story is a leela (Divine play) created by one's own Beloved Shakti-Lalita (the playful one), who creates the appearances of countless turns, decisions, choices, exits and portals, but who also leaves here and there an abundance of clues in the form of scriptures, the words of sages, rishis and yogis, sciences, sacred plants, satsangs etc.. Intelligently tracing such clues back to its source, Shiva - your True Self, finds his way back to his incomparable kingdom of Bliss, which he has temporarily forgotten. The returning of the king to His Eternal Kingdom of Love and Bliss is the greatest joy, like that of recovering a dear treasure that was presumed lost. His outlook on life's unfolding has also changed and he begins to see a growing number of synchronicities, considering each turn of the life-play as a lesson teaching something valuable about one's real nature.

In the evenings of my fasting routine I usually had a very hot bath, which also helped me with the elimination of toxins. Before going to sleep, my beloved Tara read me a chapter from the great *Tripura Rahasya*, after which, plugging my ears with ear plugs for the additional silence, I went to sleep.

I Do Believe in Fairies

After five days of fasting, I noticed that the quality of my dreams changed dramatically. My dreams became increasingly vivid, meaningful and fantastic. Beginning on the fifth night with the eruption of a volcano and activities associated with saving people's lives, I then had many flying dreams. Every night I was mastering new ways to fly. At the beginning I was flying in an absolutely crazy manner, just like a balloon that quickly releases air, chaotically rushing in all directions. Sometimes I was flying like a shot arrow among the trees, with great speed and excitement, but more often, I was mastering smooth flight like an eagle over breath-taking landscapes and even parallel realities. The feeling of weightlessness, produced by the absolute conviction and trust that I could do it, brought immense joy to my dreams. I also had a few prophetic dreams on the subject of 'no return'. I would find myself in a city building which felt like my house, my home. After leaving this building for the exploration of the city, I would turn back and with a troubling feeling, realise that all the buildings behind me, including my home, had magically reconstructed themselves, giving me a chill that I would never be able to find my way back home, I would never be able to return. There were also dreams of a frightening nature, such as the appearance of an evil magician in a castle where we stayed, who by some dark magic gradually paralysed me, turning me into stone, unable to leave the cold, darkened room. By the mercy of God, I eventually was able to dispel this stupor and escape into the warmth, movement and light.

Sometime at the beginning of March, on one special night, after twenty-eight days of fasting and isolation, I had the most vivid and

299

unexpected dream of my entire life. I could never have expected anything like it. Although I saying it was a dream, truth to be spoken, I believe it really happened in one of the infinite dimensions of omnipotent reality. So real it was.

It was Christmas time in my dream-reality. I was in a building, which in its essence felt like our home in Niton village on the Isle of Wight. Our house, although having the same structure as in a 'real life', at the same time had an interesting replacement of certain features. I could see everything in great detail and felt slightly surprised at the alterations. Instead of the usual hutch between our kitchen and living room, a big heavy and beautiful rug separated the two rooms. Instead of our iron woodstove in the living room, there was a larger charming brick fireplace with a semi-circular segmental arch. A friendly fire, gently consuming big logs, was roaring. The room was softly lit with candles and Christmas lights, creating a very cosy atmosphere. My darling Tara, who was sitting on a rug in front of the fire, looked at me cheekily and asked: 'So, my beloved, what gift would you like for Christmas?'

Immediately desire arose in me to visit my cousin Victor in Russia. I hope you remember, my dear reader, that in 'real life' he committed suicide at the age of twenty-five. In my new dream-reality however, he was only eighteen and was to be taken to the army in a few days' time. Desire spontaneously arose in me to see him before he left for two years. I told Tara that I would like to go to Russia to see Victor. 'Okay,' she said, 'Relax and watch what happens…'

She began to chant; not her usual Sanskrit chants, but something that sounded to me like Celtic, or even Elvish. Not knowing such a language, I nevertheless, could understand the meaning of the words she chanted. It went something like this: 'O, fairies, I am calling upon you! O, fairies of earth, fairies of water, fairies of fire, fairies of air, fairies of ether, I am calling upon you, come!' As soon as she began to chant, the whole room started shimmering with thousands of little sparks of light and thousands of female voices of different timbres echoed back with their chants. It was pure magic!

The next moment I found myself outside of our house. It was snowing. Snowflakes began to circle around me, turning into a snow tornado dance. I felt that I was gradually losing gravity and became noticeably weightless. The power of the fairies' magical dust began to lift my body from the ground. I was a little bit concerned by and was trying to get hold of the corner of the building, before I completely took off into the air. I couldn't grasp anything however, and was lifted into the sky, where suddenly, pop! I was gone!

I couldn't tell you, my dear reader, where I disappeared to. It is a great mystery to me too. I cannot say how long I was 'absent', but the next thing that happened was that the skies opened up and, materialising from there, my body fell on a big soft snowbank in Russia. I realised that I was not far from my cousin's house. Time reversed during this unbelievable journey. In England, it was just before midnight on Christmas eve, when I magically departed. In our normal life perception, Moscow is three hours ahead, therefore it must have been around three o clock in the morning. In my magical dream-reality however, time mirrored itself, and when my body fell from the sky onto the Russian street, it was around nine in the evening. I met a few people there who were greatly surprised to see me and told me that I had been working in a restaurant there, but then one day, had mysteriously vanished, disappeared into a thin air.

I made my way towards my cousin's house and when I approached it, I was greatly surprised to see that he had a little sister about five or six years old. Magically, two beautifully crafted boxes with some surprise gifts in them materialised in the palms of my hands. Together with these boxes, two beautiful Christmas cards appeared, one of which I handed down to the smiling, intrigued, but slightly suspicious girl. 'Do you believe in fairies?' I asked, smiling. She didn't reply, but gently opened the card that I gave her. I can't remember now the exact text of this crafted card, but it was written in the most beautiful calligraphic style in golden ink and signed: 'Queen of Fairies, Princess Elisabeth'. I do believe in Fairies! I do believe in Fairies! I do believe in Fairies!

At that moment, for whatever reason, I woke up and found myself lying in our bed in England. When Tara woke up that morning and saw me in my meditation corner, she said I was grinning from ear to ear, beaming childlike joy from my heart. I still couldn't comprehend the possibility of my most unexpected night-adventure. I looked through the window, and although it was March, it began to snow, making it a full circle of connections. O, yes, I do believe in Fairies. To add a fairy dust of synchronicity to all of the above, even today, the 1st of March of 2018, when I am writing these very words, it is snowing, a rare event in the south of England.

Together with the unusually vivid dreams, I experienced a surge of creativity during my fasting days. It is a matter of fact that when we isolate ourselves from the outside world and direct our attention towards the divinity within ourselves, our inner world begins to blossom and creativity is taken to an entirely new level, exploding with the new elegant solutions to previously unresolved problems. I received instructions in the form of Divine revelations during my sadhana, to start giving satsangs (Abidance in Truth gatherings). I was able to visualise these satsangs in my creative imagination, seeing the most efficient ways to guide people beyond their self-imposed limitations towards the emergence and rapture of unifying Divine Consciousness.

As you have already probably heard, my dear reader, the first three days are the most difficult days of fasting. The second and third days you may feel very weak and depressed. If, however, you have the strength and the willpower to continue your fasting sadhana, it will get easier and easier with every passing day. In my case, during the first ten days of fasting I lost about a kilo a day, less after the tenth day. After ten days of fasting, I was indifferent to food, having no cravings at all, and was filled with the sparkling, renewed energy. Sometimes, after cooking meal for herself or her family, Tara would bring me her plate of food to smell it. This was enough to appease my hunger. The most attractive smell for me was the smells of freshly-cut cucumbers. It probably had something to do with my childhood, where all our village folk grew cucumbers to sell at Moscow's farmers markets. After ten to fourteen days of fasting I would sometimes experience uncomfortable tension in my calves. Possibly, the toxins were moving through these regions, creating an uneasy, irritating, muscle-twisting sensations. Thank God, I have my gracious guardian angel Tarananda, who lovingly massaged my legs, releasing the uncomfortable tension. In the later stages of my Tapas, she would look at my skeletal body with the tears coming out of her eyes and ask me to be gentle with myself, not push too much and learn to enjoy relaxation. And I began to notice through my sadhana, into which I put so much effort, that it eventually led to a breakthrough point into an unearthly level of relaxation, which we do not experience even in deep sleep.

These Nirvana-like states of relaxation blossomed when, after intense pranayama, I entered Kumbhaka, squeezing all of my muscles tightly (closing my eyes, rectum, fists, curling my toes) and entering into the very source of this tension and bodily sensations; into my psychosomatic world. Staying with this voluntary tension, I observed sparks of light turning into a psychedelic display of sacred geometry in the region of my third eye. In a matter of seconds this tension led my consciousness beyond the psychedelic threshold to profound relaxation with the loss of body and world perceptions. The old dense shell of the body and world appearance with its coarse vibrations was shattered by the emergence of a new level of expanded consciousness filled with the rarefied vibrations of intelligent energy. The tension was no longer there, for the very 'I'-ego responsible for this tension was gone.

Pure relaxation is achieved when the sense of 'I' (the ego) no longer exists. There is only pure Is-ness without any tension.

Man = Tension

It became so obvious to me that 'man' is 'tension', or rather, 'tension' is another word for a 'man'. Just as a soap-bubble exists only because surface tension keeps its temporary form intact, so man's very existence relies on tension. What is this tension? It is the appearance of the ego. Although we may assume that at times we are totally relaxed, a massive amount of tension in a form of worrying about future events, unresolved emotional issues, readiness to react to unexpected stimuli, nervous and muscle tensions, unregistered, but deeply rooted fears, suspicion and doubts, concern about others' opinions, tensions to stay within the rigid frames of our adopted taboos, etc., are going on in a background of our being all the time. Even the simple act of seeing requires certain amount of effort.

Abidance in the True Self on the other hand is absolutely effortless. Having said that, my dear reader, don't make the mistake of assuming that if you are already, at all times, the very Self that you are looking for, there is no need for effort. I see so many fake gurus with their intellectual convictions, which are no better than blind beliefs, preaching their misleading assumptions to their open-mouthed disciples. Yes, it is Truth that the real You is always pure unblemished Sat-Chit-Ananda (Existence-Consciousness-Bliss), but at the same time it is also truth that you are wrongly identified with your body, ego and the character you are playing in this life-game. You are sleeping Shiva, who got carried away on the waves of his dreams from his Incomparable Kingdom of Bliss by the power of his own Shakties – energies to this comparatively imperfect dream-world of limitations.

Fright and Temptations

Although illusory, it is not so easy to shake this dream of limitations away. The wrong, but strong identification with the body-mind cannot be broken without deliberate effort, for what we are taking ourselves to be wants to exist, to live. Although the idea of completely and unreservedly merging into and being consumed by Reality, might be genuine and strong, this final sacrifice of the ego is nevertheless very difficult, for the ego gets strength from the numerous vasanas (mental habits and tendencies) accumulated during countless reincarnations. It is frightened by 'death' of the so familiar world and by the loss of all its objective knowledge to which every jiva (soul) clings for safety and protection from the terrifying unknown. The ego (what we take ourselves to be) and the whole Maya (that which does not exist yet appears to be) wants to exist and will not easily go away.

While we are enjoying our lives and trying to make the best of them, while we are sharing our love and our hearts with the whole world and the Creator, giving thanks for such an amazing gift, we are also slaves of Maya, for our very existence as human beings is far from independent. We totally dependent on Maya, who provides our temporary 'selves' with food, water, air, space, gravity, directions, shelters, entertainment etc.

Our Real Self – God Absolute – on the other hand is svatantrya (Self-dependent and sufficient) and does not require the help of Maya for Its existence, for It itself is absolute fullness and the very source of all creation. The resolve to offer oneself (the ego – I) as a sacrifice on the altar of Truth must be unshakable. The entrance to the Kingdom of God is carefully guarded by both sides of Reality – 'good' and 'evil'.

Fright and Temptations

Do you remember the scenes from the movie *Little Buddha* with Keanu Reeves, just before Siddhartha's final Awakening as Buddha in Nirvana?

Demon Mara, who could be compared with Maya, and can also be linked to Satan – the Deceiver – is a power that snares and deludes souls.

As the about-to-be-Buddha, Siddhartha Gautama, sat in meditation, Mara brought his most beautiful daughters to seduce Siddhartha. Siddhartha, however, remained unmoved in meditation. Then Mara sent vast armies of monsters to attack him. Yet Siddhartha sat still and untouched.

Then Mara appeared as the very reflection of Siddhartha and spoke thus: 'You go where no-one else dare. Would you be my God?'.

'Architect, finally I've met you. You will not rebuild your house again,' said Siddhartha. 'But I am your house and you live in me' Mara replied.

'Oh, lord of my own ego, you are pure illusion, you do not exist.'

Then Siddhartha reached out his right hand to touch the earth, 'The Earth is my witness,'[35] he said, and Mara disappeared.

Everyone who tried to break away from Maya at the very threshold of enlightenment, was either tempted, or frightened. In a story of Jesus's forty days of fasting in the dessert, at the end of his sadhana, the 'tempter', the 'deceiver', Satan appears and begins the temptations. 'Then Jesus was led by the Spirit into the wilderness to be tempted by the devil. After fasting for forty days and forty nights, he was hungry. The tempter came to him and said, "if you are the Son of God, tell these stones to become bread." Jesus answered, "It is written: 'Man shall not live on bread alone, but on every word that comes from the mouth of God.'" Then the devil took him to the holy city and had stand on the highest point of the temple. "If you are the Son of God," he said, "throw yourself down. For it is written: 'He will command his angels concerning you, and they will lift you up in their hands, so that you will not strike your foot against the stone.'" Jesus answered him, "It is also written: 'do not put the Lord your God to the test.'" Again, the devil took him

---

[35]"Little Buddha" directed by Bernardo Bertolucci 1993

to a very high mountain and showed him all the kingdoms of the world and their splendour. "All this I will give you," he said, "if you will bow down and worship me." Jesus said to him, "Away from me, Satan! For it is written: 'Worship the Lord your God and serve him only.'"[36]

We may ask ourselves what Satan was trying to achieve with such temptations? If Jesus was to accept Satan's offerings, it would have meant that the true nature of Jesus was one of incompleteness. And to complete himself he must depend on the power outside of himself. In this way he would become a slave of Satan and Satan would remain his master.

Although Maya-Shakti (The Energy of Illusion, which creates the appearance of the world and a life-stories) could be considered the great-granddaughter of the Creator and even thought by some people as no different from the Absolute Intelligence, those who begin to see her cunning ways, notice that she is like a spider spinning invisible webs around her unaware victims.

As Anandamayi Ma expressed very eloquently, 'What appears delightful to the senses later develops into a hotbed of poison, generating inner turmoil and disaster, for it belongs to the realm of death. Relative happiness, which is happiness depending on anything, must end in grief.'[37]

It would be unwise however to openly rebel against the Maya's slavery, rather we must thoroughly understand that Maya appears in our ignorance only and with the rise of True Knowledge, (not impotent intellectual knowledge, but Jnana – Real Knowledge – Being), Maya, just like Mara, will disappear, unveiling the Perfect Bliss of Reality.

We must carefully observe and learn how Maya spins her invisible webs around the countless somnambulists inhabiting this imperfect dimension of Infinite Reality.

---

[36] Gospel of Matthew 4:1
[37] Anandamayi Ma "Matri Vani" (Ananda Varta)

307

Dream-reality

'We are such stuff as dreams are made on;
and our little life is rounded with a sleep.'

~ William Shakespeare ~

I feel that some sense of protest suddenly erupted within your chest, my dear reader, after I used the word 'imperfect' for the description of the 'reality' we are all living in. We like to protect our feelings and our point of view that the world is beautiful, intelligent and even that it is perfect and above all, real. After all, God is Its source and the whole universe is the body of His intelligence and energy and as such, is no different from the Creator himself.

But if we do not want to be hypocrites, we must be honest with ourselves and admit that the world and its affairs are simply far from perfection. Of course, we may argue saying that all these imperfections are specifically designed this way and on a bigger scale, the whole Architects plan, including all its imperfections, is perfection itself.

Only those who have broken through the threshold of Maya to the inner higher levels of Infinite Reality know for sure that the world-appearance, however marvellous, intelligent and beautiful, is only a veil covering the real beauty of Truth. Those who have glimpsed the Truth have lost their doubts about the unreal nature of the world-appearance. Those who have glimpsed the most beautiful radiant face of the Beloved, when the Maya matrix temporarily crashed, want nothing but liberation from 'untruth'.

Dream-reality

Of course, the ideas that the world is not real will never be popular. After all, who wants to know, and who would agree that all our nearest and dearest; our friends, husbands, wives, daughters, sons, mothers and fathers, everyone including ourselves and all of this convincing display of intelligent laws holding together the entire cosmos are all just figments of God's imagination. We must give it some sense of reality, otherwise it would be simply unbearable to live life with such knowledge.

As long as I am not liberated, I cannot simply dismiss this world-game altogether. Although I am drawn to Truth and naturally making all possible efforts of yoga (union) towards the final Liberation, I am not yet free from my life story. I play the game of life fairly, joyfully and gracefully in this 'dream-reality' helping less fortunate ones, sharing love and goods with those in need, inserting sparks of inquiry into the Truth within my friends' hearts, following the Ahimsa (do no harm) rules, and learning from life's lessons. I fight for justice and equality, share my joy and creativity and walk with great respect on this beautiful illusion of Mother Earth.

While we are dreaming, we are playing by the dream rules and if we see someone in pain, we do not just walk away from this person within our dream, for our very nature is kindness and compassion. We naturally want to help and relieve the pain. Our life-stories are dreams of the Dream-maker – our Real Self.

What is the nature of a dream? Is it real, or unreal? We cannot say that it is totally unreal, for we are experiencing it. We are sensing, feeling, seeing, hearing it. Therefore, there must be some degree of reality to it. We cannot say that it is real either. For we know that when we wake up, a dream disappears. It wasn't real after all, but just a mental creation. As long as a dream lasts, however, it appears to be real. Again, dreams are different in their quality. Some are vague, while others have a far greater lucidity. This life-story in which the whole universe appears with all its countless intelligent details in great lucidity is nothing but a dream.

Those convinced of the reality of this dream, and the reality of their persona, due to a lack of inquiry, are searching for happiness in the objects of this illusive appearance. Searching for a greater satisfaction, they look for things this dream may offer. Seduced by the pleasures of power, money, and fame, they plunge deeper and deeper into the invisible webs of a dream-nature. Considering it to be real, they are attached to their objects of pleasure and pain, and also to their individuality.

When woken up suddenly by the death of their physical body, they fear the most the loss of their individuality, not knowing the nature of their mind, and frightened by the terrors of the Bardo states (the intermediate states between death and rebirth). They desperately search for rebirth into another dream, which could be on any plane of the multi-dimensional dream-reality. And the samsara (repetitive dream-existence) goes on and on until the desperate desire for the Absolute Truth and liberation from the illusory limitations forces them to inquire into the true nature of Reality.

There are also dreamers who dream of the spiritual evolution of a mankind. Certainly, this is very positive, noble and plausible dream. The only evolution however is not the betterment of a dream, but the Awakening from the dream to Reality in which the dream dissolves and disappears. Awakening again can be into another dream of greater lucidity, or into the highest realm of Supreme Reality – The Blissful Wakefulness, The Ecstasy-Euphoria-Bliss and Boundless Freedom of the Creator of all dream-realities. Knowing this world-appearance to be just a dream, wise ones take it very easy, gratefully, gracefully and unattached. Knowing themselves to be the dream-makers, they search for any opportunity to wake up to Reality, but at the same time they are not desperate, but content and at peace, trusting the hand of Divine Grace and the wisdom of the Supreme Intelligence.

If we dig even deeper, we must come to realisation that all dreams, and Maya itself, depends on the awareness of the dreamer. It is only when 'I' arises in consciousness that you, she, he, them, us and the whole world arises also. From all *malas* (stains, impurities) such as Mayaya, Karma and Anava malas, it is the Anava mala which is the most primordial and the most elusive and deluding. It is the sense of a separate 'I' that is different from the rest and from God which is at the source of all troubles.

It must be clearly understood that as long as the 'I'-ego exists, this 'I' is bound to go through alternating experiences of pleasure and pain, joy and sadness etc. (pertaining to the Earthly plane), and extreme experiences of ecstasy and terror etc. (pertaining to numerous other realms).

As long as this 'I' seems to exist, the Absolute Truth cannot be experienced. As long as this 'I' seems to exist, doubts and fear exist also.

To realise the full identity with the Infinite intelligence – unborn, uncreated Absolute Brahman – this 'I'-ego must be uprooted. The ego, however, cannot be killed, for its existence is ignorance itself.

As a picture exposed for a very long time to the sunlight loses its pigments and becomes white, so is with the practice of Self-inquiry, as advised by Ramana Maharshi. When the rays of consciousness are withdrawn from thoughts and external objects, and are directed and held on its very source, where the 'I' sense arises (Hrdayam – the Spiritual Heart - the Centre), the mind with the 'I' sense finally gets drowned and destroyed (manonasha) in the luminous bliss of the Self.

But it is not an easy process. The habitual tendency of the mind is to move towards external objects. Like bees' rush towards the nectar in flowers, the mind rushes towards external objects.

The 'I'-ego is incomplete. It is always feeling a lack of something and searching for happiness and completion in external objects or activities. Complete happiness can only be found in the True Self, where the search for the absolute happiness is over, and one is established in the absolute fullness (Purnam) with the total absence of any desire.

To steadily hold the totality of one's awareness on its source is also not easy because of the movements of the two battling forces of Prana and Apana.

The movements of Prana and Apana agitate the lake of the mind and create the ripples of thoughts that appear to an 'I' as external objects moving within the space-time continuum. As long as these two battling forces move, Awareness will be unstable and not homogenous. Again, Prana and Apana that are experienced by the 'I' as inhalation and exhalation are only visible manifestations of the Goddess Prana Shakti.

When one adopts pranayama (the expansion of life-force), together with Self-inquiry, one begins to be initiated step by step

Dream-reality

into the secrets and mysteries of the inner dimensions of Prana Shakti.

Uniting Self-inquiry with pranayama, one finally realises on deeper levels the identity of Prana and the mind.

Energised by pranayama, Bhairava mudra (simultaneous extroverted and introverted intense awareness) and Self-inquiry, the Prana-Mind opens completely, fully embracing and permeating the totality of the Universe in a state of Mauna (total inner silence).

Bhairava mudra, Self-inquiry, openness of inner dimensions of Prana Shakti and Mauna brings one into a state of infinite expansion in which the desire or necessity to breathe ceases.

One is then established in Kevala Kumbhaka – the absolute cessation of breath.

The unborn, uncreated Absolute (the Real Self) is the fullness of being, complete unalloyed happiness that lacks nothing. It is independent, needing nothing for its existence and happiness. Supreme Intelligence (Absolute Knowledge), Infinite Energy (Absolute Sufficiency) and the Highest Bliss (Divine Ecstasy, Euphoria, Amazement, Wonder, Joy, Love and Freedom) is the true nature of Reality.

Only when the 'I' is lost, consumed, merged into the Reality in which there is neither 'I' nor the 'other', but rather non-dual fullness, absolute happiness is regained.

Don't worry though, my dear reader; you will not become nothing or someone else after losing yourself, but on a contrary, regain your True Self which has been temporarily forgotten through the identification with the dream-character. Just like a bubble bursts, destroying its form, releasing its tension, and returning to its original nature of water and soap, so it is with the final liberation; there is a sense of tremendous relief from all fears, worries and other forms of tension, like that of dropping a heavy load, which one unknowingly carried on one's head.

My nervous system become extremely purified and very sensitive as days of my fasting continued. One day I decided to have an experiment with simple valerian tea. Oh God, I had an almost psychedelic experience after drinking it.

I cannot say for sure what the main reason was for my decision (probably a combination of many factors), but after thirty-one days of fasting, I decided to introduce fruit juices into my system. After couple of days, I added a couple of cups of vegan bullion to my diet. On the last couple of days, I also had some vegan broth. I did have a little feeling of regret for not completing all forty days, especially knowing that the major revelations usually happen to our heroes on the fortieth day of their fasting. Nevertheless, what was done was done. I accepted it and let it all go.

Healthy Diet and Breatharianism

As we are on the subject of fasting, which could be related to the subject of healthy diet and general good health, I would like very briefly to share my views on this subject. Obviously, 'good health' is a massive subject in itself, with so many intricate details, that big books can be written on this subject alone. I am not going into the depths of it but will simply mention the most rational way of eating from my point of view.

Otto Warburg, the 1931 Nobel Prize winner for cancer discovery wrote: 'No disease, including cancer, can exist in an alkaline environment.'[38] Many people have a high level of acidity level in their bodies. This is due to a diet of processed foods, refined sugars, and GMOs. However, many people do not know that an acidic body is a breeding ground for cancer, excess weight, pain and many other health issues. Highly acidic foods and pathogen-laden foods are mucus-forming, and the increased production of mucus throws the body out of a state of homeostasis (tendency towards a relatively stable equilibrium between interdependent elements).

According to my friend Alexandra Cousins, whose views I share; to live a vibrant life without dis-ease we must first clean obstructions from the organism. There are no great benefits in taking nutritious food and food supplements if it cannot be properly assimilated by the intestines. As Alexandra puts it: 'All dis-ease is created by mucus accumulated in the body through wrongful

---

[38] Otto Warburg

eating. The mucus hardens in the body and creates obstruction. Removing the obstruction and staying mucus free leads to a life free of dis-ease. We need so much less food than we think we do. We eat to cover up our unfelt emotions. We eat to celebrate because we do not know how to express our joy. We eat so that we don't have to feel our sadness/boredom/frustration/anger/stuckness/pain. We eat to avoid taking action on what intuition tells us.

'What truly feeds us is our highest joy, living our purpose and expressing the fullness of who we are. We are no different to any of the saints, ascended masters, gurus, and yogis who could fast for months and/or live on very little food. It's all about consciousness! Matter doesn't matter, it's all about energy. What we eat affects our consciousness! It's not so much about what food is good or bad, healthy versus not healthy, it's all about what degree of obstruction food creates in our body. The less obstruction, the easier it is assimilated, digested and eliminated'.

'Making our diet 80% fruit and high-water-content vegetables is the best thing we can do for our health. Fruit sugar is not the enemy, for we are made to run on carbon. Fruit will put the body into detox mode like nothing else. Many of us are too toxic to jump straight into a high fruit diet and so leafy greens and high-water content vegetables are a great way to slow detox down. Fasting teaches you about yourself in the most direct and profound ways.'[39]

The major points of a diet and the lifestyle recommended by Alexandra is as follows: Avoid eating acidic mucus-forming food such as animal products, dairy, mucus-forming grains. After an early dinner, she recommends 14, 16, or 18 hours of dry fasting, which is the best way to cellular detoxification. Dry fasting (no food and no water) induces the process of 'autophagy', during which the weaker cells are burnt for fuel and stem cell production increases by 300%. The best way to break fast is to eat fruits. Raw vegetables are good at lunch time, or dinner. If cravings for food are strong you can add lightly steamed vegetables to your diet. Of course, there is so much more that you can add to your diet, such as certain nuts and seeds, dates, sprouted seeds, tinctures, etc. Alexandra also recommends doing enemas, especially one with

---

[39] Alexandra Cousins

lemon juice in it. In this way, obstructions and parasites will be removed from the colon. Obviously, what I write here on this subject is just the tiny tip of the iceberg.

Disregarding natures laws equals dis-ease. Lack of ease in the body means there is an obstruction which is caused by one thing with many expressions: mucus. The breakdown of the mucus membrane and mucus-forming foods create acids. Acids break down the body and rob it of calcium, potassium, magnesium, iron and other essential alkaline minerals. Acids cause inflammation. These mucus-forming foods leads to lack of oxygen, through obstruction of various pathways in the body (the blood, the tissues, the colon, the head, the cells). Lack of oxygen is the most crucial factor in disease expression. Starch, flesh (meat), dairy, processed foods and hybrid plants (starch) are slave foods. Why? Because they are poisons that cause you to not be able to think straight or think for yourself correctly!

They make man submissive and prone to thinking against himself. They make him easy to control and manipulate. They make him angry, aggressive, lustful, hateful. He even hates himself, not to mention his own brother. These substances make man a beast. They cause beasty expression that is not on par with his place in nature and evolution.

Man's electrical brain and nervous system is highly advanced and requires the same in food substances. There must be affinity. Carbon body, carbon food. Electric body, electric food. Alkaline body, alkaline food. All of these so-called foods people eat that do not fall into this category are either man-made acid-based, or not for humans to consume. Fruit is the highest evolution of a plant, and the most electrical. Fruit sugar requires no insulin to be carried to the cells. It causes no blood sugar issues. Once man switches to a diet of lots of fruits, leafy plants, some seeds, occasional nuts and sprouted ancient grains, he will see a vibrant, whole energy flowing through him that is happiness and love itself.

A few years after my forty days of fasting, I discovered that it was possible to become 'breatharian'. Breatharians are those who do not eat solid foods but live only on fruit juices and vegetables juices (often diluted with water) and prana energy. There are apparently around thirty thousand of them in the world. There are even more radical few people who abstain not only from eating, but also from drinking any liquids. To mention just a few that I am aware of: Argentinian Victor Truviano, who hasn't been eating or drinking liquids for about 12 years now, Russian Zinaida Baranova, who abstained from food and liquids for 18 years and Indian yogi Prahlad Jani (Mataji), who hasn't eaten or drunk for 65 years, since the age of 7. Surely, there must be many more yogis who abstain from food and water, living in remote places away from people.

Hearing that it was possible to gradually stop eating, then abandoning even drinking altogether to stay absolutely free of anything that Maya offers, and living only on prana energy, I thought that it would be a very good step towards the absolute independence from Maya, finally going beyond even the necessity to breathe as in Kevala Kumbhaka.

You would probably argue that it would be quite miserable existence, for there is much joy in tasting food, wine etc., and it's such a big part of our lives; one of the factors of our human interactions that glue us all together. Those who start eating healthy foods such as raw fruits and leafy vegetables, those who stay only on juices and those who live only on prana, however, feel really good, cleansed and purified!

First of all, the mental fog created by the obstructions disappears. Secondly, they become more refined and attuned to higher levels of intelligence and energy. Thirdly, they become free of aches, heaviness, discomforts, cravings, and are filled with ever-fresh energy, which pours out from their translucent eyes and purified being as love and joy. And finally, as I have mentioned many times before, the greatest joy, happiness and satisfaction can only be found in realisation and unity with One's True Self which lacks nothing, wants nothing, and desires nothing, for it is Absolute Fullness Itself.

The major difficulty of become breatharian in my experience and the experiences of many others; is not the craving for food or water, nor the feeling of sickness and uneasiness of the transitional phase, but the withdrawal from the social interactions built around food consumption. Eating together is such a major part of our lives.

People often become breatharians following what is known as the 'twenty-one-day initiation process'. This includes seven days of dry-fasting (no food, or water) and another fourteen days of staying on diluted juices. I've read very interesting accounts of those who have gone through this initiation. Some of them, after four days of dry fasting underwent 'astral surgery' by the 'beings of light' to adjust their body organs for a new level of functioning. This so reminded me the operation on my cranium by the 'being of light' on one of my first psilocybin journeys.

I decided to become breatharian, but instead of twenty-one days, I took a shortcut and followed Ray Maor's ten-day initiation process. I went through self-initiation, having fruits on the first day, fruit juices on the second, water on the third, followed by four days of dry fasting and then returning to diluted juices. During the following days, once a week I was dry-fasting and the rest of the week I stayed on diluted fruit juices. I felt very good for the transitional period, which is supposed to take up to three or four months at least but lasted for me only for twenty days.

I could not bear to see my darling Tarananda slightly isolated and unhappy eating her food alone and after twenty days of breatharianism, on the 13th of June – our wedding anniversary – I surrendered to the celebration of this event with food and wine. We went to a lovely café on the sea-front and had some nice green salads with a glass of white wine, after which I gently returned to eating.

At the end of my forty days of fasting we also had some lovely green salads and a bottle of exquisite red wine. Sitting in front of our fireplace on a soft duvet, for a first time in forty days we were sharing our experiences, insights, inspirations as also our plans for the future.

Satsangs and Prana Yoga

During the next few weeks, we prepared and distributed leaflets around our island, inviting people to attend series of three satsangs (Abidance in Truth) starting in May.

Slightly shy and nervous at the beginning and silent for a good part of the satsang, we nevertheless created, with the help of Divine Grace, an atmosphere of trust, openness and sparkling vibrant energy, the beauty of which forced tears from a few people who came.

Some of the Isle of Wight's yoga teachers, and also practitioners and teachers of transcendental meditation attended my first satsang and became regular attendees and also our friends. We moved our satsangs to a new venue in the Unitarian Meeting House in the centre of Newport, and also changed their format.

Tarananda began the satsangs with a beautiful introduction, followed by the dynamic chanting of mantras, which greatly prepared the space and our consciousness for my part.

We led satsangs twice a month, expanding the circle of our grateful friends.

Sometime later, Tarananda began to teach mantra yoga classes, often leading weekend or three days workshops. She always spent a great amount of time and effort in preparation, compiling her knowledge into pages and pages of workbooks, which she used as a guideline for her three-day session.

She is undoubtedly one of the greatest mantra yoga teachers of our time. Usually the two days of mantra yoga gradually built an energy in everyone gathered, leading to an emotional catharsis towards the end of a third day in which the gates of emotion swung wide open and a previously inaccessible flood of real joy, love and bliss poured out, together with tears and the unstoppable laughter. Mantra yoga is an immensely healing and enlightening process.

Later, we also formed the 'Soul-Garden Kirtan Band' sharing our joy and love through the blissful chanting of kirtans at various venues and festivals.

I greatly enjoyed leading Satsangs and participating in Tara's workshops, but at the same time I felt that the satsangs' format was not adequate for the full Shaktipat – the transmission of liberating Shakti Energy. Prana-Shakti energy, whom I consider as my satguru (inner spiritual teacher) wasn't involved in this format. I longed to share my knowledge and conscious energy through the engagement of participants in intuitive dynamic breathing sessions in which, through the means of intense pranayama, the awakening of inner guru Prana-Shakti occurs.

First, I decided to conduct a holotropic breathing session in which Tarananda and I played the role of sitters. I was very meticulous in choosing the soundtracks for the holotropic breathing journey, for the sound of music also plays the role of a guide and guru for the journey into the inner dimensions of Infinite Reality.

Having uploaded to Soundcloud my jaw harp compositions and songs, which I wrote together with Tara, I had made a few good friends there, whose music I really liked. I felt that much of it was perfect for our holotropic journey.

It took me a long time to carefully select an appropriate playlist. I then experimented with it on myself, listening to it through headphones, while diving into the depths of meditation by means of intuitive dynamic pranayama and the expansion of consciousness to comprehension and being one with all sounds and sensations. In my expanded state, I could feel precisely how the sounds of my chosen soundtrack were influencing my consciousness and energy and which ones were leading me into the density of conscious ecstasy to break through the psychedelic threshold.

Not only was the energy of each separate track important, but the overall structure of complete music journey had to be taken care of. I excluded all compositions which had any form of familiar language in it, for language inevitably leads to formation of ideas and concepts, which are obstacles to the liberation of consciousness.

Satsangs and Prana Yoga

For the beginning of our breathing journey, when participants are advised to breathe deeply but slowly and consciousness is yet dwelling on habitual objects, I decided to choose soundtracks of the greatest beauty with the idea that such pleasant sounds would allure and seduce the mind through the sheer power of their beatitude, and so the mind would gradually abandon thoughts and memories and would lean towards the vibrations of sounds and identify with them.

An exquisite sitar composition called 'Sitar Satori (Momentum)' was my choice for the opening of our journey. Unfortunately, I cannot find the name of an author of this superb piece of music.

With the progression of the musical journey, to add an emotional aspect to the seducing power of sound, I chose a fascinating Sufi song by Ustaad Raees and Abida Parveen.

After slowly building up the tempo of breathing, while listening to such charming sounds I wanted to tie the minds of the breathers to repetitive tribal shamanic drumming with a didgeridoo to take the mind even further into possession by the sounds. Byron Metcalf, Kolo, and many other tribal musicians whom I discovered on SoundCloud and YouTube were my choice for this part of a Journey.

Sn Karma, whom I also found on SoundCloud would entice the attention of the breathers into a new level of expansion with her alluring 'Naturelement – According to 2012' composition.

At this point I decided that participants' expanded consciousness would be ready to receive guidance into the even greater depths of mystery through the magical spellbinding chants of Uma Mohan 'Ganapati Prarthana & Ghanapaath' and 'Namaskaratha Mantra' with which I personally had the most astonishing revelations. I will write about this further later in this book. After Uma Mohan's magical chants, tribal Kalander, with amazing tabla player Denis Kucherov added some tempo with their 'Independence', leading to explosive tribal-psychedelic trance from my favourite Belgian cousins Gowax and Tikki Masala, specifically their 'Bedouin Dance' and 'Redhead' compositions.

At this point, the breathing pattern of the gathered 'trippers' would supposedly become very dynamic and intense, changing from the medium-tempo 'Bastrika' to very fast 'Kapalbhati' pranayamas. With the purely psychedelic and very fast Kalki's 'Varanasi' and Tikki Masala's 'Om Sahana Vavatu' at around the one hour and ten-minute mark of the journey, the breathing tempo would reach its culmination, leading to an explosion of consciousness. This was to be accompanied by the heavenly Makyo with its '21(Night Flight mix)' in which angelic female voices sing the vowel 'A-A-A' as the waves of bliss takes one into the state of Nirvana. It was as though the breathing souls, led by the fast psychedelic trance were speeding towards the end of a cliff, and had now jumped off it and discovered that they could fly!

The journey finished at around one hour and forty minutes with the magnificent heart-wrenching flute sounds by Mohamad Naiem in his composition 'El-Fagr'.

Around ten people came to our holotropic breathing workshop, which we held in the acoustically perfect Unitarian Meeting House. One of the participants; my friend Bill who teaches transcendental meditation on the Isle of Wight brought his high-quality Bose speakers for this journey.

After about forty minutes of satsang, an introduction and guidelines for the breathing session, the journey begun. It was very interesting to observe the different breathing patterns, overall behaviour and body movements of different participants. Some started to breathe very rapidly at the very beginning and after about twenty minutes had burnt out, exhausted themselves and were forced to change their breathing pattern to a much slower tempo.

Many suffered cramps in their hands and wrists. Tarananda helped to release the tension by massaging their hands. Some didn't take up the challenge of breathing and just enjoyed the music, breathing deeply but slowly. Those who followed the guidelines and naturally progressed from the slow deep breathing into a more dynamic pattern while the music was speeding up, took the greatest benefits from the journey. They were taken into the possession of the emerging sat-guru Prana-Kundalini Shakti, who took them into the ecstatic unfolding of their body movements.

One relatively young lady, who in her day-to-day life had unintentionally created an older image of herself, literally transformed at the end of this amazing journey. She appeared ten to fifteen years younger, radiant with beauty and joy. Shakti energy was oozing out of her sparkling eyes and the entirety of her liberated being. Tarananda, highly impressed with the transformation of 'ugly duckling' into 'beautiful swan', even asked if she could paint her, so beautiful she appeared.

Although I loved the holotropic breathing, which ideally, after prolonged unstoppable breathing leads to a catharsis, I found that with the additional pauses in my breathing journeys for profound 'Kumbhakas', I was not only heading towards one big catharsis at the end of a journey, but was greatly expanding the capacity of comprehension and beholding far greater levels of intensity of intelligence and energy. I found that combining intense dynamic pranayama with periods of retention of breath is a more sufficient way to expand consciousness than breathing without any stop as in holotropic breathing.

The other point I wasn't fully satisfied with was that I myself wasn't participating in breathing session and therefore wasn't sharing the liberating Shakti Energy with the participants. I knew without shadow of a doubt that from all the so-called talents and gifts of creativity, such as an art, music, poetry, performance, inspirational talks, etc., my major gift was shamanic guidance. It is here in the very depths of the bewildering psychedelic experience, in the proximity of death, that I was the most helpful. Not helpful as to save egos, but to blow away the clouds of fear and doubts, slay inner demons, shatter the illusory appearance of frightening nature and with the help of my beloved Prana Shakti, arrive at the holy feet of the ever-radiant Shiva.

Knowing that all is one and everyone's state of consciousness affects everyone else's, I knew also that I was capable of transmitting liberating Shakti energy to the whole group. In other words, as I was capable through the means of dynamic intuitive breathing meditation to achieve non-ordinary states of consciousness, I was also changing the state of consciousness of all gathered.

In view of these points, I adjusted the format of my teachings. At the same time, a couple of our spiritual friends who were attending our satsangs and sessions built a beautiful yurt in their garden capable of accommodating up to twelve people. I thought that the round space of a yurt would be the ideal venue for my workshops. Not yet having a name, I called these gatherings 'Dynamic Intuitive Breathing Meditation'. After our very first breathing journey in Sue's yurt, I had very interesting feedback ranging from how easy and blissful it was to stay in 'breathlessness' without any rising desire to breathe at all, to a total loss of the limiting senses of gravity and direction.

One of our friends attending this workshop was an artist and musician, the lead singer of Isle of Wight band Weatherkings. He was very impressed with 'breathing meditation'. He said that, regardless from how many sources and how many times he had tried to learn about meditation and tried to stop his mind from wavering, he had never been able to calm the chatter of his 'monkey-mind'. But with this breathing session, he experienced for the first time the ease of maintaining thought-free awareness, great clarity and absolute stillness of his mind.

He asked me where I had learned it from and what the source of this teaching was. Upon learning from me that it came directly from the revelations I had received under the guidance of magic mushrooms, he suggested I give it a proper name.

Although there are many yoga practices which involve different types of pranayamas, such as Kundalini Yoga with its major 'Breath of Fire' pranayama, which is very similar to Kapalbhati pranayama, Kriya Yoga with Kriya pranayama, Hatha Yoga with its Bhastrika, Plavini, Murcha, Sitali and Sitkari pranayamas, Tantric 'Cobra Breathing', Anulom-Vilom or Nadi-Shodhana or alternative nostril breathing pranayama, along with holotropic breathing and rebirthing breathing techniques, my teaching is independent of all of these.

It came in the form of a Divine revelation as a result of Self-remembering, Self-inquiry and surrender, while under the influence of magic mushrooms, before I knew anything about yoga or pranayamas.

Although influenced by Gurdjieff and Ramana Maharshi, it is magic mushrooms and Prana Shakti herself who are my direct teachers. So, to the question: 'Which lineage do I follow?' my answer would be 'The lineage of magic mushrooms, Prana Shakti and ultimately, Shiva-Shakti'.

Thinking of the name for my yoga, I mostly wanted to separate it from the thousands of types of physical gymnastics ironically called yoga. I also wanted to stress that it mainly dealt with Prana and is also concentrated around the retention of breath:

'Kumbhaka'. So, I came up with the name: 'Kumbhaka Prana Yoga'. Although, I've already mentioned the major aspects, or limbs of Kumbhaka Prana Yoga such as Bhavana, Bhairava Mudra, Atma Vichara, Kumbhaka Pranayama and the encouragement of spontaneous body movements, I will return to a fuller description of it a little later in this book, for Kumbhaka Prana Yoga truly contains within itself the most fundamental keys to the Kingdom of Bliss. It is the quintessence of spiritual practice; the most efficient vehicle towards the ecstasy of Truth – a direct path to the supreme joy of boundless freedom.

If to the above-mentioned five limbs of Kumbhaka Prana Yoga we add the help of psilocybin gurus, who work as portals into the higher dimensions, these six would complete the teaching! There would be nothing more advanced on Earth in my opinion, than such a triumphant vehicle towards the ecstasy of liberation.

Ayahuasca, Magic Mushrooms and a Vision of Ganesha

I've heard many spiritual teachers reply smilingly to a question about the role of psychedelic substances on their spiritual discoveries. They claim they did lots of psychedelics when they were young, and these psychedelics served their purpose, but now there is nothing more that they can teach them.

This wasn't and isn't my case. Each time, regardless if it is blissful and ecstatic, or scary as shit, psychedelics teach me new valuable lessons.

In fact, I have a request: instead of numbing me with morphine, I would prefer an injection of a big dosage of psilocybin into my bloodstream on my deathbed just before I leave this body and the world behind.

My experimentations with magic mushroom teachers continued. Another musician who participated in my Kumbhaka Prana Yoga journey, Paul Butler, the lead singer of the Isle of Wight band The Bees invited me and my friend Sean to have a shamanic journey in his newly-rented house in St Lawrence. We didn't manage to collect a great amount of liberty caps, but it was enough for a mild journey. Paul made a mushroom tea. If taken as a tea, mushrooms start their magical work earlier, but I have found that they don't last as long as if they were eaten fresh or chewed dried.

Ayahuasca, Magic Mushrooms and a Vision of Ganesha

In light of this, my preference is to chew and eat them fresh or dry.

I must admit that it was a difficult journey in Paul's house for it gradually became cold there, and practically all my energy went towards sustaining my inner body-fire. I reiterate that cold is not a good companion for the magic mushroom journey. At the beginning of our journey, before the mushrooms started to perform their magic, Paul played a beautiful composition on sitar after which we continued our trip in silence. With spontaneous pranayama, my body went into a rocking and swaying mood. My Rudraksha beads knocked into each other with the rhythm of my swaying body, creating an interesting rhythmic pattern, as though I was playing Shiva's damaru (a two headed drum), enticing my mind into shamanic trance through the power of the beat.

Somewhere in the middle of our session I heard the guys moving into the kitchen and starting to talk, obviously feeling that the effect of the mushrooms was wearing off. Ignoring this, I continued my trance using everything I had for the penetration into the fields of higher frequency. When I finally joined guys in the kitchen, Paul, who had recently made a few trips to the Amazon and had a few good ayahuasca sessions there with famous Peruvian shamans, told me: 'Wow, Shiva you are a legend! You are the real shaman! Your breathing, swaying and especially the rhythm of your Rudraksha beads guided me into the depths of Reality.'

After yet another mushroom journey with my friend, who was teaching transcendental meditation on the island, Bill confessed that he had never imagined that one could take a mushroom trip to such a high level. He said that it wasn't an ordinary trip, but a real spiritual sadhana.

The time arrived for me to try ayahuasca, about which everyone was making so much noise. My friend Sean, who had participated in many ayahuasca retreats, ordered the brew from his Peruvian shaman. The effects of the ayahuasca brew was strong. I had intense visuals of psychedelic geometrical patterns accompanied by a strong electro-magnetic current rushing through my hands and wrists. But, to be honest, in my experience, the effects of ayahuasca did not come close to the power of a good dose of magic mushrooms. Yes, ayahuasca is medicine, but mushrooms are magic!

Ayahuasca, Magic Mushrooms and a Vision of Ganesha

The magic mushroom is the quintessential psychedelic on this planet! It is far older than ayahuasca, which requires fire and a water pot for its preparation. Psilocybin is a complete, organic, knowledge-based technology of non-human intelligence. As Terence Mckenna says: 'Psilocybin is 4-phosphoryloxy-n n-dimethyltryptamine. This is the only naturally occurring 4-substituted phosphorylated indole in all organic nature on this planet. Psilocybin has a unique molecular signature that says: "I am not from here, I come from outside!"'

Soon, we had another journey with Sean. This time it was around one hundred and fifty dry liberty caps each. After we ate mushrooms and were sitting in meditation, Tara read us Chapter Twenty-six from the great *Song of Ribhu*. The mushrooms were strong, enhanced by the powerful words of sage Ribhu. Spontaneous pranayama led the way into the density of the psychedelic experience. Tara had chosen the music for us this time. After some familiar sounds, going deeper and deeper into the intensity of energy, I began to hear unfamiliar music and chants.

Suddenly, my rapidly changing psychedelic patterns of sacred geometry broke down, revealing the most astonishing vision of elephant-headed Lord Ganesh!

Ganesha (Lord of the Beginnings) is the son of Shiva and Parvati. He is not only the Lord of Gunas (Rajas, Tamas, Sattva – the ever-changing qualities of Prakriti [Nature]), not only the removal of obstacles, but the child of Shiva/Shakti i.e. the manifested universe itself. We may think of Ganesha, who is the Pranava (the primal sound AUM), as the very birth and unfolding of the cosmos from the Shiva-Shakti Union. Ganesha is said to be of Infinite Intelligence – the originator of art, letters and numbers. In other words, Lord Ganesha is the creative intelligence behind the visible cosmos itself.

Ganesha is also said to be the Lord of the Muladhara Chakra (root chakra). The Muladhara Chakra is the root centre of physical experience, located at the base of the spine, the sacral plexus. The square represents the earth element, the four dimensions and the four directions. Four allows for completion, and the Earth embodies the elements and conditions for human completion on all levels. The Muladhara Chakra is the meeting place of the three main nadis: Ida, Pingala and Sushumna. The downward-pointing

Ayahuasca, Magic Mushrooms and a Vision of Ganesha triangle indicates the downward movement of energy and the three main nadis. The seed mantra is Lam, the yellow square represents the earth element. The Muladhara Chakra is governed by the vital breath, Apana. An inverted triangle in the centre of the square encloses the unmanifested Kundalini, represented as a snake wrapped in three and a half coils around the svayambhu (self-born) linga.

Because her mouth faces downward, the flow of energy is downward. The opening at the entrance of the sushumna is called Brahma-dvara, the door of Brahma, which is closed by the coils of the sleeping Kundalini. As soon as one begins working with the Muladhara Chakra, this dormant energy awakens, raises its head and flows freely into the channel of sushumna, the central nerve canal that runs along the spine. These two aspects of Kundalini: sleeping and waking, are identified as her 'poison' and her 'nectar'. The Kundalini is poison when she remains asleep in the lower abdomen; she is nectar when she rises up through sushumna, the medial channel, to reunite with Shiva, the Absolute, in the yogi's cranial vault.

The Lord of Infinite Intelligence was riding his rat-vehicle on what I can only describe as the waves of joy rising from the sea of knowledge radiating from his magnificent being and scattering dazzling sublime numbers, mystical symbols and letters of the Divine alphabet across this grand dimension.

The sounds, rhythms and sequences of mantras I had never heard before were taking me deeper and deeper into the most secret mysteries of Creation. I was sure that they were unfolding directly from Shakti's Supreme Intelligence, like a sacred password. The language was the vehicle towards the Source. This language led my consciousness into the Divine Ecstasy of the core of Infinite Reality, leaving all limitations pertaining to the world and body behind.

Sean and I didn't experience any ego battle this time, but on the contrary, Sean admitted that we were intimately connected, and that I led him through the mind-mazes towards the blissful heart of Reality. After the effect of the mushrooms wore off, we were filled with indescribable elation and childlike joy. Sean said that it was the highest experience of his entire life and that it was incomparable to any of his previous experiences with ayahuasca.

Ayahuasca, Magic Mushrooms and a Vision of Ganesha
He learned many great lessons and was very humble and filled with gratitude.

Learning from Tarananda that these magical chants which led our consciousness into the Divine Ecstasy of the core of Reality were 'Divine Chants of Ganesh' by Uma Mohan, I included the most influential chant 'Ganapati Prarthana & Ghanapaath' in my playlist for Kumbhaka Prana Yoga. Although throughout the years I have been working endlessly toward the betterment of the tracks on my playlists, always trying to find the perfect soundscapes for the journey, I always keep 'Ganapati Prarthana & Ghanapaath' as a my central masterpiece, sometimes adding Uma Mohan's Shiva chant 'Namaskaratha' next to it.

Labour of Love

My Kumbhaka Prana Yoga workshops continued in a couple of different yurts owned by my yogi friends. As part of my background was my temporary life as a sadhu, who use the smoking of charas as an essential part of their sadhana, I decided to incorporate the smoking of chillum into our Kumbhaka Prana Yoga sessions.

This decision was formed not only because I followed the sadhus' tradition, but most importantly, because throughout my continuous experiments and experimentations I found that a few good drags of cannabis vapour before pranayama meditation greatly assisted the meditator in his/her journey into the inner realms of reality. Paradoxically, inhaled cannabis vapour purifies the main nadi channels, making breathing much easier, thus assisting with the expansion of consciousness.

I anticipate that quite a few people may argue this point, saying that yoga must be clear of use of any substances. It is my opinion however, that in the deepest longing for the union (yoga) with the Beloved Truth, the sincere seeker should use any possible help, including the tremendous and unique help of plant teachers. Due to negative impositions from various influential sources, however, some individuals participating in smoking charas before meditation, could be under the influence that they are associating with something 'unclean' which induces feelings of guilt, shame and blame.

Fortunately, during all my Kumbhaka Prana Yoga sessions, there were only couple of cases of participants leaving the group when they discovered that we were planning to smoke cannabis. There were also couple of people who didn't partake in smoking

331

chillum due to previous addiction to cannabis. So, they simply skipped this step and journeyed with the rest of us without the help of sacred plants.

One of the reasons for my joy and satisfaction with the new format was that now I could fully participate in the session, breathing and guiding the gathered beautiful souls to the summit of ecstasy, not just play the role of independent observer and sitter. As all is One, without a shadow of doubt, I could feel and experience how my own state of consciousness affected everyone else's. This is one of the main purports of this teaching which is known as 'Shaktipat' – the direct transmission of conscious energy (Shakti).

The part that included words at these workshops was about forty to fifty minutes at the begging of our session, in which we had a brief satsang, followed by introduction into the mysteries of Prana-Shakti and the guidelines for our Kumbhaka Prana Yoga journey. After the guidelines, we smoked chillum, passing it around. After this, all participants lay facing upwards on soft blankets with their heads towards the centre where the speaker was situated and our magical journey into the Heart of God began.

Direct experience is the teacher of teachers! No words are needed to explain how reality works to those who have experienced its mysteries and revelations first-hand. The atmosphere of these gatherings was filled with sparkling, crackling electrical energy growing in intensity with the unfolding of our sacred journeys. Sometimes, people breaking through certain psychedelic thresholds would make incredible dramatic sounds, some started crying, shedding profuse rivers of tears. A few people couldn't break through their fears and retreated into the temporary safety of an ordinary state of consciousness but were nevertheless grateful for the lessons they received.

For those courageous souls whose longing for Truth is so strong that no matter what, they are ready to sacrifice themselves for it, ready to die for Truth, Kumbhaka Prana Yoga is the perfect vehicle towards the Heart of the Beloved!

Truly, Kumbhaka Prana Yoga is a labour of Love!

It is fuelled by Love, moved by Love, and oriented towards Love! It requires unshakable courage, strenuous efforts, willpower and the purest heart which is ready to die for Love! Love is the way to freedom and Love is freedom itself. If there is anything everlasting in existence, it is Love. Love is eternal. To give one's life for Love, to die for Love and in Love is to lose the fears and limitations of the ego-self and be reborn as everlasting infinite Love herself. Love is the greatest paradox; it grows not by containing itself, but by pouring itself out. The more it gives, the bigger it grows and so it is the inexhaustible perennial flood. It is eternal because it sacrifices itself, it dies for Truth and in this sacrificial fire, like a phoenix, it is renewed and reborn again. Truth and Love are synonymous. Truth is Love! To Love means to forget about ourselves, to offer, to sacrifice our ego-selves to the Goddess Truth. Love is not always gentle and meek. Sometimes she can be terrifying in her rage, for although her submissive character allows un-truth to exist temporarily, when she gets furious, she shatters un-truth into a cloud of dust.

Although, she is as gentle as loving mother to her child, she is the greatest force in existence, capable of destroying crores of universes in one big bang! She is the Creator; she is the protector and she is also the destroyer! She assumes forms and plays within them, and in her longing to experience her highest might she rips these suffocating clothes into pieces. Love is the origin and destination. Love is the meaning of life. Without sweet love, life is a burden.

Why do you want to know the Truth? Because Love is calling for you!

Love is the best gift ever! This universe exists only because of Love. Without Love it would submerge into darkness. Because of Love there is light! The sun of Love burns eternally, transforming pain into light. Love absorbs into itself darkness, coldness, and evil, turns them into the light and joy and radiates as a brilliant supernova. Love is the order and she is also chaos. Love is sanity and she is madness. Choose Love, my dear friend, she is the highest reward. Burn like a candle on the way to Love. Mount the sacrificial fire, enter the scorching flames, die and find your True Self in a cool breeze of heavenly paradise, the wonderland of Love! Become Love!

After the music stopped, everyone would usually continue lying down for another ten to fifteen minutes, unable to speak or move and having no desire to return to playing the world-game.

Labour of Love

We didn't discuss what everyone experienced, for firstly, we all were sharing One experience and secondly, words were too clumsy, heavy and pretentious to use. However, we bowed to each other in gratitude, blending our voices in one continuous sacred AUM and then we gave each other big hugs, which proved our interconnectedness and the magic of our expanded energy, for when, after such mind-blowing journeys, wide-open hearts come into close proximity as in hugging, people often temporarily lose the usual body senses such as gravity and direction, and for a few minutes may not be able to move, staying absolutely stunned. Sometimes, in such a hug of two wide-open hearts, a fusion may occur, which can temporarily destroy the so familiar world and the bodies in it. This, for me, is undeniable proof of Oneness.

Although in Truth we are One, we appear as separate entities who have an unspoken agreement, that you are you and I am me. We usually like to keep it that way. When we are trying to directly experience the Truth of Oneness, the sense of growing intimacy and unconditional Love that is about to destroy all taboos, all conditioning, and all barriers, frightens us. True Love destroys the illusion of separation. In our willingness to experience the Truth of Oneness, we become frightened to destroy each other. Satsangs and Kumbhaka Prana Yoga sessions provide very special conditions in which we agree to try to destroy the illusion of separation and realise that you are me and I am you. The actualisation (direct experience) of the realisation: 'I am you and you are me' requires unshakable courage. Self-realisation is the most courageous of all undertakings, for with Self-realisation the awakening soul destroys the very world it is living in.

Many people participating in my workshops admitted that it was the highest experience of their entire life! A few people asked me after our journey finished if I had added anything except cannabis to the chillum, for their experience was truly psychedelic, like those of LSD, or even DMT. Some participants described how our communal Shakti-Kundalini energy was dancing up the poll of the yurt and raining down from the roof with the droplets of Amrit (Divine nectar). One of the participants described how the floor dissolved under his body and he was flying weightless among the stars. I will write one of the many feedbacks below. I received it

Labour of Love

from one young lady named Kirstin, who experienced the Kumbhaka Prana Yoga journey for the first time:

'Hello Shiva. Again, thank you for yesterday. It was a completely profound experience! Similar things have happened before, but not of that intensity or realness. I'm usually slightly disconnected from my body, or it feels like almost a shadow happening with my soul if I have much bodily awareness – but yesterday I was fully present, body and soul. It started almost immediately from laying down, with rapid heartbeat and extreme energy tingling all throughout my body. I felt very enclosed in my skin at first, and slightly panicked, but gave myself to the process. I then started stretching and tensing the energy throughout and into my muscles. I felt it going through each chakra and dispersing in different ways in each. The fizz of the energy went from a dense vibration to very fast, free-flowing, and set into my body. My breathing naturally slowed. My body felt higher resolution. Then I had my first continual kundalini awakening. The energy from the music, and people in the room, flowed up and through my chakra, pausing (but still vibrating) and dispersing through each. In my mind throughout all this, I was dancing, almost formless, energy fluctuating... Going on a primal, tribal journey with a Scorpio woman in a jungle... I went through the bodies of each of my close relatives and understanding them... Making love with the universe... Then melting, slowly coming back into my own body and senses, not so aware of my astral body... It took me many hours to be able to talk again properly! Although I felt fully back within myself at the end of the session, I was very sensitive to energies and easily frazzled for the rest of the day. I would happily do it again!'

I have a feeling, my dear reader, that we have reached the appropriate moment in our story to give a fuller description of Kumbhaka Prana Yoga. I feel that it would be appropriate to write a whole chapter with expanded descriptions, specifically dedicated to the practice.

Kumbhaka Prana Yoga

*'Everything that was, is, or shall be, is
nothing but the different modes of expression of
the universal force. The universal Prana is thus
the Para- Prakriti (Highest, Pure Nature),
immanent energy or force which is derived from
the Infinite Spirit, and which permeates and
sustains the universe.' ~ Yogananda*

Before we go into the details of KPY practice, I am moved
to sing the praises to my Beloved Goddess sat-guru, Prana-
Shakti!

Prana Gita – Song of Prana

'Before Time and Space are born, I am – eternal!

Beyond logical comprehension, I am – infinite!

Ungraspable by my own child – the mind, I am – limit-less!

Having myself no origin, beginning-less, everything has its
origin in me!

Imperishable, death-less, end-less, I swallow creations at the
end of their cycles.

Returning to the source, all that appeared to be different loses
their distinctions in the Ecstasy of Oneness.

The Heart of Reality has no differentiation, I – The Supreme
Energy - Para Shakti are one and the same with The Supreme
Intelligence - Shiva.

336

Some say that we (Shiva and Shakti) are "One", yet others say that we are "Two", but in truth we are both "One" and "Two" at the same time, for we are beyond logical constrictions and the limitations of laws.

We are the unsolvable mystery, infinite and eternal!

As Shakti, I am the Mother of Creation.

I do not think, or plan how to create, for my very nature is Divine Intelligence and as such I do not require an effort to manifest.

The Divine Intelligence simply streaming on the currents of my fluid energy like a divine nectar streaming perpetually from the inexhaustible source.

I am "The Mover", but I move effortlessly!

I am Love that moves!

I have no will of my own, for I am (Purnam) - The Absolute Fullness itself and there is nothing I can possibly want, or desire, for I possess everything and lack nothing.

As the very nature of Love is to give, to shine, to radiate, my ecstatic fullness surges, floods, and expands into infinity.

My Movement is the incomparable Ecstasy!

As I move in ecstasy, the Supreme Language is born!

This Creative Language is nothing else, but the expression of my ecstatic movements.

This Supreme Language (Para-Vak, Logos, Malini, Matr'ka, Mantra) is the origin of all 'knowledge' and the building blocks of all apparent creations.

By the potency of this Divine Language the unfolding creations are both: pre-determined and yet free to change!

As the Spanda (creative vibration-throb) ripples from the Heart of Reality and produces Divine Language creating the Ideation and the Knowledge, the objective manifestations shapes into perceptions.

I am known by thousands of names, each attributed to one of my arrays of qualities.

As Lalita, I like to play my favourite game of "hide and seek" by temporarily blinding my beloved Shiva with my marvellous display. By the power of identification with the objectified image, I lead him into the belief and the sense of temporarily identity with the separated object (Jiva) in one of the lower orders of my infinite creation, simultaneously veiling our True Nature.

My Magical Language entraps such sparks of intelligence (Jivas) in the bubble of the "objective knowledge".

My daughters Shakties – energies presiding over the letters of my Supreme Alphabet are free to choose which Jivas (Souls) to drawn further into the deep waters of Samsara (cyclic existence) by the power of arranging of words and sentences conveying the meanings into some certain sequences forming certain types of knowledge and which to save from the illusory creation according to theirs (Souls) predispositions, desires and longings.

Every Jiva (Soul) in reality is of course Shiva himself, who under my spell has temporarily forgotten his real nature.

Experiencing the limitations of lower planes of creation, he is no longer free and spontaneous.

Like a fly trapped and cocooned in a spider-web, he is now cocooned in "objective knowledge" and the "body-experience" woven by the multitudes of words and meanings.

This Creation, although unsubstantial and ephemeral like a dream, nevertheless appears as a solid reality due to the infinite capabilities of Supreme Intelligence-Energy.

To free himself from these illusory restrictions, Shiva, who temporarily takes himself to be an "individual" separated from the whole, must apply the discriminative logic and right efforts, for although the walls of Maya are illusory, they cannot be broken without the right discrimination and correct efforts.

I have eternity at my disposal, and so my games are infinite!

I leave many clues in my games for Jiva-Shiva to find his way back to the ecstasy of our Union.

I myself am the ultimate Satguru!

For those who begin to know me better, for those who, with their sacred efforts penetrate deeply into my inner dimensions, I – The Supreme Energy am the surest guide to the Divine Rapture of Sublime Truth!

O, what a joy it is, when after the years of exile on lower planes of existence, after his unquenchable longing and search for truth, Shiva finally wakes up from the dream to Reality!

This triumphant moment is worth of a life-game of uncertainty and difficulties.

Kumbhaka Prana Yoga

I – Shakti am always present and reside as the very essence of all creation as Prana Shakti – the life-energy.

I as Indra – Lord of Indriyas (senses) project myself outwardly through the senses and appear as the solid outside world.

At the time of death, I withdraw senses one by one back within myself.

Not knowing my Supreme State, ignorant see me in my gross form of 'Vayu' (wind, air) of inhalation and exhalation.

Wise, who worship me, who begin to know me as their Satguru (inner guru), who, falling in love with me, who seek union with me, directly realise me through the Yoga of Supreme Identity to be their very Self.

When riding on my powerful currents into the source of life – mystery, into the origin of creation... my beloveds, who are longing wholeheartedly for the union with me realise me as their own Supreme Reality.

Through the growing identity with me they lose their sorrows, their boundaries, their wrong knowledge, their minds (the seeds of misery) and their illusory 'identities' in the ecstasy of my True Nature.

Plunging deeply into the subatomic expansion of awareness, my beloveds realise me as "Para-Vak"– the Supreme Language – the source of all Knowledge.

Their sweet efforts of offering their minds and their very lives to me melts my heart, and I am rushing towards them, tormented with the pain of separation.

When the illusion of duality melts away as a result of their courageous efforts of self-sacrifice, of offering their very "sanity" unto me – "The Unknown", I take over their beautiful efforts and begin to shower them in the delightful Soma Rain.

I am washing off their persistent delusions in my refreshing Amrita.

I am brushing off all suffocating dust of wrong knowledge.

I am purifying their being from the remnants of fears, doubts and uncertainties.

As Kundalini, I am rising upward through the main Sushumna Nadi from the Muladhara to the Sahashrara, melting with my heat all-satisfying Amrita Nectar in the cranium and burning with my Radiant Purifying Fire all veils of illusion.

Kumbhaka Prana Yoga

I dance as Kali, playing with the Garlands of Letters of my
Supreme Alphabet, destroying the notions of time and space.

I am Malini, Matr'ka – (Mother of Realities) pregnant with
True Knowledge, Wisdom and Infinite Creativity.

I am the very Life of Awareness, the agitator of Consciousness,
the "Spandana – throb".

I am Shiva's heartbeat!

I am Kumari – the most desirable One, the sweetest Love-
maker.

I am Lalita – the playful One.

I am Bala – Sodashi – forever young.

I am Tripura Sundari – Goddess of Transcendental Beauty in
all three worlds.

I am the Creatrix of All that Is and all that appears to be.

Union with me is Divine Ecstasy!

Knowledge of me is Euphoria!

I am Your very Life!

I am Your very Self!

I am You!

Oh, My Beloved!!!

You are Supreme Shiva!

I am Your Eternal Spouse.

Your Shakti!

Your Creativity!

Your True Love!

Your Dance!

Your Uma-Parvati!

Your Wish-fulfiller!

Your Prana!'

Although prana, due to our limited understanding capacity and
inability to fully comprehend its real significance, appears to our
senses and mind as simple inhalation and exhalation only, or as a
mechanism that allows us to bring in rejuvenating oxygen and
expel carbon dioxide from our body organism, for those who,
through their spiritual effort began to know prana better, she
reveals herself as the Supreme Energy and Intelligence of Absolute
Reality – Shakti Devi of Shiva!

Kumbhaka Prana Yoga

Prana appears to our limited logic less significant and inferior to mind, only because of our lack of direct experience of her inner dimensions. In the love-affair with Goddess Prana, led by her grace into her glorious inner reality, the yogi crosses over the boundaries of differentiation between prana and mind and realises that on the deeper level they are identical, i.e., prana is the energy and the very essence of intelligence (mind). Prana truly is the soul of the universe!

"Prana and vak (speech) are two faces of the same underlying Reality. Prana is unmanifested speech, and speech is manifested prana. Prana is spirit, which is formless, while speech is the basis of form and matter through the naming process. Name and form arise from speech while being and consciousness are sustained by prana. Prana and speech are intertwined, like husband and wife. They always move together. Prana is the energy behind speech, which moves through the breath.

The Vedas define the two fundamental forces in the universe as prana or life-energy and vak (speech). Prana is the spirit of mantra. Mantra in turn is the expression of prana."[40]

'In the beginning was the Word, and the Word was with God, and the Word was God' – begins the Bible.[41]

Kashmir Shaivism also equates Svatantrya (Free Will and the sufficiency of the Absolute) with Para Vak (Supreme Speech).

But what is the Word? What is the Speech?

It is the movement of Supreme Energy (Prana-Shakti)!

Prana is also Indra – the Lord of Indriyas (senses). Senses are born of prana. The movements of prana agitate the lake of the mind, creating thoughts, meanings and images. Prana is life itself!

When Prana snaps its link with the body, we say that a person is dead. Prana-Indra, the Lord of senses (indriyas), blazing forth from the ungraspable singularity of the Spiritual Heart (Hrt - Hrdayam – the centre), like a spider, emits her holographic webs of the universe outward through the senses, and also by agitation of the nadis (subtle nerve-energy channels) and by the churning the lake of the mind with its rhythmic pulsating (Spanda – Sphurana) essence. By the rhythms of her Divine sequences, she creates Para

---

[40] David Frawley "Mantra Yoga and the Primal Sound: Secrets of Seed (Bija) Mantras" p.48

[41] John 1:1

Vak (Supreme Language) and Matrikas (pregnant Mothers of Cosmos/ the energy forces forming phonemes/ letters of the Divine Alphabet), which bring about all sorts of limited knowledge. At the time of death of the physical body, Prana-Shakti withdraws the senses one by one (taste, smell, sight, touch and hearing) together with the great elements (earth, water, fire, air and ether) back within herself.

In the individualised consciousness, that is swallowed, absorbed by the non-referential, non-local, ungraspable homogenous Prana, the basic tendency to grasp begins to form. Due to its habitual tendencies, the desire to be someone forms and develops into the experience of separation and localisation within the all-pervading, non-local wholeness. If something unacceptable is detected within the display of its own mind, then a sense of rejection or anger may surge to the surface of consciousness and the fight against its own creation begins. Blinded by growing ignorance to the fact that he/she is fighting against its own projections, some of the individualised consciousness may enter and become trapped in dimensions of cold hell, frightened and isolated from its own Divine Source – God.

The 'I am Brahman' Bhavana and the courageous act of complete surrender to Lord Yama – Lord of Death – and his act of annihilation of individuality, together with limited objective knowledge pertaining to individuality, and a willingness to 'cease to exist', are very important, intelligent spiritual attitudes.

The growing love-affair with Prana-Shakti awakens in response her Love! When all the illusionary defences of the ego are burnt to ashes by the fire of Devotional Love for the Absolute Truth, when one throws oneself into the grace of Her mercy, She the Compassionate One absorbs him/her into infinite Ecstasy – the Bliss of the Highest States of Infinite Reality! Regardless of how advanced and sophisticated the logic and intellect, lying only on the surface of reality, gazing and trying to penetrate its mysteries, can never take one all the way into its depths. But Prana Shakti can take those united with her yogi's consciousness all the way to its mysterious core, the very nucleus of God Absolute!

As we look at the Yoga of Patanjali, we will see that he did not limit yoga to six limbs only (asana, pranayama, pratyahara, dharana, dhyana and samadhi) but he also included important aspects such as the right conduct of living (dharma), yamas (restraints/ right harmonious living with others) consisting of ahimsa (nonviolence), satya (truthfulness), asteya (not stealing), brahmacharya (non-excess), aparigraha (non-possessiveness) and niyamas (observances – an adult harmonious relationship with one's mind and thoughts) consisting of saucha (purity), santosha (contentment), tapas (self-discipline), svadhyaya (self-study), ishvara pranidhana (surrender). It shows us that yoga is not only occasional exercises of body and mind, but it also a way of living.

Further, if we analyse Yoga of Malinivijayottara Tantra we also find that the practice of yoga and its accomplishment requires a very substantial amount of time. It is suggested in Purva-Tantra (Malinivijayottara) that the perfection of one tattva would take around three years of regular uninterrupted practice. Proceeding further, with three years of concentration on each of five mahabhutas (great elements), the yogi must also ascend through seven levels of 'perceivers' (pramatrins) from Sakala experient to Pralayakala pramatri, Vijnanakala pramatri, Suddhavidya with Mantra pramatri, Isvara with Mantresha pramatri, Sadasiva with Mantra-Mahesvara experient, and finally, Siva as experient in oneness with the Shiva experience.

As we can see, it would take almost the entirety of our lives, to achieve perfection in the practice of yoga.

Born into different circumstances of our lives, specifically into Western culture of the modern age, we must admit that only a rare handful of people born into favourable circumstances, or real heroes with utmost dedication to the highest goal can afford the luxury of a life dedicated solely to yoga. For the rest of us living amid busy society, engaged in the fight for survival and a search for entertainment, it is better to find such yogic tools that can be used on a daily basis amidst countless everyday tasks and interactions, to quickly resume the satisfying connection with the Sublime Source – our True Self. Also, it would be great to find the most powerful spiritual technologies, which allow us to bypass countless obstacles and, in one quantum leap, find ourselves in the beatitude of Supreme Truth.

Kumbhaka Prana Yoga could be considered one such shortcut!

Regardless of whether we consider our lives as a dream or as reality, as long as we are not free from the perception of the objective world it would not be wise, or even possible to just simply dismiss and ignore it. Rather, we should joyously participate in the life-play, knowing it for what it really is – a play of consciousness and energy.

As Krishna instructs Arjuna in Bhagavad Gita in Chapter Three on 'Karma Yoga':

'All men are forced to act helplessly according to the impulses born of the modes of material nature; therefore no one can refrain from doing something, not even for a moment.

One who restrains the senses and organs of action, but whose mind dwells on sense objects, certainly deludes himself and is called a pretender (hypocrite).

On the other hand, he who controls the senses by the mind and engages his active organs in works of devotion, without attachment, is by far superior.

Perform your prescribed duty, for action is better than inaction. A man cannot even maintain his physical body without work.

Work done as a sacrifice for Vishnu has to be performed, otherwise work binds one to this material world. Therefore, O son of Kunti, perform your prescribed duties for His satisfaction, and in that way, you will always remain unattached and free from bondage.'[42]

In the light of all mentioned above, I happily advise that, although I didn't include Patanjali's yamas and niyamas in Kumbhaka Prana Yoga, I nevertheless am in full harmony with their teachings and practices and consider them a very essential part of yoga and the rightful conduct for harmonious living.

Wise men never disregard and reject something valuable but extract the very essence of the teaching and would use it for their own gain.

In this way, Kumbhaka Prana Yoga could be regarded as a quintessence of many different teachings, combined into one most powerful spiritual technology.

Some people are focused on one aspect of spiritual practice, without paying too much attention to other practices which could be of a great assistance to the main one.

---

[42] "Bhagavad Gita" Chapter 3 Karma Yoga verse 5,6,7,8,9.

Kumbhaka Prana Yoga

For example, I know many people who follow the main teachings of Ramana Maharshi (the direct path of Self-inquiry), disregarding such practices as pranayama etc... Followers of Gurdjieff and Ouspensky concerned mainly with Self-remembering and the transformation of negative emotions, disregard practices of meditation etc... *Ribhu Gita* is dedicated to the practice of Bhavana (creative contemplation), missing the other helpful links assisting with Awakening. And almost all spiritual aspirants shy away from using the most valuable help of sacred plants and spirit-molecules.

It is true, that if practiced vigilantly with utmost dedication, all such practices could be efficient enough to deliver the aspirant into the bliss of Truth, but as I mentioned before, it would require total dedication and a considerable amount of time to achieve perfection.

In my Kumbhaka Prana Yoga, I combined the most powerful aspects of all kinds of spiritual practices to make this system one of the most powerful and efficient for Self-realisation!

As I mentioned a few times before, Kumbhaka Prana Yoga consists of five major parts or limbs. They are:

1) Bhavana (I am Brahman certitude – conviction)

2) Bhairava Mudra (simultaneously extroverted and introverted awareness of the totality of all phenomena. The expansion of consciousness towards the cognition and comprehension of all external and internal impressions simultaneously)

3) Atma-Vichara (Self-inquiry – tracing the I-thought/ I-feeling to its source, turning attention within and focusing on the I-sense

4) Kumbhaka Pranayama (dynamic intuitive spontaneous breathing with the periods of majestic Kumbhakas)

5) Shamanic Trance-dance. The encouragement of spontaneous movements of the body and its parts including fingers and tongue (spontaneous formation of asanas and mudras).

Bhavana and Atma Vichara

Aham Brahmasmi Bhavana and Atma-Vichara do not require any special circumstances in their initial stages and can be practiced continuously, anywhere at any time. One must constantly, or whenever one remembers it, keep reminding oneself that 'all this that I perceive now is only a display of my own consciousness. It is a projection of my own mind, it is a dream, Maya, illusion. It exists

345

only in ignorance and it does not exist in Reality.' This is the first part of Bhavana – negation: This does not exist. Only I – the True Self exists.

Who, or what am I? Whence am I? This is the beginning of Self-inquiry.

I am Brahman – Immortal Infinite Reality – God Absolute! Here is the second part of Bhavana – affirmation.

The attention turns within towards the very source of awareness and gets fixed on the sense of 'I'. When I say 'I', where do I feel it? Whence is this 'I' arising from? (Atma-vichara).

I am beyond this Maya's display; I am the unperishable Truth! (Bhavana).

One must totally open oneself up to these words of Truth and through the immense power of unshakable trust in this Truth, feel this statement with one's whole being. Feel oneself identical with this Sublime Truth!

However, with the deepening of the Self-realisation initiated by Bhavana and Atma-Vichara, it becomes increasingly difficult to be simultaneously engaged with the daily tasks of the life-game, for one's consciousness is greatly withdrawn from the 'play'. So, for a deeper penetration into the mysteries of Reality, one should be alone. Bhavana is a very powerful practice enabling one to ascend from the words of Truth and their meaning to the actual experience of Truth. When it has deeply penetrated one's own being, Bhavana turns into 'Sat-tarka'. Sat-tarka can be translated as 'true logic', or 'intuitive reasoning'. The great Kashmiri sage Abhinavagupta, Malinivijayottara Tantra and the Trika system of Kashmir Shaivism tradition considered Sat-tarka as the last stage of Awakening. Intuitive reasoning is not based on an ordinary thinking process, but rather it is the emergence of pure intuition. It is the blossoming of innate knowledge. Sat-tarka therefore must be regarded as pure gnosis (Pure Knowledge), emerging at the level of Suddhavidya (pure wisdom).

Bhavana can be practiced and experienced on different aspects of Reality such as feeling 'I am the field of energy', or 'I am pure joy', 'I am amazement and wonder', 'I am All', 'The gleaming picture of the world is within me', 'The world is the materialisation of my energy-intelligence, it is my body', 'I am Infinite Love', 'I am Prana – all permeating conscious energy', 'I am The Self – the

Substratum of all', 'All is I', and also 'What I perceive does not exist', 'Space and time do not exist', 'Directions do not exist', 'Gravity does not exist', 'Temperature does not exist', 'Limitations do not exist', 'Distance does not exist', 'I permeate all', 'I do not exist' etc. As best as one can, one must fully identify with the given quality of each affirmation and realise it as an aspect of One's True Self. In other words, 'Be That'.

Regular Bhavana allows one to embody the words of Truth and leads to direct experience of this Truth. Direct experience, even momentary, strengthens one's conviction in 'I am Brahman' certitude. And so, these two: Bhavana and the direct experience of Truth to which it points leads to unshakable certainty that 'I am Brahman – the imperishable, indestructible unblemished wonderful Reality – God Absolute!'

Established in such diamantine certainty, one begins to see life as the secondary creation of one's own consciousness – a game-play with many deliberately created clues, which lead one to awaken from the dream, to the final liberation from self-imposed limitations. One begins to notice the abundance of synchronicities and Divine providence in life and starts to regard the life-story not as a mechanical accident, but as orchestrated by Supreme Intelligence!

Having such an attitude, one becomes a quick learner from all the lessons that life offers. In other words: harvesting the energy of every given situation and using it as a fuel for the conscious rocket takes one out of the prison of the gravitational field into the freedom of pure beatitude and the bliss of Highest Truth!

Atma-Vichara

When Kavyakanta Ganapati Muni a prominent scholar, well versed in Vedas, approached the feet of young muni, Venkataraman (Ramana Maharshi) and asked him from the depth of his heart: 'What is Tapas?', Ramana broke his years-long silence and answered: 'If one watches whence the notion "I" arises, the mind gets absorbed there; that is Tapas. When mantra is repeated, if one watches whence that mantra sound arises, the mind gets absorbed there; that is Tapas.' This, in a nutshell is the very essence of Ramana Maharshi's teaching, called 'Atma-Vichara' (Self-inquiry), also known as the 'Direct path'. Self-inquiry must be considered as the very heart of all spiritual teachings! As I mentioned before; even in the midst of the most bewildering psychedelic experience Self-inquiry is possible and even unavoidable if one tries to realise the Self, for as long as there are any sorts of perceptions, there is also the perceiver. Who am I who is perceiving this? Always turning and fixing the attention on the perceiver, the mind merges into its own source and gets swallowed by the True Self.

However, due to the mind's tendency to cling to the objects of perception and produce thoughts, and also due to the continuous battle of Prana and Apana, agitating nadis and the lake of the mind, success in Self-inquiry is not an easy achievement.

As Yogiraj Gurunath Siddhanath expressed very eloquently:

'The dual breath is a storm that creates form waves (sensations) in the lake of the mind. These sensations also produce body consciousness and duality and thus obliterate the unified consciousness.

So long as this light is flowing up and down as the two battling currents of Prana and Apana, the breath of inhalation and exhalation, they lend their Life and Light to the sensory perceptions, and to the mortal process of growth and decay.

Life force withdrawn from the senses becomes concentrated into a steady inner Light in which Spirit and its Cosmic Light are revealed.

The Yogi consciously experiences without dying, the death process by which energy is switched off from the senses (causing the disappearance of body consciousness).

When breath ceases, Yogi realises then that it is a storm of human breath that is responsible for the creation of the dream wave of the human body and its sensations, it is breath that causes body consciousness.

When, with the cessation of breath, the life force is switched off from the senses, the mind becomes detached and interiorized, able at last to perceive consciously the inner astral worlds and supernal spheres of Divine Consciousness.

Yogi then perceives the illusion of the body dream dematerialising into the Reality of God.

When a Yogi has fully understood the ideational body, he is able to withdraw his consciousness from the three bodily prisons and Unite himself with the Dreamless Blessedness of God'.[43]

From the thousands of people practicing Self-inquiry, however, only few can claim that their mind has been annihilated (Manonasa).

If the practice of Self-inquiry goes hand in hand with the practice of Bhavana, Bhairava mudra, Kumbhaka Pranayama and the encouragement of spontaneous movements of one's body and its parts (spontaneous asanas and mudras), the success rate would multiply dramatically.

Bhairava mudra.

I hope you are familiar with stereograms, my dear reader. To be able to see a three-dimensional picture on a two-dimensional stereogram, one needs to let go of one's habitual focus. One must un-focus one's gaze. In the intermediate stage, while one's focus is shifting from its usual fixated point in search of another perspective, the perception is very abstract and hazy. But once one's eyes find a new focus; one begins to see a three-dimensional image with great clarity. One may then move one's eyes all around the picture, investigating the smallest details without losing one's new perspective.

In the same way, our awareness is scattered everywhere, but the focus of our attention is fixed on a particular object at any one time. So long as the focus of our attention is glued to the objects of perception, it is not possible to see the wider picture. To be able to simultaneously grasp all at once, we should let go of the fixed focused of our attention. There will be obviously a transitional period between one level of focus and the next. There will be a state of blur, a state of abstraction between the two levels of perception, between the two focuses, between the parallel realities.

Bhairava mudra is a perfect example of un-focusing or refocusing and so is Gurdjeff's and Ouspensky's 'divided attention'.

---

[43] Yogiraj Gurunath Siddhanath

Kumbhaka Prana Yoga

The rays of our awareness are diluted and scattered throughout the space of so-called 'objective reality'. Our precious attention, like a hungry caterpillar, without abandoning one object, searches for a new one with which to entertain itself. Rarely do we bring our attention back to where it came from; to the sense of 'I'; 'I' the seer, 'I' the experiencer. Without abandoning 'objective reality' by simply shutting our eyes, but rather with our eyes wide open, like an archer pulling the string of a bow, we must pull the gravity of our awareness, containing the world-picture, to its centre – the Seer, the Experiencer, the 'I'. Not giving attention to thought, we must begin to feel the pure energy! The energy (Shakti) is the satguru (inner teacher) and the guide to the ecstasy of Truth. Now, we must enter the tremor, the shaking, the faintness, enter our psychosomatic world of energy! Enter the temple of our body-cosmos. With all our might and courageous efforts, we must swim against the outgoing currents, like a salmon, upstream into our Divine Source – Hrt, Hrdayam.

Swami Lakshmanjoo encourages us to look at one point uninterruptedly without blinking until the perceptions of world-appearance disappear. 'In concentrating on Karana through the sense of sight, you have to look at a particular thing. You must go on looking without the blinking of your eyes. You should go on seeing that one point with unbroken awareness. And when that point vanishes, and it should and will vanish when you enter into that vastness of the centre, that is the end. When the perceiver exists, the perceived is also found in the background; not vividly but it is there. While rising from the state of perceiver to the state of Super-perceiver you fall in voidness (pralayakala state). When you are in a pralayakala state, it is almost certain that you will lose consciousness. When you do not lose consciousness of your Being you are carried automatically to the state of Siva. You must apply effort only up to the crossing Maya,' says Swami Lakshmanjoo in *The Secret Supreme*.[44]

Although he doesn't mention expanded unqualified awareness, only concentration on one spot, if one undertakes such a practice, it will become evidently clear that while the gaze is fixed on one spot, the rest of unqualified awareness will be spread all around,

---

[44] "The Secret Supreme" Swami Lakshmanjoo

permeating outer and inner and fusing all perceptions of apparently dual nature into one homogenous awareness.

Vigilant practice of Bhairava Mudra expands consciousness to its utmost limits, crossing which a new mode of vision opens: 'non-referential perception'. In such as state, there is no one point of reference, but instead there are multiple points or sources of awareness in every atom of existence.

Ramana Maharshi points out that it is difficult to realise Self because the mind, like a bee rushing towards the nectar in flowers, rushes towards its lovers – the objects of perception. Mauna (the absolute silence), he says, is not a state of indolence and inactivity. On the contrary, it is a state of immense activity in which the mind opens 100% and is able to destroy illusion at the very moment of its conception, or appearance. In our ordinary state of consciousness, we use only a fraction of our mind, and so do with frequent breaks, but in the state of Mauna, or a state of Oneness with the Self, the mind opens completely and perceives all outer and inner impressions simultaneously. Obviously, in such a mode of perception, the very nature of impressions changes dramatically and is no longer ordinary, but extraordinary!

As long as one perceives two dimensions, one is simply unable to perceive three dimensions. As long as one perceives a snake in a rope, one is unable to perceive the rope. As long as one perceives the world, one is unable to perceive the Self – the Reality!

When one meditates with the eyes closed, although it is easier at the beginning, eventually one has to open one's eyes and then one is back to the experience of the world-illusion. Bhairava mudra (eyes wide open gazing into the one spot with the panoramic perception of all impressions at once, thought-free attention turned within and fixed on the Seer) is a far more advanced way of meditation! The intensity of awareness is such that it is capable of destroying illusion!

Through the power of Bhairava Mudra, the yogi splits atoms and releases the tremendous sub-atomic energy needed for the breaking through the Maya's threshold into the vastness of the Higher Realms of Supreme Intelligence. With the eyes wide open, he uses the totality of perceptions as a fuel for the rocket of Self-knowledge. Sharply cutting off the impressions of the past and the expectations of the future, the yogi penetrates deeper and deeper into the narrow gap of Now-ness. With such penetration, the Now widens, leading yogic awareness into the timeless origin of Time.

The words of Hermes Trismegistus in his *Hermetica* describe the 'I am Brahman' Bhavana and the Bhairava Mudra very appropriately: 'If then you do not make yourself equal to God, you cannot apprehend God; for like is known by like. Leap clear of all that is corporeal and make yourself grown to a like expanse with that greatness which is beyond all measure; rise above all time and become eternal; then you will apprehend God. Think that for you too nothing is impossible; deem that you too are immortal, and that you are able to grasp all things in your thought, to know every craft and science; find your home in the haunts of every living creature; make yourself higher than all heights and lower than all depths; bring together in yourself all opposites of quality, heat and cold, dryness and fluidity; think that you are everywhere at once, on land, at sea, in heaven; think that you are not yet begotten, that you are in the womb, that you are young, that you are old, that you have died, that you are in the world beyond the grave; grasp in your thought all of this at once, all times and places, all substances and qualities and magnitudes together; then you can apprehend God.'[45]

Like a crazy scientist preparing for the moment of his major experiment all his life, and now about to witness the pure miracle of it, like a child seeing a magician's trick, struck with astonishment, one must intently bring oneself to a state of great wonder!

When one is suddenly struck by the recognition of majestic beauty, one's jaws part, pupils dilate, and the breathing abruptly stops, for what one is witnessing is breath-taking. So the yogi practicing Bhairava Mudra must attentionally bring himself to a state of absolute amazement, recognising that what he is witnessing now is nothing ordinary, but rather, a pure miracle!

As it is said in *Spanda Karikas* by Ksemaraja, describing Bhairava Mudra: 'He sees the totality of objects appearing and disappearing in the ether of his consciousness like a series of reflections appearing and disappearing in a mirror. Instantly all his thought-constructs are split asunder by the recognition, after a thousand lives, of his essential nature surpassing common

---

[45] "Hermetica" Hermes Trismegistus

experience and are full of unprecedented bliss. He is struck with amazement, as though entering the mudra of amazement. As he obtains the experience of vast expansion, suddenly his proper, essential nature comes to the fore.'[46]

I used to practice sitting meditation with my eyes closed, entering the thought-free stillness of inner being. What such silent meditation lacks is the sufficient amount of energy for Awakening. The greatest advantage of Kumbhaka Prana Yoga over silent meditation with one's eyes closed is the amount of available energy.

The way to Shiva is through Shakti!

The Spiritual Energy (Shakti) is the vehicle towards the explosion of pure Intelligence (Shiva)!

I hope by reading about Bhavana, Atma-Vichara and Bhairava Mudra, you, my dear reader, are already beginning to feel that all these spiritual practices combined lead to the release of the tremendous amount of energy needed to shatter the illusory walls of Maya and enter the high-vibrational fields of the inner dimensions. Released, awakened energy picks such a yogi and carries him/her on its powerful currents to the summit of Reality. This energy purifies the mind and the field of consciousness of all accumulated dross and makes it shine like a diamond.

Although, Bhavana, Atma-Vichara and Bhairava Mudra in themselves can be efficient enough for the awakening to Highest Reality if practiced vigilantly, the most powerful tool for the awakening from my experience is what I call Kumbhaka Pranayama.

Prana is Energy. Therefore, working with Prana Shakti, learning from Prana Shakti, falling in love with Prana Shakti, the sadhaka (spiritual aspirant) makes acquaintance with the most powerful force in the universe!

Kumbhaka Pranayama.

It's not a big secret that if you begin to breathe with greater vigour and amplitude, something very interesting is going to happen. After as little as thirty or forty rounds of inhalations and

---

[46] "Spanda Karikas" Ksemaraja

exhalations you will begin to feel lightheaded, almost to the point of faintness, or the point of losing of normal consciousness. If at that moment, you arrest your breathing, entering into the firm Antar-Kumbhaka (retention of breath after inhalation), or Bahya-Kumbhaka (retention of breath after exhalation) and if at that magical moment you expand your awareness-consciousness through the previously described Bhairava Mudra, Bhavana and Atma-Vichara, you will enter a field of highly accelerated energy where everything is possible!

The process of Awakening is an opening of the bottomless inner reservoirs of energy. It is the shooting of prana through all the branches, capillary and miniscule passages of the nadi system, delivering refreshing energy and the light of awareness to every particle in the body-cosmos, as well as to the whole field of cognition. It is a breaking by the flood of prana of all restrictions and blockages. It is the penetration of consciousness-awareness into the ever-expanding, vital vibratory fields of the inner dimensions. It is an exposure of the sense of 'I' to the intensely bright light of Supreme Intelligence.

In principle, Kumbhaka Prana Yoga is very similar to the ignition of a car engine. In older cars, one must apply one's actual strength and force to start an engine. One must rotate a hand-crank at a certain speed to trigger the engine. Only when there is enough speed in the rotation will the motor kick in and start working on its own.

As Gurdjieff taught, we do not have a one brain (centre of intelligence), but several; intellectual, instinctive, moving, emotional and sexual brains (lower centres), all working on different types of fuel, and at different speeds. Together with the lower centres, he taught, there are also two higher centres (higher emotional and higher intellectual) which are fully developed and work constantly at higher speeds. These are considered to be a higher order of intelligence, which stands above the body functions (lower centres). Due to a complete identification with the functions of the lower centres, however, and the wastage of energy on its own activities, we do not have a connection with the high-speed workings of the higher centres under ordinary circumstances.

Many spiritual traditions take a similar position. For example, in Hindu philosophy and specifically in the Kashmir Shaivism tradition, the True Self is always present as the Divine bliss of the timeless Now, and yet the limited sense of 'I', which every individual fully identifies with, doesn't feel connection with this ever-present, all-satisfying, all-knowing higher level of Intelligence. On the contrary, almost every individual feel cut off from God, from the Divine Source.

As I have mentioned, the main reason we feel cut off from Divine Source lies in the insufficiency of our speed of perception, or our inability to accelerate our frequency. We are trapped in a bubble of lower frequencies. To escape from this bubble into a higher frequency domain we must accelerate the frequencies of our perception, accelerate our energy.

As you can see; all the practices described above directly lead to the acceleration of the speed of perception, to the acceleration of the frequency of energy.

All efforts in KPY are directed towards igniting innate wisdom, towards making a connection, towards triggering dormant Kundalini intelligence-energy. And so, the analogy of 'igniting of a car engine' works perfectly here.

Self-remembering, according to Gurdjieff, creates the first conscious shock that triggers the food octaves to proceed further and to produce higher hydrogens (a higher frequency field) and therefore make connection with the higher order of intelligence of the higher centres which are already perfect.

Although, Bhavana, Atma-Vichara, Bhairava mudra and Self-remembering are all very powerful spiritual techniques that trigger reconnection with Higher Intelligence, it is the Kumbhaka Pranayama above all, in my experience, that has the most powerful impact on our state of consciousness. It is able to release the tremendous amount of energy needed for reconnection. But the best results can be achieved when all the above-mentioned sadhanas are combined and practiced simultaneously, especially when they are practiced under the graceful influence of sacred plants.

As I have mentioned, prana energy – Love – is not stiff like the mind, but flexible, fluid. Because of that, I cannot give you firm instructions as to how to breathe, but rather can only offer you guidelines, for the major point of such dynamic breathing is the awakening of dormant intuition. In other words, you are already God-Absolute. You are already filled with Divine Knowledge and all these techniques, including dynamic breathing serve only for the purpose of reconnection with already intelligent active energy.

It is important to understand that the movement of prana is directly linked to the state of consciousness. When there is a sudden emergence of fear, or when one is awed by majestic beauty, breathing spontaneously stops. And so, sometimes when I begin to practice KPY, I am already in a quite heightened state of consciousness and therefore start KPY with a prolong Kumbhaka, simultaneously practising Bhavana, Atma-Vichara and Bhairava mudra.

If, however, you are in your 'normal' state of consciousness I advise to begin your breathing with the relatively slow but deep and round breathing, without stopping at the end of inhalations or exhalations. Listening to your innate body intuition, however, you may decide to begin breathing with great vigour from the very start.

For the first five to ten minutes, you even can forget about Bhavana, Atma-Vichara and Bhairava mudra. The most important thing is to concentrate and to continue your round breathing, very slowly increasing the tempo and widening the depth of your breathing.

Your practice of Bhavana, Atma-Vichara and Bhairava mudra should emerge by themselves when you proceed further with your dynamic breathing. It is impossible to say with precision when you need to stop for a retention. Sometimes, you just get tired of breathing and you feel that you need to take a little break. In this case there are three possible scenarios at that moment:

1) You arrest your breathing after the inhalation and enter Antar Kumbhaka, but you stay in rest of Kumbhaka for only two to three seconds and then resume your breathing. These two to three seconds should be enough to give you a little rest, with the help of which you will proceed to the next desirable station.

2) You arrest your breathing after the inhalation and settle into a very firm Kumbhaka (you may lock your throat and perineum with Jalandhara and Mula bandhas). If you decide to settle in this Kumbhaka, now is a good time to bring in the power of your affirmations, your Self-inquiry and to expand your consciousness with the Bhairava mudra, even if you decide at the beginning to practice KPY with your eyes closed. In this case, you can still use Bhairava mudra internally, expanding your consciousness,

simultaneously experiencing all inner bodily sensations and feeling the play of energies permeating the body.

Pull the rays of your awareness towards the place behind your eyes, where you feel the seer abides, then further towards the back of your head, the back of your neck and your spinal cord. Feel that you are pulling the whole world towards your centre.

At the beginning the sensation of centre (Hrdayam) will experience two digits to the right side of your chest on the front part of your body, but with the deepening of your sadhana this sensation of the centre should sink deeper within your body towards the sushumna channel.

The very moment you are entering Kumbhaka is truly magical. All portals are wide open in this moment of great potentiality. Cherish this magical moment! Use what you've learned so far to expand your consciousness, penetrating deeper and deeper into the Now, gradually widening this bottomless gap of Now.

3) You may find the willpower to break through this seemingly needed interval. In this case you may find that with the continuation of your breathing for another three to five minutes, nothing extraordinary happens in terms of altered states of consciousness. You just may feel that regardless of how long you breathe, you are still in your ordinary state of consciousness. My advice to you if you reach this stage is to continue using your willpower to proceed with your breathing. Avoid sabotaging thoughts telling you that it is impossible to breathe in such a manner for a very long time. These thoughts are lies. Sooner or later, you will reach the stage of emergence of greater energy. Sometimes it can be overwhelming. You should develop your intuition of these stages. The moment of entering Kumbhaka is right when you feel the sudden flood of energy permeating your being. Go into Kumbhaka and enter (embody) the field of energy – the field of prana. Expand your consciousness, uniting it with energy. Be conscious energy or energetic consciousness.

At the moment of entering into Kumbhaka, there are also a few choices available:

You lock your throat by slightly tucking your chin close to the chest (Jalandhara bandha) but relaxing your body, gradually releasing all noticeable tension.

Kumbhaka Prana Yoga

When you enter Kumbhaka after the inhalation, tightly squeeze all the muscles of your body, your skull and your mouth. Firmly shut your eyes, creating dense pressure in your head. Your hands might form tight fists, your toes curl, you lift your pelvic floor, squeezing your perineum. You can also push your tongue above the soft palate of your mouth towards the nasal cavities, forming Khecari mudra. Stay in this tension as long as you can, observing the psychedelic display of lights and patterns, firstly in the region of your third eye, gradually spreading towards the back of your body. Gradually this tension will begin to release itself, bringing a sense of ease.

This stay in voluntary tension warms up and purifies the nadi channels, releasing trapped energy and allowing prana to flow more freely and vigorously up and down the nadis, especially the main Ida, Pingala and Sushumna channels at the spinal cord.

I also cannot provide you with a precise measure of time that you should stay in Kumbhaka for the reasons I have already mentioned. With the continuation of dynamic breathing your intuition will come to the fore and gradually start to help you with the breathing navigation. Most people who attended my workshops found that when they entered Kumbhaka after prolonging dynamic breathing, time stretched dramatically, they lost the desire to breathe and could stay in this state of breathlessness for ages.

My advice for the initial stages of the Kumbhaka Prana Yoga journey is not to attempt to forcibly hold Kumbhaka, but to resume breathing as soon as you feel the urge for it. You can experiment with forcibly holding Kumbhaka in later stages, when your entire nadi system has thoroughly warmed up. To hold forcibly Kumbhaka is not easy. When the urge to exhale has developed, you may decide not to continue breathing, but to hold your retention to the utmost limits.

The power forcing you to exhale can seem almost unstoppable and might make you feel as though you have no other choice but to exhale. With practice however, you can find the necessary willpower to stay firmly in retention for some extra seconds, or even minutes. When you decide to resist the urge to breathe out, it might be helpful to sway your head from side to side, to move your body, creating contraction and release of your muscles, What you will observe as a result of your super-human efforts to hold

Kumbhaka Prana Yoga

Kumbhaka by force is a gradual fusion of Prana and Apana into homogenous Vyana. You will find that, by some miracle your exhale, although almost explosive, at the same time will be disproportionally shallow, for the breath of inhalation diffused throughout the entire nadi system of your body. I advise you to quickly pick up a more intense rhythm of breathing after this explosive exhalation, feeling that Shakti herself is beginning to breathe for you.

Listening attentively to the wisdom of your body and your emerging intuition, you may find that your round breathing now tends towards deeper, prolonged inhalation and much shorter and rapid exhalation, like in Bastrika Pranayam. Follow this pattern of breathing if you feel that its suits you. Bastrika Pranayam is very powerful.

You might find also at a later stage that your breathing tends towards a very deep inhalation to the full capacity of your lungs, after which you can pause in retention just for a second, followed by a very deep exhalation, at the end of which you can hold retention for another second. You can proceed with this breathing pattern until the new tendency develops.

Another type of breathing may also be helpful for stimulating your Muladhara Chakra. The reverse of Bastrika Pranayam, this type of breathing involves short and fast inhalation. You have a very prolonged exhalation to your utmost capabilities, entering Bahya Kumbhaka at the end of your exhalation, then you lock your perineum with the Mula Banda.

This prolonged pause in Bahya Kumbhaka creates a brief period of low oxygen levels known as 'hypoxia'. According to some research this 'intermittent hypoxia' stimulates stems cells to come out of their niches and move around the body to places where they can heal and regenerate healthy cells.

While in Bahya Kumbhaka you also can rhythmically tighten and release your pelvic flor, visualising sexual intercourse and the arousal of sexual energy rising up your sushumna channel from Muladhara towards Sahashrara at the top of your head. After staying long enough in Bahya Kumbhaka, you may surprisingly find that you can squeeze a little bit more air from your lungs now. Lock your bandas again and stay in Bahya Kumbhaka as long as you can. You may gasp for air after prolonged retention. Follow this with a short, but full capacity inhale and a slow, deep exhalation.

Your major currency, your trump card in this process is your sacred efforts to vigorously breathe rooted in your Love, your longing for freedom and union with the Beloved Truth! You are ready to sacrifice yourself for Love!

With practice you will begin to intuitively feel which moments of your dynamic breathing are the most suitable for entering Kumbhaka. I recommend that somewhere around twenty to thirty minutes of intuitive breathing, when you begin to feel that the moment is just right for entering retention, skip it and proceed breathing. You may find that after you skip this desire for Kumbhaka, your consciousness drops to the lower (ordinary) frequencies and no matter how long you proceed with breathing it does not change into the waves of new overwhelming energy. But I assure you, if you patiently proceed with your breathing, the energy will finally build up to the new, far more powerful level than before and will deliver you to the moment of a new and extremely potent Kumbhaka.

With the most powerful spiritual weapon of Kumbhaka Prana Yoga you are piercing the veils of illusion. One by one you are crossing the energy thresholds, as you break through the emotional and psychosomatic barriers and blockages. Your sacred efforts to breathe with great vigour and your courage to face and to enter your fears and the dense energy fields, take you safely through the psychological defences into the blossoming super-consciousness.

Just as a marathon athlete can get out of breath and 'hit the wall', but with the extra effort discover a 'second wind' which allows him to fly almost effortlessly, so it is with the practice of Kumbhaka Pranayama. With the extra effort to break through emerged blockages, one finds the inner power (Awakening Prana-Kundalini Shakti) taking over one's initial efforts.

One is then surprised at one's own abilities to breathe with greater vigour.

The sensations of body then become gradually replaced with the sensations of a powerful electro-magnetic field with the Sushumna channel at its core, radiating tremendous energy as a column of golden light.

Kumbhaka Prana Yoga

The experience then simultaneously becomes the play of electro-magnetic currents, psychedelic geometry, liquid energy, overwhelming intimacy and the purely organic.

The initial efforts of the intellectual nature such as the 'I am Brahman' certitude, the expansion and stabilisation of consciousness (Bhairava mudra) and the pull of awareness from external objects towards the inner reality transform the experience into a display of pure energy (Shakti).

The energy on this stage is more intelligent than the intelligence of a limited mind rooted in thought.

The sensations of Prana as inhalation and exhalation (Prana-Apana) transform into the sensations of Prana being intelligence itself (the throbbing, all-permeating Vyana), the very essence of 'I'-consciousness.

Energy in turn transforms gradually into a different sort of intelligence – The Supreme Intelligence.

The sensations of dual nature, such as the outside world and the experiencing subject, along with all pairs of a dual nature blend into one homogenous experience of Awakening.

With the regular practice of Kumbhaka Prana Yoga the True Nature of Reality becomes apparent and clear.

All scriptures and spiritual teachings have now served their purpose and are no longer useful for the practitioner of KPY. One can only find confirmation in the highest scriptures of what one already has experienced by the grace of Kumbhaka Prana Yoga.

Prana-Shakti is recognised to be one's ultimate guru.

KPY prepares the practitioner for the next levels of 'initiation' – initiation into the further mysteries of Reality with the help of the wisdom of sacred plants, and also the initiation by the Goddess Kali and Lord of Death – Yama.

All-permeating Vyana, shimmering with the Universal Consciousness, also gets absorbed into Udana (fifth Prana) taking one's consciousness into the seed mystery of Infinite Singularity – the very Heart of Shiva-Shakti's union.

What happens at the Heart of Reality, no words can describe, and no parallels can be found.

Highest Realty is indescribable, incomparable and even unthinkable!

Kumbhaka Prana Yoga

Returning to the analogy of the ignition of a car engine, I would like to say that, with the deepening of the practice of KPY you will begin to learn not only how to start the car engine, but also how to change gears.

I hope you agree that it is not a great fun to drive only in a lower gear.

When you are diving within the increasing energy fields you will be met with resistance (blockages, barriers) on your way, which you must break through using your courageous efforts and your willpower. When you successfully break through these obstacles, you find yourself within a new level of energy fields, suddenly refreshed and energised. You begin to directly experience the helping hand of your inner guru - Prana Kundalini Shakti, and aligning your efforts, you feel the emergence of great power. This allows you to continue dynamic breathing with doubled zeal and proper knowledge.

Just like a supersonic plane breaks through the sound barrier, when breaking through energy barriers, you learn how to change your gears and shift into the higher speeds and higher energy levels. Driving, or rather flying at higher speeds creates tremendous momentum – the awakening force which takes over your efforts and carries passengers into the higher planes of Infinite Reality. When your awareness merges into the Awakening Prana, pulling with it the whole cognised world, mind and prana unite.

Energised by the Awakened Prana, mind purifies itself of illusion and limitations and becomes magnificently radiant.

If needed however, you can switch your engine on lower gears. Sometimes during your breathing sadhana you just need to drop the tempo of your breathing into very shallow but relatively fast breathing. It is important to find the most suitable and well-balanced way of breathing; one with which you can be comfortable for a long period of time. What usually happens is that this shallow but relatively fast breathing gradually gains strength and amplitude and often turns into fast and very energetic breathing like Kapalbhati Pranayam. From my experience, for the successful breakthrough of all limitations, this very fast dynamic Kapalbhati style of breathing is a must. Usually it happens by itself after breaking through accumulated resistance.

It must be crystal clear, my dear reader, that as long as you have body consciousness, even if it's only the awareness of your breathing, you cannot experience the pure freedom of Reality. Think of it! How can you? To be fully liberated is only possible when all bodily and world sensations, all notions and all limiting conditions are gone from one's Awakened consciousness!

All the above-mentioned efforts lead to the emergence of spontaneity orchestrated by Her Majesty Supreme Energy-Intelligence (Shakti).

The other aid for igniting the inner engine lies in the awakening of intuition of how your body wants to move.

I call this part 'Shamanic Trance-Dance.'

Shamanic Trance-Dance.

After ingesting a sacred plant, or sometimes without it, a shaman begins to sway, to rock, to roll, to whirl and gradually induces a non-ordinary shamanic trance state of consciousness in which his body gets possessed by the awakened higher power. This leads his body into a sacred dance, or a spontaneous utterance of unknown words, or convulsive movements. So, it is with the practice of KPY. I advise on a certain stage of your journey to intuitively listen to your body's desire to move and to encourage these movements by gently swaying and rocking your head, entwining and twisting your fingers, forming spontaneous mudras, and later, whirling, twisting, sticking out and drawing in your tongue.

I am sure that the majority of yoga and meditation practitioners are of high opinions about silent meditation with eyes closed in which they keep their bodies still and immovable. I would not argue much about this method of achieving Samadhi. It is surely one of the effective ways to enter the Kingdom of God through what can be called the 'the peace that passeth understanding'.

The practitioner of Kumbhaka Prana Yoga on the other hand enters the Kingdom of God through the Dynamic Ecstasy of Samavesha (Divine Possession).

In the Kashmir Shaivism tradition also, liberation is achieved not through Samadhi but through Samavesha.

Kumbhaka Prana Yoga

It is advised in a few yogic scriptures that it is helpful to fix one's attention on the tip of one's nose. I found that concentration on the tip of the nose, although helpful, creates unnecessary pressure on the area below the forehead just behind the eye-sockets. If practiced often, this can also lead to eyesight damage. From my experience, which I recommend in Kumbhaka Prana Yoga, it is much easier and more effective to fix the focus of your attention on the point of external 'dvadasanta' (end of twelve); approximately twelve finger-widths from the tip of your nose. In yogic scriptures, this point is often mentioned as the point at which the breath of exhalation (Prana) dies out and reverses into breath of inhalation (Apana). It is often suggested as the point of concentration together with the internal dvadasanta; twelve finger-widths from the tip of nose towards the Spiritual Heart (Hrt), where Apana terminates and Prana rises. Fixing and holding the focus of your attention on this point, with the simultaneously expanding awareness of the peripheral vision helps to withdraw awareness from the otherwise persistent objects of perception. Such steady gazing brings a sense of abstraction. There are perceptions, but they are undefinable, just as in abstract art there is no representation of external reality, but rather indefinable shapes and colours stimulating imagination. In such a position, the mind is abstracted from objects and their names.

When you begin to sway and roll your head, obviously the focus of your gaze will start to move also. My recommendation here is to glide your gaze with such speed and movement that the mind won't have time to define what it has just perceived. It is a good way to keep the mind free of thought. Instead, the mind can be engaged in retrospection, observing and merging with the energy of prana.

With the intensification of breathing and the gradual awakening of intelligent energy (Shakti), the movements of the body will intensify also. At this stage I suggest using the alteration of tension and release of body muscles. With the exhalation, twist your tongue inside your mouth, then stick it far out with the production of a hissing sound, simultaneously entwining your fingers, squeezing your pelvic floor muscles and curling your toes. Then pull your tongue back, twisting and rolling again, into your mouth with the inhalation, simultaneously relaxing your muscles. These tension

364

and release movements stimulate energy, which will gradually take over these initial movements.

All the above described yogic techniques lead to SAMAVESHA (Divine Possession)!

Kumbhaka Prana Yoga can be also called Samavesha Yoga (Yoga of Divine Possession).

All these spiritual efforts called yoga are needed only for the Awakening of the innate intelligence-energy, which is already present and perfect, but with which we, as apparent separate individuals, have lost connection.

With the continuation of KPY, the sadhaka (spiritual aspirant) arrives at the point where all his/her previous affirmations and negations become impossible. Instead with his/her full identity with Prana, having no thought constructs, one feels that only inhalation and exhalation remains, and shortly these two distinctions are also going to disappear into homogeneity.

Undoubtedly, if one practices this extremely powerful Samavesha Yoga vigilantly with all his heart, will, determination, perseverance, tenacity and courage, it can take one all the way to the incomparable bliss of Highest Reality.

However, due to accumulated vasanas (mental predispositions, habits) binding one to the wheel of samsara (repetitive history), final liberation is not an easy achievement.

Therefore, for those whose long for union with the Beloved Truth, for those who cannot wait any longer and are ready to use any shortcuts and any possible help for the realisation of Truth, I would advise incorporating the most valuable and unique help of sacred plants.

Intelligent use of Sacred Plants gives Kumbhaka Prana Yoga a greater depth and an entirely new dimension.

And so, the incorporation of sacred plants into the one's sadhana could be considered as a sixth limb of Kumbhaka Prana (Samavesha) Yoga!

Sacred plants are the teachers, and as such, require utmost respect!

As I have mentioned many times, my major gurus had been and are the magic mushrooms.

I am sure that other substances such as peyote and mescaline, ibogaine, ayahuasca or yopo snuffs can be also a very powerful allies in the process of liberation, but I have not had enough experience with them to speak of them with authority.

If, my dear reader, you wish to avoid the terrifying lessons of hell's dimensions, you must prepare yourself physically and psychologically and prepare a space in which you decide to experiment with these powerful gurus.

It is highly advisable to undertake a few days of fasting before your journey with the sacred plants of your choice. Over these few days you should, in the best possible way, psychologically prepare yourself for the intensity of the upcoming journey. Practice of the above described methods of Kumbhaka Prana Yoga will help clear the space of your consciousness from the contamination of fear and doubt. Your nadi system will be greatly purified, ready to handle the release by the magic mushrooms of tremendous energy. Your mind will strengthen to focus on the imperishable Self – the Reality.

One thing that you must avoid at any cost is a cold and damp environment. These conditions can easily trigger a bad trip of cold hell. Either chose a beautiful warm spot in nature, or a pleasant, clean, warm and cosy room, safe from the interference of unwanted people.

I prefer to take psychedelic journeys on my own, but you may choose a close friend as a sitter, who can take care of your needs. It is important, however, that he/she does not interrupt your journey, but sits quietly, observing, or occasionally change the music you have chosen. If you want to have some extra security and peace of your mind in case if your trip goes wrong, you may have some Valium, or Xanax at hand which should help to relax and calm you down.

You must also make sure the space in which you are planning your 'trip' doesn't have any sharp corners, or objects which may accidentally hurt you if you become possessed by the awakened energy which can start to move your body unpredictably.

I would also advise you or your sitter to make a puja ceremony, inviting benevolent presences, or at least to purify (smudge) your body and the space around with burning incenses of juniper, sage, sweetgrass, cedar or frankincense resin for cleansing negative energies and triggering good visions. You should keep your guru or chosen God/Goddess close to your heart and in your prayers.

Kumbhaka Prana Yoga

A 'normal' dose of dry psilocybin mushrooms for 'normal' people is somewhere between 1 to 3 grams. Of course, such a dose can release spiritual energy which can amplify the experience, intensifying and widening the range of colours and creating a certain metamorphosis of 'reality'. But when I am talking of Samavesha Yoga, the aim is a full breakthrough of all limiting conditions and thresholds into a freedom of Samavesha (possession) by Shiva's Shakti. With this aim in mind and heart, I recommend a minimum of 5 grams of dry psilocybin mushrooms, preferably around 10 or even 20 grams for full Samavesha.

Of course, many people might be concerned with their physical and mental safety if they undertake such terrifying journey. Some might be even concerned with the safety of just Kumbhaka Pranayama without the incorporation of magic mushrooms. To such people I can only offer a quote from Nisargadatta Maharaj: 'The search for Reality is the most dangerous of all undertakings, for it destroys the world in which you live.' Undoubtedly, it is dangerous, but so is Death itself!

Divine grace, evoked by your utmost devotion to your Beloved, your longing for Truth, your courage and your sacred efforts will take you to the utmost depths, where you will be initiated into the greatest mysteries and Divine secrets by Lord Yama (Lord of Death) and Mother Kali Herself.

When the approaching death becomes reality, then what was known as life totally loses all its importance and zooms away from awareness. Everything which seemed so real, valued and cherished, everyone who was so dear and loved, all life's promises, meanings, purposes become irrelevant and unreal. This crucial life/death situation, in which one tiny wrong choice can unleash the terrors of hell, demands the totality of one's attention. All opposites sit side by side here. Heaven and hell are separated only by a miniscule movement of consciousness. Will one be claimed by the darkness or the light? In this intensity of battling forces, one is never sure on which side the coin will land. The fear of insanity and hope for enlightenment unfold simultaneously.

The words 'I am not afraid of death' are realised as nothing but one's empty bravado. Even one's conviction that death is not real is gone, for even the person who had this conviction is no longer there. The mind and the intellect are too slow to catch up or to cancel this instinctive primordial fear.

However, death is not an obliteration of all cognition and experiences. It is not the extinction of life, but rather mystical point of singularity – the meeting point of all planes of Infinite Reality. Never does one feel more alive than in this magical and terrifying moment of infinite possibilities - the timeless and spaceless moment where absolutely everything is possible. Death is an open portal to countless space-time vortexes. Which portal one's soul is destined to enter is determined by the karma one has accumulated and the lessons learned in one's lifespan.

For those whose longing for the Ultimate Truth is great, the moment of death is the culmination, the most exciting crescendo of life. For the lover of Truth, death is a long-awaited possibility. All portals are wide open here. Fools closing their eyes, dismissing and ignoring death, learn nothing from life and are subjects of a continuous Samsara (repetitive cyclic existence). Death is the greatest guru. Nachiketa (the hero from the Katha Upanishads) learned a most valuable lessons from Lord Yama (Lord of Death). Death mercilessly destroys the false conviction that life in this world is the only Reality.

Shiva and Kali are known for their destructive nature. Kali is the destroyer of the demon Kala (Time), who has stolen the elixir of immortality. Adi yogi Shiva is the destroyer of illusions. At the moment of death or Awakening, they bring about cosmic dissolution in which all appearances, all décor, all falsity and pretence gets shattered into obliteration. They return to the eternal madness-ecstasy of their boundless freedom, beyond any laws, rules, taboos and limits. They are naked and unashamed, for they are without stains (malas). They are innocence and purity. Their nakedness is the most beautiful thing in all the worlds. They are the very Self of all - The Reality. As it is said in the "Bhagavad Gita": 'The unreal has no existence. The Real never ceases to be. Men possessed of the knowledge of the Truth fully know both these'[47]

So, if you have your doubts and fears about it, you better wait for the unfolding of the natural course of events. Samavesha Yoga (KPY) is only for those who know with all fibres of their being that

---

[47] "Bhagavat Gita" Chapter 2 (part-2)

the True Self is deathless and imperishable and whose courage and longing for Truth is unshakable.

I have given you now with Kumbhaka Prana Yoga (Samavesha Yoga) the most essential tools and the most efficient techniques which, if applied intelligently and with great zeal and courage, can certainly take you through the mazes of Maya into the incomparable glory of your magnificent Eternal Kingdom of Highest Bliss!

It is now your choice, my dear reader, to apply it in practice or leave it just on intellectual level.

Let us now return to the continuation of my life story.

Shabda Brahman

At least once a year, usually somewhere towards the end of January after all the Christmas puddings and New Year's Russian salads have been eaten, after all the whiskey, brandy, port and vodka has been drunk, I undertake seven to ten days of fasting. As in my previously-described forty days of fasting, I usually go to complete isolation from all external sources of information, resorting solely to KPY. While immersed in this intense breathing sadhana, I often listen through my headphones to either already-chosen playlists, or some new interesting soundtracks which I find on YouTube or Soundcloud. In January of 2011, while on my fasting sadhana, I found very powerful binaural beats on YouTube which I began to listen to regularly while intensely breathing. The combination of fasting, Kumbhaka Prana Yoga and listening to the binaural beats culminated in a very loud Shabda-nada within my head.

The Shiva-Shakti ecstatic dance generates a rhythmic spiritual sound which the Vedic Rishis (seers) term as Shabda or Nada Brahman; the initial primordial sound of extremely high frequencies that are beyond one's imagination.

The evolution of the material world from pure consciousness has been conceived as taking place in three stages – the seed stage, the mixed stage and the final stage. This evolution involves four categories – Parameswara, Shakti, Para-nada, and Para-bindu. Parameswara-Shiva is the Supreme Being with whom Shakti is in inseparable relation. The appearance of Shakti causes an unmanifest sound called Para-nada, which concentrates itself to a point called Para-bindu. Para-bindu evolves into three parts – Apara-bindu, Bija, and Apara-nada. The Shiva element dominates

370

in the Apara-bindu and the Shakti element in the Bija. In Apara-nada, Shiva and Shakti are in equilibrium. The sound caused by the division of Para-bindu is called Sabda Brahman. The inseparable Shakti of the Supreme Being in the modes of Iccha (will) and kriya (functioning/activity) is responsible for these transformations.

Shabda is the transcendental sound of the Divine Word (Om, AUM); the very essence of God, the sound of Creation. At times, especially after chanting mantras, or being immersed in pranayama, or after listening to binaural beats, one can hear it very clearly and loudly within one's head. Although, one initially hears Shabda or Nada ringing in the middle of one's head, if maximum attention is concentrated on this sound and one traces the sound to its source, it eventually leads to its origin, which is right in the middle of one's chest in the Heart chakra - Anahata Chakra. Anahata means 'unstruck' and Anahata Nada refers to Vedic concept of 'unstruck sound' (the sound of the celestial realm). If one continues concentrating, the attention eventually shifts slightly to the right towards the Hrt chakra or Hrdayam (The Centre). Shabda (Divine Word) or Nada (Divine Sound) is the high-pitched sound belonging to the electromagnetic waves of vibratory energy.

As Ramana Maharshi stated 'The breath starts from the heart abode of pranavayu. If we exhale and do not inhale immediately, the need to take a new breath will start in the middle of the chest, rather than down towards the solar plexus. That is the seat of pranavayu. That is also the place of the "lower akasha", the space of the heart "upper akasha" is in the head, where the vibration of the omkara dhwani, the Anahata Nada resonates. He who meditates on it feels it. There are ten kinds of Nada. After the final thundering Nada, the man gets "laya" (absorption, dissolution). That is his natural and eternal state. Nada, Jyothi and enquiry (vichara) take one to the same point. Meditation on Nada is one of the several approved methods. The adherents claim a very special virtue for the method. According to them it is the easiest and the most direct method. Just as a child is lulled to sleep by lullabies, so Nada soothes one to the state of Samadhi. Again, just as a king sends his state musicians to welcome his son on his return from a long journey, so also Nada takes the devotee into the Lord's abode in a pleasing manner. Nada is said to be subtle sound with light (tejas) in it. This light is said to be the body of Shiva. When it develops, and sound is submerged, it becomes Bindu (the transcendental silent point from which Creation originates and where it is ultimately unified)'.[48]

Although Ramana Maharshi says here that concentration on Nada soothes one to the state of Samadhi, I would say that this process is not without the emergence of great fear, which one must courageously face in the later stages of following Shabda-nada. As it is said in Nada yoga and other yogic scriptures dealing with concentration on Nada, there are several (usually ten) distinctive sounds which can be heard in the process of penetration into the Shabda-Nada, the last of which is like the sound of thunder.

When one's nadi system is thoroughly purified by prolonged intense pranayamas, when it's vitalised by the prolonged chanting of mantras, or listening to binaural beats, then, in a state of inner and outer silence, one can hear a very loud, high pitched ringing sound within one's head. This is Shabda-nada! If then, firmly established in the thoughtless unwavering Bhairava mudra, one gives all one's attention and concentration to listening and fully identifying with it, the sound will grow louder and louder, becoming higher pitched. If one keeps one's identity with this sound, one will begin to experience the mighty vibrations of this sacred sound resonating within the marrow of one's bones, trembling and shaking one's entire being. With the sound turning into that of thunder, all 'objective reality' (world and body) begins to shake, fracture and finally gets shattered.

Gurdgieff taught that every note of each octave has within it the whole octave of inner vibrations, and so, with the penetration of consciousness within the increasing Shabda-nada, one begins to experience these released inner vibrations which are recognised not as sound but as a revelation of Supreme Knowledge itself. Shabda-nada then stops being perceived as audible and is perceived as Jyoti (light) of higher vibrations.

As you can imagine, deep concentration on Shabda-nada releases the tremendous energy of the inner octaves and can lead to the dissolution of the so familiar world and body. Because of that proximity to the unleashed energy, which is about to annihilate the

---

[48] Sri Ramana Maharshi/Nada Yoga

world, an intense fear will emerge which must be faced and embraced.

I simply didn't have guts to plunge fully into this frightening dissolution, but I was standing on the very edge of the shattering of illusions, the explosion of intelligence-energy and had a profound insight into the nature of Shabda Brahman as also the approach, the practice and the possibilities of Nada Yoga.

Lessons from the Dying Process

At the beginning of 2013, one of our dearest friends was diagnosed with lung cancer and after a couple of months, she was taken to hospice. Tara and I visited her often, and as gently and diplomatically as we could, we gave her little hints of spiritual instructions for facing death. We didn't read her *The Tibetan Book of the Dead* directly, but nevertheless, talked to her about her true immortal nature and reminded her that she was, in truth, ever-existing, ever shining Love.

For a first time in my life I had the opportunity to closely observe the dying process of terminally ill person. The most interesting discoveries in this process for me were related to her breathing patterns. A couple of weeks before she died, I noticed that she had very long exhalations, ending with long retentions of breath. At these points we sometimes even felt that she was about to leave her body. It seemed though, that at this crucial moment of her soul's departure from the body, she encountered something extremely frightening, and her body suddenly, like in the cases of sleep apnea, took very rapid inhalations, often accompanied with a call for safety and protection; 'Mum, Mum.'

I have to say that she was in a state of denial of death. She did not accept the idea that she was going to die, but rather concentrated on fighting the cancer and feeding her illusions of even going to the music festivals in the approaching summer. Her husband didn't encourage her to prepare psychologically and to face the fact of her approaching inevitable death either. So, it wasn't a wonder that, during her last hours, she was in a state of great psychological and spiritual distress.

At midnight on the 15th of May, we received a call from the hospice saying that her breathing pattern had changed and that in their opinion it would be her last hours. We drove to the hospice and found a few relatives gathered in her room. Her breathing pattern had changed dramatically and now appeared as intense holotropic breathing without any pauses for retention and rest. The breathing also was accompanied by the loud rattling sounds known as a 'death rattle'.

I sat at her feet in deep meditation. It was somehow obvious, and not only to me, that she was facing something extremely horrifying and was battling with demonic forces dragging her into their scary dimension. It seemed to me that her life energy - her prana, was involuntarily forcing her soul into the deepest state of meditation by the means of this intense breathing. From the external observation, it was exactly like a prolonged session of holotropic breathing.

After witnessing five hours of her breathing struggles, her husband decided to leave room for a quick cigarette. It appeared, that she had not dared to leave her body in her husband's presence. As soon as he left the building, she seized the opportunity. Her last deep inhalation followed her last exhalation. Her eyes rolled up (which was a good sign), and her relatives leaned towards her, expressing their grief.

Tara immediately tapped the crown of her head to divert attention from the lower regions and to attract it towards Sahashrara. In an instant it was clear that the life force animating her body had now pierced the mysterious singularity Bindu and left it, leaving behind a lifeless corpse.

This dying process so reminded me of my own Kumbhaka Prana Yoga practice, with the one, but very essential difference; that at the end of her six hours of intense breathing, she breathed her last, or we may say she entered Maha Kevala Kumbhaka (the great permanent cessation of breath). Kumbhaka Prana Yoga may also be considered as the way to consciously enter death, or at least approach death and learn the greatest lessons from her terrific presence.

Samavesha (Divine Possession)

My dear reader, I am now approaching the culmination of my story, but neither I nor anyone else would be fit for the task of description of the indescribable. My attempts to somehow put into words of what is beyond the wildest imagination are bound to fail. Even if I could masterfully juggle a voluminous vocabulary like a great linguistic wizard, I still would fail. For although construction of letters into words and words into sentences can greatly stretch our imagination, pluck the strings of our souls and our inner knowing and widely stretch our capacity of understanding, they are not able to transmit the real astonishment and amazement of the Divine Revelations that I was blessed to receive, for the finite and the limited can never describe the infinite and the unlimited and no comparisons can apply to the incomparable.

Ideally, I would have liked to take you all the way with me into this unthinkable, unimaginable Divine Rapture of Truth. It would be the only solution to my problem, for you would experience it for yourself and there would be nothing more to say or add to it.

Nevertheless, if I would like to somehow share the faint flavour of it with you, I have no other choice but to use our limited language to paint a pale picture.

My dearest reader, following my writings, you have visited in your imagination various fascinating, incredible and even unbelievable places and dimensions, but the event I am about to describe now is simply incomparable with anything that you have read so far, for it is of unparalleled quality. It is owing to these

376

Samavesha (Divine Possession)

Divine Revelations, which completely destroyed all my doubts and uncertainties, that I dare now to write a book and talk of Highest Truth.

Before I proceed with my pale descriptions of this Divine Epiphany, I would like again to draw your attention to the subject of 'knowledge'. How do we acquire knowledge? On what is our 'knowledge' is based? Is it our 'knowledge', or is it borrowed from other sources, assimilated into our understanding to became, as we believe, ours? I would say that knowledge, or even if we dare to speak or think of it; the 'knowledge of reality' comes to us in a few different ways.

Firstly, knowledge is received or derived from external sources such as holy scriptures, yogic or tantric texts, findings and the conclusions of scientists, the words of the maharishis (the great seers), sages, jnanis, and gurus who claim to have 'knowledge of reality'.

Secondly, knowledge is formed through the ability to carefully and attentively observe the workings of the inner and outer worlds. Knowledge is extracted by deep inquiry, with the keen intellect establishing deep intellectual conclusions, philosophical and psychological understanding of the workings of Reality.

Thirdly, knowledge is based on the intense thinking, comparisons, analyses, attempts to put all the jigsaw pieces together and build a harmonious structure of knowledge of Reality.

Then, there is knowledge as a result of sharpening intuition (intuitive knowledge) and insights.

And lastly, there is knowledge received as direct experience of Divine Revelations.

I do not see the need, my dear reader, to convince you that the highest form of knowledge comes from the direct experience of Divine Revelations, for in this case this knowledge is not borrowed from someone supposedly possessing it, nor it is a product of your limited mind and logic, but it is your first-hand knowledge and it comes directly from the Divine Intelligence!

As Leonardo Da Vinci put it again and again very eloquently; 'Avoid the precepts of those thinkers whose reasoning is not confirmed by the direct experience', 'Wisdom is the daughter of experience' and 'Experience is the teacher of teachers'. And so, it

Samavesha (Divine Possession)

is. The direct experience of Reality is the teacher of maharishis or even Shiva Himself.

Of course, the knowledge received as the direct experience may also vary, and one who was once convinced in the knowledge of his/her direct experience may later receive new revelations on a far deeper level, which may cancel or make secondary the inferior knowledge received previously.

There are however revelations of such tremendous clarity and power that they cannot allow any doubt or uncertainty to exist any longer. These revelations irreversibly and totally annihilate all remaining doubts and uncertainties.

For those who have been blessed with such revelations, the search for Truth is over!

They cannot add anything to their understanding of Reality from extra teachings or teachers, because all this knowledge is now inferior and secondary to the knowledge of direct experience. At best, they can find that some of the best teachings, point out or describe that which they directly experienced in these Divine Revelations. Those who've been graced with such revelations, directly experiencing the Divine Mysteries of Higher Realms, have realised that the way to know and experience the Truth is not through the deepening and widening of understanding, but through the initiation of Samavesha (Divine Possession). The methods of igniting the Divine fire of Prana-Kundalini Shakti leading to Samavesha I have described before.

There are two possible ways to a further unfolding for those who have been blessed to receive this Highest Knowledge:

Final Liberation /Moksha/Kaivalya – an untangling from the webs of Maya (illusion), isolation from Prakriti (nature), gunas (changing qualities of Prakriti), karma and anava malas (stains) and a severing of the Hrt-granthi (Heart-knot). If this happens, the Self is awakened from the sleep of the temporal dream-reality to its Highest State – the unparalleled Divine ecstasy, euphoria, wonder, amazement, astonishment, joy, love, freedom, the bliss of its True eternal, incomparable, unimaginable, unthinkable state in which the world illusion and the 'illusion of other' does not exist in the least. Isolated from the dream-world and established in One's own True Nature, the Self – God Absolute – does not perceive anything different than the Self.

378

Samavesha (Divine Possession)

Although directly experiencing the Highest Ecstasy of Truth and temporarily realising full identity with it, Jiva (the individual), due to unresolved karma and vasanas (mental habitual tendencies) can be thrown back into the illusion of body, space and time restrictions.

If this happens, one will not become super intelligent and all-knowing, but will return to limited experience of the unfolding of one's life story as before, but with full knowledge of the path that leads towards the final liberation.

In the depths of the inner dimensions (in sadhana, psychedelic journey or death), where many individuals can be confused and frightened, such a person would find his/her way to Shiva's radiant light with great ease, for he/she has received the Diksha (Initiation) Upadesha (Teaching) on the deepest levels of Reality from Mother Shakti Herself.

Having had the Realisation that no 'other' exists in the highest realm of Infinite Reality, the need to prove something or to argue with someone is rendered useless. If One Self exists only, to whom, how and why is there a need to give explanations or teachings, never mind arguing about the true nature of Reality? And so, one becomes quieter and quieter, graciously and gracefully accepting the gifts of unfolding life, knowing it with utmost certainty to just be a dream.

He/she sees satisfaction only in his/her spiritual efforts to tear off the illusory curtain between the ego and God. He/she is melting his/her heart and mind in ever increasing devotion to the Beloved Truth. Although rejoicing in life and accepting everything as a gift from the Beloved, they are patiently waiting for death to come, knowing that it shall be their real chance to unite with their Immortal Beloved!

On a one full moon night of the 14th December of 2013, as a result of a Kumbhaka Prana Yoga sadhana in combination with the wisdom of sacred plant teachers (around three hundred of liberty caps) I was blessed with the Samavesha (full possession of my limited individual body-mind-soul by the Goddess Prana-Kundalini Shakti, who is also known by many other names such as Kali, Malini, Saraswathi and Tripura Sundari. I cannot fully distinguish them, for they, in their essence are One Svatantrya Shakti – the Supreme Intelligence – the energy of Absolute Shiva.

Samavesha (Divine Possession)

All limiting conditions were broken and washed away. Individuality was lost. The indescribable, incomparable, unimaginable, unthinkable highest rapture, ecstasy and bliss of pure Reality was experienced.

I became 'the unfolding' of the spontaneous Self-awakening. I realised my Self as having a mantric Body, as the dance of the letters of the Divine Language, Pashyanti and Para Vak, as the pregnant mother of all manifestations, Matrika Shakti.

In a state of Samavesha (complete identity with the Ultimate Reality), I experienced absolute radical freedom, freedom from all limitations, a freedom of absolute sufficiency, independence and sovereignty. This unrestricted freedom is the inexhaustible eternal source of the excessive joy that pours out as all of Creation.

Trying to give you somehow a fuller picture I must describe it from the three points of view; 1) from the Absolute Reality itself 2) from the point of view of my individuality and 3) from the point of view of the 'others' who were partially witnessing the 'event'.

From the Absolute viewpoint: Reality has no origin! It never began, was never been created, has never been born and it can never be destroyed or annihilated. It can never die, and it can never end!

In the density of Divine Ecstasy, the world-illusion or the illusion of 'others' does not exist!

There are no such things as 'enlightened individuals'. If an individual gets enlightened, he/she will cease to perceive illusions of the world and life stories. He/she will lose their individuality to the absolute ecstasy of Reality. Reality has no limitations, oppositions, boundaries, laws, taboos, others, or anything that can limit it in any way whatsoever.

This Absolute Freedom would not be Absolute if it was just a passive, impotent freedom of witnessing consciousness, or 'being' only. Absolute Freedom means Absolute Sufficiency!

In other words, nothing is impossible for the Absolute, everything is possible! Absolute Freedom means that it has full capacity of knowledge and the means to create or destroy anything and everything by a mere wish, and so Iccha Shakti (Divine Will), Jnana Shakti (Divine Knowledge) and Kriya Shakti (Divine Action), who are the expressions of Svatantrya Shakti (Unimpeded

380

Freedom and Absolute Sufficiency) can create anything and
everything without any restrictions.

There is no sense of doership however, or any sort of effort.
Absolute Intelligence effortlessly unfolds the experience of highest
bliss as the very nature of infinitely creative freedom. Almighty,
Omnipotent, Omniscient, Omnipresence! Nothing is impossible for
Absolute Intelligence. This unborn, uncreated, ever-existing
Absolute Intelligence, the source of all is eternally immersed in the
unparalleled ecstasy of its own infinite might, of its own Supreme
Intelligence and inexhaustible energy. The Supreme Intelligence of
the Absolute is incalculably more intelligent and magnificent than
limited human intelligence. From the perspective of human
intelligence, such Supreme Intelligence is unimaginable,
unbelievable and unfathomable.

Highest Reality is in the never-ending journeying from Divine
ecstasy to far greater depths of Divine ecstasy. This flooding joy,
cascading bliss, highest wisdom, and inexhaustible infinite energy
is the very nature of Reality, the very nature of Self as the meaning
is not separate from the word, as the heat is the nature of fire, as a
liquidity is the nature of water, as movement is the nature of wind,
as expansiveness is the nature of space....

The best description of Reality from my point of view is Shiva-
Shakti! Masculine and feminine, passive and active, different but
the same, separate but One, Shiva-Shakti is beyond apprehension!
Shakti is the very nature of Shiva, his Svabhava (own nature).
Svatantrya Shakti, the unimpeded freedom and sovereignty of
Shiva is the very essence and the Svarupa (Own Form) of Absolute
Shiva.

Shakti can polarise herself and split into two: 'Aham' ('I') and
'Idam' ('That'), becoming both the observer and the observed.
Then, she has the power to locate the sense of identity into a
reflected image, simultaneously drawing a veil over her real nature.
In this sense She becomes a separate actor on her own stage.

Why she does so? Firstly, because Reality is eternal and
infinite, and in infinity and eternity every possibility must be
realised. Everything is therefore possible and even inevitable. All
possibilities can be manifested and experienced.

Secondly, the Absolute is the greatest player of all and one of
his favourite games is Hide and Seek. Knowing his own might and

intelligence, he can deliberately throw his sense of identity into a life story on any plane of infinite creation for the sake of the game and adventure of Self-discovery. After being voluntary tormented by the storms of Samsara, desperately longing for the home of everlasting Love, the greatest oceanic joy envelops Shiva, when finally, all seemingly-real prisons collapse, and the heavy weight of cares, problems, frustrations and unhappiness gets shaken off, delivering our hero into His eternal home – the incomparable Kingdom of Highest Bliss.

And so, from the Absolute viewpoint, Shiva, who temporarily forgot His Real nature and assumed my identity, on this epiphanic night, untangled himself from the illusory webs that his Shakti had woven around him.

From the point of view of my temporary identity (the ego): On this auspicious full moon night, somewhere around ten o clock in the evening, I decided to undertake a shamanic journey with the help of around ten grams of dry liberty caps. My journey began as usual with the intense dynamic breathing of Kumbhaka Prana Yoga while the magic mushrooms began their mysterious teachings. I was listening through headphones to music specially selected for KPY.

I cannot say at what point I took my headphones off, but at certain moment I found my body kneeled in prostration with my forehead on a floor as in Balasana (child's pose) not in a passive state though, but intensely rocking and rolling from side to side. I saw a stupendous, vibrating unearthly colours, shapeshifting, transforming, rotating and sub rotating multidimensional mandala on all sides of my vision. I heard an encouraging female voice somewhere in the depths of my being saying: 'Shiva, enter! You can do it!'. And I took it as a sign and an invitation to enter a new dimension and to fully break out of the cocoon of my body consciousness and the restrictions of the world-prison.

What happened next no words can describe…

I asked myself: How can I – God Absolute – can feel bound by this breath of inhalation and exhalation? And, using all my willpower, I decided to use all that I had to breathe through all fears, restrictions and pain to absolute victory. I was breathing intensely in and out, in and out, in and out, until I could no longer differentiate between the inhalation and the exhalation. My efforts to breathe gradually faded away for it was no longer I who had been breathing but the power residing in me.

The gates of conscious energy swung wide open and instead of breathing, the spontaneous effortless flood of Divine language gushed in and through...

And I asked myself: How can I – the Absolute Freedom – feel the boundaries of space-time, body and objects? And I allowed myself to lose my mind, to become insane and careless, to swing, to sway, to growl, to roar, to shake, to push, to bite, to spit, to let my body express itself bizarrely, madly, insanely but freely...

At this moment I felt that I was moving out of the womb of illusion and about to be born into the perfect freedom. I was pushing the birth canal apart, and I began to push apart everything that felt like boundaries, impediments and limitations...

I tore apart the mandala that the floor had become and lost sense of directions, gravity and solidity. The floor gave way and transformed into an ocean of magnificent letters of the Divine alphabet. These Divine letters were not only around me but were passing through my body and coming out as some sort of superstrings from my mouth.

My tongue transformed into the long, thin tongue of Goddess Kali and became capable of moving freely through the spaces between my teeth, pulling out these superstrings of Divine letters.

If I sensed any kind of restriction or objects, I pushed them away, throwing them around, and all these flying objects transformed into unbelievable surprises, some new revelations of this emerging Intelligence. All the usual laws of nature, such as gravity, directions, velocity, form, temperature, solidity, sensations of touch, weight etc., were gone. Instead, there was the play of radiant knowledge and energy. There was the awe and wonder of the astonishing metamorphosis of energy into substances or letters, or events in a multi-dimensional Reality.

Reality is not material as we usually perceive it in our 'dream-world', but also it is not non-material, for the substance of Reality is not nothing, but rather the Supreme Energy Intelligence.

Probably the best way to get to an approximation of what was really happening would be to use analogy. The best analogy I can come up with to describe this miraculous unfolding is the most sophisticated computer animation or virtual reality game. If only

Samavesha (Divine Possession)

you can imagine that this incredible animation was not only visual and auditory, but also tactile, olfactory, gustatory, kinesthetic and organic. If only you can imagine that these sensory images weren't perceived as apart from you as though projected on a screen, or were not even perceived as three dimensional visuals with surround sound, but that all these incredible sensations were in fact if they were the very body of yours – the body of your intelligent energy, and this body was all there is.

The other analogy with the reference to the movements of the letters of the Divine alphabet would be the flight of starlings. Have you ever observed how a flock of starlings can create astonishing displays of fantastic moving forms? When you observe a flock of starlings in flight you can surely sense that every one of them moves not by its separate will, but that all of them get moved by a unified intelligent energy which creates majestic moving patterns. If instead of grey and white starlings, you imagine the magnificently coloured letters of the Divine alphabet flying in all directions it would give you a pale approximation of the experience. To add to this, if my body were temporarily relaxed, the letters were flying outwards, but as soon as the intelligent energy governing all the movements of my body squeezed my muscles tightly, the letters came closer, causing the Amrit (Divine nectar of Gods) to pour out down the nasal cavity and soft palate from the Sahashrara (thousand petalled chakra on the top of the head) and Ajna (third eye chakra) or pineal and pituitary glands.

If my hand was to touch an object, then there was the sensation of this thing scattering like bubbles or balls of living energy, opening and presenting some astonishing surprises.

What was happening I can only describe as a total breakthrough through all the illusionary layers into the primal Reality of Mantra, Malini and Matr'ka – the Alphabet Goddesses (the Creatrix of all manifestations).

With the heightening of the experience there was a total loss of control, effort, choice and uncertainty.

I could no longer make any effort or choice, for I broke through the threshold of illusion of separate identity onto the lap of the Divine Mother, who began to shower me with her sweetest grace and overwhelming love!

Samavesha (Divine Possession)

She, my True Beloved, gently delivered me from the womb of illusion in her loving embrace. She took over my efforts. She fully possessed me, taking me on an astonishing ride by means of her Divine language (Pashyanti and Para Vak) into the glorious heart of love and ecstasy. I became Her!

Note: It is a paradox, but what we consider to be freedom of choice in truth is not freedom at all, for to make a choice requires effort or energy, regardless how tiny or big this amount of energy is. Also, choice affirms the illusion of separation from the will of God. When one finally breaks through the resistance of individuality and becomes one with Shakti (the Mover), one is not restricted any longer by the tasks of making choices. Choices and efforts are no longer possible there, for the separate individuality with its resistance no longer exists. Shakti, with whom one is now in inseparable union, takes one on an astonishing ride into the never-ending festival of Divine Ecstasy and glory.

O, majestic radiant Goddess of Pure Knowledge!!!

Who can describe Your, beyond mind, speech and beliefs, magnificence?

Nothing can prepare one for the experience of Highest Reality. When one's sadhana, spiritual efforts and self-sacrifice awakens the grace of Devi and she allows access to her Real Nature and strips herself of all clothing, revealing her majestic nakedness, one would never believe that such beauty, such love, such intelligence, such ecstasy and such wisdom are possible... for it is beyond imagination!

She – The Mover – began to move my body and its parts in the most astonishing, intelligent and unmistakable pattern. She was moving my body by means of Her Divine alphabet. The sequences of the garlands of Divine letters passing through my body were responsible for my extraordinary movements. These unfolding sequences forced my body through yogic asanas, forming mudras, and moving my tongue, the organ of speech and creativity.

I must say that the language I experienced on this Pashyanti level wasn't Sanskrit as we know it at the Vaikhari level, but was far more mysterious, primordial and Divine. Each letter was Shakti Herself; a living force endowed with eternal intelligence. It is possible, however, that when this Pashyanti level of speech

Samavesha (Divine Possession)
descends onto Madhyama and further onto Vaikhari level it
becomes known as a Sanskrit as we know it.

Some Vedic, yogic and tantric scriptures refer to what I
experienced as the 'Pashyanti Vak'. It is said in some scriptures
that the ripples of Samashti-Pranas (the entirety of Pranas) produce
semi-cosmic vibrations which are visible through cosmic sight
alone. Pashyanti is said to be the visual language, the language that
is seen. On the level of Pashyanti there is unity of language and
consciousness. Pashyanti is the state of seeing, the perceptive or the
illumined word; it is the sound that perceives and reveals the Truth.
Pashyanti refers to the visible sound which is ordinarily
experienced as a feeling or a mental image. The sound that leaves
its audible nature and manifests as a feeling, a wordless idea or
some visual imagery is named Pashyanti Vak, which is intuitive in
nature and beyond defined linguistic forms and frameworks.
Pashyanti is the finest relative level where there is no distinction
between the word and the meaning and there is no temporal
sequence.

There are some discrepancies among different schools and
scholars regarding the vowels and the consonants. Some spiritual
teachers ascribe vowel sounds to Shakti and others to Shiva. I agree
in these with regards to the position of Abhinavagupta, who in his
Paratrisika Vivarana, which greatly elaborates on the creative
alphabet (Malini and Matr'ka), says that vowels are Shiva's bijas
(seed sounds 'germs') which, through the creative process of
entering Shakti's consonants (yonis/female organs) and their
copulation triggers the birth of Creation. As far as I can remember
and recollect, the letters that were coming out of my mouth were
predominately Shakti's consonants (they were not audible but
rather sentient energy objects).

The passage of these Divine letters was felt as an indescribably
pleasant inner massage. The passage of these letters through all the
channels of my body was cleansing my entire being. I felt like I
was being thoroughly washed, not only externally but my every
organ, every passage, including my lungs, my brain, my spinal
cord, my every particle. I was washed not in water but in some kind
of amazing balm. I was purified of all negative, dark qualities,
reaching a state of utmost clarity. I felt these Divine letters as solid
objects, as masterfully carved wood or ivory beads coming out of

Samavesha (Divine Possession)

my mouth, so I could spit them out and feel all the tactile sensations they produced. These letters were dancing on every strand of my hair. These letters at the same time weren't just letters of insentient matter, but they were embodiments of living energy, supreme joy, love and intelligence.

There weren't any mistakes in further events, nor was there any shadow of doubt. I knew that this was final, total, perfect Awakening to the unthinkable Reality. The Supreme Mystery was unfolding itself effortlessly, naturally and spontaneously.

Imagine yourself to be the greatest treasure wrapped up in very long sequences of the Divine alphabet. To reveal your true essence, you must be unwrapped. Your beloved Shakti begins this unwrapping process, rocking and rolling your body, pushing your limbs, fingers and tongue through the most amazing postures and mudras (formation of fingers and tongue 'seals'). Your own awakened intelligence-energy begins to move, to push you, sometimes gently, sometimes outrageously funny, through the most astonishing patterns. She is lovingly shaking off all the silly beliefs provided by your senses that you temporarily regarded as truth, freeing you from gripping stiffness. She is blowing off the dust of all your hazy perceptions, purifying your true vision, and forcing you to purge yourself of all accumulated impurities, to spit out all deluding objective knowledge.

She is washing away all your doubts and fears. She purifies you from the contamination of unhappiness, misery, illusions, limitations, rules, false pride and vanity in her delightful Amrita. She is snapping the strings of attachments to the unreal. She is pulling off the countless plugs by which you were plugged into the matrix. She is untangling your radiant essence from the sticky cobwebs of persistent delusions, freeing you from all accumulated tension. She is brushing off all sense of duty. She is removing from your consciousness the illusion of 'others'. She is stripping you off all binding concepts and delivering you into Absolute Freedom. With each unwrapped layer you feel more freshness, more clarity, more vitality and aliveness, more joy, more love, more freedom.

One of the most pronounced qualities of this Divine experience is the sense of incomparable freshness. To say that thousands of roses, gardenias, hyacinths, jasmines and lilies suddenly blossom within your being, releasing their sweetest fragrances would be a great underestimation of the incomparable freshness I was experiencing. The freshness of a rose garden at the break of dawn, far away from pollution of civilisation would not even come close to the Divine freshness of Self-realisation. The most sophisticated wizardly blends of the most seductive pheromones and essences of cedar, musk, oud, frankincense, amber, figs, dates, patchouli, sandalwood, orange blossoms… could never compare to the Divine fragrance of the True Self, which alone can make one insane with ecstasy!

In every instant you are newly born into the sweetness of Divine fragrance and heavenly tasting Amrit.

There is the quality of all-permeating liquidity as in the sense of liquid energy, liquid light, or liquid intelligence. It is no wonder that Mahamrityunjaya Mantra describes Shiva as 'Sugandhim pusti vardhanam' (the essence of fragrances, the flourishing nourishment).

In our ordinary perceptions of life, the visual perceptions are the most dominant, but as one enters deeper and deeper into the Samavesha, the moonlight of our ordinary five senses fades away with the opening of super-senses of pure experiencing. It is not that sight and the other four senses become dimmer, on the contrary, they are sharpening and become crystal clear, but the very mode of seeing is changing from our ordinary subject-object division into the wholesome embodiment of experiencing; being one with seeing, having eyes in every atom, being the energy of seeing. And although the visuals are mind-blowing; the visual aspect is not dominant.

What is dominant is the utmost intimacy with the movements of Conscious Energy. The tactile sensations of the experience are probably the most pronounced sensations! It is not the sensations of touch as such, but again the sense of embodiment with the movements of this intelligent energy, the sense of utmost intimacy with your own energy!

Another rarely spoken of quality was the most hilarious Divine humour!

Here is a great paradox again, but when Awakening is unfolding, you will be laughing your socks off at the hilarity of the simplicity of Awakening! You simply will not believe how stupid you were, trying to figure out how to awaken, for now, you realise that it is the easiest thing of all! When the awakening is unfolding, and you see how you have created all these stories which brought you back to your Self, and now you are experiencing the astonishingly beautiful nakedness of your Supreme nature, you simply will not believe your ability to be so extremely funny. The Absolute is the funniest joker ever! I will dare to say that side-splitting laughter is at the very core of Reality.

Every passing letter was the embodiment of the greatest fun and joy. Each instant was filled with hysterical humour. There wasn't time to ponder over one Divine joke, as immediately there was another hilarious unfolding. This ridiculous fun is born out of the inexhaustible sufficiency of the Supreme Intelligence-Energy to always amuse itself!

The next quality was the sense of never-ending and never-diminishing surprise. With a dropped jaw and wide eyes, just like a baby amazed to see something for a first time, everything was new and unbelievable. I could never ever have imagined that I possessed such infinite capabilities.

Another profound quality was the sense of utmost relief from the previously unregistered burden, just like a dropping heavy load of stuff which I was unknowingly carrying on my head. There was the utmost release of all accumulated tension, freedom from all fears, cares, problems, senses of duty and maintenance of self-image, relief from all doubts and uncertainties.

Yet another Divine quality was the utmost clarity. It was obvious to me that what was happening was the perfect and final liberation, the return from an illusory imprisonment to the absolute freedom and ecstasy of reality. This utmost clarity of Self-knowledge, clarity of realisation of my True Self, who after so many struggles and efforts, finally just realised that he is the highest eternal reality – Shiva-Shakti. The Self is unconditional Love! This overwhelming purest Love is gushing with tears of gratitude and excessive joy.

Yet another quality is the identity with the might of infinite intelligence. You know without a shadow of doubt that nothing is impossible for the Awakened you, the Self-realised God Absolute. Your infinite knowledge (Intelligence), infinite might (Energy), and unrestrictable action (Kriya Shakti) can do or manifest anything and everything effortlessly and without any limits of what

Samavesha (Divine Possession)

is possible or not possible. Everything is possible for Absolute Reality!

But by far, the most impressive quality of all is the quality of Absolute Freedom. There is no one and nothing exists to limit You in any aspect. There is no Lord over You!

And this freedom is not the impotent 'freedom' of witnessing consciousness, but the freedom of the absolute sufficiency of your Beloved Svatantrya Shakti. She, your inseparable consort, your Lalita Tripura Sundari, is the wish-fulfiller who keeps you forever newly born into the purest joy, gentleness, freshness, wonder and love. This boundless perfect freedom is the very source of purest joy. The infinite potency and might of Reality keep the True Self in a state of perpetual amazement and childlike wonder at its own abilities to do and to experience anything without reserve.

I see now, that as I predicted earlier, I have failed to adequately describe the incomparable Divine Revelations that I was graced to receive. My hope is that at least you caught some faint glimpses of its flavour.

All I can summarise is that I was God-Absolute in a mind-blowing state of Self-realisation!

At a certain point however, somewhere far in the background, I began to hear a hum, which gradually assumed more definition and finally appeared as voices of unknown people. One voice somehow struck a sense of worry in my being. 'Shiva do you know what you are doing?' Immediately a sense of slight panic crept into me. These words incepted my consciousness and brought the feeling that I'd done something terrible (possibly destroyed the universe, or something like this). I refocused my eyes and saw a few policemen standing in front of my convulsing body.

It was like being trapped back in the matrix and seeing Agents Smith.

I could still remove them from my consciousness however, and my body still was immersed in the spontaneous movements until the policemen greatly solidified, pressed my face to floor, bent my arms behind my back and put handcuffs on my wrists. My body was trying to break out of the handcuffs. I was hissing in tongues.

Oh, it was truly heart-breaking to be dragged back into the tenets of Maya.

Samavesha (Divine Possession)

For some reason, Karmic forces brought me back into this earthly plane…

Now, I would like to describe the aforesaid situation from the point of view of the other angle of illusion: from the point of view of 'others'.

My wife was horrified and absolutely distressed at what was happening. She was trying to protect my possessed body. My body was throwing and kicking objects across the room. The carpets were covered in the blood that was coming out of my nose, after it had been burned by the friction on the carpet. The whole room was a complete mess, with two broken lamps, torn cushions and a TV lying on a floor. Tara said that foam was coming out of my mouth. She thought I was dying. Not knowing what to do in this dramatic situation, she called our friend Sean to come and help her, and later she called the ambulance, describing to them what was happening. Four or five policemen arrived together with the ambulance. And so, our house was full of policemen and medics.

After I gave up the struggle, I was taken to hospital in the ambulance.

'That's going to hurt like hell tomorrow,' said one of the medics, pointing to my skinless, bleeding nose.

My tongue was also swollen enormously, almost occupying the whole cavity of my mouth.

'I must say that we were very impressed with the movements of your body,' said the medic.

'I've never seen anything like it in my entire life! So, what was your experience?' he asked.

'You would never believe it anyway, even if I was able to somehow describe it. It was the Divine ecstasy of Truth' I replied.

When we arrived at the hospital and I was given a bed, I heard this doctor saying to another doctor that he had never seen anything like it and that he wished he had recorded it on camera.

They put me on glucose drips and quite soon Tara and Sean arrived. 'Thank God you are back with us' said Sean.

'You just don't have a clue about the whole situation, I am not happy to be back in this moderately endurable prison at all,' I thought, but didn't express it outwardly.

Samavesha (Divine Possession)

Another doctor arrived later, saying a phrase that seemed hilarious to me: 'You have to be very carefully with the mushrooms, you could die.'

'Isn't it just certain that everyone dies?' I thought.

I was discharged from the hospital after couple of hours. Tara drove me home. It was the middle of the night, and a beautiful full moon was shining very brightly. I realised that my Divine trip into the ecstasy of Reality had been forcibly interrupted somewhere around two and half hours after the ingestion of the magic mushrooms.

I knew from my countless previous mushroom trips that the pinnacle of my shamanic experience was somewhere around four or five hours after ingestion. From that, I concluded that if I hadn't been so violently interrupted, it was almost certain that I would not have returned to my body consciousness but been fully absorbed into the Divine Ecstasy of Reality.

I agree with Swami Lakshmanjoo, who in his interview titled 'Final Goal in Kashmir Shaivism' says: 'I have a theory that if this super-sexual excessive joy of God consciousness remains for one hour, then this body would not exist. You will die, for you simply cannot tolerate this intensity of Joy in this limited body'.[49]

He also says in *The Secret Supreme*: 'The Supreme Kundalini is so vast and universal that the body cannot exist in its presence. It is only experienced at the time of death. It is the heart of Shiva. This whole universe is created by Para Kundalini, gets its life from Para Kundalini, and is consumed by Para Kundalini. When this Kundalini creates the universe, Shiva conceals his real nature and is thrown into the universe. When the universe is created, he becomes the universe. There is no Shiva left which is separate from the universe. This is his creative energy. And when Kundalini destroys the universe, Shiva's nature is revealed'.[50]

Depending on the degree of possession, one's karma can be fully burnt by the intense ecstasy of Reality, vasanas (mental impressions and habitual patterns) can be totally annihilated, Maya and Anava malas (stains) wiped clean and the Hrt-granthi (heart-knot) severed. Or, if the degree of possession doesn't reach its

---

[49] Final Goal in Kashmir Shaivism. Swami Lakshmanjoo (YouTube)
[50] "The Secret Supreme" Swami Lakshmanjoo

Samavesha (Divine Possession)

utmost intensity, some threads of connection to illusory appearances may still remain intact and therefore bring jiva (the individual soul) back to the play of Maya.

Well, I know now with utmost certainty that it is simply not possible to experience Reality and at the same time have a body. These two simply cannot co-exist, for as long as there is the sensation of a body, there will always be sensations of limitations and the sensations of something 'other' than Self, nor it is possible to perceive the world in the radiant ecstasy of Self-realisation.

Virtual Reality and Simulation Theories

My dear reader, this book is not an attempt to create the Theory of Everything. My view is that it is simply impossible for limited mind and logic to understand infinite Reality. More than that, no system can ever completely understand itself, for when it attempts to comprehend itself, by this very act it infinitely increases its own complexity. As I mentioned before, to fully comprehend itself is to stop the unfolding, stop the dynamism. Self-comprehension therefore is a never-ending process. There is always something new beyond the boundaries of accumulated knowledge and understanding.

That's why Reality is infinite, as is Self-knowledge. And, my dear reader, that's some very good news, for existence is eternal and wonder and novelty is never-ending!

Theoretical knowledge can only offer us a model of Reality and at best can prepare us for the direct experience, but to truly understand Reality, knowledge must be applied and made practical. In other words, one can understand Reality only by 'Being It'.

As Elizabeth Haich put it very eloquently in her *Initiation*: 'The first source of all truth and all manifestations is the eternal being – God. But God is in the unmanifested state beyond time and space, and only his manifestations appear as projections in the three-dimensional world. Therefore, in order to understand these laws correctly, we must begin with God. In order to talk about God, however, we always have to cope with the fact that God stands above the recognizable world. For this reason, every living creature can only understand God to the extent to which it itself is able

394

consciously to experience, manifest and realize God, that is, to the extend, to which it itself can be God. In everything God is living, and everything living in God. Nevertheless, God in His own complete perfect being can be understood only by one who has himself become God – or who has never fallen out of God. God can be understood only by God'[51]

For this reason, I am not interested so much in bringing the theoretical explanations, but in showing the practical way leading to Self-discovery. No amount of theoretical knowledge can show you the Ultimate Truth or God, but practice and spiritual experiments can strip the clothes of illusion and reveal the naked beatitude of Her Majesty Truth.

If you've never seen the sky before, I can try as best as I can to describe it to you and you may have some glimpse of it in your imagination. If however, I shout 'FIRE!' and run away from the room into the street, maybe you will follow me and, finding yourself outside, you will see the sky for yourself and there will be nothing else for me to explain.

Having as my foundation and authority the Divine revelations which provided me with first-hand experience of the highest states of Reality, I would like now to point you to the teachings and the scientific theories which either harmoniously resonate with my direct experience, or at least have much in common with it.

As you have seen from my Divine experience, Reality has much to do with the unique Divine language. Naturally, after experiencing it first-hand, I was drawn to do more research in the teachings that emphasise the significance and creative role of this Divine language. And although even the Gospel of John begins with the grand opening: 'In the beginning was the Word (from Greek 'Logos' which is not only Word of God but principal of Divine reason, creative order and logic) and the Word was with God, and the Word was God'[52], the centrality of 'The Word' and the significance of 'creative language' I found in the teachings of Kashmir Shaivism, specifically in *Paratrisika Vivarana* and *Tantraloka* by Abhinavagupta.

---

[51] "Initiation" Elizabeth Haich
[52] Gospel of John 1:1

Virtual Reality and Simulation Theories

Para Vak – the Supreme Word – is equated with the Svatantrya Shakti (Divine Sovereignty, free will, Self-dependence, Shiva's irresistible will). Two alphabet Goddesses; Matr'ka and Malini, which have as their basis different arrangements of the sequences of letters, seem to interact, influence and reflect each other. Matr'ka, which can be translated as 'misunderstood divine mother pregnant with creation' has a 'regular' order of alphabet. She begins Her Creation with the letter 'A', generating a series of vowels, ending with the consonants. Each of these 50 letters are the living forces (little mothers) meeting each other they generate ideas, thoughts, meanings, concepts, feelings and emotions.

'Oh Goddess, the whole universe from Brahman until the earth is filled with Matr'ka, which is filled with the glory of the Supreme Consciousness' (*Tantrasadbhava*).

'Matr'ka (the power of sound inherent in the alphabet) is the source of unlimited knowledge.' (Shiva Sutra).

Matr'ka Shakti – the power behind the words has a tremendous influence on life. She can bind, create confusion and illusion, generate ignorance, but she can also liberate!

Malini Shakti has a different arrangement of her alphabet, known as Nadiphantakrama. (The alphabet begins with 'na' and ends with 'pha'). The most mysterious Goddess Malini has an irregular order of Her alphabet in which vowels and consonants are intermingled in a hitherto unexplained and, at first sight, random order.

I would like to quote here a very intriguing passage from Malinivijayottara tantra:

'Thus, following proper procedure, the self-born one created Rudra's energy in the form of Nadiphanta (sequence), using the phonemes generated from his own body.

The Goddess comprising all phonemes, provided with all (auspicious) marks, being born blazing with great splendour, stood before Bhairava.

Malini said: 'Who are you?'

'I am God'

'Why have you come?'

'How can you not know me, O Goddess? Who created you? You have been brought forth by me, my dear, for the sake of incarnation in the sport which is creation.'

'Who has created you? Tell me, Bhairava!'

'I am the array of phonemes, O lucky one, (I am) self-born, the lord of the world. I created you with the seed (syllables) produced from my limbs. Therefore, you are lauded "She who has a sequence of heroes" (virvali), the power of Rudra!'

Malini furious, said: 'Have I been produced by the phonemes originating from your own body? Take your phonemes here!'

Throwing out the garland of phonemes she assumed her elemental own – nature, a body preceding seed (syllables), the sleeping deathless coiled one (amrtakundali).

'Where are all the phonemes gone?' The Lord of the Gods was puzzled. Utterly astonished, he reasoned for a moment.

The Lord of the universe reflected: 'Becoming unstable, they have all dissolved into the principle of soul. Lo! The power of the Goddess!'

The God praised the world-supporting Goddess (Bhuvana-Malini) with various hymns'.[53]

I tend to think that in my Divine experience of Samavesha, I was possessed by the mysterious Goddess Malini!

As I was drawn towards the ideas centred around Divine creative language, I also discovered that pioneering scientific thought also moved towards new interesting ideas closely connected with these ideas.

As father of quantum theory Max Planck said: 'Science progresses one funeral at the time'.

While science and technology evolve, a new radical scientific view on the nature of Reality is emerging, which in its essence is not too far from the ideas of the ancient yogic and tantric scriptures; the ideas that the universe is only appears to be real, in reality being only Maya (illusion), i.e. 'That which appears but doesn't exist'. There has been a significant shift among the pioneering thinkers in the last decades towards the ideas that the world we are living in is not 'real', but it is a 'virtual or simulated reality!'

With the development of technology and computer science, it is clear now that in the near future it will be possible to create virtual

---

[53] Malinivijayottara Tantra

reality or simulation games of such quality and complexity that it will be impossible to distinguish between 'reality' and 'simulation'.

The ideas that we are living within the simulated reality - 'the Matrix' has become overwhelmingly popular and convincing and, from my point of view, represents science at its best in this moment of time. These ideas go against the materialistic, physicalistic view of reality.

Local realism, which claims that physical objects have definite values of their physical properties like position, momentum, spin and charge and that those definite values, if they are not observed, have influence that propagates no faster than the speed of light, are found to be false by countless experiments of quantum mechanics.

Space-time is no longer considered fundamental, but rather the 3D desktop of a supercomputer in which objects are just icons on a 3D graphic user interface that hides the Truth, for the Truth is too complex to comprehend. The whole point of this desktop interface is to not show us the truth of the computer.

Professor of Cognitive Science Donald. D. Hoffman proposes the monistic theory which he calls 'conscious realism' or the 'theory of conscious agents' in which the vast dynamic network of 'conscious agents' of different complexities is the fundamentality and space-time is just a data compression scheme, a user interface that we use because the network of social interaction of the conscious agents is infinitely complicated and we can't deal with that. So, we must dumb it down and use space-time as our data compression scheme.

Similar ideas of our universe being 'virtual reality' and us being consciousness completely identified with our avatars (body-minds) and fully immersed in this 'virtual reality' I found also in the works of physicist Thomas. W. Campbell, the author of '*My Big T.O.E.*' (*Theory of Everything*).

According to Thomas. W. Campbell: only consciousness which is finite and imperfect self-modifying evolving digital information system is fundamental. Everything else including "physical reality" is virtual. There are many virtual reality frames and we exist in several of them. There is no such thing as objective reality, all reality is interpreted. Evolution, love and spiritual growth defined in terms of entropy (the less chaos and more order equals to evolution, love and spiritual growth).

Virtual Reality and Simulation Theories

There is also an 'emergence theory'; the work of Klee Irwin and an L.A. quantum gravity research team to which I became attracted, specifically due to its ideas regarding creative language.

To avoid all the complexity of explanations, I only would like to highlight some of these ideas very briefly.

According to the quantum gravity research team: 'Emergence Theory weaves together quantum mechanics, general and special relativity, the standard model and other mainstream physics theories into a complete, fundamental picture of a discretised, self-actualising universe.

At the root of emergence theory's formalism is a concept quickly taking hold in the theoretical physics community – that all of reality is made of information. What is information? Information is meaning conveyed by symbols. Languages and codes are groups of such symbols that convey meaning. The various possible arrangements of these symbols are governed by rules. The language user makes free-will choices regarding how to arrange the symbols, in order to produce meaning, according to these rules.

Fundamentally, then, the existence of information must therefore imply a "chooser", or some form of consciousness, for it to be actualized. Reality is experimentally observed to be geometric at all scales, from the Plank level to the largest structures. A central feature of reality behaving geometrically is that all fundamental particles and forces in nature, including gravity, can transform into one another, through a process called gauge symmetry transformation, in a manner that corresponds precisely to the vertices of the 8-dimensional polytope of a crystal called the E8 lattice.

Emergence theory focuses on projecting the 8-dimensional E8 crystal to 4D and 3D. In a way we can consider three-dimensional appearance as a shadow of a higher-dimensional reality. On a TV or computer screen the smallest indivisible unit is a 2D pixel. In our 3D quasicrystaline (quasicrystals are derived from projecting from different angles E8 crystal into 4D and 3D) reality, the tetrahedron is the smallest possible 3D shape that can exist in this reality. Each tetrahedron is the smallest possible 3D shape that can exist in this reality: the length of each of its ages is the Planks length (over 10^{35} times smaller than a meter). These 3D pixels combine with one another according to specific, geometric rules, to populate all of space. These 3D pixels act as a binary language: in any given moment, each tetrahedron can be chosen by the code operator to be either 'on' or 'off'. If it is 'on', it can be in one of two states: 'rotated left' or 'rotated right'. If in a movie we have normally 24 frames per second, in the emergency theory model one second contains 10^{44} frozen frames.

Emergence theory views spacetime in a way that builds on Einstein's spacetime model, in which the future and past exist simultaneously in one geometric object. This object is a system in which all frames of spacetime interact with all other frames all the time. In other words, there is a constant, dynamic, causality loop relationship between all moments in time, in which the past influences the future and the future influences the past.

Emergence theory view consciousness as both emergent and fundamental. In its fundamental form, consciousness exists inside every tetrahedron/pixel in the 3D quasicrystal in the form of something called viewing vectors. Think of viewing vectors as micro-scale observers in the traditional quantum mechanical sense. These observers actualise reality by making ultra-fast, Plank scale choices about the binary states of the pixels (on, off, left, right) at every moment in time. This fundamental, primitive, yet highly sophisticated form of consciousness steers the pattern on the quasicrystaline point-space toward more and more meaning.

Eventually consciousness expands into higher degrees of order such as nature and life as we know it. From there life and consciousness keep expanding, growing exponentially, into all corners of the universe. There are no known laws in physics that place an upper limit on what percentage of the universe can exponentially self-organize into freewill systems such as humans. Indeed, physics allow the possibility that all the energy of the universe can be converted into a single, conscious system that itself is a network of conscious systems. Given enough time, what can happen will eventually happen. By this axiom, universal emergent consciousness has emerged via self-organization somewhere ahead of us in 4D spacetime. And because it is possible, it is inevitable. According to the evidence of retro-causality time loops, that inevitable future is co-creating us right now just as we are co-creating it'.[54]

Although all these new-age theories seem far more intelligent than materialistic views on reality, they all have their flaws in my opinion. Firstly, all three of them are based around the idea of 'evolution'. The idea of evolution implies progress within time frames. It is okay to think in terms of evolution within the virtual reality; however, the idea of evolution does not apply to that which is timeless!

Unborn, uncreated Absolute Supreme Intelligence does not aim for evolution and perfection. It is already and always eternally and infinitely evolved and perfect!

Because our thinking process is rooted in our limited logic, we cannot conceive eternity and infinity and project our limited familiar ideas of evolution on the Absolute.

If we look back at history, we will find that many great civilisations collapsed for one reason or another at the height of their social, cultural and technological evolution. As day and night and seasons follow each other in circles, so human evolution rises and falls in circles or spirals. As according to Gurdjieff's law of octaves, which states that no impulse proceeds without deviation, so evolution takes us to certain heights and then, for one reason or another, stops its development and leads us to degradation or even extinction. Then again, there are different types of evolution, and let's say that technological evolution will not necessarily lead to a far more important spiritual evolution. Many new-age people dream nowadays that humanity at this moment of highly evolve technology stands at the threshold of a quantum leap in human evolution and the rise of the collective consciousness. All these dreams of a new wave of evolution, however, are happening within the dream (Maya – Matrix) itself, and the only real evolution is waking up from the dream to Reality!

According to Hindu philosophy, everything goes in cycles; human beings are born, live and die and then they are reborn again in one of the numerous planes of reality. They are cycling on a wheel of samsara (repetitive existence) until the longing for Truth

---

[54] Emergence Theory: General Overview in Layperson Terms (Quantum Gravity Research)

and liberation develops so strongly in them that they can burn their karmic bonds and residual impressions and wake up to Reality.

According to ancient Vedas, for example, the current age of the universe is around 155.521972944 trillion years. There are 4 ages on Earth which keeps circulating: Satya Yuga – 1.728 million years, Treta Yuga – 1.296 million years, Dwapara Yuga – 0.864 million years, Kali Yuga – 0.432 million years. This Yuga cycle is called Maha (Great) or Divya (Divine) Yuga.

One thousand such cycles form one day of Brahma. So, one day of Brahma is 4.32 billion human years. Each day of Brahma is called a 'kalpa'. His night also constitutes 4.32 billion human years. During his day, life exists in the universe. At night-time, no form of life exists. So, day and night each last for 8.64 billion human years.

The Age of Brahma is 100 years. Each year of Brahma has 360 days and the same number of nights. Thus, the total age of Brahma is 311.04 trillion human years. This period is called 'Maha kalpa'. The life span of the universe is one 'Maha kalpa' i.e. 311.04 trillion human years.

This time span is also the duration of one breath of Vishnu!

When Vishnu exhales, thousands of universes emerge, and one Brahma is born in each universe.

When Vishnu inhales, all universes get sucked in and Brahma dies.

This cycle is non-ending and eternal in Vedic science.

I know it's quite a stretch of the imagination, but why we must assume that there was ever a beginning? Why must there always be 'nothing' prior to 'something'? We simply cannot think outside of the box! Our very logic is this box of limitations. However, regardless how far back our mind can take us, before the birth of stars and galaxies, before the so called 'Big Bang', we cannot find the beginning of Reality, we cannot find the beginning of God – Supreme Intelligence. This Supreme Intelligence that gives birth to all cognition, time, spaces, minds, senses, the myriad forms, countless universes with their countless details, itself has no beginning! We simply cannot conceive such an infinite being within the ordinary frames of our limited minds.

The intelligence of human beings, regardless of our sophistication is simply incomparable with the Supreme

Intelligence, and yet Supreme Intelligence is the very Self of every living being.

Eternal Absolute does not require evolution, for He/She is forever wise!

The next flaw I see in the work of Thomas Campbell when he tries to equate Love to the lowering of entropy. Where there is more order he says, there is more love.

Sorry, but Love who is God does not operate this way. Although Love, in one of her phases, creates forms and order, in another, finding herself restricted by its own creation, she shakes off all limitations (forms and order), freeing herself and returning to her original state; prior to and beyond any laws or limitations, which, from the human perspective could be called 'chaos'. Love is equally the source of both order and chaos.

The other inadequacy of all three theories is that their ideas of evolution depend on cooperation and widening of the vast dynamic social network of conscious units.

The yogi immersed in the bliss of Self-knowledge does not require cooperation with other conscious agents or the widening of his circle of conscious interaction, and yet, his evolution and knowledge of Reality is far greater than of those who spread and receive the ideas through wide interactions.

Regardless of the amount and the quality of information and its manipulation, it doesn't drastically change the level of one's being. On the other hand, intelligent yogic practice, discipline and self-sacrifice born out of devotion and unquenchable longing for the union with God can take one all the way to a first-hand experience of Ultimate Truth, Love and Freedom in which one realises complete identity with God!

And lastly, all these beautiful theories suggest and are based on the ideas that consciousness i.e. fundamental Reality, although very complex, is finite and imperfect.

I know that to be untrue. This simulation, dream, matrix, Maya we are experiencing and living in, truly, is far from perfection, but God, the Self, Reality is eternal, infinite and perfect!

Light on Common Misconceptions

*'The fullness and splendour of Being has no
analogy in the empirical trifles; our thought
can perceive no parallels to the bewildering
richness of Reality. Nothing partial or
piecemeal can demonstrate the entirety and
integrity of the Real. A Reality which is
Satyasya Satyam (real of all reals), Purnam
(full), could not be an essence-less vacuum.'*

~ Ista – Siddhi of Vimuktatman ~

My dear reader, in this chapter I would like to focus our attention on common misconceptions about the true nature of Reality. Through social media, I have noticed many common misconceptions about the nature of Reality to which I would like to bring your attention.

To begin with, let me define of what I mean by Self-realisation, for there are so many interpretations of it. My point is that Self–realisation is nothing less than God–realisation!

Now, in realising oneself as God, one enters a Divine ecstatic bliss of such density that it presses all impurities, imperfections and limitations out of its perfect existence. There are no limitations of body, world or others in the real freedom of Highest Reality. There are no lords or authorities over awakened Self. There are no power

404

that can restrict this perfect freedom and there are no others who require help to be awakened.

Many spiritual teachers mistakenly take establishment in the so-called 'witnessing consciousness' to be Self-realisation. From this misconception, the other follows too.

Freedom then, according to some of those who maintain that they are awakened is practically equal to 'acceptance' of what is. Obviously, if we are not free and still within the Maya's game and are unable to change events for lack of will and knowledge, it is wisest to accept with gratitude everything as it is without trying to reshape the situation, but would I call it freedom? Far from it.

Some of these 'enlightened' teachers proclaim that freedom is not necessarily exciting, it's just free, and freedom is not 'from' but 'to', meaning that you are not running away from the difficulties and pain, but easily and freely accepting whatever comes to you.

It's all okay, but all this is just within the dream itself.

When I am talking of freedom, I refer to Absolute Freedom which we can equate with the irresistible, limitless, unstoppable will of God!

This Ultimate Freedom is not the impotent 'freedom' of witnessing consciousness while unable to change anything. God's Absolute unrestrictable freedom is based on His/Her complete sufficiency. Absolute sufficiency is the major power behind this true illimitable freedom!

God is not subject to any law!

He/She does as He/She pleases, and no-one can stop Him/Her!

Laws (physical, mathematical, social, etc.) envelope this unstoppable flood of excessive love, joy and creativity into dynamic forms.

This freedom and sufficiency is the most exciting thing in all the worlds. It is the real source of the excessive outpouring of joy and love.

Together with the confusion about the freedom, there are also confusions about the primacy of either stillness or movement.

Thanks to the blessed experience of Samavesha, I know that at the ultimate level of reality, the difference between movement and stillness is nullified.

Light on Common Misconceptions

The ecstatic movements of consciousness/intelligence/energy are purely spontaneous and do not require any amount of effort. As such they are no different from stillness.

Absolute stillness without any movement whatsoever, cannot be the highest reality. That which does not move is dead.

Shiva (God-Absolute) is a shava (corpse) without the vibrating energy of Shakti!

Then, there is an idea that is popular among spiritual teachers that every experience comes and goes, but the reality is beyond experience and unchanging.

The absence of any sort of experience is not different than the state we can call 'non-being' or insentience!

It might be desirable state for those who are constantly tormented with sorrow and suffering, for in such a state, these things are absent, but so are all positive qualities such as joy, love, wonder, etc... The state of absence of any experience, which we can call 'non-being' surely cannot be the highest reality.

Highest reality is full of positive qualities: Supreme joy, love, bliss, knowledge, effortless activity, ecstatic dance!

Oh, what a boring and dead reality it would be if it was ever unchanging.

The Absolute is forever newly born into freshness and wonder!

Such a commodity as memory, although very useful in our lives, creates a sense of nostalgia. Some cherished moments that are lost in time and will never return produce a sense of loss and sadness. Memory also confirms that things just keep repeating itself, going around and round; night follows day and winter follows autumn. After enough repetitions, this creates feelings of boredom.

Nothing is remembered in the highest state; everything is new, renascent and full of wonder and amazement!

Selfish, we might say, but this would only be a projection of our limited understanding and our sense of incompleteness onto that which is beyond limitations, complete and satisfied.

At the end of the day, when you look closely, attentively and with greater clarity and love at your Self, you realise; it is always only You ... You are the dearest friend, the lover, love and beloved to your Self. Everything else, regardless how hard you are trying to hold it or save it, slips through your fingers, crumbles away and

406

loses its importance. Only the eternal essence of all – your True Self is forever your true Beloved! Realising this, you fall more deeply in love with your Self!

Another misconception is around the duality of subject and objects or observer and observed. For some reason, many people are unable to grasp that in order to perceive, to cognise, there is no need to split the observer from the observed or the subject from the objects. This misconception has become rooted in people's minds through the popularisation of ideas that consciousness must be similar to a white screen on which a movie is projected, or to a piece of blank paper on which a script is written, or to an empty container within which the whole Universe appears.

By the grace of Samavesha, I see no difficulty in comprehending how subject and objects can be one.

Supreme Dynamic Intelligence-Energy – Shakti – is the very body of Shiva-Absolute.

Awakened Self sees not 'not-Self'!

In this ultimate state there is not the slightest division between the observer and the observed. There are no objects separate from the subject, but the subject is not devoid of the experience of Self-knowledge and Self-manifestations. On the contrary, His/Her experience is Divine euphoria and ecstatic bliss.

We may say that at the level of Ultimate Reality, the Absolute Intelligence Energy has woken up from the dream of embodiment on the earthly plane facilitated by Maya Shakti. It isolated itself from the Prakriti (Nature) and Gunas (Nature's ever-changing qualities) and became established in its 'aloneness' (Kaivalya).

We may ask ourselves; what happens in this case with the Earthly plane, all its inhabitants and the whole universe? Would this plane of reality still exist, somehow separate from the Awakened Shiva? What will happen to you, my dear reader, if I awaken?

Wouldn't it be the height of egotism and narcissism to say that you are nothing but a figment of my imagination? And if I awoke, you would simply… puff… disappear?

I know on 100% from my experience of Divine possession that no 'other' and no limitations can ever exist in the state of Self-realisation, that is why there is Ultimate Freedom, for nothing other than Self exists. But it does not exclude the possibility that on different frequency domains, the other conscious agents, with their virtual universes may exist, but be isolated from the awakened Shiva.

The space of pure intelligence has none of the limitations of the physical space does. In our so-called physical reality, two solid objects cannot occupy the same space simultaneously. In the space of pure intelligence, countless universes can occupy the same space without the need to interact with each other. In fact, pure intelligence doesn't need to occupy any space at all. Space is said to be the first veil drawn upon reality. The space-time continuum, like a dream, is unsubstantial, having at its substance the language of intelligence. The space of pure intelligence could be filled with countless parallel realities. Pure intelligence has no limitations of physical space, nor any limitations of time.

The ether of our physical space is filled with many TV programmes, phone or Skype conversations, radio waves, and countless pieces of digital information, but we do not perceive all this information with our naked senses. To receive all these countless signals and channels, we need appropriate receivers which can tune in to the same wavelengths and frequencies as the transmitters. We must also lend a portion of our awareness to it.

In the same way, our consciousness can slide, so to speak, between parallel realities, through the hierarchical ladder of Tattvas from the lowest hells to the Divine Ecstasy of Oneness by changing the frequencies of our perceptions.

You are not your body, my dear reader, but rather a spiritual being – a soul animating your body. The soul in Hindu philosophy is known as Atma. Atma is both the individualised consciousness and the totality known as Para Brahman. Atma can move among the parallel realities and the levels of perceivers. When Atma is closely associated with the body it is known as Jivatma. The word 'Jiva' means to live or to move in transmigratory existence. Longing for the Ultimate Truth, Jivatma, who in reality is none other but shrunken into an anu (point, point of view), Shiva, who temporarily forgot his true nature, moves towards the light of Self-knowledge. On its way it loses the shackles of Maya and Karma and wipes off the anava mala stain, together with the ego-self and finds itself in the egoless Oneness. It is then known as Paramatma, which is identical with Brahman.

Light on Common Misconceptions

Jivatma is the soul of yourself, so to speak, and Paramatma is the Self of your soul. And so, when you wake up to the utmost reality, my dear reader, shedding all your illusory coverings, you will arrive egoless into the incomparable Kingdom of Oneness. There will be neither 'you' nor 'me' but the undifferentiated bliss and glory of God Absolute who is our very innermost real Self. At this ultimate level, we are One Ultimate Reality.

When talking about the reality or unreality of our 'waking' state on this earthly plane it is appropriate to compare it with a dream state. What is the nature of a dream? Is it real or unreal? We cannot say that it is totally unreal, for we are experiencing it. We are sensing, feeling, seeing, hearing it. Therefore, it has some degree of reality in it. We cannot say that it is real either, for we know that when we wake up, the dream disappears. It wasn't real after all but just our imaginary, mental creation. But as long as the dream lasts, it appears to be real.

As Elizabeth Haich wrote in *Initiation*: 'The difference between dream and reality is only that what you accept on one level of consciousness as reality immediately turns into a dream when you awaken on a higher level of consciousness and realise that it wasn't reality at all, but merely a projection of the self, in other words a dream. Every dream is reality as long as you believe it to be real. The one and only reality is the Self: God!'[55]

It is also possible to have recurring dreams. Although in the waking state the dream is not perceived, on some subtle levels it may exist in the form of residual impressions and one may come back to the left dream and experience its continuation. Similar to a dream-nature is our so called 'waking reality'. It seems to be a solid existence or reality and yet one can wake up from this 'waking dream'.

Although in the beatific magnificence of Oneness there are no perceptions of other planes of reality, these planes may exist for the unawaken jivas (sparks of consciousness), who are still under the spell of illusion and ignorance. They continue their march of trans-migratory existence until either repulsion to untruth or unquenchable longing for truth force them to keenly inquire into the truth and make sacred efforts towards liberation. 'The will of

---

[55] "Initiation" Elizabeth Haich

409

Light on Common Misconceptions

Absolute does not reach directly the earthly plane but manifested here as a number of mechanical laws' says Gurdjieff.

So many modern 'gurus' greatly oversimplify Enlightenment, Awakening and Self-realisation, mistakenly taking it to be just a shift of the sense of identity into the 'witnessing consciousness'. Being established in this delusion, they trivialise and belittle mystical Experiences.

Those who have broken through the threshold of Maya into the inner dimensions of infinite reality know without a doubt that Reality is hierarchical. On each higher level, the degree of lucidity and freedom grows exponentially until at the stage of the Shiva-Shakti union, intelligence and energy lose all impediments and limitations and are found to be infinite and eternal.

The 'world-appearance' is perceived by our senses operating only within a limited frequency field. Just as a piece of wood can be saturated with water and water can be saturated with gas, just as each note of an octave has within it the whole octave of greater density, so is Reality saturated with the fields of greater density of vibrations (Spandana); the inner dimensions.

The pure will of the Absolute is not directly manifested and experienced at this stage of creation which we call our universe. It is light-years from the Big Bang of the Eternal Now to the perception of 'world-appearance' (the collapse of the wave function into a one certain pattern). What is experienced on this plane of Infinite Reality is the result of deviations and divisions of the descending octave of creation.

Maya Shakti, the 'great-granddaughter' of Adi (primal) Shiva-Shakti, inherited from her eternal grandparents the power to create. But her creation is imperfect and most importantly, her convincing creation veils the Truth. If God Absolute decided to reveal His/Her real Svarupa (own form) to us, not only we, but all steps in the hierarchical structure of creation would be annihilated by Hers/His terrific beatitude.

'Oh, who if I cried out, would hear me among the Angels' hierarchy? And if one of them suddenly pressed me against His Heart, I would be consumed in this overwhelming being,'[56] says Rilke. When Krishna began to reveal His universal form to the

---

[56] "Duino Elegies" (The First Elegy) Rainer Maria Rilke

410

opened yogic vision of Arjuna, Arjuna, whose hair was standing on end and who was trembling with fear, began to beg for mercy, asking Krishna to assume His human form.

Self-realisation is none other than God-realisation, for God is the very Self of all. This is not some insignificant shift of the sense of identity into a 'witnessing awareness' but an awakening from the dream of limitations and imperfections into the perfectly free, magnificent and incomparable Reality!

Parting Words of Advice

My dear reader, I sincerely hope that this book has touched your beautiful heart and soul and churned within it a sense of longing for the all-satisfying union with Her Majesty Sublime Truth! I hope the path towards our True Beloved, which I have laid down in this book is seen clearly now by you.

It's time for me to say farewell and leave you with my parting words of advice.

Leaving aside endless philosophy, hypotheses and theories, resort to spiritual practice. It alone can reveal the Truth, not countless words and thoughts.

Human birth is a rare gift! Don't foolishly waste your precious time on trivial achievements and unimportant endeavours but put all your zeal and efforts towards the realisation and actualisation of your highest potential; knowledge and experience of your True Self who is none other but eternal Truth – God Absolute!

As long as you perceive this plane of reality, it is best to live it with deep gratitude, being thankful to Beloved God for this crazy gift of your human life and the lessons, which can teach you something very important and useful about yourself.

As Jesus said: 'Thou shalt love the Lord thy God with all thy heart, and with all thy soul, and with all thy mind. This is the first and great commandment. And the second is like unto it, thou shalt love thy neighbour as thyself. On these two commandments hang all the law and the prophets.'[57]

---

[57] Matthew 22 v.37 to 40 Bible, King James Version

Parting Words of Advice

Immersed in the contemplative 'I am Brahman' Bhavana, look upon the whole world and every creature as thy own Self.

Love Thyself, for if you cannot love yourself you cannot love others.

Knowing this life to be just a game, play it consciously, happily, joyfully, gracefully and fairly.

Clean your mind with the cloth of wisdom, erasing the contamination of thought, and fix steadily its gaze on the Wonderous Source of All.

Polish your beautiful heart with the elixir of Love, removing the stains of negative emotions. God loves to enter clean things.

Empty yourself of all accumulated knowledge, be ready to receive Divine Grace.

Open wide your brilliant mind and your beautiful heart to receive God's Love and let this Love pour freely and unobstructed through your heart, mind, eyes, lips, throat and hands towards the whole creation.

Become like God who in His perennial flow of giving, wants nothing for Him/Her Self. Filled to the brim with Love, keep spilling it out.

Also, keep pouring the light of your loving awareness into the ocean of Love within your heart. These loving streams of your attention will churn out the Love that you really are, and it will bubble as champagne and begin to expand, often coming out with sweet purifying tears. Gently leaving anything that restricts you, let yourself flow with these loving streams into Love.

Knowing that attention is the most precious commodity, don't feed it to negative states, doubts and fear, but turn it within and fix it on Truth.

Unable to avoid choices, make the best ones, listening attentively to the voice of your conscience.

Follow the right conduct of Dharma (Righteousness).

If you are still eating meat, change your diet to vegetarian or vegan, for even though you are not killing our little brothers and sisters (animals) yourself, by buying meat you are supporting it.

Ahimsa (non-violence) is a very important principle to follow.

With the sharp sword of discrimination, discern between that which is impermanent and perishable and therefore not real, and that which is everlasting and eternal. Realise what is more important to you.

Remember Death! Don't foolishly bury your head in sand like an ostrich, pretending that Death won't find you. Instead, with great reverence, take Death to be an equal partner to your Life.

Death is the greatest teacher! Don't miss the opportunity to learn from her, she is the bottomless well of Divine wisdom.

With the help of Kumbhaka Prana Yoga, make an acquaintance of Death. She will teach you the greatest secrets of life. She will teach you Love!

When you accept Death as an equal partner to Life, your sense of scale will expand dramatically. From this expanded perspective of scale and relativity, all human dramas can be accepted with great ease, detachment and a smile.

Knowing this life story to be just a game, do not get engrossed in the human drama. These dramas and the negativity surrounding them are the easiest way for the spider Maya to weave another thread over her victims, plunging them deeper and deeper into the darkness of ignorance.

Nevertheless, stand firmly against injustice and bullying, be compassionate to those less fortunate than you, for your very nature is kindness, justice and love.

Do not hate Maya for holding you prisoner in her relatively beautiful, but deceitful creation, for hatred is just another thread of Maya's spiderweb. Instead, use the most powerful weapon in this universe – your unconditional Love – to absorb illusion into your expanding consciousness.

Do not be naïve however, thinking that all is godliness and goodness. On this imperfect plane of duality, evil also exists, as you have probably noticed. Although your True Self is unblemished and immaculate, within your lower psyche, together with the light, there is also a shadow world of darkness and evil tendencies. Do not disown these shadows, for they will poison your wellbeing and stir up troubles, but as best as you can expose these shadows to the loving light of your consciousness.

When one indulges oneself in inappropriate actions and harmful habits, the body can be possessed by demons and other evil entities.

Parting Words of Advice

Jesus said: 'This kind does not go out except through prayer and fasting'.[58]

Do not run away but courageously face your deepest fears. Harvest their compact energy to reconnect with your True Self.

Learn to transform suffering and negativity into love, light and joy by cultivating a sense of deepest gratitude towards the Creator for this insane gift of life. Regardless if it is painful or pleasurable, awaken gratitude for whatever comes. For those who have mastered the art of transformation of suffering and negativity into Love, everything, regardless of its nature, appears as a gift. Suffering is food for the growing Soul.

Let 'Inshallah' (God willing) be your moto. Why worry about a thing if everything is in God's hands?

Learn mantra yoga from a qualified teacher. It will protect you from endless mind-chatting and will reharmonize your body.

With the help of mantra-japa, zikr, or inner Jesus prayer, tie your mind to mantra. It will be your guide towards the Supreme.

With the help of Holosync technology, binaural beats and nadi-shodhana, known also as anulom-vilom (alternative nostril breathing), balance and harmonise the left and right hemispheres of your brain.

Keep purifying your nadi system (subtle nerve channels) with Kumbhaka Pranayama.

Using nada yoga, follow your Shabda Nada into its inner octaves, which will lead to the highest divine language; Pashyanti and Para Vak.

Keep experimenting with different types of Pranayama and other breathing techniques. This could take you all the way into the density of Divine Ecstasy.

With a persistent and steady Bhairava Mudra, open your brilliant mind to its full capacity to Behold the Ineffable Glory of your True Beloved!

Following Ramana Maharshi's Direct Path, dive into the Self; the heart of Creation.

Keep experimenting wisely and reverently with Sacred Plant Teachers, combining this with Kumbhaka Prana Yoga.

---

[58] Gospel of Matthew 17:21

Parting Words of Advice

Resort to sadhana (spiritual practice) for there is nothing in this whole world more satisfying than your sacred efforts, self-sacrifices and offerings to your Beloved God. Through sacred sadhana, you are reconnecting with God and that brings the greatest satisfaction, happiness and joy.

From time to time, engage in spiritual Tapas (heat of inner energy). This could be prolonged fasting or sacrifice of other comforts. This is your advanced payment to the Creator, who in turn awakens Hers/His Love.

Remember that absolute happiness and satisfaction can never be found in fleeting external objects, but only within your eternal True Self.

Regardless of what you think, my dear reader, your True Self – the Reality – cannot cease to exist! Sooner or later you will realise your Self!

If your longing for Truth and union with your Beloved is strong, there is no need to wait for the natural unfolding of evolution. Take a shortcut by engaging in sacred sadhana!

May Divine Grace always shine on you brightly!

May your sacred efforts triumph in Self-realisation!

May you rediscover your True Self and may you be immersed in the never-ending ecstatic bliss of your True Nature!

Glory! Glory! Glory to Shiva-Shakti, eternal lovers from whom creation with all its bewildering complexity, ripples effortlessly into existence!

Aum.

Appendix 1

'The Monad is a monarchy with nothing above it. It is he who exists as God and Father of everything, the invisible One who is above everything, who exists as incorruption, which is in the pure light into which no eye can look.

He is the invisible Spirit, of whom it is not right to think of him as a god, or something similar. For he is more than a god, since there is nothing above him, for no one lords it over him for he does not exist in something inferior to him, since everything exists in him. For it is he who establishes himself. He is eternal, since he does not need anything. For he is total perfection. He did not lack anything, that he might be completed by it; rather he is always completely perfect in light. He is illimitable, since there is no one prior to him to set limits to him. He is unsearchable, since there exists no one prior to him to examine him. He is immeasurable, since there was no one prior to him to measure him. He is invisible, since no one saw him. He is eternal, since he exists eternally. He is ineffable, since no one was able to comprehend him to speak about him. He is unnameable, since there is no one prior to him to give him a name.

He is immeasurable light, which is pure, holy [and] immaculate. He is ineffable, being perfect in incorruptibility. [He is] not in perfection, nor in blessedness, nor in divinity, but he is far superior. He is not corporeal nor is he incorporeal. He is neither large nor is he small. There is no way to say, 'What is his quantity?' or, 'What is his quality?', for no one can know him. He is not someone among [other] beings, rather he is far superior. Not that he is [simply] superior, but his essence does not partake in the aeons nor in time. For he who partakes in an aeon was prepared

417

beforehand. Time was not apportioned to him, since he does not receive anything from another, for it would be received on loan. For he who precedes someone does not lack, that he may receive from him. For rather, it is latter that looks expectantly at him in his light.

For the perfection is majestic. He is pure, immeasurable mind. He is an aeon-giving aeon. He is life-giving life. He is a blessedness-giving blessed one. He is knowledge-giving knowledge. He is goodness-giving goodness. He is mercy and redemption-giving mercy. He is grace-giving grace, not because he possesses it, but because he gives the immeasurable incomprehensible light.'[59]

---

[59] Apocryphon of John (The Secret Book of John)

Appendix 2

a) The Tattvas of the universal experience 1-5

As it has been said, Parama Siva has two aspects: transcendental and immanent – creative. This creative aspect of Parama Siva is known as Siva Tattva. Sakti is not something separate from Siva. Siva in His creative aspect known as Sakti. She is His ahamvimarsa (I-consciousness), His unmukhata or intentness to create.

1) Siva Tattva and 2) Sakti Tattva can never be separate. Sakti – the creative energy of Siva begins the process of creation by polarizing consciousness into Aham - 'I' and Idam – 'This', or Subject and object. We can find parallels to this 'beginning of creation' in 'Quantum mechanics', when pregnant with tremendous energy and infinite possibilities 'Void' splitting itself into the asymmetrical particles and antiparticles, matter and antimatter, or in the process of divisions of cells.

3) Sadasiva Tattva is the first manifestation. In this Universal Experience, both the subject and object are consciousness. Consciousness in this aspect becomes perceptible to Itself. The Ideal Universe (object) is perceived as an indistinct from the subject. In Sadasiva Tattva the 'I' side is predominant. The experience of Sadasiva is 'I am This'.

4) Isvara Tattva. With the next stage of unmesa (opening out) the Creation becomes more defined as a distinct blossoming. The experience of Isvara is: 'This am I'.

5) Sadvidya or Suddhavidya Tattva. In the Sadvidya Tattva, the 'I' and the 'This' side of experience are equally balanced. The 'I'

419

and the 'This' are recognized with such equal clarity that while
both 'I' and 'This' are still identified; they can be clearly
distinguished also. The experience of this stage may be called
diversity-in-unity i.e. while the 'This' is clearly distinguished from
'I', it is still felt to be part of the 'I' or Self. The experience of this
stage is known as Parapara dasa. It is intermediate between the Para
or higher and Apara or the lower.

b) The Tattvas (principles) of the limited individual experience

6 - 11) Maya Tattva. In the next stage of Creation begins the
'play' of Maya Shakti. From this stage onward begins an impure
order in which the ideal nature of the Divine is veiled. The word
Maya is derived from the root 'ma', meaning to measure out. That
which makes experience measurable i.e. limited and severs the
'This' from 'I' and 'I' from 'This' and excludes things from one
another is Maya. Up to Sadvidya, the experience is universal; the
'This' means 'all this', the total universe. Under the operation of
Maya, 'This' means merely 'this', different from everything else.
From now on starts sancosa or contraction, limitation. Maya draws
a veil (avarana) on the Self, thus he forgets his real nature, and
Maya generates a sense of difference. The products of Maya are the
five Kancucas, or coverings. Their functions are given below:

7) Kala. This reduces the sarvakartratva (universal authorship)
of the Universal Consciousness and brings about limitation with
respect to authorship or efficacy.

8) Vidya. This reduces the omniscience (sarvajnata) of the
Universal Consciousness and brings about limitations with respect
to knowledge.

9) Raga. This reduces the all-satisfaction (purnatva) of the
Universal Consciousness and brings about desire for particular
things.

10) Ka'la. This reduces the eternity (nityatva) of the Universal
Consciousness and brings about limitation in respect of time i.e. the
division of past, present and future.

11) Niyati. This reduces the freedom and pervasiveness
(svatantrata and vyapakatva) of the Universal Consciousness and
brings about limitation with respect to cause, space, and form.

Appendix 2

c) The Tattvas of the limited individual

12) Purusa (ego connected with subjectivity). Shiva, through Maya Shakti, who limits His universal knowledge and power becomes Purusa or the individual subject. Purusa in this context means every sentient being. Purusa is also known as 'anu' in this system. The word 'anu' is used in the sense of limitation of Divine perfection.

13) Prakriti (nature). While Purusa is the subjective manifestation of Shiva, Prakriti is the objective manifestation. Prakriti is the matrix of all objectivity. Prakriti has three 'gunas' or genetic constituents; sattva, rajas and tamas. In her unmanifest state, Prakriti holds these gunas in perfect equipoise. In the order of being, sattva is characterised by brightness and lightness, in the psychological order it is characterised by transparency, joy and peace; in the ethical order, it is the principle of goodness. In the order of being, tamas is the principle of darkness, inertness; in the psychological order it is characterised by dullness, delusion and dejection, and in the ethical order it is the principle of degradation, debasement. In the order of being, rajas is characterised by activity; in the psychological order it is characterised by craving and passion; in the ethical order it is the principle of ambition and avarice.

According to Pratyabhijna (the Kashmir Shaivism system of Self-recognition), Prakriti is the Santa (Peace) Shakti of Shiva, and the gunas: sattva, rajas and tamas are only the polarisation of His Shakties of Jnana, Iccha and Kriya respectively. Purusa is the experient (bhokta) and Prakriti is the experienced (bhogya).

d) The Tattvas of mental operation

14-16 Buddhi, Ahamkara, and Manas
Prakriti differentiates into antahkarana (the psychic apparatus), indriyas (senses) and bhutas (matter). Antahkarana means the inner instrument, the psychic apparatus of the individual. It consists of the Tattvas; buddhi, ahamkara and manas.

14) Buddhi (intellect) is the ascertaining intelligence. The objects that are reflected in buddhi are of two kinds; a) external, e.g., a jar which is perceived through the eye, and b) internal; the images built out of the samskaras (the impressions left behind on the mind).

15) Ahamkara (ego connected with objectivity). This is the product of buddhi. It is the I-making principle and the power of self-appropriation.

16) Manas (mind). It is the product of 'ahamkara'. It co-operates with the senses in building perceptions, and by itself builds images and concepts.

e) The Tattvas of sensible experience

17-21 The five powers of sense perception. Jnanendryas or Buddhindryas, which are products of ahamkara, are the Tattvas of sensible experience. The five powers are those of smelling(ghranendriya), (ghrana – nose, organ of smelling), tasting(rasanendriya), (rasana – tongue, organ of tasting), seeing(caksurindriya), (caksu – eye, organ of seeing), touch (sparsendriya), (tvak – skin, organ of touching), and hearing(sravanendriya), (srotra – ear, organ of hearing).

22-26 The five Karmendriyas or powers of action. These are also products of ahamkara. These are powers of speaking(vagindriya), (vak – speech), handling(hastendriya), (pani – hand), locomotion (padendriya), (pada – foot), excreting (payvindriya), (payu – excretion), sexual action and restfulness (upasthendriya), (upastha – creative).

The indriyas are not sense organs but powers which operate through the sense organs.

27-31 The five tanmatras, or primary elements of perception. These are also products of ahamkara. 'Tanmatra' literally means 'that only'. These are the general elements of sense perception. They are 'sound as such'(sabda-tanmatra), 'touch as such'(sparsa-tanmatra), 'colour and form as such'(rupa-tanmatra), 'flavour/taste as such'(rasa-tanmatra), 'odour as such'(gandha-tanmatra).

f) The Tattvas of materiality

32-36 The five Bhutas (great elements).

The five gross elements, or the panca-mahabhutas are the products of the five tanmatras.

32) 'Akasa' is produced from 'sabda-tanmatra' (ether).

33) 'Vayu' is produced from 'sparsa-tanmatra'. (air)

34) 'Teja' (Agni) is produced from 'rupa-tanmatra'. (fire)

35) 'Apas' is produced from 'rasa-tanmatra' (jala – water)

36) 'Prithvi' is produced from 'gandha-tanmatra' (earth)[60]"

Reference and further readings: *Siva Sutras* by Jaideva Singh.

---

[60] "Shiva Sutras" Jaideva Singh

Appendix 3

Escape into the Higher Order

'The sound neurotechnology create great fluctuations in electrical brain wave activity. As one moves from the beta brain wave pattern of normal consciousness to the slower brain wave pattern of alpha, then deeper into theta, and finally to the deepest delta, the fluctuations in the brain are constantly increasing. Here is the important point, though: these fluctuations give the nervous system input, or stimulus, beyond its ability to handle, the way it is currently structured. In order to handle these fluctuations, nervous system is forced to reorganize itself at higher, more complex levels of functioning, evolving a new structure that can handle the input it originally could not handle. As the brain continues to receive this input, the nervous system will continually reorganise itself, in a series of quantum leaps – some at the micro-level of functioning and some at a much more global level – until a new structure has been created that can easily handle this input. This model of change is based on the work of scientist Ilya Prigogine, the winner of the 1977 Nobel Prize for work on the growth and evolution of what scientists' call "non-linear open systems". Neurophysiologically, this reorganization in the brain causes the creation of new neural pathways, resulting in communication between parts of the brain that previously were not communicating, or were communicating only a minor amount. One of the unique things about the Holosync technology is its ability to create synchronisation between two hemispheres of the brain, over time making this kind of cross-hemispheric communication permanent. This increase in communication within the brain leads over time to what scientists' call "whole brain thinking, or whole brain functioning".

Change is the one constant in this universe. One of the first things the Buddha noted when he began to teach was that everything changes. For that reason, understanding change, how it happens, what makes it difficult and what makes it easy, is of crucial importance to anyone on a spiritual or personal growth path.

But how does change work? Why does it happen? And, how can we allow it, without resisting and suffering?

The answer is found in the Nobel Prize-winning work of Russian-born Belgian theoretical chemist, Ilya Prigogine. Prigogine, working in the field of thermodynamics, became intensely curious about what seemed to be a contradiction between one of the basic laws of science and some equally basic observable facts, including the existence and evolution of life itself. This contradiction, though seemingly unrelated to our everyday lives, contains the seed of profound practical wisdom for anyone committed to mental, emotional, and spiritual growth.

The second law of thermodynamics states that whenever work is done, some energy is irretrievably lost. When expanding steam causes a piston to move, for instance, some energy is lost from the system in the form of heat radiation due to friction. In addition, the machine itself, unless energy is added to the system in the form of an overhaul, new parts, etc., will wear out and eventually break down.

This fact of nature is called the law of increasing entropy. Entropy, simply put, is a measure of the amount of randomness or chaos in a system, and the law of increasing entropy is an expression of the fact that the universe is irreversibly moving toward a state of increased disorder and randomness. Left to itself, with no energy input from the outside, any system will break down and become increasingly disordered. A car will turn to rust and fall apart, a mountain will be worn down, and so on. Even the expansion of the universe is a movement in the direction of increasing disorder, increasing entropy.

Yet, we can see that many things in the universe tend toward increased order—the opposite of what—the second law of thermodynamics predicts. Life has evolved as atoms became molecules, then amino acids, proteins, cells, multi-cellular life, social systems, and so on—definitely a process of increasing order, and against the flow of increasing entropy. This seeming paradox puzzled scientists for over a hundred years until Prigogine discovered the key: that order arises not in spite of entropy, but because of it!

The experiments with the "open systems" proved his hypothesis that order emerges not in spite of chaos but because of it – that evolution and growth are inherent in far-from-equilibrium (open) systems. The key to such systems is their ability not only to take in energy and matter from the environment, but also to dissipate the resulting entropy to the environment, creating an overall energy dynamic that does follow the second law of thermodynamics.

Prigogine called these open systems that evolve and grow by taking in energy and matter from their environment and dissipating the resulting entropy "dissipative structures". Prigogine's discoveries apply to every open system in the universe, whether a chemical system (as in Prigogine's original experiments), a seed, a highway system, a corporation—or a human being.

Such structures, to maintain their existence, must interact with their environment, continually maintaining the flow of energy into and out of the system. And, rather than being the structure through which energy and matter flow, dissipative structures are, in fact, the flow itself. In other words, this is not a universe of independent things, but rather one of process, a changing, flowing, evolving, and intimately interconnected system of interactions.

Dissipative structures (such as human beings) flourish in unstable, fluctuating environments. The more ordered and complex a system becomes, the more entropy it must dissipate to maintain its existence. Conversely, each system has an upper limit, due to its level of complexity, of how much entropy it can dissipate. This is a key point. If the fluctuations from the environment increase beyond that limit, the system, unable to disperse enough entropy into its environment, begins to become internally more entropic, more chaotic.

If the excessive input continues, the chaos eventually becomes so great that the system begins to break down. Finally, a point is reached where the slightest nudge can bring the whole system grinding to a halt. Either the system breaks down and ceases to exist as an organized system, or it spontaneously reorders itself in a new way. The change is a true quantum leap, a death and re-birth, and the main characteristic of the new system is that it can handle the fluctuations, the input from the environment, that overwhelmed the old system. In Prigogine's words, the system "escapes into a higher order!"

Out of chaos comes a new order, a more evolved system. This new system has a new stability and is able to more easily exist in the previously overwhelming environment. But if input increases again, to a level beyond the system's new and higher capacity for dispersion of entropy, the process will repeat, resulting in new internal chaos and another reorganization at an even more evolved level.

The human brain as a dissipative structure. High frequency brain wave states, such as the beta state (that of normal, non-meditative consciousness), have very low amplitude. The wave form has little difference from its highest to its lowest point—a small amount of fluctuation. Lower frequency alpha and theta brain waves—those of traditional meditation (and the even deeper delta brain waves created by Holosync)—have very high amplitude—a large amount of fluctuation.

Since the amount of environmental fluctuation determines a system's possibilities for evolutionary change, a beta state does not push the brain to evolve. In the alpha, theta, and delta states, however, the brain experiences larger fluctuations, which, as we have seen, stimulate evolutionary change in dissipative structures. When an open system like the human brain is exposed to such low-frequency, high - amplitude fluctuations, it can (and will) make the quantum leap to the next higher level.[61],[62]

---

[61] "Holosync Neurotechnology" Bill Harris
[62] "Order out of Chaos" Ilya Prigogine

Glossary of Sanskrit Terms

Abhinavagupta: One of the major gurus (spiritual teachers) of the Kashmir Shaivism tradition, the founder of the Trika system, which is the quintessence of Kashmir Shaivism. Author of *Tantraloka, Paratrisika-Vivarana* and other books on the True Nature of Reality.

Advaita ('non-duality'): The truth and teaching that there is only One Reality (Atman, Brahman), see Upanishads and Vedanta.

Agamas, Agama Shastra ('of Divine Origin'): There are Shiva Agamas and Shakti Agamas. Holy Scriptures attributing authorship to Shiva or Shakti.

Aham: 'I' or 'I am'.

Ahamkara ('I-maker'): the individualisation principle

Ahimsa ('non-violence'/'non-harming'): The single most important moral discipline (yama), the moral principle of living (dharma).

Ajna, Ajna Chakra: The psycho-energetic centre in the middle of the head, behind the 'third eye' area in the region of the pituitary and pineal glands. It is often associated with psychic abilities.

Akasha ('ether/space'): The first of the five material elements of which the physical universe is composed. Also used to designate 'inner' space, that is, the space of consciousness (cid akasha).

Amrit, Amrita ('immortal, immortality'): Nectar of immortality, the Divine nectar of the Gods that oozes from the psycho-energetic centre at the crown (Sahashrara chakra).

Anahata, Anahata chakra: Psycho-energetic centre in the middle of the chest (heart chakra).

Anahata Nada: Unstruck sound.

Ananda ('bliss'): The condition of utter joy, which is the essential quality of ultimate Reality.

Antar Kumbhaka: Retention of breath after completion of inhalation.

Anu ('an atomic point'): Universal consciousness shrunken into a microscopic dot – the ego-individuality.

428

Glossary of Sanskrit Terms

Anulom – Vilom: Alternative nostril breathing pranayama.

Anuttara (an+uttara): Nothing higher, incomparable, unsurpassed, second to none, the highest reality.

Apana, Apana Vayu (Wind): Outgoing breath. Most active in the pelvis and lower abdomen, apana governs the eliminative functions (excretion, urination, menstruation) and the downward and outward flow of energy in the body.

Apara (non-supreme): One of the three Goddesses of the Trika of Kashmir Shaivism.

Asana ('seat'): A physical posture.

Ashtanga yoga (eight-limbed union): The eightfold yoga of Patanjali, consisting of moral disciplines (yamas), self-restraint (niyamas), postures (asanas), breath control (pranayamas), concentration (dharana), meditation (dhyana), and absorption into Reality (samadhi), leading to liberation (kaivalya, moksha).

Atma, Atman ('Self'): The transcendent Self, or Spirit, which is eternal and superconscious; our true nature or identity; distinctions made between Jivatma (individual soul) in connection with Jiva and Paramatma (universal soul), that is identical with Brahman.

Atma-Vichara: Self-inquiry.

Atma-Vyavahara: The act of communion with the Self.

Avadhuta ('he who has shed everything'): A radical type of renouncer (samnyasin), free of bondage.

Avidya ('ignorance'): Avidya, also called ajnana, is not an absence of knowledge, but rather 'wrong knowledge', which is the root of suffering.

Bahya Kumbhaka: Retention of breath after completing exhalation.

Bardo: The intermediate state between death and rebirth.

Bardo Thodol ("Liberation in the intermediate state through hearing"): Commonly known as *The Tibetan Book of the Dead/*

Bastrika pranayama ('bellows' pranayama): A dynamic form of breathing in which one inhales air with a moderate tempo to the full lung capacity, after which one rapidly expels air, returning to relatively slow, but full lung capacity inhalation.

Bhakta ('devotee'): A disciple practising bhakti yoga.

Bhakti ('devotion/love'): The love of the bhakta toward the Divine or a guru as a manifestation of the Divine.

Glossary of Sanskrit Terms

Bhakti yoga ('Yoga of devotion'): The way of union with the Beloved Reality through the means of devotional love.

Bhairava: In |Shaivism, a fierce manifestation of Shiva associated with annihilation. In the Trika system, Bhairava represents Supreme Reality, synonymous with Para Brahman.

Bhairava Mudra: A spiritual practice in which awareness is extroverted and expanded with the eyes wide open, perceiving maximum impressions with the attention simultaneously turned within and fixed on the seer.

Bhavana: Conviction, certitude.

Bija, Bija Mantra ('seed', 'seed syllables'): Bija is the seed from which everything originates. Bija mantras are one-syllable sounds (seed mantras). The potency of the seed syllables owes to the conceived undifferentiated unity of nada and bindu in them. (See below)

Bindu ('seed/point'): The creative potency of anything where all energies are focused.

Brahma ('he who has grown expansive'): Creator of the universe, the first principle (Tattva) to emerge out of the ultimate Reality (Brahman).

Brahman ('that which has grown expansive'): Ultimate Reality

Buddhi ('she who is conscious, awake'): The higher mind (intellect).

Chakra ('wheel'): One of the psycho-energetic centres of the subtle body (sukshma-sharira). In Hindu yoga, there are often seven chakras mentioned: Muladhara, Svadishthana, Manipura, Anahata, Vishuddha, Ajna, and Sahashrara.

Chillum: A pipe, often made of clay, for smoking charas (marijuana pollen).

Cit: Consciousness.

Darshan: seeing, sight.

Dharma: The way of righteous living.

Dhuna: An open fireplace.

Diksha: Initiation.

Gandharvas: Celestial musicians.

Ganesh, Ganesha: Elephant-headed god Ganapati (Lord of Gunas). God of beginnings. Remover of obstacles.

Gorakhnath: the founder of hatha yoga, a disciple of Matsyendranath.

430

Glossary of Sanskrit Terms

Gunas: Qualities. The three primary qualities or constituents of nature (prakriti) are tamas (the principle of inertia), rajas (the dynamic principle), and sattva (the principle of lucidity).

Guru: Spiritual teacher.

Hatha ('force', 'effort'): 'Ha' means 'sun', 'tha' means 'moon'. Hatha yoga is a tantric practice as it attempts to bring about harmony between the two energies of life: the pranic and the mental. This pair can also be described as the Shakti, or female, cool current which travels through the Ida nadi, and the male hot current which travels through the Pingala nadi. When their union takes place in the central channel (Sushumna nadi) it is the union of Prana and Mind, and this is the awakening of higher consciousness.

Hrdayam ('this is the centre'): The spiritual heart centre.

Hrt, Hrt chakra: The spiritual heart centre located two finger widths to the right side of the chest.

Hrt-granthi: Heart knot.

Iccha, Iccha Sakti ('will'): The will energy of Absolute Shiva.

Ida ('comfort'): Ida is associated with lunar cooling female energy. One of the three major nadis.

Idam ('this, here'): Refers to something near.

Ishvara, Isvara, Isvara-tattva ('excellent ruler, God'): Personal God. 'I am this, this am I' (aham-idam-idam-aham). Associated with Jnana-Sakti, the Power of Knowing. Ishvara-tattva is the fourth level representation of God's power of pure, infinite knowledge whereby He is able to know all things. At this stage God begins to conceive in His Mind the Universe to be created.

Jalandhara Bandha ('jala [web] + dhara – [holding] + bandha – [bond]'): This bandha is performed by extending the neck and elevating the sternum before dropping the head so that the chin rests on the chest. Meanwhile, the tongue pushes up against the palate in the mouth.

Japa ('muttering'): The recitation of mantras.

Jiva ('individual self'): The individual consciousness, as opposed to the ultimate Self (paramatman).

Jivatma: Individualised soul, self.

Jnana: True knowledge, real wisdom.

Kailash: Mountain in Tibet, abode of Shiva

431

Glossary of Sanskrit Terms

Kaivalya ('isolation'): The state of absolute freedom from conditioned existence, isolation from nature (prakriti) and gunas (qualities of nature).

Kali: Goddess of the dissolution of apparent manifestation, destroyer of the demon kala (time) who stole the elixir of immortality.

Kaksyasotra: Ode, eulogy, hymn of praise in the Kashmir Shaivism tradition.

Kapalbhati ('shining scull'): Very fast and dynamic form of pranayama with the stress on rapid exhalation after which inhalation happens automatically.

Karma ('action'): The sum of a person's actions in this and previous states of existence, viewed as deciding their fate in future existences. Karma mala is one of the three impurities (stains) that prevent the yogi from seeing his/her true nature or pure consciousness.

Kartrtva: Doership

Kashmir Shaivism: Non-dual philosophy that gives primacy to Universal Consciousness (Chit or Brahman). In Kashmir Shaivism, all things are a manifestation of this Consciousness, but the phenomenal world (Shakti) is real, existing and having its being in Consciousness.

Katha Upanishad: One of the *mukhya* (primary) Upanishads, embedded in the last short eight sections of the Katha school of the Krishna Yajurveda. It is the legendary story of a boy, Nachiketa, who meets Yama, the Hindu deity of Death. Their conversation evolves to a discussion on the nature of man, knowledge, Atman (Soul, Self) and Moksha (liberation).

Kaula: Family, Clan

Khecari-mudra ('space-walking seal'): The tantric practice of curling the tongue back against the upper palate in order to seal the life energy (prana).

Kevala: Isolated, alone, only, pure, whole, complete.

Kirtan: Devotional singing, chanting.

Kriya: Activity, action

Kriya Shakti: Creative cosmic power of action. Kriya Shakti is one of three parts of the creative cosmic power. The other two parts are Iccha Shakti (willpower) and Jnana Shakti (the power of knowledge).

Glossary of Sanskrit Terms

Kaula, Kula (community, clan, tribe): Kula can also mean Shakti whereas Shiva is known as Akula. Kula is also an essential (tantric) part of the Kashmir Shaivism Tradition.

Kumbh ('pot'): A body could be considered as a kumbh.

Kumbhaka: Retention of breath, suspension of breath.

Kundalini ('coiled one'): A form of divine energy (Shakti) located at the base of the spine in the Muladhara chakra.

Lalita: 'She who plays, playful mother'

Lalita Tripurasundari: Adi Parashakti (original, primal, highest Shakti), one of ten Mahavidyas.

Mahamrityunjaya: Great liberation from death, mantra.

Maharishi: Great seer.

Mantra: Sacred utterance, numinous sound, phonemes.

Mantra-maheshvara: The state of the energy of a superperciever (pramatrin) standing above Mantreshvara and below Shiva.

Mantreshvara: The state of the energy of a superperciever (pramatrin) standing above Mantra-pramatri and below of Mantra maheshvara.

Matrika, Matr'ka ('misunderstood Divine mother of the cosmos'): Alphabet goddess, the matrix, the source (yoni) of all mantras, all knowledge and creation itself.

Matsyendranath ('Lord of the Fishes'): The creator of hatha yoga.

Mauna: Absolute silence (silence of speech and silence of thought).

Maya ('illusion'): That which does not exist yet appears to be. The power by which the universe becomes manifest, the illusion or appearance of the phenomenal world.

Malini ('the garlanded one'): The Goddess Malini is one of two alphabet deities prominent in the Tantric system called the Trika. The mantric identity of this Goddess is the Nadiphantakrama, the order of the alphabet beginning with na and ending with pha; a particular rearrangement of the Sanskrit syllabary in which vowels and consonants are intermingled in a hitherto unexplained and at first sight random order.

Malinivijayottara Tantra: Sacred tantric, yogic text. Abhinavagupta considered Malinivijayottara Tantra as the Highest Tantra. He puts this Tantra at the very heart of the Trika system of the Kashmir Shaivism tradition.

Glossary of Sanskrit Terms

Moksha ('emancipation, liberation, release'): Moksha refers to various forms of emancipation, enlightenment, liberation and release. In its soteriological and eschatological senses, it refers to freedom from samsara, the cycle of death and rebirth. In its epistemological and psychological senses, moksha refers to freedom from ignorance: Self-realisation, Self-actualisation and Self-knowledge.

Mudra ('seal'): A mudra is a spiritual gesture and an energetic seal of authenticity. While some mudras involve the entire body (including the tongue and eyes), most are performed with the hands and fingers. Mudras are often used (or spontaneously formed) in conjunction with pranayama (yogic breathing exercises). Mudras are generally internal actions, involving the pelvic floor, diaphragm, throat, eyes, tongue, anus, genitals, abdomen and other parts of the body.

Mula Bandha ('root lock'): A posture where the body from the anus to the navel is contracted and lifted up towards the spine.

Muladhara ('root and basis of existence'): The root chakra Muladhara is said to be the base from which the three main psychic channels or nadis, Ida, Pingala and Sushumna, emerge. Muladhara is also the subtle abode of the Hindu God Ganapati (Ganesh). Its graphic representation includes a square, in the centre of which, below the seed syllable of the Muladhara chakra is a deep red inverted triangle. The Kundalini Shakti is said to sleep here, waiting to be aroused and brought back up to Brahman, the source from which it originated. It is represented by a snake wrapped three and half times around a smoky grey lingam.

Nachiketa: A hero from the Katha Upanishad, who was sent to Lord Yama (Lord of Death) before his appropriate time. Nachiketa, who was very keen on the true knowledge of Reality, rejected Yama's offerings of material possessions and the satisfaction of material desires and learnt the highest secrets on the true nature of Reality, Self-realisation and Moksha (liberation) from the Lord of Death.

Nada ('subtle sound'): The entire universe consists of subtle vibrations called Nadas. Nada is hidden energy that connects the outer and inner cosmos. Nada is also Consciousness about to manifest as the universe. The transcendent sound-principle is Nada, from which articulate speech, letters, syllables, words and

434

sentences evolve. Nada is the sound energy in motion rather than of matter and particles which form the building blocks of the cosmos. Nada is linked to pulsation, light and essential rhythm.

Nadi ('river'): Nadis are rivers of conscious energy, the subtle energy channels within the body through which Prana flows. There are said to be seventy-two thousand nadis radiating from the Spiritual Heart. Three main Nadis are the left Ida, associated with lunar, calming, feminine energy, the right Pingala, associated with solar, masculine, active energy and the central Sushumna Nadi in the spinal cord through which awakened, conscious Kundalini energy may rise from the Kanda (bulb) to Brahmarandrha at the top of the skull.

Namaskar: Traditional Indian greeting or gesture of respect, made by bringing the palms of the hands together before the chest and bowing. Namaskaram or Pranam could be a full prostration.

Nath ('Lord, protector, master'): Adi Nath means 'first' or 'original' and refers to Shiva, the founder of Nathas.

Nidagha: Disciple of sage Ribhu.

Nirvana ('blown out'): A transcendent state in which there is neither suffering, desire, nor sense of self, and the subject is released from the effects of karma and the cycle of death and rebirth. It represents the final goal in Buddhism.

Nirvikalpa, Nirvikalpa Samadhi ('unwavering, doubtless, changeless, unqualified'): Absorption in Reality without the support of mind and thought.

Ojas ('vigour'): The inner glow of bodies' pure energy, the seat of which is the heart.

Para ('highest, supreme'): Supreme Goddess in the Anuttara Trika system of Kashmir Shaivism. The other two are Para-para (supreme con non-supreme) and Apara (non-supreme).

Para Kundalini: According to Swami Lakshmanjoo, Para Kundalini is the very heart of Shiva. Everything is born of Para Kundalini, exists in Para Kundalini and gets absorbed by Para Kundalini.

Para-para: Supreme con non-supreme.

Para-Trisika-Vivarana: Tantric text of Abhinavagupta, Kashmir Shaivism of Trika.

Paramatma: Absolute Atman or supreme Self, equal to Brahman.

Glossary of Sanskrit Terms

Parasamvit: The highest consciousness.

Pingala: Right, sun, masculine Nadi.

Prakasha ('light, splendour, light of consciousness'): Prakasha in Kashmir Shaivism is Shiva's light of consciousness which gets reflected, so to speak, in the mirror of Shakti-Vimarsha, creating a Self-reflection, Self-knowledge.

Prakriti ('nature'): The material part of creation driven by changing qualities (gunas). Counterpart of Purusha (Spirit, Self).

Pralayakala: State of voidness. Pralayakala Pramatri (the perceiver) stands above Sakala Pramatri and below Vijnanakala Pramatri.

Prana ('life-force, breath'): A vital principle, the primary energy which permeates Reality on all levels. Prana is not only the basic life-force, but the original creative power. It is the master form of all energy working at every level of existence.

Pranam: Prostration.

Pranayama: Expansion of life-energy, also restraint, control and suspension of breath (yogic exercise).

Pratyabhijna-hridaya: Direct knowledge of oneself, Self-recognition. System of knowledge of Anuttara Trika of Kashmir Shaivism.

Purana ('ancient'): Sacred writings on Hindu mythology. Primarily in Sanskrit, but also in Tamil and other Indian languages.

Purusha ('the universal soul, spirit'): Purusha is a non-material (Spiritual) part of creation. 'Splendid and without a bodily form is this Purusha, without and within, unborn, without life breath and without mind, higher than the supreme element. From him are born life breath and mind. He is the soul of all beings,' says the Upanishads.

Rajas: Guna (changing quality) of Prakriti (nature). Rajas represent passion, activity, agitation, etc.

Ribhu: Sage Ribhu, who received darshan (vision) of Shiva on the Kailasam mountain (the abode of Shiva) and Shiva's teaching on non-duality, expounds this teaching to his disciple Nidagha and other assembled sages through the scripture called *Ribhu Gita* (Song of Ribhu).

Rishi ('seer'): Refers to those great seers of Vedic and Upanishadic lore, who through yogic visions perceived the greatest secrets of the inner dimensions of Reality.

Glossary of Sanskrit Terms

Sadashiva, Sadasiva: Sadasiva is the omnipotent, subtle, luminous Absolute. The highest manifestation of the Almighty who blesses with Anugraha or grace, the fifth Panchakritya – 'Holy five acts of Shiva.' Sadashiva is usually represented in the form of Mukhalingam, having five faces which are: Ishana, Tatpurusha, Vamadeva, Aghora and Satyojata. These faces are known as Panchabrahmas (the five creators), emanating in the four directions and upwards from the nishkala (formless) Parashivam.

Sadhak ('to accomplish'): One who follows a particular sadhana (spiritual discipline) towards the realisation of the goal of one's ultimate ideal, whether it is merging with one's eternal source, Brahman, or realisation of one's personal deity.

Sadhana: Spiritual practice or discipline which leads to perfection, these being contemplation, asceticism, worship of God and correct living.

Sadhu: A holy man, sage, ascetic.

Sadvidya, Suddha Vidya ('pure knowledge'): Considered to be part of the yogi principles, known as the Five Pure Tattvas, sadvidya represents pure spirit and consciousness that occurs between the Self and the universe when they are in a balanced state. The acknowledgement of 'I am this,' or universal consciousness, is accomplished during suddha vidya.

Sahashrara: The thousand-petaled, or crown chakra is generally considered to be the most subtle chakra in the system, relating to pure consciousness. When a yogi is able to raise his/her kundalini, energy of consciousness, up to this point, the state of Nirvikalpa Samadhi is experienced.

Samadhi: Meditative absorption in Reality.

Samana: Third prana which located in navel and connects Anahata and Manipura chakras, distributes the energy of nutrition throughout the human body.

Samavesha: Spiritual practice (abhyasa) as a goal. Samavesha is Divine Possession. Immersion into the body of consciousness, permanent eradication of individuality. 'Submerging of the individual un-enlightened mind and the consequent identification with the Supreme Shambhu who is inseparable from the primordial Shakti' (Abhinavagupta). Perfect entering into one's own true nature. In Kashmir Shaivism, liberation is achieved not through Samadhi, but through Samavesha.

Glossary of Sanskrit Terms

Samsara ('wandering'): Cycle of deaths and rebirths.

Samskara, Sanskara: Mental impression or psychological imprint. Samskaras create an input into the formation of Karma. Every action and intent by an individual, leaves a samskara in the deeper structure of the person's mind. These impressions then await volitional fruition in that individual's future, in the form of hidden expectations. These samskaras manifest as tendencies, karmic impulses, subliminal impressions, habitual potencies or innate dispositions.

Sara: Essence.

Saraswati: Goddess of knowledge, music, art, wisdom and nature. She is part of the trinity of Saraswati, Lakshmi and Parvati.

Satsang: Association with truth, abidance in truth, being together in truth.

Sattarka ('true logic, intuitive reasoning'): Resulting from Bhavana (creative contemplation, certitude), Sattarka is an emergence of pure knowingness (gnosis).

Sattva: One of the three gunas (modes of existence). Sattva guna's qualities are clarity, serenity, harmony, goodness, purity.

Savichara ('reflective'): The citta (mindset) is concentrated upon a subtle object of meditation, which is not perceptible to the senses, but arrived at through interference, such as the process of cognition, the mind, the I-am-ness, the chakras, the inner breath (prana), the nadis, the intellect (buddhi).

Savikalpa (samadhi): Associated with deliberation, reflection, bliss, and I-am-ness. Deliberation and reflection form the basis of the various types of savikalpa.

Shabdha: (sound, resonance)

Shabdha Brahman: (transcendental sound or sound vibration, creative cosmic sound)

Shakti ('power, energy'): The primordial cosmic energy, dynamic forces that create the appearance of manifestations. Shakti is Shiva's conscious energy and power. She is his ability to create. Shakti is also the concept or personification of divine feminine creative power, sometimes referred to as 'The Great Divine Mother'.

Shaktipat: (transmission of Shakti – energy)

Shavasana: (corpse pose)

Glossary of Sanskrit Terms

Shiva ('the auspicious one' also known as Mahadeva 'the great god'): is one of the principal deities of Hinduism. He is the supreme being within Shaivism.

Shiva lingam (mark, symbol): Symbol of creation representing all the energies of the world and beyond

Shree Vidya ('supreme knowledge'): a Hindu Tantric religious system devoted to the Goddess as Lalita Tripurasundari (Beautiful Goddess of the Three Cities), Bhuvaneshwari, Bala Tripurasundari, etc.

Siddha ('perfected one'): Perfected master who have achieved a high degree of physical as well as spiritual perfection or enlightenment.

Siddhi: (supernatural powers)

Siva: see Shiva

Soma: (Intoxicating drink described in Vedas, Divine nectar)

Spanda: Divine pulsation, vibration, throb

Sphurana: Throbbing, quivering, trembling. Aham-Sphurana: throb, pulsation of self-awareness.

Sphuratta: creative impulse, radiant pulse, glittering.

Suddha Vidya ("pure wisdom"): fifth tattva associated with Kriya Shakti. "I am this" is a mantra of conscious reality.

Sushumna, Susumna ("most gracious"): central nadi channel in the spinal cord.

Svabhava: ("own nature")

Svatantrya ("self-dependency, free will"): Svatantrya shakti – independence, autonomy, free will of Shiva.

Tamas ("darkness"): Inertia, dullness, lethargy. One of the three Gunas (changing qualities of Prakriti)

Tantra ("an instrument for expansion"): a Hindu (specifically Kashmir Shaivism) mystical texts as also set of spiritual practices involving mantras, meditation, yoga and rituals.

Tantraloka ("light on Tantra"): magnum opus of Abhinavagupta.

Tapas ("generation of spiritual heat and energy"): practical spiritual discipline that involves self-effort, deep meditation, austerity, self-discipline, sacrifice of comforts.

Tathagata: In Vajrayana Buddhism are the emanations and representations of the five qualities of the Adi-Buddha Vairocana, which associated with Dharmakaya. In "Bardo Thodol" peaceful and wrathful deities of a bardo (intermediate between death and rebirth) states.

Tattva ("that-ness"): a plane, stage of reality. In Kashmir Shaivism there are 36 Tattvas from Parama Shiva down to Earth element.

Trika ("triple, threefold"): the most esoteric system of Kashmir Shaivism.

Tripurasundari ("she who is beautiful in the three worlds"): the highest Shakti of Srividya tradition.

Udana ("upward-moving breath"): fifth prana which takes soul to higher or lower realms of existence after death.

Upadesha: ("teaching")

Valmiki: Sage and poet, composer of "Ramayana" and "Yoga Vasishta"

Vamadeva: refers to one of the five faces of Sadashiva that revealed the Agamas (sacred texts) this face/aspect of Shiva is considered the peaceful, graceful and poetic one – the lord of the female aspect of it is associated with water.

Vamakeshvara Tantra: one part of "Nityashodashikarnava" (ocean of the 16 Nityas). The other part is known as "Yogini Hridaya" (Heart of the Yogini). Vamakeshvara Tantra is said to be the most important tantra for Sri Vidya worship. This tantra discusses on internal worship of Shakti. Vamakeshwari is said to be the source of this Universe.

Vasanas: ("wishing", "desiring"): behavioural tendency or karmic imprint which influences the present behaviour of a person.

Vasishta: one of the oldest and most revered Vedic rishis. Vasishta is credited as a chief author of Mandala 7 of Rigveda.

Vijnanakala: in ascending towards Parama Shiva order, Vijnanakala is the third after Sakala and Pralayakala level of experient.

Vimarsa, Vimarsha ("representation", "reflection"): power (Shakti) by which Divine represents itself to itself. Power of Self-Awareness. The power by which we know ourselves. Prakasha (Light of Consciousness) is associated with Shiva. Vimarsha is associated with Shakti. It is reflection of the Absolute in a mirror of awareness. Manifestation, maintenance and reabsorption of the universe attributed to Vimarsha – Para Shakti (Super-power).

Glossary of Sanskrit Terms

Viveka ("right discrimination"): one of the correct functions of the intellect.

Vyana: fourth prana. Expansive, homogenous, all-permeating prana.

Yama: Lord of Death.

Yoga ("union"): union of seemingly separate parts such as individual and the supreme, prana and apana etc, Various spiritual practices.

Yoga Vasishta: Sacred text attributed to sage Valmiki.

Yogi: one who practice Yoga.

Yogini: 1) a female yogi. 2) women endowed with supernatural powers (divine, semi-divine or human origin).

Yogini Hrdaya, Yogini Hridaya: "Heart of the Yogini" tantric text, one part of the "Nityashodashikarnava". The other part of which is Vamakeshvara Tantra.

Made in the USA
Middletown, DE
18 July 2020

13073191R10267